New PERSPECTIVES IN EDUCATIONAL LEADERSHIP

EDUCATION MANAGEMENT EM:C³
Contexts, Constituents, + Communities

M. Christopher Brown II
GENERAL EDITOR

Vol. I

PETER LANG
New York • Washington, D.C./Baltimore • Bern
Frankfurt • Berlin • Brussels • Vienna • Oxford

New PERSPECTIVES IN EDUCATIONAL LEADERSHIP

Exploring Social, Political, AND Community Contexts AND Meaning

EDITED BY **Sonya Douglass Horsford**

FOREWORD BY **Fenwick W. English**

CONCLUSION BY **Linda C. Tillman**

PETER LANG

New York • Washington, D.C./Baltimore • Bern
Frankfurt • Berlin • Brussels • Vienna • Oxford

Library of Congress Cataloging-in-Publication Data

New perspectives in educational leadership:
exploring social, political, and community contexts and meaning /
edited by Sonya Douglass Horsford.
p. cm. — (Education management: contexts, constituents, and communities; vol. 1)
Includes bibliographical references and index.
1. Educational leadership. I. Horsford, Sonya Douglass.
LB2806.N395   371.2—dc22   2009036727
ISBN 978-1-4331-0747-4 (hardcover)
ISBN 978-1-4331-0746-7 (paperback)
ISSN 1947-6256

Bibliographic information published by **Die Deutsche Nationalbibliothek**.
Die Deutsche Nationalbibliothek lists this publication in the "Deutsche
Nationalbibliografie"; detailed bibliographic data is available
on the Internet at http://dnb.d-nb.de/.

A version of Chapter 13 appeared in *Shaping the Future:
Policy, Partnerships and Emerging Practices (NCPEA Yearbook 2003)*
edited by F. Lunenburg and C. Carr, © Rowman & Littlefield.
Reprinted with permission.

The paper in this book meets the guidelines for permanence and durability
of the Committee on Production Guidelines for Book Longevity
of the Council of Library Resources.

© 2010 Peter Lang Publishing, Inc., New York
29 Broadway, 18th floor, New York, NY 10006
www.peterlang.com

Printed in the United States of America

✠ TABLE OF CONTENTS

PART 3 **Looking to the Future**

✠ FOREWORD

New Voices, New Perspectives, New Spaces for Educational Leadership Thought and Practice

Fenwick W. English

For too long, the field of educational leadership has been mired in various forms of scholasticism. Scholasticism represents "the worshipping [of] exalted texts from the past which are regarded as containing the completion of all wisdom" and "eminence here goes to those persons who make themselves the most impressive guardians of the classics" (Collins, 1998, p. 31).

Our field has seen the elongated and elaborate codification process involved with the creation of the Interstate School Leaders Licensure Consortium (ISLLC) and Educational Leadership Constituent Council (ELCC) Standards for the preparation of school leaders. This effort represented the culling of a limited number of job skills followed by a sort of census taking of selected practitioners upon which a national examination was created and used by the states in the licensure process. The leaders of this movement were engaged in scholasticism upon which the standardization process was subsequently constructed. The result has been not only the miniaturization of the field, but its resultant stagnation intellectually and conceptually (English, 2003, 2008; English and Papa, 2009).

Collins (1998) has indicated that the intellectual growth of a field or an area is centered on conflict rather than consensus because "conflict is the energy source of intellectual life..." (p.1). It is with this caveat in mind that I welcome the publication of *New Perspectives in Educational Leadership: Exploring*

Social, Political, and Community Contexts and Meaning edited by Sonya Douglass Horsford as a vital new source to re-energize our field. In this volume, we have new voices and perspectives, which hopefully will initiate new themes, strands for inquiry, and significant alternatives to those which stand dominant today.

This is a propitious moment, for as Collins (1998) indicates: "At founding moments, spaces open up which are filled not merely by individuals but by a small number of intellectual movements which restructure the attention space by pressing in opposing directions" (p. 6). It is my hope that this book is such a "founding moment" and new spaces are opened up in which to push out the boundaries of our field. It is long overdue.

As I examined the chapters I found it fitting that the contributing scholars were taking up the themes of equity, culture, critical servant leadership, multiculturalism and diversity, urban regime theory and social justice. For too long, some scholars in our ranks thought that such spaces were not part of the "legitimate" so-called "scientific" pursuit of knowledge in educational leadership. But what we have learned is that a science, which leaves out these themes, does a grave injustice for a field that is centered in moral issues.

Culture and context are not anecdotal appendages to scientific inquiry; they enshrine it and shape it profoundly. Scientists are not immune to prevalent social values enshrined in our culture, and those exist long before scientists even become scientists. The same is true for professional educators and leaders. We bring the "whole human being" to work in the schools and we deal with children who are also whole human beings. I view the perspectives pursued in this book as part of learning who we are as whole human beings and how we can enable the schools to become more human and humane.

I hope the themes and perspectives proffered by the thoughtful colleagues in this volume have strong legs, and continue to resonate and trigger thoughtful discussions (and conflict) in the years ahead.

Fenwick W. English
R. Wendell Eaves Distinguished Senior Professor of Educational Leadership
School of Education, University of North Carolina at Chapel Hill

References

Collins, R. (1998). *The sociology of philosophies: A global theory of intellectual change.* Cambridge, MA: The Belknap Press of Harvard University Press.

English, F. (2003, March). Cookie-cutter leaders for cookie-cutter schools: The teleology of standardization and the de-legitimization of the university in educational leadership preparation. *Leadership and Policy in Schools, 2*(1), 27–46.

English, F. (2008). *Anatomy of professional practice: Promising research perspectives on educational leadership.* Lanham, MD: Rowman & Littlefield Education.

English, F., & Papa, R. (2009). *Restoring human agency to educational administration: Status and strategies.* Lancaster, PA: Proactive.

✠ INTRODUCTION

Re-Imagining Educational Leadership: New Perspectives and Contextual Considerations in the Field

Sonya Douglass Horsford

Strong schools require strong leaders. And as public schools and systems of schooling continue to generate heated criticism from a variety of educational, political, and community stakeholders, educational leaders have the unique challenge and opportunity of serving as both the object of study and conduit for meaningful change in education.

Increasingly, leaders of schools and school systems are faced with a complex set of responsibilities and challenges in which they must navigate multiple and varied contexts with skill, sophistication, and conviction to meet the demands of high-stakes accountability standards, public scrutiny, and the leadership our children, schools, and communities deserve. With a firm grounding in leadership studies and research from business and management, public administration, and interdisciplinary approaches drawn from history, sociology, anthropology, and psychology, etc., the study of educational leadership continues to yield new and insightful perspectives that are important in light of the dynamic social context of education, which warrants and requires new ways of imagining theory, research, and practice in the field.

The purpose of this volume is to offer a collection of new perspectives in educational leadership grounded in a much-needed focus on the social, political, and community contexts in which education management, administration, and leadership are located. Educational leadership is no longer limited to a knowledge base of instructional leadership, site-based management, and organizational development. Rather, the current state of the field requires an exploration and examination of the more complicated and complex dynamics associated with the contexts in which managers manage and leaders lead. Attention to these contemporary contextual considerations is critical to the work, meaning, and subsequent success of educational leaders in our increasingly diverse society and global community, which directly affects the learning experiences, academic achievement, and educational success of students.

Unlike many texts on educational leadership, this volume offers a blend of chapters representing various philosophical, conceptual, theoretical, and disciplinary approaches, which endeavor to reflect the broad array of contexts and perspectives that represent the educational leadership field of the twenty-first century. The chapters included in this text advance research and discussions presented in others areas of education research more broadly, but that in most cases, have yet to fully explored or imagined in the field of educational management or leadership. With particular attention to the implications and larger contexts of shifting racial, ethnic, and cultural demographics; immigration; and globalization realized by schools and societies in the twenty-first century, this book endeavors to advance lines of inquiry grounded in the research on organizational and school culture and climate; transactional and transformational leadership; reflective practice; the politics of equity, adequacy, and high-stakes accountability; school-family-community engagement; and social justice within the domain of educational leadership.

More specifically, *Part One: Theory, Research, and Practice* presents new perspectives on traditional and time-honored organizational and leadership theories with implications for practice in schools. In Chapter 1, Brooks and Miles offer an informative overview and cogent critique of the organizational and school culture literature, followed by Chapter 2 where Peters "rethinks" transformational leadership and its often tenuous relationship with transactional leadership approaches, as determined by immediate contexts and circumstances. In Chapter 3, McKenzie and Locke argue the importance of instructional leadership as it pertains to advancing educational equity and excellence in schools, and in the following chapter, Barnett and O'Mahony present a discussion of how reflective practice helps to build capacity in school leaders, which in turn, improves student learning and achievement. The final chapter in this section features McClellan's exploration of the possibilities of applying critical theory to our understanding of well-established constructs of servant leadership in order to inform educational leadership preparation and practice.

Extending the theoretical and practical applications of leadership in schools and school communities, *Part Two: Contextual and Cultural Considerations* emphasizes the social, political, and cultural contexts of education important to the work of educational leaders. Chapter 6 presents Lewis and Fusarelli's examination of the contemporary political context of "change" and the shifting nature of accountability in education policy, followed by Alemán's overview and critique of public school funding in (post)racial America in Chapter 7. In Chapter 8, Dancy and Horsford explore the possibilities associated with advancing culturally proficient leadership in both school and campus communities to resist the reproduction of social inequality from system to system, followed by Cooper's call to engage families and communities through cultural work and transformative leadership in Chapter 9. This section concludes with Chapter 10 by Murakami-Ramalho who puts forth a concept of advocacy leadership that she argues is essential to the successful preparation of students for increasing internationalization and globalization in twenty-first-century schools.

Part Three: Looking to the Future provides a collection of chapters that chart new directions for educational leadership. In Chapter 11, Jean-Marie, Ruffin, and Burr explore the role of principals as cross-boundary leaders in school reform, while Royal and Davis, in Chapter 12, explore the development of teacher-leaders as a strategy for educational change. In the following chapter (Chapter 13), Brunner, Hammel, and Miller present a leadership preparation tool designed to promote educational equity by addressing issues of power and identity.

Chapter 14 presents Theoharis' work on the messy, but necessary, work of advancing educational access, equity, and opportunity through social justice leadership and is followed by a concluding chapter by Tillman who challenges the field to continue to move from new perspectives to *new practices.* Together, these chapters push our thinking as it relates to the future of educational leadership and how the field must engage scholarship and praxis that equips and supports educational leaders in their efforts to better serve students, families, and school communities.

A collection of cutting-edge empirical and conceptual research, representing views of both emerging and leading scholars in the field, it is my hope that this book not only will provide students, professors, researchers, practitioners, community-based education leaders, policy makers, and other education stakeholders with new perspectives in educational leadership, but also will offer ways of thinking about educational management, administration, and leadership that actively improve the way we educate, prepare, and support students and their families, and in turn, the quality of life of our citizens and society. *New Perspectives in Educational Leadership: Exploring Social, Political, and Community Contexts and Meaning* is the beginning of an important conversation that I believe offers exciting possibilities and opportunities in the study, practice, and re-imagination of both leadership and education.

Sonya Douglass Horsford
Editor
University of Nevada, Las Vegas

✠ PART ONE

Theory, Research, and Practice

✠ CHAPTER 1

Educational Leadership and the Shaping of School Culture: Classic Concepts and Cutting-Edge Possibilities

Jeffrey S. Brooks and Mark T. Miles

Research on educational leadership and school culture has largely focused on how administrators understand and influence the norms, behaviors, mores, values, beliefs, visions, and missions of schools (e.g., Fullan, 2001; Deal & Peterson, 1999). Schools are primarily conceived as organizational groups (e.g., Cunningham & Gresso, 1993; Deal & Peterson, 1991; Westheimer, 1998), and to a lesser extent, loose collections of organizational subgroups (e.g., Brooks & Jean-Marie, 2007). While certainly useful and insightful in some respects, these foci have shortcomings. In particular, studies of the social and cultural dynamics of school leadership can be critiqued in at least five ways: (a) the business leadership is not school leadership critique; (b) the difference-blind critique; (c) the rhetoric over reality critique; (d) the lost individuality critique, and (e) glocal critique.

At best, such shortcomings are simply gaps in the literature that help point the way for future scholars. At worst, the shortcomings of this knowledge base mean that it has potentially been harmful to generations of students and educational leaders who have based their practice on irrelevant or misconceived research that may even do *harm* to students under the pretense of helping improve their educational experience. The purpose of this chapter is to review literature in educational leadership focused on two primary conceptual frameworks used to understand social and cultural dynamics in schools: organizational culture and school culture. Then, we critique the shortcomings of the two major bodies of literature and finally suggest possibilities for future inquiry and practice.

Social and Cultural Dynamics of School Leadership: Organizational Culture and School Culture

For some time, educational leaders have framed their understanding of social and cultural dynamics of schools through two main bodies of literature: organizational culture and school culture. In this section, we review basic concepts and findings in each of these areas.

Organizational Culture: Key Concepts for School Leaders

According to Trice and Beyer (1993), organizational culture may be described as a unique combination of six related factors. First, because cultures are created by interactions between individuals, cultures are *collective*. Second, organizational culture involves helping members make meaning of their work and the management of chaos, and as a result, it is *emotionally charged*. Third, since culture develops over time, it is based upon a unique set of *historical circumstances*. Fourth, culture also focuses upon the expressive side of the organization and is inherently *symbolic*. Fifth, cultures undergo a continual evolution and are *dynamic*. Finally, because organizations operate in complex environments, the cultures of these organizations are often ambiguous and challenging to interpret.

Kilmann, Saxton, and Serpa (1986) define organizational culture as "the shared philosophies, ideologies, values, assumptions, beliefs, expectations, attitudes, and norms that knit a community together" (p. 89). Culture is manifest in attitudinal and behavioral norms, hidden assumptions, and human nature. These authors also contend that culture can have an impact on the organization in three ways: direction, pervasiveness, and strength. The organizational culture provides a direction for the organization to follow. The pervasiveness of the culture is the degree to which the culture is shared among organizational members. The strength of the culture is the amount of pressure exerted on organizational members to behave in a certain way.

Several studies conclude that variables of organizational culture may predict organizational performance, making the concept of particular interest to school leaders seeking to improve organizational outcomes such as student achievement scores. Marcoulides and Heck (1993) tested a model concerning how an organization's culture affects organizational performance. In their study, 392 participants in 26 different organizations responded to structured interview questions and completed a follow-up questionnaire. The researchers identified five variables of organizational culture: (a) organizational structure and purpose; (b) organizational values; (c) task organization; (d) organizational climate; and (e) individual values and beliefs. Their analysis revealed that these variables of organizational culture had a direct or indirect effect on organizational performance. They concluded that managers or leaders within the organization may directly influence many cultural variables and have an indirect impact on overall organizational performance.

Lessons from Corporations

Deal and Kennedy (1982) describe the elements of corporate culture as the business environment, the values of the organization, the heroes with whom the organizational members identify, the rites and rituals of the organization, and the cultural network of informal communication that carries the values and heroic stories. Successful corporations possess products to distribute and have profits to make; moreover, many of these successful corporations focus on the organizational members as well. Individuals within these corporations pass on values and beliefs to other organizational members, tell stories to one another, and emulate heroes of the organization. As a result, a strong culture guides employee behavior by providing a system of informal rules that defines how employees should behave and enabling these employees to feel a sense of accomplishment as they perform organizational tasks.

Deal and Kennedy (1982) found that successful corporations shared three characteristics in relation to corporate values: (a) the company had articulated a philosophy about how they conduct business; (b) managers spent time shaping values and communicating them to others within the organization; and (c) values were known and shared by all organizational members. Corporate values also present unique challenges. If the business environment changes, values may become obsolete if the values do not change. In addition, values may become entrenched within the organization that organizational members are resistant to change. Managers or leaders within the organization may appear inconsistent if their actions do not conform to espoused values. Leaders' consistency and inconsistency are manifest in particular types of organizational activities.

Organizational Culture and Leadership Activity

Rites, rituals, ceremonies, and other symbolic actions may have an impact on organizational success (Deal & Kennedy, 1982). Various forms of play within the organization such as jokes, teasing, brainstorming, and strategizing create a sense of community and reduce conflict. Rituals are rules that guide behavior within the organization and emphasize the company's cultural values. While rituals are taken for granted, ceremonies are more elaborate events to celebrate employee achievements, heroes, myths, symbols, and organizational milestones. The cultural network is the primary means of communication within the organization. This cultural network can "reinforce the basic beliefs of the organization, enhance the symbolic values of heroes by passing on stories of their deeds and accomplishments, set a new climate for change, and provide a tight structure of influence for the CEO" (p. 86).

Effective managers and leaders recognize the existence and importance of the cultural network and maintain appropriate contacts with key persons within the cultural network. These leaders maintain a visible presence within the organization and frequently communicate with all organizational members. In addition, they seek key friendships and utilize time with organizational members to communicate stories and anecdotes (Deal & Kennedy, 1982). Beyond effectiveness, symbolic leaders play an important role within the organization.

Symbolic Leaders and Organizational Culture

Bolman and Deal (1997) contend that meaning, belief, and faith are essential to a symbolic perspective of organizations. According to Bolman and Deal, symbols embody and express an organization's culture. Organizational culture is "the interwoven pattern of beliefs, values, practices, and artifacts that define for members who they are and how they are to do things" (p. 217). Organizational symbols include myths; stories and fairy tales; rituals; ceremonies; and metaphors, humor, and play. Myths provide a sense of organizational greatness and a connection to the past. Stories and fairy tales perpetuate organizational values and traditions and are the mechanism through which heroes and their exploits are remembered and shared with other organizational members. Rituals and ceremonies "create order, clarity, and predictability" (p. 223) within the organization. Rituals and ceremonies also create opportunities to communicate with the external environment. Finally, metaphors, humor, and play within the organization allow informal processes of communication to emerge to simplify complex issues and contend with ambiguity. Symbolic leaders are sensitive to culture and its importance to long-term success. In addition, these leaders are very trusting of other organizational members and rely on them to ensure success. Symbolic leaders see themselves as scriptwriters, directors, and actors in the daily drama of company affairs (Deal & Kennedy, 1982). According to Rafaeli and Worline (2000), symbols serve four functions within organizations. They reflect underlying aspects of culture, elicit emotional responses for organizational members, and represent the organization's values and assumptions. Symbols link organizational members' emotional responses and interpretations to organizational actions and provide a frame of reference and allow organizational members to communicate about vague and complex issues. Finally, symbols provide a unified system of significance for organizational members.

Summary

In summary, leaders play both a substantive and symbolic role in shaping and guiding organizational culture (Deal & Kennedy, 1982). Leaders should consider how they shape—and can reshape—organizational culture when the environment is changing rapidly and the organization is value-driven. Ultimately, leaders should focus upon organizational culture for three essential reasons: (a) the environment of schooling is becoming more complex; (b) the rate of change is accelerating; and (c) competition is intensifying and becoming more global (Brooks & Normore, in press).

Linking Organizational Culture to Leadership

Edgar Schein's (1992) often-cited work defines the link between organizational culture and leadership. He contends that leadership is closely associated with the creation and management of culture. In fact, he goes so far as to assert "the only thing of real importance that leaders do is to create and manage culture and that the unique talent of leaders is their ability to understand and work with culture" (p. 5). After acknowledging the variety of culture definitions present in the organizational literature, Schein provides a synthetic definition of organizational culture:

A pattern of shared basic assumptions that the group learned as it solved its problems
of external adaptation and internal integration, that has worked well enough to be
considered valid and, therefore, to be taught to new members as the correct way to
perceive, think, and feel in relation to those problems (p. 12).

Schein (1992) further suggests that culture is comprised of three interrelated
components: (a) artifacts, (b) espoused values, and (c) basic underlying assumptions. Artifacts include all of the things a person sees, hears, and feels upon
entering an unfamiliar organization. These artifacts may include the physical
environment, language, technology, products, and style of clothing as well as
the visible behavior of organizational members and organizational processes.
Espoused values are the set of values that become an essential part of organizational philosophy and serve as a guide in dealing with a variety of situations.
Basic underlying assumptions are taken for granted and are neither confronted nor debated. As a result, these assumptions are very difficult to
change.

According to Schein (1992), culture is a pervasive organizational phenomenon and encompasses organizational members' concerns and their approaches to dealing with those concerns. Thus, cultural assumptions develop
as a result of interactions between organizational members and their environment. To perform effectively, organizational members must achieve consensus
to perform effectively and enhance internal integration. Culture provides sta-
bility, predictability, and meaning in an uncertain environment as a result of
organizational decisions in the past. Schein contends the leader should focus
upon the internal and external interactions to ensure management, survival,
and growth of the organization and its members.

Developing and maintaining appropriate internal integration requires organizational members to define and elaborate upon certain concepts and
processes. They must create a common language and conceptual categories.
This allows organizational members to communicate with one another, interpret events in a similar fashion, and build a consensus of mission and meaning. Organizational members must define organizational membership and
establish the criteria for inclusion and exclusion. In addition, organizational
members must determine how power and status is distributed throughout the
organization. Developing norms of intimacy, friendship, and love creates appropriate boundaries for peer relationships within the organization. Organizational members must define what constitutes a reward and a punishment and
establish a process for administering them. Finally, organizational members
must establish processes for dealing with and giving meaning to uncommon

events. Leadership serves to provide an original source of ideas for the development of these concepts and processes (Schein, 1992).

As organizations evolve, they inevitably develop shared assumptions of more abstract organizational issues (Schein, 1992). Organizational members develop shared basic assumptions about the nature of reality and truth, time, space, human nature, human activity, and human relationships. As a result, leaders must learn to decipher a variety of cultural clues to maintain constructive relationships within the organization and to ensure organizational productivity. Schein also contends that leaders must acknowledge the complexity of organizational culture as well as the power they possess to influence the creation and development of that culture.

Schein (1992) alleges that the difference between management and leadership is the leader's concern with culture. An organization's founders may have a profound impact upon the development of the organization's culture as a result of their strong assumptions, self-confidence, and determination. These founders tend to select and recruit other organizational members who have similar personal attributes and impose their assumptions upon these new organizational members. Because of the founder's unique position within the emerging organizational structure, he/she will possess much influence in organizational decision-making processes.

Leaders use various mechanisms to embed and transmit culture within the organization (Schein, 1992). The issues that leaders pay attention to, measure, and control send a powerful message to other organizational members. The way in which a leader reacts during an organizational crisis may establish new norms or values and communicate other underlying assumptions. Leaders also embed culture through the budgetary process and allocation of scarce resources. Leaders also serve as role models, teachers, and coaches to communicate values and assumptions to other organizational members. Organizational members learn what type of behavior the organization values through the allocation of rewards and status. A subtle way in which leaders within the organization maintain the culture is to recruit, select, and promote individuals with similar values and beliefs. Organizational design and structure; systems and procedures; rites and rituals; physical space; stories about important events and people; and formal statements of organizational philosophy, mission, and vision may also be used by leaders to embed and transmit culture.

School Culture and Leadership

School culture affects every part of the organization. Collaborative cultures may have an impact on several aspects of the school. A school focused on school effectiveness and productivity provides teachers with opportunities for success. A collegial and collaborative culture improves communication among stakeholders and enhances problem-solving processes. A school culture may promote successful change and improvement efforts.

Sarason (1966) defined school culture as "those aspects of the setting which are viewed by school personnel as 'givens' or essential features, which would be defended strenuously against elimination or marked change, and which reflect psychological concepts and value judgments" (p. 3). Stolp and Smith's definition of school culture (as cited in Stolp, 1994) is "the historically transmitted patterns of meaning that include the norms, values, beliefs, ceremonies, rituals, traditions, and myths understood, maybe in varying degrees, by members of the school community" (p. 1). Thus, school culture refers to "the character of a school as it reflects deep patterns of values, beliefs, and traditions that have been formed over the course of its history" (Deal and Peterson, 1991, p. 7).

A productive school culture may improve school productivity. Several studies suggest that an organization that possesses a strong identity, adapts to the changing environment, and responds to the needs of its members will be more productive (Deal & Kennedy, 1982; Ouchi, 1982; Peters & Waterman, 1982). Successful schools share similar cultural characteristics to include organizational members who share strong values promoting safety and the primacy of learning, establish high expectations for students and teachers, believe in the importance of basic skills instruction, develop performance standards and feedback procedures, and value strong leadership (Deal & Peterson, 1991). Faculty, staff, students, and administrators may identify with the school with a productive school culture. A supportive, caring school environment may increase the energy and motivation of faculty, staff, students, and administrators. Finally, a purposeful culture allows organizational stakeholders to focus upon key values and behaviors and what is important (Deal & Peterson, 1999).

School Culture and Collaboration

Purkey and Smith (1985) describe the characteristics of a healthy school culture. In a school with a healthy culture, faculty members are given responsibility for increasing academic performance and are involved in democratic deci-sion-making processes. Collaborative relationships and a sense of community foster faculty involvement in these decision-making processes. Strong leader-ship within the school emerges to initiate and maintain school improvement efforts. Students spend a majority of their time engaged in active learning ac-tivities related to a well-articulated, coordinated curriculum. Ongoing staff development addresses the specific organizational and instructional needs of faculty and students. Parents are actively involved in the school community. Schoolwide recognition is provided to students achieving academic excellence. The district office supports the efforts of the faculty, staff, and administration. The mission and vision of the school are clearly articulated, leading to clear goals, high expectations, order, and discipline.

A collaborative school culture may impact the school in many ways. A col-laborative school culture fosters school effectiveness and productivity. In addi-tion, collegial and collaborative activities that foster better communication and problem-solving activities develop. This culture, in turn, promotes successful change and improvement efforts. Faculty, staff, students, and administrators commit to and identify with the organization. As the culture increases the en-ergy and motivation of faculty, staff, students, administrators, and community, these stakeholders increasingly focus upon what is important and valued (Deal & Peterson, 1999).

Collaboration and collegiality are very important for school improvement efforts (Barth, 1990). Barth suggests that most educators exhibit congeniality toward each other, not collegiality. In a collegial environment, educators talk openly about best practice. Teachers observe one another in their respective classrooms, work together in planning and designing curriculum, and teach each other about new and innovative teaching practices. Collegiality results in better decisions, higher morale, and trust among educators; sustained interest in adult learning; and increased motivation on the part of students. These col-laborative cultures are created and maintained through structures deliberately created by individuals within the organization (Hopkins, Ainscow, & West, 1994). Most often, the positional leaders have the greatest ability to modify these structures, though this is not always the case.

School Culture and School Improvement

Cunningham and Gresso (1993) offer similar suggestions for enhancing school improvement efforts through school culture. School culture may be enhanced by providing all organizational members with the opportunity to communicate about organizational issues on a regular basis. Quality information is provided to all organizational members to promote quality decision-making. The development of a collective vision allows for collective action toward a common goal. Collegiality and collaboration foster cohesion between organizational members and develop common understandings. Trust and support among faculty, staff, and administration is prevalent. When conflict emerges between individuals or groups, a spirit of compromise emerges. Individual empowerment and lifelong growth are promoted within the school. Finally, these processes contribute to sustained inquiry and continuous school improvement efforts.

School improvement occurs when teachers strengthen their teaching skills, the curriculum is renovated, the organization improves, and parents and citizens are involved in a partnership with the school (Saphier & King, 1985). The school culture may enhance these efforts or undermine them. According to Saphier and King, the 12 norms of school culture that affect school improvement are (a) collegiality; (b) experimentation; (c) high expectations; (d) trust and confidence; (e) tangible support; (f) reaching out to the knowledge bases; (g) appreciation and recognition; (h) caring, celebration, and humor; (i) involvement in decision-making; (j) protection of what is important; (k) traditions; and (l) honest, open communication

Leadership plays a role in the development of these norms. Without quality leadership, school culture will not develop or endure over time. Whenever these norms are present within a school, leaders, teachers, students, and other stakeholders reflect them in the discussion of values and in their behavior.

Types of School Cultures: "Forward-Moving" vs. "Stuck"

Each school has a unique culture and may be characterized as "forward-moving" or "stuck" (Rosenholtz, 1989), and in some instances, schools seem to be doing both at the same time (Brooks, 2006a; 2006b). Forward-moving schools are characterized by an emphasis on values and beliefs that are used to guide decision-making processes. Within these schools, stakeholders collaborate extensively and trust one another. Teachers emphasize student achievement, work together, and share instructional strategies.

On the other hand, in stuck schools, teachers do not achieve consensus on educational goals. Teachers are isolated from one another, self-reliant, and reluctant to collaborate. Most schools lack a shared technical culture and, thus, are "stuck" (Glickman, Gordon, & Ross-Gordon, 2001). These "stuck" schools are characterized by teacher isolation, lack of dialogue, inadequate induction, and a lack of involvement in the school's decision-making processes. Glickman asserts that schools would benefit by becoming advanced professional communities with a shared technical culture. Stakeholders in a shared technical culture have a common purpose, share expertise, and utilize methods for analyzing and solving problems. In addition, stakeholders use sophisticated performance standards for assessment and communicate through a shared technical language.

A Typology of School Culture

Fullan and Hargreaves (1996) describe various types of school culture as fragmented, balkanized, contrived collegiality, comfortable collaboration, and collaborative. A fragmented culture is characterized by teachers being isolated from other teachers and being insulated from outside interference. Teachers are autonomous and self-reliant and unaware of the activities in other teachers' classrooms. While individualism is encouraged, collaboration is discouraged. Because teachers are content with existing teaching practices, new and innovative teaching practices are not considered. Administrators are seldom available to assist, and when they do, teachers perceive the assistance as arrogance on the part of the administrator and incompetence on the part of the teacher.

In a balkanized culture, teachers collaborate and share only with friends or groups that are like-minded. These subcultures of teachers are strong and compete for position, resources, and territory. Members of these subcultures create shared perceptions of learning, teaching styles, discipline, and curriculum. Conflict results when teachers attempt to collaborate outside their respective subculture. The balkanized culture is characterized by poor communication, indifference, and divergent groups of teachers (Fullan & Hargreaves, 1996).

Contrived collegiality results when school leadership creates the processes of collaboration and determines structures. School leaders attempt to force teacher collaboration by controlling school structures. As a result, teachers are regulated and predictable. While this culture is meant to support new and innovative approaches to teaching, it actually reduces teacher motivation to cooperate beyond normal expectations. While the culture initially discourages true collegiality, it provides a credible starting point for the development of a true collaborative culture (Fullan & Hargreaves, 1996).

In a comfortably collaborative culture, teachers engage in conversations about schooling; however, these conversations do not involve critical questions about their work or how to improve the work. The conversations result in comfortable support for one another without constructive criticism. Teachers are aware of other teachers' classroom activities and discuss strategies for dealing with problem students (Fullan & Hargreaves, 1996).

A collaborative culture exists when teacher development is facilitated through interdependence. A majority of teachers agree on educational values and are committed to change and improvement. Teachers help, support, and trust one another and are aggressively curious about teaching and learning. Conversations among teachers focus upon school improvement. Teachers frequently observe other teachers in their classrooms. As a result of this observation, teachers engage in a critical analysis of teaching practices. School leaders challenge ineffective teaching practices while encouraging the professional development of individual teachers (Fullan & Hargreaves, 1996).

Certainly it is important to point out that each of these school culture "types" paints an unrealistically simple portrait of the complex cultural dynamics found in schools. While we find these types helpful in understanding school culture in the broadest sense, it is important to recognize that schools are mosaics of subcultures within the larger school—it is ultimately critical that school leaders seek to understand how these subcultures operate and interact with one another (Brooks & Jean-Marie, 2007).

School Leaders and School Culture

Leaders play a valuable role in shaping school culture. Norris (1994) suggests that shaping the school culture requires understanding, patience, and human relations and communication skills on the part of the leader. In addition, leaders must learn the existing culture by studying heroes, rituals, ceremonies, and cultural networks. Establishing communication linkages allows a leader to understand facets of the school culture. In order to learn about the school's culture, a leader must

1. meet the social and psychological needs of teachers by documenting accomplishments and providing encouragement and resources necessary for teaching and learning to occur;

2. create opportunities for individual teacher growth by promoting professional development and challenging teachers to expand their learning;

3. be open to self-examination and reflection, model desired behaviors, and hire new teachers who share the same educational philosophy as the school; and

4. communicate compelling ideas and the meaning of those ideas for organizational members (Sergiovanni, 1994).

The leader's principles, values, and beliefs and how they are communicated to organizational members are extremely important. As an important enculturation agent, school leaders shape school culture and must establish the link between mission and practice, focus on solutions, be creative, acknowledge the needs of others, promote staff development, create learning networks, and focus on student achievement as the primary goal of schooling (Krajewski, 1996; Saka, Southerland, & Brooks, 2009). Cultural leadership on the part of the leader requires the leader to stir human consciousness, interpret meanings, articulate key cultural strands, and link organizational members to them (Sergiovanni, 1984). The leader's long-range vision is also a key factor in the building of culture (Sashkin & Sashkin, 1993).

Fullan (1992) contends that leaders should enable other organizational members to become problem solvers. In facilitating the development of teachers as problem solvers, leaders create a collaborative school culture. To realize the development of the collaborative school culture, leaders should foster vision-building; create norms of collegiality while respecting individuality; develop problem-solving skills and conflict resolution strategies; promote lifelong teacher professional development that encourages teachers to be inquiring, reflective, and collaborative; and support school improvement initiatives.

Maehr and Midgley (1996) contend that two reasons exist for examining school culture. First, school culture makes a difference in the motivation and learning of students. When students sense and understand the mission of the school and recognize the salient elements of a collaborative school culture, student motivation and learning increases. Second, school culture is a manageable variable. For managing the culture, leaders may enhance the investment teachers and students make in their educational endeavors. However, for all the interest in understanding and influencing school culture, it is perhaps a poorly conceived idea in need of both critique and intense investigation. In the subsequent section, we examine some contemporary critiques of the themes and findings discussed above.

Critique of Classic Concepts of School Culture and Leadership: Five Points to Consider

In this section, we briefly discuss each of five critiques that can be leveled against the body of conceptual and empirical research discussed above. We do not explore each critique in great detail, and rather offer them as points for you to consider as you evaluate whether each or any combination of our "critiques" simply constitutes the identification of a gap in the literature or an omission that casts doubt on the accuracy and validity of the corpus of research in the social and cultural dynamics of educational leadership.

Critique One: Business Leadership Is Not School Leadership

The field of educational leadership has had a love/hate relationship with the business world. At times, researchers and practitioners alike have marveled at efficiency-based process models, bureaucratic structures, and hard-line tactics about organizational production. More recently, they have also admired some emerging business models that promote democratic principles and practices. However, scholars have pointed out that while we might borrow ideas and concepts from business, a basic difference between businesses and schools is that the foundation of educational leadership is *education*, not *management* (Murphy, 2002), which demands emphasis on, at least, "child development, learning theory, classroom management, effective teaching, motivation and discipline, and the appropriate use of instructional technology" (Siegrist, 1999, p. 200). Many of these ideas and concepts are absent in business literature, but are foundational to education.

Murphy further cites Evans (1991) and contends that "the deep significance of the task of the school administrator is to be found in the pedagogic ground of its vocation" (p. 17). . . and that a key to reculturing is changing the taproot of the profession from management to education" (Murphy, 2002, p. 168). The bottom line is that the field of educational leadership has long been influenced by business literature without questioning either the foundations on which business ideas rest or potential problems with transference of ideas from one field to another.[1] Other educational scholars likewise catalog issues related to problems with adopting business approaches to educational leadership (Bates, 1984; Gelberg, 1997; Greenfield, 1988; Griffiths, 1995, 1997).

Critique Two: The Difference-Blind Critique

In their 2002 chapter in the *NSSE Yearbook*, Larson and Murtadha point out some limitations of the knowledge base that undergirds educational leadership. In particular, they note that educational leadership research has been conceptualized as "difference-blind" in that it does not take into account how individual and group differences such as race, gender, sexuality, ethnicity, and social class influence leadership behavior. They argue that by ignoring these sociocultural differences, the knowledge base of the field is inherently flawed, since extant research suggests the importance of these factors (see Brooks et al., 2007 for a discussion of this). If you revisit much of the empirical and conceptual base reviewed in the previous section, you will find these dynamics conspicuous by their absence. Given that researchers have found that these factors, and still others, have a great deal of influence on leadership, it calls to question whether the entire knowledge base described above is completely inaccurate for these omissions.

Critique Three: The Rhetoric over Reality Critique

The rhetoric over reality critique centers on the way educational leaders speak about cultural and social dynamics, and while we might call on sociolinguistic theorists to support our position, we will offer this critique from lived experience and from our own research (Brooks, 2006a, 2006b; Brooks, Scribner, & Eferakorho, 2004; Brooks, Hughes, & Brooks, 2008; Brooks & Miles, 2008). Simply stated, this critique suggests that there is a distance between the way educational leaders and researchers generally discuss social and cultural dynamics and how said dynamics operate in practice. This is perhaps as much a matter of logistical convenience as it is misconceptualization, in that educational leaders are commonly charged with the responsibility to lead exceedingly large organizations and organizational units. It is simply easier to ignore the complex concepts of race, ethnicity, social class, subcultures, gender, sexuality, and many others and make decisions based on the supposition that there is a single culture or a few distinct subcultures in a school. However, as with so many areas of educational research and practice, it is essential that leaders embrace intricacy rather than eschew it and endeavor to comprehend that school decisions need to be made based on the notion that students, staff members, administrators, counselors, and teachers each have their own culture and that decisions must be sensitive to a plurality rather than a plenum, which leads us to the concept of propriespect.

Critique Four: The Lost Individuality Critique

Propriespect is the notion that each person has a unique cultural experience rather than necessarily adopting or assimilating group and/or organizational values and norms to form a single group with a single group of cultural and social dynamics. Put differently, everyone has an individual culture and everyone experiences society in a unique way. Wolcott (1991) suggested that propriespect was useful in that it challenged the idea that people's culture was merely "a complement to all the information aggregated within an entire cultural heritage" and recognized a "need to specify the particular information that any particular human, who must therefore be a member of a particular subset of human groups, actually knows" (p. 257).

Building on this basic concept to argue that while educators are quite happy to base their instructional work on the premise that all students learn in a unique manner, *we must likewise embrace the notion that each person in the school has a unique culture.* This individual culture, in turn, greatly influences the way that educational leaders should think about their work as instructional and cultural leaders. Moreover, leaders should understand that they have the potential to influence the social and cultural context of a school, and this in turn influences the dynamic action that occurs between people when they interact through education and the way the collective concurrently subverts and marginalizes the importance of the way *individuals* experience, construct, influence, and are influenced by these dynamics.

While we as a field are quick to proclaim our belief that each student learns, behaves, and develops in a unique manner, we are less willing to accept the possibility that each student is likewise unique with respect to other important educational characteristics, culture being one of these. This is of course a daunting prospect, yet consider this—while educational leadership scholars continue to emphasize the collective (e.g., Fullan, 2001; Schein, 1992, and the entire literature reviewed above), anthropologists (Wolcott, 1970) and sociologists (Lortie, 1975) have argued for some time that a deeper investigation of individual culture will lead to key breakthroughs, and as we argue in this chapter—they allow us to serve *every* student in a culturally relevant and powerful and individualized manner while also making teaching a personally meaningful profession for those in schools.

Critique Five: The Glocal Critique

The literature we reviewed at the onset of this chapter does not take into account any issues related to globalization and glocalization. Glocalization (Courchene, 1995; Weber, 2007; Spring, 1998, 2008) is a meaningful integration of local and global forces, which properly considered can help educational leaders inform and enhance their pedagogy and practice. While it is beyond the scope of this chapter to go into much detail here about the complexity of glocalization, we refer readers to another article (see Brooks & Normore, in press) and suggest that contemporary educational leaders must develop glocal literacy in at least nine domains of practice: political literacy (Cassel & Lo, 1997), economic literacy (Stevens & Weale, 2003), cultural literacy (Lechner & Boli, 2005), moral literacy (Normore & Doscher, 2007), pedagogical literacy (Maclellan, 2008), information literacy (Abdelaziz, 2004), organizational literacy (Earle & Kruse, 1999), spiritual and religious literacy (Dantley, 2005), and temporal literacy (Marx, 2006). Further, we note other scholars identifying other forms of literacy, such as racial literacy (Guinier, 2004; Horsford, 2009) and that it is important to understand that each of these domains is dynamic, ecologically interconnected, and can be influenced by the discrete agency of leaders (Capra, 1996).

What's Next? Toward Culturally Relevant Leadership

Given the extant knowledge base and critiques we have discussed in this chapter, it is important for us to consider what kind of educational leadership practices and research agendas might better serve students. Certainly, there is a need to conduct historical, philosophical, qualitative, quantitative, and mixed-method research on the social and cultural dynamics of educational leadership using various forms of critical theory, such as critical race theory, critical feminist theory, queer theory, and critical studies of how ethnicity, social class, political and social capital, and other characteristics and social forces influence the practice of educational leadership. This approach would help deconstruct and interrogate the perhaps incorrect assumptions upon which much of our (mis)understanding of the field is based and point the way toward new practice and research possibilities.

A second and equally important avenue of exploration is to connect our research and practice more directly to that of our colleagues in other fields of education and in the social sciences (Bogotch et al., 2008). In particular, the possibilities and ideas advanced in the area of culturally relevant pedagogy might ultimately suggest a culturally relevant leadership that could revolutionize the way administrators are trained and developed (see Brooks, 2009). Leadership of this sort is an other-oriented (or loving) approach that emphasizes service, humility, compassion, listening, and observing (Liable, 2000). It begins with establishing high-quality individual relationships and then sustains them through meaningful and protean working networks. Culturally relevant leadership is critical and proactive rather than status quo and passive. Culturally relevant leadership is driven by both hard and soft data (Ladson-Billings, 1992, 1995a, 1995b, 1995c, 1997, 1998). By beginning our exploration of culture and considering and working toward a culturally relevant leadership, in scholarship and practice, we might begin to understand the way the social and cultural dynamics of educational leadership shape the lives of children in ways we have not yet discovered.

Note

1   A fascinating exploration of this is Mintzberg's (1993) analysis of education's use of strategic planning. Mintzberg found that there is no solid evidence for this practice in the business world, but that educators have—and continue to—adopt these processes uncritically.

References

Abdelaziz, A. (2004). Information literacy for lifelong learning. Paper presented at the World Library and Information Congress: 70th IFLA General Conference and Council, p. 4. Retrieved on June 6, 2009 from: http://www.ifla.org/IV/ifla70/papers/116e-Abid.pdf

Barth, R. S. (1990). *Improving schools from within: Teachers, parents, and leaders can make the difference.* San Francisco: Jossey-Bass.

Bates, R. J. (1984). Toward a critical practice of educational administration. In T. J. Sergiovanni & J. E. Corbally (Eds.), *Leadership and organizational culture: New perspectives on administrative theory and practice* (pp. 260–274). Urbana: University of Illinois Press.

Bogotch, I., Beachum, F., Blount, J., Brooks, J. S., & English, F. W. (2008). *Radicalizing educational leadership: Toward a theory of social justice.* Rotterdam, Netherlands: Sense Publishers.

Bolman, L. G., & Deal, T. E. (1997). *Reframing organizations: Artistry, choice, and leadership* (2nd ed.). San Francisco, CA: Jossey-Bass.

Brooks, J. S. (2009). The miseducation of a professor of educational administration: Learning and unlearning culturally (ir)relevant leadership. In A. K. Tooms & C. Boske (Eds.), *Bridge leadership: Connecting educational leadership and social justice to improve schools* (pp. 153-169). Charlotte, NC: Information Age Publishing.

Brooks, J. S. (2006a). Tinkering toward utopia or stuck in a rut? School reform implementation at Wintervalley High. *Journal of School Leadership, 16*(3), 240–265.

Brooks, J. S. (2006b). *The dark side of school reform: Teaching in the space between reality and utopia.* Lanham, MD: Rowman & Littlefield Education.

Brooks, J. S., Hughes, R., & Brooks, M. C. (2008). Fear and trembling in the American high school: Educational reform and teacher alienation. *Educational Policy, 22*(1): 45–62.

Brooks, J. S., & Jean-Marie, G. (2007). Black leadership, white leadership: Race and race relations in an urban high school. *Journal of Educational Administration, 45*(6): 756–768.

Brooks, J. S., & Miles, M. T. (2008). From scientific management to social justice...and back again? Pedagogical shifts in educational leadership, in A. H. Normore, (Ed.), *Leadership for social justice: Promoting equity and excellence through inquiry and reflective practice* (pp. 99–114). Charlotte, NC: Information Age Publishing.

Brooks, J. S., Normore, A. H., Jean-Marie, G., & Hodgins, D. (2007). Distributed leadership for social justice: Influence and equity in an urban high school. *Journal of School Leadership 17*(4): 378-408.

Brooks, J. S., & Normore, A. H. (in press). Educational leadership and globalization: Toward a glocal perspective. *Educational Policy.*

Brooks, J. S., Scribner, J. P., & Eferakorho, J. (2004). Teacher leadership in the context of whole school reform. *Journal of School Leadershipm, 14*(3), 242-265.

Capra, F. (1996). *The web of life: A new scientific understanding of living systems.* New York: Anchor Books.

Cassel, C. A., & Lo, C. C. (1997). Theories of political literacy. *Political Behavior, 19*, 317–335.

Courchene, T. J. (1995). Glocalization: The regional/international interface. *Canadian Journal of Regional Science, 18*(1), 1–20.

Cunningham, W. G., & Gresso, D. W. (1993). *Cultural leadership: The culture of excellence in education.* Needham Heights, MA: Allyn & Bacon.

Dantley, M. E. (2005). African American spirituality and Cornel West's notions of prophetic pragmatism: Restructuring educational leadership in American urban schools. *Educational Administration Quarterly, 41*(4), 651–674.

Deal, T. E., & Kennedy, A. A. (1982). *Corporate cultures: The rites and rituals of corporate life.* Reading, MA: Addison-Wesley.

Deal, T. E., & Peterson, K. D. (1991). *The leader's role in shaping school culture.* Washington, DC: United States Department of Education.

Deal, T. E., & Peterson, K. D. (1999). *Shaping school culture: The heart of leadership.* San Francisco: Jossey-Bass.

Earle, J., and Kruse, S. (1999). *Organizational literacy for education: Topic in educational leadership.* Mahwah, NJ: Lawrence Erlbaum Associates.

Evans, R. (1991, April). *Ministrative insight: Educational administration as pedagogic practice.* Paper presented at the annual meeting of the American Educational Research Association, Chicago, IL.

Fullan, M. (2001). *Leading in a culture of change.* San Francisco: Jossey-Bass.

Fullan, M. G. (1992). Visions that blind. *Educational Leadership, 49*(5), 19–22.

Fullan, M. & Hargreaves, A., (1996). *What's worth fighting for in your school?* New York: Teachers College Press.

Gelberg, D. (1997). *The "business" of reforming American schools.* Albany: State University of New York Press.

Glickman, C. D., Gordon, S. P., Ross-Gordon, J. M. (2001). *Supervision and instructional leadership: A developmental approach.* Needham Heights, MA: Allyn & Bacon.

Greenfield, T. B. (1988). The decline and fall of science in educational administration. In D. E. Griffith, R. T. Stout, & P. B Forsyth (Eds.), *Leaders for America's schools* (pp. 131--159). Berkeley, CA: McCutchan.

Griffiths, D. E. (1995). Theoretical pluralism in educational administration. In R. Donmoyer, M. Imber, & J. J. Scheurich (Eds.), *The knowledge base in educational administration: Multiple perspectives* (pp. 300-309). Albany: State University of New York Press.

Griffiths, D. E. (1997). The case for theoretical pluralism. *Educational Management & Administration, 25,* 371-380.

Guinier, L. (2004). From racial liberalism to racial literacy: *Brown v. Board of Education* and the interest-divergence dilemma. *Journal of American History, 91*(1), 92-118.

Hopkins, D., Ainscow, M., & West, M. (1994). *School improvement in an era of change.* New York: Teachers College Press.

Horsford, S. D. (2009, Summer). The case for racial literacy in educational leadership: Lessons learned from superintendent reflections on desegregation. *UCEA Review, 50*(2), 5-7.

Kilmann, R. H., Saxton, M. J., & Serpa, R. (1986). Issues in understanding and changing culture. *California Management Review, 28* (2), 87-94.

Krajewski, R. J. (1996). Enculturating the school: The leader's principles. *NASSP Bulletin, 80*(1), 3-8.

Ladson-Billings, G. (1998). Teaching in dangerous times: Culturally relevant approaches to teacher assessment. *The Journal of Negro Education, 67*(3), 255-267.

Ladson-Billings, G. (1997). *The dreamkeepers: Successful teachers of African-American children.* San Francisco, CA: Jossey-Bass.

Ladson-Billings, G. (1995a). Toward a theory of culturally relevant pedagogy. *American Education Research Journal, 35,* 465-491.

Ladson-Billings, G. (1995b). Toward a critical race theory of education. *Teachers College Record, 97,* 47-68.

Ladson-Billings, G. (1995c). But that's just good teaching! The case for culturally relevant pedagogy. *Theory into Practice, 34*(3), 159-165.

Ladson-Billings, G. (1992). Liberatory consequences of literacy: A case of culturally relevant instruction for African American students. *The Journal of Negro Education, 61*(3), 378-391.

Larson, C. L., & Murtadha, K. (2002). Leadership for social justice. In J. Murphy (Ed.), *The educational leadership challenge: Redefining leadership for the 21st century* (pp. 134-161). Chicago: University of Chicago Press.

Lechner, F., & Boli, J. (2005). *World culture: Origins and consequences.* Malden, MA: Blackwell.

Liable, J. (2000). A loving episetmology: What I hold critical in my life, faith, and profession. *International Journal of Qualitative Studies in Education, 13*(6), 683-692.

Lortie, D. C. (1975). *Schoolteacher: A sociological study.* Chicago, IL: University of Chicago Press.

Maclellan, E. (2008). Pedagogical literate: What it means and what it allows. *Teaching and Teacher Education, 24*(8), 1986-1992.

Maehr, M. L., & Midgley, C. (1996). *Transforming school cultures.* Boulder, CO: Westview Press.

Marcoulides, G. A., & Heck, R. H. (1993). Organizational culture and performance: Proposing and testing a model. *Organization Science, 4*(2), 209-225.

Marx, G. T. (2006). *Future-focused leadership: Preparing schools, students, and communities for tomorrow's realities.* Alexandria, VA: Association for Supervision and Curriculum Development.

Mintzberg, H. (1993). *The rise and fall of strategic planning: Reconceiving roles for planning, plans, planners.* New York: Simon & Schuster.

Murphy, J. (2002). Reculturing the profession of educational leadership: New blueprints. *Educational Administration Quarterly, 38*(2), 176-191.

Normore, A. H., & Paul Doscher, S. (2007). Using media as the basis for a social issues approach to promoting moral literacy in university teaching. *Journal of Educational Administration, 45*(4), 427-450.

Norris, J. H. (1994). What leaders need to know about school culture. *Journal of Staff Development, 15*(2), 2-5.

Ouchi, W. G. (1982). *Theory Z.* Reading, MA: Addison-Wesley.

Peters, T. J., & Waterman, R. H., Jr. (1982). *In search of excellence: Lessons from America's best-run companies.* New York: Harper and Row.

Purkey, S. C., & Smith, M. S. (1985). School reform: The district policy implications of the effective schools literature. *The Elementary School Journal, 85*(3), 353-389.

Rafaeli, A., & Worline, M. (2000). Symbols in organizational culture. In N. M. Ashkanasy, C. P. M. Wilderom, & M. F. Peterson (Eds.), *Handbook of organizational culture and climate* (pp. 71-84). Thousand Oaks, CA: Sage Publications.

Rosenholtz, S. J. (1989). *Teacher's workplace: The social organization of schools.* White Plains, NY: Longman.

Saka, Y., Southerland, S. A., & Brooks, J. S. (2009). Becoming a member of a school community while working toward science education reform: Teacher induction from a cultural historical activity theory (CHAT) perspective. *Science Education, 93*(3): 1-30.

Saphier, J., & King, M. (1985). Good seeds grow in strong cultures, *Educational Leadership, 42*(6), 67-74.

Sarason, S. (1966). *The school culture and processes of change.* College Park, MD: University of Maryland.

Sashkin, M., & Sashkin, M. G. (1993). Leaders and their school cultures: Understanding from quantitative and qualitative research. In M. Sashkin & H. J. Walberg (Eds.), *Educational leadership and school culture* (pp. 100-123). Berkeley, CA: McCutchan Publishing.

Schein, E. H. (1992). *Organizational culture and leadership* (2nd ed.). San Francisco, CA: Jossey-Bass.

Sergiovanni, T. J. (1984). Cultural and competing perspectives in administrative theory and practice. In T. J. Sergiovanni & J. E. Corbally (Eds.), *Leadership and organizational culture: New perspectives on administrative theory and practice* (pp. 1-17). Urbana: University of Illinois Press.

Sergiovanni, T. J. (1994). *Building community in schools.* San Francisco, CA: Jossey-Bass.

Siegrist, G. (1999). Educational leadership must move beyond management training to visionary and moral transformational leaders. *Education, 120*(2), 297-303.

Spring, J. (2008). Research on globalization and education. *Review of Educational Research, 78*(2), 330-363.

Spring, J. (1998). *Education and the rise of the global economy.* Mahwah, NJ: Lawrence Erlbaum.

Stolp, S. (1994). Leadership for school culture. *ERIC Digest #91*. Eugene, OR: ERIC Clearing-house on Educational Management.

Stevens, P., & Weale, M. (2003). *Education and economic growth*. London: National Institute of Economic and Social Research.

Trice, H. M., & Beyer, J. M. (1993). *The culture of work organizations*. Englewood Cliffs, NJ: Prentice Hall.

Weber, E. (2007). Globalization, "glocal" development, and teachers' work: A research agenda. *Review of Educational Research, 77*(3), pp. 279–309.

Westheimer, J. (1998). *Among school teachers: Community, autonomy, and ideology in teachers' work*. New York: Teachers College Press.

Wolcott, H. F. (1970). An ethnographic approach to the study of school administrators. *Human Organization, 29*(2), 115–122.

Wolcott, H. F. (1991). Propriespect and the acquisition of culture. *Anthropology and Education Quarterly, 22*(3), 251–273.

✠ CHAPTER 2

Rethinking Transformational Leadership in Schools: The Influence of People, Place, and Process on Leadership Practice[1]

April L. Peters

Leadership theory is an important aspect of organizational development. Oftentimes, the success or failure of an organization is attributed to its leader's approach or style. Many believe that successful, effective leadership can occur at many different levels of the organization. For example, Bass and Riggio (2006) assert that it is critical for leaders to develop leadership skills among their subordinates, an idea central to the theory of transformational leadership, a term first coined by Downton (1973) and further developed by political sociologist James MacGregor Burns (Bass & Riggio, 2006). But while transformational leadership has enjoyed increasing popularity as a leadership style, effective transformational leadership should be examined and understood in light of the various elements that impact leadership within an organization, including the context, the people, and the processes through which leadership occurs, including exchanges between the leader and constituents.

Thus, the purpose of this chapter is to demonstrate the ways in which transformational leadership is dependent upon a leader's deep understanding of how these elements of people (personnel), place (context), and process (transactional leadership) are also important to the work of principals and school leaders. The chapter first reviews traditional understandings of transformational leadership. Next, the concept of transformational leadership is unpacked by using a practical example to explicate the nuances of this leadership style and its interaction with people, place, and process. Finally, a discussion and implications for school leadership are provided.

Transformational and Transactional Leadership

Transformational leadership is a leadership style in which the leader engages constituents in a manner that transforms, or changes, them (Northouse, 2007). As Burns (1978) developed the concept of transformational leadership, he made the distinction between transformational and transactional leadership. Transactional leadership is primarily concerned with the exchanges that take place between leaders and their followers. In contrast, transformational leadership is focused on the relationship that the leader fosters in order to inspire others toward increased motivation and higher levels of morality (Northouse, 2007). This chapter examines the ways in which these leadership models are inextricably linked and work together to influence effective leadership.

Transformational Leadership

According to Bass (1990), transformational leadership exists when "leaders broaden and elevate the interests of their employees, when they generate awareness and acceptance of the purposes and mission of the group, and when they stir their employees to look beyond their own self-interest for the good of the group" (p. 21). Another definition of transformational leadership explains it is "a leadership that facilitates the redefinition of a people's mission and vision, a renewal of their commitment, and the restructuring of their systems for goal accomplishment" (Leithwood, 1992). Thus, transformational leadership is concerned with the effect of the leader's behavior on his or her followers (Yammorino, Dionne, & Chun, 2002). Bass (1990) outlines the characteristics of a transformational leader as follows: (1) *charisma*, which draws the confidence of employees; (2) *inspiration*, which excites employees; (3) *individual consideration*, where close attention is paid to each employee; and (4) *intellectual stimulation*, where creativity and "rational" solutions to problems are explored.

Transactional Leadership

An alternative but related type of leadership is transactional leadership. Bass (1990) defines transactional leadership as "transactions between managers and employees" and identifies three predominate styles that transactional leaders rely on: (1) *contingent reward*—rewards and recognition for employees that perform well; (2) *active management by exception*—searching for poor performance and disciplining those employees who do not perform; and (3) *passive management by exception*—intervention occurs only when standards are not being met. There is a fourth measure of transactional leadership, *laissez-faire leadership*, which can actually be considered a measure of nonleadership (Hinkin & Schriesheim, 2008), and describes someone who avoids leadership responsibility altogether (Bass, 1990).

The Relationship between Transformational and Transactional Leadership

According to Burns (1978), the difference between transformational and transactional leadership is the relationship between the leaders and their followers. In his book, *Leadership*, Burns (1978) explains that transactional leadership occurs when "one person takes the initiative in making contact with others for the purpose of an exchange of valued things," and transformational leadership "occurs when one or more persons engage with others in such a way that leaders and followers raise one another to higher levels of motivation and morality."

There are, however, differing opinions on the relationship between transformational and transactional leadership. While Burns states that transformational and transactional leadership fall at opposite ends of the continuum (Tejada, Scandura, & Pillai, 2001), Bass disagrees, arguing "transformational and transactional leadership are conceptually separate and independent dimensions that appear simultaneously in the behavioral repertoire of leaders" (Tejada et al., 2001). In other words, leaders who are transformational also engage in transactional leadership behaviors (Howell & Avolio, 1993).

Some researchers believe that the two leadership styles are complementary, as transactional leadership is more concerned with the day-to-day tasks that keep organizations operating while transformational leadership is "value-added" (Leithwood, 1992). Bass also notes that transformational leadership augments transactional leadership (Tejada et al., 2001) and suggests that "transactional leadership is a necessary precondition if transformational leadership is to be effective," and because it is based on clear directions, transactional leadership makes transformational leadership "less confusing and ambiguous" (Hinkin & Schriesheim, 2008). Bass and Riggio (2006) explain that transformational leadership can be viewed as an extension of transactional leadership in that it takes the basic exchange between leaders and followers and "raises it to the next level" through inspiration, by creating a shared vision between the two, and finally, through the development of the followers' leadership skills.

Bass and colleagues (2003) find that as a result of transformational leadership, "followers' feelings of involvement, cohesiveness, commitment, potency, and performance are enhanced" (Bass et al., 2003). Further reports indicate that transformational leadership was positively correlated with employee evaluations of managers, recommendations for promotions, and research and development innovations (Bass et al., 2003). When influenced by a transformational leader, followers are motivated to do more than they originally expected to do. They become more aware of the importance of the task and outcome and are "induced to transcend their own self-interest for the sake of the organization" (Yukl, 1999). Bass and Riggio (2006) explain that, through motivation and more challenging expectations set for their followers, transformational leaders are able to elicit higher levels of performance for followers as well as increased levels of follower satisfaction. Transactional leadership has been defined as simply a process of leader–follower exchange, and is considered, by some, as either ineffective (Yukl, 1999) or less effective than transformational leadership (Bass, 1990). Bass (1990) describes transactional leadership as a "prescription for mediocrity" and finds that employees of a transactional leader are more likely to exert less effort than those of a transformational leader.

Laissez-faire leadership, the fourth aspect of transactional leadership, has been described by some researchers as "the antithesis of the leadership construct" (Tejada et al., 2001). Unlike the other styles of transactional and transformational leadership, Hinkin and Schriesheim (2008) explain that laissez-faire leadership is the only type of leadership that is not reliant upon the performance of subordinates, but is characterized entirely by the leader's avoidance of decision-making. Research by Skogstad, Einarsen, Torsheim, Aasland, and Hetland (2007) label laissez-faire leadership as "a destructive leadership behavior" (Hinkin & Schriesheim, 2008).

Assessing Leadership Style

Researchers understand the need to assess leaders along several dimensions of leadership and have developed tools to do so. The Full Range of Leadership model combines the four aspects of transformational leadership with the three styles of transactional leadership as well as laissez-faire leadership (Bass & Riggio, 2006). To assess the three leadership styles and analyze leadership traits, organizations use the Multifactor Leadership Questionnaire (MLQ) created by Bass (Avolio, Bass, & Jung, 1999). The MLQ is still in widespread use today among researchers and throughout organizations. It is the most widely used instrument to assess transformational leadership and is considered "the best validated measure of transformational and transactional leadership" (Muen- john & Armstrong, 2008). Survey research done using the MLQ (5X) supports the idea that charisma is an essential component of transformational leader- ship. There is no consistent research on the relationship between transforma- tional and charismatic leadership (Yukl, 1999); however, charismatic leadership is often considered in tandem with transformational leadership. Charisma is defined as "special personality characteristic that gives a person superhuman or exceptional powers...and results in the person being treated as a leader" (Weber cited in Northouse, 2007). However, charisma is not a neces- sary condition for transformational leadership. Yukl (1999) suggests transfor- mational leadership has been broadly defined to include almost any type of successful and effective leadership, regardless of the influence process, and contends that leaders can be transformational without being charismatic.

The MLQ is comprised of two forms—the Leader form, that asks the leader to rate his/her leadership styles, and the Rater form, which asks follow- ers (i.e., subordinates or direct reports) to rate the frequency of the leader's leadership behavior (Bass & Riggio, 2006). Bass and Riggio (2006) explain that the Rater form is actually the more important of the two MLQ forms, as raters are usually more unbiased than leaders. The Rater form is most com- monly used in research relating to transformational and transactional leader- ship (Bass & Riggio, 2006).

Originally, the MLQ consisted of 73 items based on data compiled by James MacGregor Burns used for his description of transformational leader- ship (Bass & Avolio, 2006). Criticisms of the MLQ arose, including those fo- cused on "problems with item wording, lack of discriminate validity among certain leadership factors, and the incorporation of behaviors and attributions in the same scale" (Avolio et al., 1999). The MLQ was eventually revised to the MLQ (5X), which is presently used. The MLQ (5X) consists of 36 items that assess the leadership dimensions defined by the Full Range of Leadership model, as well as nine additional items that measure outcomes relating to the leader's effectiveness, follower satisfaction, and a measurement of the extent to which followers exert effort (Bass & Riggio, 2006).

Transformational Leadership in Schools: What the Research Says

There have been many studies in the past in order to understand the effects of transformational leadership on organizations. These studies have typically involved businesses or the military, and recent research has emerged attempting to understand transformational leadership in schools. As federal school reform policies and politics trickle down to the local level, school leaders are faced with a changing educational landscape. Leithwood (1992) found that transformational leaders in schools are in constant pursuit of three goals: "1) helping staff members develop and maintain a collaborative, professional school culture; 2) fostering teacher development; and 3) helping them solve problems together more effectively" (pp. 9–10).

Effects of Transformational Leadership on Teaching and Learning

Leithwood and Jantzi (2006) conducted a study to test the effects of transformational school leadership on teachers and their classroom practices and on student learning. Almost 2,300 teachers from 655 primary schools were included in the study. Their study included three broad leadership categories, each with three specific practices. The first category, setting directions, included building a school vision, developing goals, and setting high performance expectations. The second category, developing people, included intellectual stimulation, individualized support, and modeling professional practices. Finally, the third category, redesigning the organization, included developing a collaborative school culture, designing structures that encourage collaboration, and creating productive community partnerships (Leithwood & Jantzi, 2006).

Their study found that transformational leadership had a very strong and direct effect on teachers' work settings and motivation and a moderate but significant effect on teachers' classroom practices. However, their study did not produce results that explained the variation in student achievement gains (Leithwood & Jantzi, 2006). Based on these results, Leithwood and Jantzi (2006) concluded that transformational leadership has an important influence on the "likelihood that teachers will change their classroom practices," but they also state that there is a difference between classroom practices that are changed, and those that lead to greater student learning and achievement. They point out that an area for possible future research would be to understand the variety of sources of transformational leadership throughout a school, and to determine which sources are best for which practices (Leith-wood & Jantzi, 2006).

Impact of Transformational Leadership on Teacher Satisfaction and Commitment

Additional studies aim to understand whether a principal's transformational leadership style impacts teacher satisfaction and teacher commitment. Research by Leithwood, Jantzi, and Steinbach found that teachers in schools with a transformational principal are more likely than teachers in other schools to express satisfaction with their principal, report that they exert extra effort, and are more committed to the organization and to improving it (Ross & Gray, 2006). Hinkin and Tracey found that transformational leadership is "positively correlated with satisfaction with the leader, effectiveness of the leader, role clarity, mission clarity and openness of communication" (Lunenberg, 2003). Further research done by Leithwood found that the contribution of leadership to the development of a strong school culture was essential for supporting a collective school identity. Leithwood also proposed that transformational leaders "raise the aspirations of followers and align their goals more closely to organizational intents" (Ross & Gray, 2006).

Impact of Principal Leadership on Teacher Agency and Outcomes

Using 3,074 responses from 218 schools in two large school districts in Ontario, Canada, Ross and Gray (2006) conducted a study of the impact of principal leadership on teacher outcomes. The results of their study found that the principal's role "offers a variety of opportunities to improve the agency beliefs of staff" and that transformational leadership directly and indirectly influenced worker satisfaction and organizational commitment (Ross & Gray, 2006). Ross and Gray outlined three specific ways in which principal leadership can affect teachers. First, principals should overtly influence teacher interpretation of school and classroom data, helping them to identify relationships between achievement and teaching and to take responsibility for success and failures in the classroom. Second, principals should help teachers set realistic goals to increase the likelihood of "mastery experiences." Lastly, principals should provide teachers with access to high-quality professional development and provide feedback on their skill acquisition (Ross & Gray, 2006).

Effects of Charisma in Stable School Organizations

In 2003, Lunenberg developed two studies to assess the relevance of charisma in stable school organizations using, in total, 207 superintendents, 634 principals, and 277 teachers. His research results provided empirical support for three behavioral dimensions of transformational leadership, and are consistent with past theoretical findings and found that while charisma may not be relevant for leaders in stable organizations, the other three dimensions may be very important. Using schools as an example, he discovered that educational leaders should communicate "a sense of where the organization is going, develop the skills and abilities of subordinates, and encourage innovating problem solving." Lunenberg (2003) also suggested expanding the dimensions in order to provide for a more accurate understanding of leadership behaviors. First, through the dimension of intellectual stimulation, he suggested inclusion of nontraditional approaches to problems. Second, through the dimension of individualized consideration, he suggested a focus on individualized development. Lastly, he recommended the third dimension of inspirational motivation, which he argued should include the articulation of future orientation (Lunenberg, 2003). Lunenberg (2003) also noted the need to reduce any emphasis on charisma as a part of transformational leadership and instead focus on "identifiable" leadership behaviors.

Influence of Transformational and Transactional Leadership in Schools

Using primary schools in Tanzania as a case study, researchers Nguni, Sleegers, and Denessen (2006) used aspects of the MLQ to study the influence of transformational and transactional leadership on three outcome variables: teachers' job satisfaction, organizational commitment, and organizational citizenship behavior. Results indicated that both transformational and transactional leadership influenced teachers' job satisfaction, organizational commitment, and organizational citizenship behavior, but differed in the type and manner of the influence. Researchers determined that, overall, transformational leadership had stronger, more positive influences on the outcome variables, as compared with transactional leadership. Transformational leadership had moderate to strong positive effects, while transactional leadership had weak and insignificant effects (Nguni, Sleegers, & Denessen, 2006).

Nguni et al. (2006) found that, of the transformational leadership characteristics, charismatic leadership had the greatest influence in this study. Individualized consideration, the transformational leadership trait where close attention is paid to each employee, had a weak and insignificant effect on the three outcome variables (Nguni et al., 2006). Studies by Yukl and Geijsel attempted to explain the results, stating that individualized consideration usually consists of two dimensions, "developing" (coaching and mentoring) and "supporting (respect and admiration) (Nguni et al., 2006). In the Tanzania study, individualized consideration was more strongly represented by the "supporting" dimension, and the weak results were in line with the prior studies that show that the "supporting" dimension typically produced weak effects (Nguni et al., 2006). Intellectual stimulation, where creativity and "rational" solutions to problems are explored, was found to have a weak influence on job satisfaction and virtually no influence on the other two outcome variables (Nguni et al., 2006).

Of the transactional leadership characteristics, Nguni et al. (2006) discovered, most notably, contingent reward had a moderately strong negative influence on teachers' commitment to stay but a moderately positive influence on job satisfaction. The negative influence on teachers' commitment to stay could possibly be explained by the fact that in Tanzania, teacher rewards (pay raises, etc.) are given out by the central government (Nguni et al., 2006). Passive management by exception, when leaders intervene only when standards are not being met, as well as laissez-faire leadership, or the avoidance of leadership responsibility, both had strong negative effects on teachers' commitment to stay (Nguni et al., 2006).

Results of the Tanzanian study by Nguni et al. (2006) show that school leaders should use a combination of both transformational and transactional leadership in order to be successful. Bass suggests that these relationships between leaders and followers can be observed in a "wide range of organizations and cultures in different parts of the world, and the results of this study support Bass' assertions about "the universality of the transformational and transactional leadership paradigm across nations and societies" (Nguni et al., 2006). This particular study is also important because, in the past, most studies have been done in Western countries and this case uses a developing nation for its sample (Nguni et al., 2006).

Rethinking Transformational Leadership: Interrogating the Theory in Practice

Although transformational leadership provides an insightful manner in which to provide leadership within organizations, several factors should be taken into consideration in the implementation of this leadership approach in schools. The research on this approach seems to suggest that there is a universal method to becoming a transformational leader without considering the context, the developmental level of the followers, and the significance of transactions related to goal attainment within the organization. Research does indicate that organizational change is best facilitated by transformational leaders (Bass, 1990; Howell & Avolio, 1993). Thus several questions must be addressed in order to consider an approach to transformational leadership that: transforms the organization, inspires individuals toward a greater morality, and creates a better relationship between the leader and followers, but does not fall in lock step with the ways in which this theory has been presented in the literature. Therefore, the questions posed here are used to interrogate this theory utilizing the (1998) movie *Lean on Me* as a lens to view the tensions and complexities of effective leadership given the immediate and larger social and political context, the developmental level of constituents, and the interaction between transactional and transformational leadership. A brief description of the movie follows.

> Lean on Me *is based on the true story of a high school principal charged with changing a failing New Jersey school in less than a year before a state takeover. State law required that seventy-five percent of students pass a basic proficiency exam. Because of their consistent poor performance, the State Department of Education threatened to take over the school district. Joe Clark, an elementary school principal, was asked by his superintendent to assume the leadership of East Side High School. The school was an unsafe place, characterized by student fights and violence, drug deals, and staff assaults. The physical environment of the building was punctuated with graffiti and vandalism. Students frequently cut class. Teachers were afraid and apathetic. Mr. Clark had taught at East Side High School twenty years prior. As the principal, he utilized a very authoritarian, almost dictatorial leadership style with staff and students, initially. Right away he set about making major changes to improve the culture, including: amassing a list of student "miscreants" and having them permanently removed, appointing a head security person and a full complement of security personnel, demoting the head football coach to assistant coach and promoting the assistant to head, removing the cages in the student cafeteria, requiring faculty to be silent and take notes during staff meetings, requiring the head custodian to get rid of graffiti with permission to have detention students help in this effort, requiring all students to know and sing the school song on demand, firing certain faculty, and chastising teachers for the lack of student achievement.*
>
> *Although a formidable figure, Mr. Clark was very charismatic, often invoking an oratorical style reminiscent of a traditional African American preacher, when speaking to large groups. In addition, Mr. Clark seemed to take a special interest in individual students and often served as an advocate and/or parental figure to students, even conducting home visits of students when necessary. Over time, fear was replaced with mutual respect.*

The school culture began to change. The physical environment became healthier and more inviting with students invested in the appearance of the building as well as their own learning. Mr. Clark became famous in the news throughout the state for placing chains and padlocks over the exterior doors to protect students by keeping the drug dealers out of the school. He walked around the school carrying a bullhorn and a bat. He had several encounters with the fire marshal because of the fire code violation caused by chaining the exterior doors. Eventually Mr. Clark was arrested at the school for this behavior. However, by this point, his leadership had ignited the fire of change within the school building. His students marched down to the jail pleading for his release. Mr. Clark was successful in raising the test scores, although not to the required percentage pass rate. However, in less than a year's time he completely transformed the school from a persistently dangerous setting where learning was not a priority to a much safer environment for students and teachers to teach and learn.

Contextualizing Leadership: An Examination of the Leadership Approach of Principal Joe Clark

Transformational leadership has heretofore been understood as a leadership concept on a continuum with transactional leadership styles (Bass, 1990, 1985; Bycio, Hackett & Allen, 1995; Howell & Avolio, 1993). However, this paper suggests that transformational leadership be understood within a *context* of transactions. Therefore, transformational leadership styles can vary based upon varied factors such as context, resources, development levels of employees and the amount of transaction the leader perceives he or she must engage in to be effective. The following section interrogates the leadership behavior of Principal Clark utilizing key questions as a way to understand the challenges and effectiveness of his style of transformational leadership and the broader context of transactions as well as his use of transactional leadership within his leadership practice. A significant scenario follows each question from Principal Clark's experience, followed by a discussion of the challenges the scenario poses and the connection to transformational leadership.

Question: *How does context determine or influence the way in which a school leader implements a transformational leadership approach?*

Scenario: *Joe Clark was hired specifically to improve student achievement. He was provided less than a year in which to accomplish this formidable task. He was charged to do so in an urban context of violence and other volatile behavior, low parental involvement, low teacher morale, and lack of student engagement. His task was transformation, and while the needs of the school called for transformation, the context was not inherently conducive to such change. In fact, there is often a great deal of resistance to change, and this change was required to occur sooner rather than later.*

Leadership is exemplified differently in different contexts. The organizational context provides the foundation for addressing the questions posed in this work. That is, context includes the culture/climate, resources, developmental stages of workers, and so on. For the purposes of this discussion, context will be examined through the lens of setting and culture, as the other elements of culture are addressed elsewhere in this paper. The research on transformational leadership is silent regarding the impact of context on the leader's transformational style. Schools as organizational settings have a variety of different challenges, clientele, and settings. The needs of the people specific to the setting are most salient to the leadership approach employed. That is, there is no singular blueprint approach to the way in which to implement any leadership style within a particular setting, given the varied demographics and needs of each specific setting.

The now pervasive context of accountability significantly impacts a school leader's responsibilities and approaches to leadership. Leithwood (2007) suggests that the accountability movement and the resulting processes for achieving prescribed goals necessitate a transactional leadership style. The principalship has been influenced by national policy and an agenda of educational reform, which in turn require unique leadership approaches (Portin, 2000). Moreover, certain characteristics of urban schools make leadership in such contexts more challenging. Portin (2000) suggests several such challenges, including: "larger bureaucratic districts, higher per pupil expenditure, less local revenue, and higher percentages of students at risk for school failure, living in poverty and with limited English proficiency" (p. 496).

Question: *How is transformational leadership influenced by the developmental level of the followers?*

Scenario: *Joe Clark asserts that he was placed at East Side High School to clean up the work that the faculty demonstrated they were not able to perform based upon consistently low levels of student achievement. In addition, the culture was one of low parental involvement, fear, and apathy. This culture existed within a larger context of change. At this time, the State Department of Education mandated certain levels of student achievement, against a backdrop of sanctions for poor performance. There was therefore a tremendous uncertainty and fear among the faculty and resistance from students, particularly those who were comfortable with the status quo. While arguably many teachers may have been competent in their content areas, they needed a strong leader to help them to: believe that change was not only necessary but also possible, mobilize forces to change the negative aspects of the school culture, create a (physically and) intellectually safe environment in which to focus on student achievement, develop a learning community focused on supporting student achievement.*

Transformational leadership has several components that contribute to its whole. Idealized influence is the component that refers to the leader's attentiveness to the developmental needs of the followers and their proficiency at providing support and coaching (Bass, 1999). However, this is made challenging with certain workers in certain contexts. Typically, within an organization, workers are at various stages of development, a concept integral to the situational leadership approach. Within this approach, the leader determines his or her specific style based upon the developmental level of the workers within the organization. Ultimately, within the situational leadership approach, the leader adopts a directive or supportive relationship with workers based upon their need. However, within certain organizations, followers' developmental needs require specific attention from the leader, particularly within organizations that are reforming or overhauling the status quo. In organizations where extreme change is needed, significant levels of professional development are necessary to support the growth of employees toward the organizational goal.

Employee resistance and/or a culture that steeped in tradition may negatively impact the ability for a leader to operate from a transformational approach. Howell and Avolio (1993) assert that in such environments, "the level of support for innovation would be expected to moderate the impact of transformational leadership on performance" (p. 893). In such settings, it can be a challenge for the leader to facilitate sweeping change utilizing the support of employees.

> Question: *How does a leader's effective use of transactional leadership influence his/her ability to be transformational?*
>
> Scenario: *The biggest issue initially facing Principal Clark was that of safety for his staff and students. His environment was riddled with violence, drug sales and use, and fear and apathy. Implied in his actions is the fact that Principal Clark negotiated for certain authority with his superiors to carry out the requirements of his role. While not expressly stated within the movie, prior to agreeing to take on this role he clearly negotiated certain terms and conditions of his leadership.*

When he arrived, he unilaterally promoted and demoted certain faculty and expelled certain students. He did this to create a healthier environment for the school socially, physically, and intellectually. Additionally, Mr. Clark utilized his position to reinforce the transactional nature of his position initially. The imperative under which he operated was to improve student achievement in less than a year. Under these conditions, in order to transform this organization, he needed to use a transactional style. Bass (1999) suggests, "this transaction or exchange—this promise and reward for good performance, or threat and discipline for poor performance—characterizes effective leadership" (p. 20).

Discussion and Implications

Much of the research distinguishing between transactional and transformational leadership suggests that leaders "who are more satisfying to their followers and who are more effective as leaders are more transformational and less transactional" (Bass, 1999; Bycio, Hackett, & Allen, 1995). However, this author argues that an effective transformational leader recognizes that all interactions within a work setting occur within the context of transaction, irrespective of the priority placed upon that transaction. Workers perform their duties in anticipation of compensation (financial, verbal recognition, etc.). Organizations themselves exist within a context of transactions or exchanges. Thus, a transformational leader cannot ignore the import of various transactions. In fact the transformational leader needs to view the transactions as necessary and aligned with Maslow's hierarchy of needs. That is, the leader must meet basic needs of safety before being able to meet higher order needs of self-actualization. Often a way to accomplish this is via transactions. An effective leader can make these transactions seamless for his or her followers.

Additionally, the research consistently suggests that the transactions in which a leader engages are top down. That is to say that the transactional leader is exercising his or her authority to engage employees in exchanges or bargains through contingent reward leadership or management by exception (Bass, 1990; Bycio, Allen, & Hackett, 1995; Howell & Avolio, 1993). However, arguably, a leader must engage in transactions with his or her superiors in order to accomplish goals within the context that impact the followers.

Lean on Me provides a vehicle in which to understand transformation as an outcome of a leadership style that incorporates elements of situational, transactional, and hierarchical leadership approaches that are focused on the large goal of improving student achievement within a compressed amount of time. It presents a context in which to try to "redefine" and "rethink" transformational leadership based upon the salience of context, transactions (both top down and bottom up), and employees. These elements influence the leadership style and provide a framework in which to understand the context:

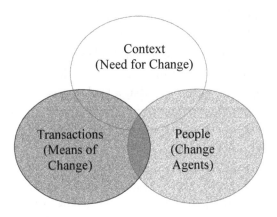

As Principal Clark's leadership is examined within the framework of the dimensions of transformational leadership, this theory can be understood more fully. Most would agree that Clark was a very hierarchical, directive leader. However, he understood a great deal about the organizational context, the imperative for increasing student achievement, and the indirect needs of the organization (those that are not directly related to student achievement, but necessary to influence a change in the culture that is conducive to student achievement). To that end, he exhibited a number of the qualities of a transformational leader: (1) *charisma*—he demonstrated a great deal of charisma amongst each constituent group (parents, students, faculty); (2) *inspiration*—some of his methods were quite untraditional, but ultimately he inspired students and teachers to focus on creating a better school culture and increasing student achievement; (3) *intellectual stimulation*—Clark implemented some very creative and rational solutions to increasing student achievement. These included: changes to the environment that would improve school culture, eliminating members of the community who were destructive, and creating a safe environment for teaching and learning.

It is not clear whether or not Principal Clark utilized the fourth dimension of transformational leadership, *individual consideration*, in which the leader engages each individual employee in a relationship of care or concern. However, it is clear that he attempted to do so with students. His decision not to fully engage employees may have been necessary given the nature of his task, the time limitations placed upon him and the volatile nature of the environment. Further, Principal Clark's actions demonstrate that transformational leadership as a leadership style is mutually inclusive, that is, it allows leaders the freedom to implement a variety of leadership styles at once.

The ability to engage in transactional leadership was a very important aspect of Principal Clark's leadership and of most leaders. This examination considered not only the transactions that a leader must make with the followers within the context, but also the "invisible" transactions that must be negotiated with the leader's superiors in order to meet the needs of the followers and realize the vision. To that end, this examination illuminates the fact that transactions must meet not only the goals of specific individuals in specific instances, but also the goals of the organization overall. In some cases, leaders must engage in transactions that are "invisible" to his or her followers because they have been negotiated at a different organizational level given that transactions flow in both directions within an organization.

Conclusion

Leadership is an integral part of any successful organization, and schools are no exception. Leadership studies conducted in schools are emerging on a more consistent basis, and it is important that educational leaders use the results of these studies to understand how to better run their schools. The public school system has long been viewed as a top-down bureaucracy where rules and policies are passed down from the federal level to the state and district levels, and eventually, to the school, where there is little room for adjustment. Policies that affect various aspects of a school environment, including curriculum, student placement, standardized testing, and teacher compensation, are being implemented on an on-going basis and principals must be able to respond effectively.

Principals are the leaders who must motivate teachers, parents, and oftentimes, the community-at-large, and are expected to increase student achievement at the same time. A transformational principal is one who has molded the school into a cohesive unit that can respond effectively and successfully to changes in the school environment, and has developed a supportive working environment where teachers, staff and parents are all focused on the end goal of students' academic success. The study of leadership theory has evolved over time, and there is still no one way to best lead an organization, or in this case, a school. As research has demonstrated, there is a relationship, although it has not been clearly defined, between transformational and transactional leadership. Aspects of both leadership styles can prove useful in creating an effective school, but one must remember to take people, place and process into account. Principals and school leaders must be aware of the importance of their actions, the resulting consequences, and the impact on their constituents.

Note

1 Dr. April Peters wishes to thank doctoral student Ain Grooms for her assistance in the development of this chapter.

References

Avildsen, J. G. (Producer/Director) & Schiffer, M. (Writer), (1998). *Lean on Me* (Motion Picture). United States: Warner Brothers.

Avolio, B. J., Bass, B. M., & Jung, D. I. (1999). Re-examining the components of transformational and transactional leadership using the Multifactor Leadership Questionnaire. *Journal of Occupational and Organizational Psychology, 72*, 441–462.

Bass, B. M. (1985). *Leadership and performance beyond expectations.* New York: Free Press.

Bass, B. M. (1990). From transactional to transformational leadership: Learning to share the vision. *Organizational Dynamics, 18*(3), 19–31.

Bass, B. M. (1999). Two decades of research and development in transformational leadership. *European Journal of Work and Organizational Psychology, 8*(1), 9–32.

Bass, B. M., & Riggio, R. E. (2006). *Transformational Leadership,* 2nd ed. Mahwah, NJ: Lawrence Erlbaum Publishers.

Bass, B. M., Avolio, B. J., Jung, D. I., & Berson, Y. (2003). Predicting unit performance by assessing transformational and transactional leadership. *Journal of Applied Psychology, 88*, 207–218.

Burns, J. M. (1978). *Leadership.* New York: Harper and Row.

Bycio, P., Allen, J. S., & Hackett, R. D. (1995). Further assessments of Bass's (1985) conceptualization of transactional and transformational leadership. *Journal of Applied Psychology, 80,* (4), 468–478.

Hinkin, T. R., & Schriesheim, C. A. (2008). An examination of "nonleadership": From laissez-faire leadership to leader reward omission and punishment omission. *Journal of Applied Psychology, 93,* 1234–1248.

Howell, J. M., & Avolio, B. J. (1993). Transformational leadership, transactional leadership, locus of control and support for innovation: key predictors of consolidated-business-unit performance. *Journal of Applied Psychology, 78*(6), 891–902.

Leithwood, K. A. (2007). Transformation school leadership in a transactional policy world. *The Jossey-Bass Reader on Educational Leadership,* 2nd ed.. San Francisco, CA: Jossey-Bass.

Leithwood, K. A. (1992). The move toward transformational leadership. *Educational Leadership, 49*(5), 8–12.

Leithwood, K. A., & Jantzi, D. (2006). Transformational school leadership for large-scale school reform: Effects on students, teachers and their classroom practices. *School Effectiveness and School Improvement, 17,* 201–227.

Lunenberg, F.C. (2003). *Emerging Perspectives: The usefulness of the construct of transformational leadership in educational organizations.* Proceedings from the Annual Meeting of the National Council of Professors of Educational Administration.

Muenjohn, N., & Armstrong, A. (2008). Evaluating the structural validity of the Multifactor Leadership Questionnaire (MLQ), capturing the leadership factors of transformational-transactional leadership. *Contemporary Management Research, 4*(1), 3–14.

Nguni, S., Sleegers, P., & Denessen, E. (2006). Transformational and transactional leadership effects on teachers' job satisfaction, organizational commitment, and organizational citizenship behavior in primary schools: The Tanzanian case. *School Effectiveness and School Improvement, 17,* 145–177.

Northouse, P. G. (2007). Leadership: theory and practice (4th edition). Thousand Oaks, CA: Sage Publications.

Portin, B. S. (2000). The changing urban principalship. *Education and Urban Society, 32*(4), 492–505.

Ross, J. A., & Gray, P. (2006). Transformational leadership and teacher commitment to organizational values: The mediating effects of collective teacher efficacy. *School Effectiveness and School Improvement, 17,* 179–199.

Skogstad A., Einarsen, S., Torsheim, T., Aasland, M. S., & Hetland, H., (2007). The destructiveness of laissez-faire leadership behavior. *Journal of Occupational Health Psychology, 12*(1), 80-92.

Tejada, M. J., Scandura, T. A., & Pillai, R. (2001). The MLQ revisited: Psychometric properties and recommendations. *The Leadership Quarterly, 12,* 31–52.

Yammarino, F. J., Dionne, S., & Chun, J. U. (2002). Transformational and charismatic leadership: a levels-of-analysis review of theory, measurement, data analysis and inferences. In L. L. Neider and C. A. Schriesheim (eds.), *Leadership*. Greenwich: Information Age Publishing.

Yukl, G. (1999). An evaluation of conceptual weaknesses in transformational and charismatic leadership theories. *The Leadership Quarterly, 10,* 285–306.

✣ CHAPTER 3

On Becoming a Leader for Educational Equity and Excellence: It Starts with Instruction

Kathryn Bell McKenzie and Leslie Ann Locke

There are no silver bullets in school leadership. No matter how much we search for the "right" program, the "right" instructional strategy, the "right" leadership style, the "right" faculty, or the "right" students, there is no single "right" way for leaders to improve schools. To improve schools, particularly in an era of high-stakes accountability and increased student diversity, takes well-prepared, smart, hardworking, reflective teachers and leaders.

In this chapter, we focus mainly on the principal as leader, although the principal is certainly not the only leader in a school. Many people in schools serve formally or informally in leadership roles. Moreover, we discuss the principalship within a context of high-stakes accountability and increased student diversity. Indeed, our schools are rich with diversity, including language differences; learning differences; ethnic, racial, and cultural differences; economic differences; gender and sexual orientation differences; etc. These differences, for us, should be embraced and considered an asset rather than a deficit. However, much of the literature, popular and otherwise, equates difference with deficit (for a discussion of deficit thinking see McKenzie and Scheurich (2004); Valencia (1997) and for an example of difference as deficit, see Payne (1996).[1]

Difference is often seen as an obstacle to overcome rather than an opportunity to learn about ourselves, others, and the relationship between ourselves and others. This concept of "diversity as an obstacle" is a fundamental problem in schools and one we will address herein. Therefore, what follows is a discussion of the principalship within a context of high-stakes accountability and student diversity that demands leadership theory and practice that establishes and sustains excellent and equitable schools.

Historical Context of Leadership Models

In the last twenty years, there has been ongoing debate regarding two leadership models: instructional leadership and transformational leadership. Hallinger's 2003 article, "Leading Educational Change: Reflections on the Practice of Instructional and Transformational Leadership," offers a thorough review of "the conceptual and empirical development" of these two models (p. 329), whereas Robinson, Lloyd, and Rowe's (2008) meta-analysis,[2] "The Impact of Leadership on Student Outcomes: An Analysis of the Differential Effects of Leadership Types," examines the impact of these leadership models on "students' academic and nonacademic outcomes" (p. 634). We relied mainly on these articles to inform and provide the theoretical frame for this work.

According to Hallinger (Hallinger, 2003; Hallinger & Heck, 1999), instructional leadership emerged in the 1980s from the effective schools research conducted by Ronald Edmonds. One of the correlates of this research specifically addressed instructional leadership. Edmonds (1982) states: "The characteristics of an effective school include... the principal's leadership and attention to the quality of instruction..." (p. 4). At that time, though, there were critics of the effective schools research and particularly the instructional leadership component of this research (e.g., Cuban, 1984; Miskel, 1982; Murphy, 1988; Leithwood, 1992). According to the critics, instructional leadership, as defined by the effective schools movement, placed the principal as the sole leader of instruction. This created a hierarchical structure that alienated teachers (Murphy, 1988). Moreover, many principals did not have the expertise to be instructional leaders (Leithwood, 1992), and there was little support to assist them in this area, which ultimately led to their failure (Cuban, 1984).

There was, however, another leadership model at this time: transformational leadership. The root of transformational leadership came from Burns (1979) and was called "transforming leadership." He distinguished transforming leadership from other forms of leadership, stating that it is moral, as it "raises the level of human conduct and ethical aspiration of both leader and led, and thus it has a transforming effect on both" (p. 20). However, it was not until the 1990s, as a result of the critique of instructional leadership and "the top-down emphasis of American school reform" (Hallinger, 2003, p. 342), that the transformational model emerged as a viable alternative to instructional leadership.

Instructional leadership was characterized as direct principal involvement in curriculum and instruction, including monitoring of classroom instruction and student progress, and working intimately with teachers to improve teaching practices and student outcomes (e.g., Bass & Avolio, 1994; Blase & Blase, 1999; Leithwood & Jantzi, 1991; Leithwood, Tomlinson & Genge, 1996; Smith & Andrews, 1989; Southworth, 2002), whereas transformational leadership was characterized as charismatic and inspirational (Bass, Avolio, & Atwater, 1996), resulting in followers feeling trust, admiration, loyalty, and respect toward the leader (Bass, 1997). The underlying influence process between the leader and the led was seen to motivate followers by making them more aware of the importance of task outcomes and inducing them to transcend their own self-interest for the sake of the organization (Bass, 1997). Then in the late 1990s and into the twenty-first century, there was an accelerated focus on student outcomes and "closing the achievement gap." This brought about a renewed interest in a more direct involvement in teaching and learning, a renewed interest in instructional leadership.

Today, with the continued emphasis on student outcomes, along with shifting demographic patterns resulting in more diversity within schools, there is a renewed interest in and debate about the efficacy of both instructional and transformational leadership. This debate is evidenced by recent works addressing these models (e.g., Alig-Mielcarek & Hoy, 2005; Brown & Keeping, 2005; Griffith, 2004; Hallinger, 2003; Leithwood & Jantzi, 2005, 2006; Marks & Printy, 2003; Nelson & Sassi, 2005; Sheppard, 1996, 2003). Included in these works is Robinson's et al.'s meta-analysis referenced earlier and titled, "The Impact of Leadership on Student Outcomes: An Analysis of the Differential Effects of Leadership Types," that won the Division A, article of the year award at the 2009 American Educational Research Conference. The next section draws from this work and discusses the findings related to the efficacy of these two leadership models.

Impact of Instructional and Transformational Leadership

In Robinson et al.'s 2008 article, the purpose of the work was to address "the paradoxical differences between the qualitative and quantitative evidence on

leadership impacts by taking a fresh approach to the analysis of the quantitative evidence" (p. 637). They stated: "Rather than conduct a further meta-
analysis of the overall impact of leadership on student outcomes, we focus on
identifying the relative impact of different types of leadership" (Robinson et
al., 2008, p. 637). The paradoxical differences they refer to are based on qualitative "case studies of 'turn around' schools" and "interventions in teaching
and learning", it was the *leaders* at the school and district level who were credited with improving instruction and student outcomes (Robinson et al., 2008,
p. 637), whereas the quantitative research on both the direct and indirect effects of leadership has shown weak impact. In other words, the qualitative
studies credit leadership with improving instruction and student outcomes
and the quantitative studies indicate that leadership has little effect on improved instruction and student outcomes. What sets Robinson et al.'s (2008)
work apart from previous work on the impact of leadership on student outcomes is that their work is a meta-analysis, where, according to them, the
works of others were reviews of literature on empirical studies (e.g., Bell, Bolam, & Cubillo, 2003; Leithwood, Day, Sammons, Harris, & Hopkins, 2006;
Leithwood, Seashore Louis, Anderson, & Wahlstron, 2004; Marzano, Waters,
& Mcnulty, 2005; Witziers, Bosker, & Krüger, 2003). Moreover, Robinson et
al.'s work focused specifically on the impact of two leadership models: transformational versus instructional.

In this work, Robinson et al. (2008) conducted two meta-analyses. The
first was a "comparison of the effects of transformational and instructional
leadership on student outcomes" and the second meta-analysis was "a comparison of the effects of five inductively derived sets of leadership practices on
student outcomes" (p. 635). With regard to the first analysis, they found that
the effect of instructional leadership on student outcomes "was three to four
times that of transformational leadership" (p. 635). Moreover, in the surveys
they analyzed, there were five sets of leadership practices that were used to
measure leadership. These included "establishing goals and expectations; resourcing strategically; planning, coordinating, and evaluating teaching and the
curriculum; promoting and participating in teacher learning and development,
and ensuring an orderly and supportive environment" (p. 635). The second
meta-analysis revealed "strong average effects for the leadership dimension
involving promoting and participating in teacher learning and development
and moderate effects for the dimensions concerned with goal setting and
planning, coordinating, and evaluating teaching and the curriculum" (p. 635).

Based on this study, one can conclude that instructional leadership has a stronger impact on student learning than transformational leadership. More specifically, when leaders promote and participate in teacher learning and development, there is a strong effect on student learning. Simply put, "the closer educational leaders get to the core business of teaching and learning, the more likely they are to have a positive impact on students' outcomes" (Robinson et al., 2008, p. 664).

Instructional Leadership, Equity Consciousness, and High-Quality Teaching Skills

In reading Robinson et al.'s work (2008), we drew a connection to our research and the research of our colleagues on the qualities of successful diverse classrooms, schools, and districts and the leadership needed to bring about success (e.g., McKenzie et al., 2008; McKenzie & Lozano, 2008; McKenzie & Scheurich, 2004; McKenzie & Scheurich, 2009; Rorrer & Skrla, 2005; Rorrer, Skrla, & Scheurich, 2008; Scheurich & Skrla, 2003; Skrla & Scheurich, 2001; Skrla, Scheurich, & Johnson Jr., 2001). This research was conducted over the last two decades and influenced by the authors' lived experiences in schools as teachers and school leaders. McKenzie, one of the authors of the current work, had a twenty-five-year career in public education, mostly in large urban schools, as a teacher, curriculum specialist, principal, and trainer of principals.

From the aforementioned research, we developed in our more recent works (Skrla, McKenzie, & Scheurich, 2009) a conceptual framework for instructional leadership for social justice (see Figure 3.1). This framework shows the relationship between instructional leadership for social justice, equity consciousness, and high-quality teaching skills. Building on Robinson et al.'s (2008) definition of instruction leadership as leadership that is focused directly on the "core business of teaching and learning" (p. 664), we added the component of social justice, which we believe is critical to achieving equity and excellence in schools. An instructional leader for social justice not only focuses directly on the "business of teaching and learning," but ensures that teaching and learning is occurring for all students. This is done through attention to equity consciousness and high-quality teaching skills.

Figure 3.1

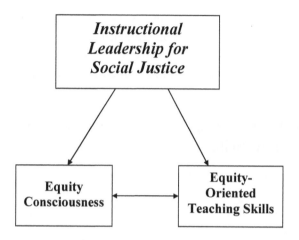

Equity Consciousness: Four Central Beliefs

To ensure equity and excellence in schools, everyone in a school, teachers and leaders, should have an equity consciousness. Inherent in this consciousness are four central beliefs. These are as follows:

1. That *all* children (except only a very small percentage, e.g., those with profound disabilities) are capable of high levels of academic success.
2. That *all* children means *all*, regardless of a child's race, social class, gender, sexual orientation, learning differences, culture, language, religion, and so on.
3. That the adults in schools are primarily responsible for student learning.
4. That traditional school practices may work for some students but are not working for all children. Therefore, if we are going to eliminate the achievement gap, it requires a change in our practices (Skrla, McKenzie, & Scheurich, 2009, pp. 82-83).

High-Quality Teaching: Nine Skills

In addition to an equity consciousness, every teacher should have high-quality teaching skills, which according to research on teaching, learning, and culture (e.g., Bell, 2003; Cartledge, Tillman, & Talbert-Johnson, 2001; Festinger,

1957; Gay 2000; Gonzalez & Huerta-Macias, 1997; Gregory, 1994; Hunter, 1994; Ladson-Billings, 1995; McKenzie et al. 2008; McKenzie & Lozano, 2008; Resnick & Hall, 2001; Tomlinson, 1999; Tomlinson et al., 2003; Valencia, 1997; Williamson, Bondy, Langley, & Mayne, 2005; Wong & Wong, 2004; Yair, 2000) should at a minimum include the following:

Skill 1: Using consistent and reliable classroom procedures and routines

Skill 2: Clearly communicating expectations for learning

Skill 3: Stimulating students with high-level and complex tasks

Skill 4: Ensuring students are actively, cognitively, engaged

Skill 5: Extending student learning through teacher-to-student and student-to-student discussion

Skill 6: Frequently assessing individual student learning

Skill 7: Differentiating instruction to meet individual student needs and capitalize on individual assets

Skill 8: Using an asset model to respond to students' varying cultures

Skill 9: Demonstrating respect and care in all interactions with all students and students' families (Skrla, McKenzie, & Scheurich, 2009, pp. 90-96).

Systemic Coherence: Taking Quality to Scale

The challenge for an instructional leader for equity and excellence, however, is to ensure that *all* students in a school are learning. This means guaranteeing that every teacher in every classroom has an equity consciousness and high-quality teaching skills. This expands the quality beyond a few classrooms. This takes quality to scale, creating systemic coherence (Figure 3.2), which means that the system will have consistent high quality. Put another way, "success begets success." Taking this further out to scale, if enough schools have systemic coherence around high-quality teaching, then the entire school district will have consistent teaching quality and high levels of student success.

We realize this sound simplistic, and furthermore we understand the complexity of teaching, learning, and leading. However, we believe, as Robinson et al.'s (2008) work would confirm, that leaders, that is *instructional* leaders, can have a direct and significant impact on teaching and thereby learning in a school. However what we typically find in the schools we work with, either through research or consultation, is that few principals are instructional leaders. Certainly, we cannot generalize our findings to all principals. There are some that are incredible instructional leaders, there are some that are trying to be instructional leaders but allow microdiversions to derail their leadership, and there are some who aspire to transformational leadership, but this does not seem to be working.

Figure 3.2

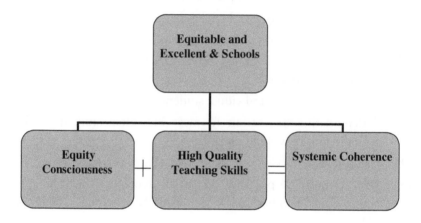

Instructional and Transformational Leadership in Schools

Drawing from multiple research projects over the last two decades, including case studies of several elementary schools (e.g., McKenzie & Scheurich, 2008), a Hewlett Foundation–funded study of U.S. school districts (Skrla et al., 2007), and a Richardson Foundation–funded study of large urban high schools (in progress), along with our consultation to dozens of schools, we have identified three types of leaders. They are: (1) strong instructional leaders, (2) leaders derailed by diversions, and (3) aspiring transformational leaders.

Strong Instructional Leaders

The principals we have worked with who are strong instructional leaders, like Steve Kinney at Tice Elementary, often lead in unconventional ways, yet they are keenly focused on and involved in "the core business of teaching and learning" (Robinson et al., 2008, p. 664). Tice is an elementary school in the Galena Park School District of Houston, Texas. One of us, McKenzie, and colleagues (Skrla, Scheurich, & Dickerson) studied the Galena Park school district in 2004–2006, as part of a Hewlett Foundation–funded project examining high-performing school districts that serve predominately low-income students and students of color. At that time, the demographics at Tice were 52% Hispanic, 43% African American, 4% White, 0.7% Asian, and 0.2% Native American. Twenty-four percent of the students were categorized as limited English proficient, and 79% were eligible for free and reduced lunch.

It was during this project that we met Steve Kinney, who had been principal of Tice for five years. Prior to Steve's tenure at Tice, the school was rated acceptable[3] on the Texas Academic Excellence Indicator System (AEIS). At that time, the superintendent in Galena Park was Dr. Shirley Neeley. Shirley later went on to become the Commissioner of Education for the State of Texas. As superintendent of Galena Park, Shirley gave the principals a directive that they needed to have their school at the "recognized" level within three years or they would be removed as principal of their campus. According to Kinney, Dr. Neeley said, "We're scoring from 50%–70% right now, and some people are happy with that, saying we're a poor district and that's just how it's going to be. We're not going to accept that any more. We're going to average 90% passing in this district, and if your school can't get recognized, I'll remove the principal after three years." She also told them that they had the autonomy to do whatever they needed to do to raise their campuses to recognized status as long as it was ethical, legal, and was in the best interest of the students.

Steve took both the charge and the latitude seriously. He reworked his school. He hired faculty of color. He took four master teachers out of their classrooms and reassigned them to a learning lab where they pulled the lowest-performing five students out of each first- to fifth-grade teacher's classroom and provided intensive small-group daily instruction in reading and math. Additionally, Kinney and the Dean of Instruction at Tice met daily with teacher teams to develop and align curriculum and pedagogy and to assess student work. In other words, he was intimately involved in "promoting and participating in teacher learning and development" (Robinson et al., 2008, p. 667). Surprisingly, he required that everyone leave the school at 3:30 p.m. every day. He said, " . . . this building's empty at 3:30 everyday. We want them [the teachers] working really hard, then going home to their families."

The work of Steve and the faculty and staff at Tice paid off. During his time as principal, the school went from an acceptable rating to exemplary, the highest rating possible, exceeding the rating required by the superintendent.

Moreover, Tice had 18–44% of their students at commended level, depending on the subject, which means the students not only passed the state examinations, but passed with high scores. Thus, Tice Elementary, which served predominantly low-income students and students of color, performed higher than most of the middle-income predominantly white schools in the state. This we believe is a testament to the instructional leadership provided at Tice.

Looking at the Tice story in relation to both Robinson et al.'s (2008) findings related to instructional and transformational leadership and our work on equity consciousness, high-quality teaching skills (Srkla, McKenzie, & Scheurich, 2009), and systemic coherence, the following can be surmised. First, Steve is an example of a principal who was an instructional leader. He exhibited the dimensions Robinson et al. (2008) found to have strong or moderate effects on student outcomes. Indeed, all the strategies he used to bring about high-quality teaching and learning, including the weekly curriculum and instruction meetings and the employment of master teachers to provide intensive instructional support to students who lacked requisite skills, were examples of "promoting and participating in teacher learning and development" and "goal setting and planning, coordinating, and evaluating teaching and the curriculum" (Robinson et al., 2008, p. 656).

Second, when the leadership of a campus focuses initially and directly on instruction, as Steve did at Tice, transformation can occur at the individual and organizational level. This direct focus on teaching and learning supports individual teachers in developing both equity consciousness and high-quality teaching skills, which scales up as more and more teachers develop these skills. We contend, however, that a focus on instruction must *precede* or at least occur concurrently with a focus on transformation. For example, when one of us, McKenzie, was a principal in a large urban elementary, she never inspired or talked any teacher into changing attitudes, that is, equity consciousness, about students whom the teacher believed were unmotivated, did not care about learning, or were incapable of learning at high levels. It should be noted that these students, typically, were students of color, those living in poverty, or those with learning differences (McKenzie, 2001; McKenzie & Scheurich, 2004).

However, with a clear and directed focus on instruction, including aligning curriculum and instructional practices, frequent assessment and monitoring of student work, monitoring teachers' instructional practices, and offering professional development and instructional support to teachers, the teachers became successful with students with whom they had not been successful.

Once this occurred, teachers began to change their attitudes toward their students and other students who were "like" their students. Therefore, a focus *first* on instruction brought about a transformation in teaching skills and equity consciousness. Again, as Robinson et al. (2008) state, "the closer educational leaders get to the core business of teaching and learning, the more likely they are to have a positive impact on students' outcomes" (p. 664). We contend that instructional leadership precedes and creates transformation, which then leads to positive impacts on student outcomes.

Leaders Derailed by Diversions

Next, we discuss principals that allow diversions, some at the macrolevel, such as true urgencies, and some at the microlevel, such as minor disruptions that can usually be handled by others, to prevent them from being instructional leaders. These principals know that they should be "promoting and participating in teacher learning and development" (Robinson et al., 2008, p. 635) but often they just cannot quite get to it, too many things get in the way, too many macro- and microdiversions. Certainly, principals must address serious issues, but we have worked with or known principals who spend much of their time on the microdiversions, the things that have nothing to do with instruction and could be delegated to others.

For example, we know one principal who spends little time in classrooms but frequently walks the halls of the school taking down outdated posters of upcoming events. Another goes around and pulls all the plastic bottles out of the trash cans for recycling. And, the most radical, one principal that makes sure that all the blinds in the building are lowered to the exact same level on all the windows at the end of the day. Yes, these examples seem extreme, but when one considers the possible psychology behind these actions, they are important to examine. Possibly these principals are under enormous stress, and therefore as a strategy to alleviate some of the stress, they focus on things they can control, like taking down outdated posters or manipulating blinds. Possibly these principals are insecure about their instructional or pedagogical knowledge and avoid working directly with teachers. There may be other interpretations, but regardless, these principals are not working on the "core business of teaching and learning" (Robinson et al., 2008, p. 664).

Beyond these extreme examples, most of what we hear from principals is that they just cannot get into classrooms or work directly with teachers on instruction because of a variety of "musts" that have to be done, including special education Admission Review and Dismissal (ARD) meetings, discipline issues, issues with teachers and parents, paperwork, demands from the central office of the district, etc. Furthermore, these diversions seem to occur more frequently in schools that serve mainly students of color or those living in poverty, that is, schools with the greatest needs. One only needs to look at the National Center for Education's Institute of Educational Statistics website (http://nces.ed.gov/) and the statistics provided therein to determine that we continue to fail our students of color and those living in poverty. In fact, students of color and those from poor households continue to achieve at levels lower than their white counterparts, are more often referred for special education, and are more often suspended and expelled from school. Therefore, in the schools with the greatest needs, there may be more diversions, making it less likely that there will be strong instructional leadership.

However, some of these diversions might dissipate, like discipline, parent, and teacher issues, if the instruction at the school were at a high level. We assert that one cannot wait for issues like discipline to get better before teaching and learning begins. It is the converse. For example, high-quality teaching that engages all students at their instructional level eliminates much student frustration that may lead to discipline problems. So, one must start with the instruction. This may require, however, that principals literally schedule classroom visits or work times with teachers. This should be done weekly, if not daily like Steve Kinney's approach at Tice, and be held sacred, which implies that only a true urgency should divert these activities.

Leaders Who Aspire to Transform

The next principal type is the principal who aspires to be a transformational leader. As we stated earlier, a transformational leader is the one who is characterized as moral, inspirational, charismatic (Bass, Avolio, & Atwater, 1996), and the one who motivates followers by making them more aware of the importance of task outcomes and inducing them to transcend their own self-interest for the sake of the organization (Bass, 1997). However, we believe, and Robinson et al.'s findings would support, that when principals keenly focus on "the business of teaching and learning" (Robinson et al., 2008, p. 636), they have a greater impact on the teaching and the learning in a school. Yet, many of the principals we work with spend most of their time and resources trying to inspire their faculty to teach better or to teach *all* their students. This is problematic particularly in schools that, according to state and national accountability data, need the most transformation, that is, schools that mainly serve students of color and those living in poverty. These are the schools where there is the greatest need for all teachers to have an equity consciousness and high-quality teaching skills, which, we contend, requires instructional leadership. Like the principals who allow diversions to derail their instructional efforts, principals attempting to inspire their faculty to transform engage in a range of strategies to inspire, from the superficial to the more substantive.

In the category of superficial, we would place the monthly token of appreciation in the teachers' mailboxes, for example, the Bar None candy bar with the attached note, "Bar None, you're the best." Here, appreciation is seen as a way to inspire. Certainly, teachers work hard for little pay and any form of appreciation is warranted. However, token appreciation will not directly improve practice. Another strategy to inspire, which is less superficial but still not substantive, is the attempt to involve faculty in the mission, vision, and goals of the school in the belief that this involvement will promote "buy-in" that will then lead to a transformation in attitudes toward students or improved teaching. We even had a student in one of our principalship classes say that at her school the faculty had been working with the principal for five years on perfecting the school mission statement. We are not saying that a principal should not involve staff and faculty in determining the mission and/or vision of the school. Indeed, the organizational literature (Boucher, 2001; Kezar & Eckel, 2002; Sherr & Lozier 1991) is clear that "buy-in" is an important factor is advancing goals of an educational organization. We are saying, however, that "buy-in" alone does not correlate to improved equity consciousness or teaching skills.

Of course, there are substantive efforts to inspire and transform, and these would include, but not be limited to, activities in which the principal engages in thoughtful discussions with faculty around their practice in an effort to enhance self-reflection, with the goal of this self-reflection resulting in improved practice. We know that self-reflection is a viable strategy for examining and improving both attitudes and practices (Schon, 1983). However, we have worked with principals and teacher leaders who get frustrated when they feel they have had these thoughtful discussions with teachers, but the teachers do not seem to become more reflective and do not change their practice.

However, based on Robinson et al.'s (2008) findings and our work in schools, these efforts toward transformation alone do not seem to make much difference in changing teachers' equity consciousness or teaching skills. It is direct involvement in teaching and learning by the principal or designated leader on a campus that makes a difference in transforming teachers' practices. Thus, we are left wondering why principals or teacher leaders continue to engage in strategies with teachers who do not appear to be working, particularly when we know that direct principal involvement in teaching and learning does make a difference. Is it because these leaders hold on to the transformational model, as it seems the more democratic way to go about leading? Is it because they want to avoid the conflict that might occur when they directly confront teachers about their attitudes and practices? Is it because they do not know enough about teaching and learning to help their teachers and do not want to delegate this work to others who have the skills to help teachers improve their practices?

Any or all of the above may be the case. Furthermore, addressing specifically the dilemma of principals who may not feel secure in their own knowledge about teaching and learning, we have worked with principals who have delegated this work to teacher leaders who, indeed, are "master teachers." In other words, they are outstanding teachers who understand teaching and learning. At one school in which we studied teacher leaders, whose responsibilities were to work with novice teachers to improve instruction, the master teacher leaders exhibited the same behaviors we observed in principals. Instead of directly addressing the practices of the inexperienced teachers they were assigned to help, they attempted to motivate teachers to improve and then got aggravated when teachers did not improve their practice.

One teacher leader explained to us that in an effort to help her mentees, she told them, "I want you all to be happy, but you need to tell me how I can help you be happy. What can I do?" It appeared this teacher leader assumed that being happy is correlated to being motivated and that motivation would improve practice. Another teacher leader explained that her mentees complained that they could not do their job because they did not have the materials they needed. The teacher leader stated, "I went to the computer, got my visa and I ordered everything they need. That still does not get them where they need to be." Here the teacher leader seemed to think that getting teachers the materials they wanted would improve their practice, but it did not. When these strategies did not improve teacher attitudes and practices, the teacher leaders became upset. One said, "These kids cannot go home and get what they are not getting at school. They cannot get crap and no one on that team [of mentees] understands that. And we don't know how to get that from them." Another teacher leader referring to her mentees said, "Nobody is thinking. And that is what kills me at night when I lie in my bed."

It appears, then, that using the strategies most often associated with transformational leadership, like motivating and inspiring others to transcend their own interests for the sake of the organization, does not improve teachers' equity consciousness, their teaching skills, or student outcomes.

Conclusion

As we stated in the introduction, there are no silver bullets for improving schools. It takes good leaders and good teachers. This is even more evident in this era of high-stakes accountability and increased student diversity. For schools to be equitable and excellent, to take this quality to scale, every teacher in every classroom must engage in equitable and excellent practices, which requires a well-developed equity consciousness and high-quality teaching skills. To help teachers develop and maintain these skills requires leadership, specifically instructional leadership. As Robinson et al.'s (2008) meta-analysis clearly revealed, the effect of instructional leadership on student outcomes was three to four times the effect of transformational leadership. Furthermore, there were "strong average effects for the leadership dimension involving promoting and participating in teacher learning and development" (p. 664). Thus, as we have similarly argued in this chapter, "the closer educational leaders get to the core business of teaching and learning, the more likely they are to have a positive impact on students' outcomes" (Robinson et al., 2008, p. 664).

The conclusions drawn by Robinson et al. (2008) and supported by our own research (McKenzie & Scheurich, 2004; McKenzie, Skrla, & Scheurich, 2006; Skrla, McKenzie, & Scheurich, 2009) have implications for research, leadership preparation, and leadership practice. First, there needs to be more research on why principals and teacher leaders are reluctant to involve themselves in the promotion of teacher learning and development, a primary component of the instructional leadership model which has direct effects on successful student outcomes. Second, programs preparing school and teacher leaders must recruit students who are already strong instructionally and then develop their knowledge, skills, and dispositions to successfully work with adults. Specifically, these leadership programs need to include courses in adult learning and conflict management. Third, leaders need to be mindful consumers of research, adopting only those practices that are supported by rigorous inquiry and which have been shown to positively affect the improvement of teaching and learning and thus student learning. Based on our work, instructional leadership is one example of research-supported educational practice, for when it comes to leading for equity and excellence, it starts with instruction.

Notes

1. It is our opinion that Ruby Payne's work, while offering some important insights into the disconnect between middle-class teachers and their students who come from families living in poverty, neglects the socio-structural aspects of poverty, is based on the illusion of a meritocracy, is ahistoric, and promotes a deficit view of those who live in poverty.
2. Robinson et al. (2008) define meta-analysis as "an empirical, knowledge-building strategy that enables the results of quantitative studies of the relationship between two constructs to be aggregated so that an estimate of the average magnitude of the impact of one on the other can be derived"(p. 639).
3. At this time, the Texas accountability system had four ratings for schools: exemplary, recognized, acceptable, and low-performing. For more information on this system or to get specifics on the criteria of each of the rating categories, see www.tea.state.tx.us/perfreport/aeis/.

References

Alig-Mielcarek, J. & Hoy, W. K. (2005). Instructional leadership: Its nature, meaning, and influence. In C.G. Miskel & W. K. Hoy (Eds.). *Educational leadership and reform* (pp. 29–52). Greenwich, CT: Information Age.

Bass, B. M. (1997). Does the transactional–transformational leadership paradigm transcend organizational and national boundaries? *American Psychologist, 52*(2), 130–138.

Bass, B. M., & Avolio, B. J. (1994). *Improving organizational effectiveness through transformational leadership.* Thousand Oaks, CA: Sage.

Bass, B. M., Avolio, B. J., & Atwater, L. (1996). The transformational and transactional leadership of men and women. *Applied Psychology: An International Review, 45*(1), 5–34.

Bell, L. I. (2003). Strategies that close the gap. *Educational Leadership, 60*(4), 32–34.

Bell, L., Bolam, R., & Cubillo, L. (2003). A systematic review of the impact of school leadership and management on student outcomes. In *Research Evidence in Education Library* London, EPPICentre, Social Science Research Unit, Institute of Education. Available online at: http://eppi.ioe.ac.uk/EPPIWeb/home.aspx?&page=/reel/reviews.htm (Accessed September 1, 2004).

Blase, J., & Blase, J. (1999). Principals' instructional leadership and teacher development: Teacher's perspectives. *Educational Administration Quarterly, 35*(3), 349–378.

Boucher, L. (2001). Why can't you buy a vegetable garden: Whole-school literacy program reform. *The New England Reading Association Journal, 37*(3), 1–9.

Brown, K. F., & Keeping, L. M. (2005). Elaborating the construct of transformational leadership: The role of affect. *The Leadership Quarterly, 16*(2), 245–395.

Burns, J. M. (1979). *Leadership.* New York: Harper & Rowe, Inc.

Cartledge, G., Tillman, L. C., & Johnson, C. T. (2001). Professional ethics within the context of student discipline and diversity. *Teacher Education and Special Education, 24*(1), 25–37.

Cuban, L. (1984). *How teachers taught: Constancy and change in American classrooms, 1890–1980.* New York: Longman.

Edmonds, R. (1982). Programs in school improvement: An overview. *Educational Leadership* 40(3), 4.

Festinger, L. (1957). *A theory of cognitive dissonance.* Evanston, IL: Row Peterson.

Gay, G. (2000). *Culturally responsive teaching: Theory, research, and practice.* New York: Teachers College Press.

Gonzalez, M. L., & Huerta-Macias, A. (1997). Mi casa es su casa. *Educational Leadership, 55*(2), 52–55.

Gregory, J. F. (1994). The crime of punishment: Racial and gender disparities in the use of corporal punishment in U.S. schools. *Journal of Negro Education, 64*(4), 454–463.

Griffith, J. (2004). Relation of principal transformational leadership to school staff job satisfaction, staff turnover, and school performance. *Journal of Educational Administration, 342*(3), 333–356.

Hallinger, P. (2003). Leading educational change: Reflections on the practice of instructional and transformational leadership. *Cambridge Journal of Education, 33*(3), 329–352.

Hallinger, P., & Heck, P. (1999). Can leadership enhance school effectiveness? In T. Bush, R. Glatter, R. Bolam, P. Ribbins, and L. Bell (Eds), *Redefining Educational Management* (pp. 178–90). London: Paul Chapman.

Hunter, M. (1994). *Mastery teaching.* Thousand Oaks, CA: Corwin.

Kezar, A., & Eckel, P. (2002). The effect of institutional culture on change strategies in higher education: Universal principles or culturally responsive concepts? *Journal of Higher Education, 73*(4), 435–460.

Ladson-Billings, G. (1995). Toward a theory of culturally relevant pedagogy. *American Education Research Journal, 32*(3), 465–491.

Leithwood, K. A. (1992). The move toward transformational leadership. *Educational Leadership, 49*(5), 8–12.

Leithwood, K., Day, C., Sammons, P., Harris, A., & Hopkins, D. (2006). *Successful school leadership: What it is and how it influences pupil learning.* London: DfES and Nottingham: NCSL.

Leithwood, K., & Jantzi, D. (1991). Transformational school leadership effects: A replication. *School Effectiveness and School Improvement, 10,* 451–479.

Leithwood, K., & Jantzi, D. (2005). A review of transformational school leadership research 1996–2005. *Leadership and Policy in Schools, 4*(3), 177–199.

Leithwood, K., & Jantzi, D. (2006). Transformational school leadership for large-scale reform: Effects on students, teachers, and their classroom practices. *School Effectiveness and School Improvement, 17*(2), 201–227.

Leithwood, K., Seashore Louis, K., Anderson, G., & Wahlstrom, K. (2004). *How leadership influences student learning: A review of research for the Learning from Leadership project.* New York: The Wallace Foundation.

Leithwood, K., Tomlinson, D., & Genge, M. (1996). Transformational school leadership. In K. Leithwood, J. Chapman, D. Corson, P. Hallinger, & A. Hart (Eds.), *International handbook of educational leadership and administration* (pp. 785–840). Dordrecht, Netherlands: Kluwer Academic.

Marks, H. M., & Printy, S. M. (2003). Principal leadership and school performance: An integration of transformational and instructional leadership. *Educational Administration Quarterly,* 39(3), 370-397.

Marzano, R. J., Waters, T., & McNulty, B. A. (2005). *School leadership that works: From research to results.* Alexandria: Association for Supervision.

McKenzie, K. B. (2001). *White teachers' perceptions about their students of color and themselves as white educators.* Dissertation, The University of Texas at Austin.

McKenzie, K., Christman, D., Hernandez, F., Fierro, E., Capper, C., Dantley, M., Gonzalez, M., Cambron-McCabe, N., & Scheurich, J. (2008). Educating Leaders for social justice: A design for a comprehensive, social justice leadership preparation program. *Educational Administration Quarterly,* (44)1, 11-138.

McKenzie, K., & Lozano, R. (2008). Teachers' zone of self-efficacy: Which students get included, which students get excluded, and more importantly, why. *The National Journal of Urban Education and Practice,* (1)4, 372-384.

McKenzie, K., & Scheurich, J. (2008). Teacher resistance to improvement of schools with diverse students: A critical naiveté in the scholarship on school change. *The International Journal of Leadership in Education* (11)2, 117-133.

McKenzie, K., & Scheurich, J. J. (2004). Equity traps: A construct for departments of educational administration. *Educational Administration Quarterly,* 40(5), 601-632.

McKenzie, K., Skrla, L., & Scheurich, J. (2006). Preparing instructional leaders for social justice. *Journal of School Leadership,* 16(2), 158-170.

Miskel, C. G. (1982). Motivation in educational organizations. *Educational Administration Quarterly,* 18(3), 65-88.

Murphy, J. (1988). Methodological, measurement, and conceptual problems in the study of instructional leadership. *Educational Evaluation and Policy Analysis,* 10(2), 117-134.

Nelson, B. S., & Sassi, A. (2005). *The effective principal: Instructional leadership for high-quality learning.* New York: Teachers College Press.

Payne, R. (1996). *A framework for understanding poverty.* Highlands TX: aha! Process, Inc.

Resnick, L. B., & Hall, M. W. (2001). *The principles of learning: Study tools for educators* [CD-ROM, version 2.0]. Pittsburgh: University of Pittsburgh, Learning Research and Development Center, Institute for Learning (www.instituteforlearning.org).

Robinson, V. M. J., Lloyd, C. C., & Rowe, K. J. (2008). The impact of leadership on student outcomes: An analysis of the differential effects of leadership types. *Educational Administration Quarterly,* 44(5), 635-674.

Rorrer, A. K., & Skrla, L. (2005). Leaders as policy mediators. *Theory Into Practice,* 44(1), 53-62.

Rorrer, A. K., Skrla, L., & Scheurich, J. J. (2008). Districts as institutional actors in educational reform. *Educational Administration Quarterly,* 44(3), 307-357.

Schon, D. (1983). *The reflective practitioner: How professionals think in action.* New York: Basic Books.

Sheppard, B. (1996). Exploring the transformational nature of instructional leadership. *Alberta Journal of Educational Research,* 42(4), 325-344.

Sheppard, B. (2003). If to do in schools were as easy as to know what were good to do. *Education Canada,* 43(4), 16-19, 31.

Sherr, L., & Lozier, G. (1991). Total quality management in higher education. *New Directions for Institutional Research, 71,* 3–11.

Skrla, L., McKenzie, K., & Scheurich, J. (2009). *Using equity audits to create equitable and excellent schools.* Thousand Oaks, CA: Corwin.

Skrla, L., McKenzie, K, Scheurich, J., Sykes, G., Thompson, C., & Opfer, D. (April, 2007). "A Study of Instructionally Effective School Districts." Paper presented at the conference of the American Educational Researchers Association. (AERA), Chicago, IL.

Skrla, L., & Scheurich, J. J. (2001). Displacing deficit thinking in school district leadership. *Education and Urban Society, 33*(3), 235–259.

Skrla, L., Scheurich, J. J., & Johnson, J. F. (2001). Toward a new consensus on high academic achievement for all children. *Education and Urban Society, 33*(3), 227–234.

Smith, W. F., & Andrews, R. L. (1989). *Instructional leadership: How principals make a difference.* Alexandria, VA: Association for Supervision and Curriculum Development.

Southworth, G. (2002). Instructional leadership in schools: Reflections and empirical evidence. *School Leadership and Management, 22*(1), 73–91.

Tomlinson, C. A. (1999). Mapping a route toward differentiated instruction. *Educational Leadership, 57*(1), 12–16.

Tomlinson, C. A., Brighton, C., Hertberg, H., Callahan, C. M., Moon, T. R., Brimijoin, K., Conover, L. A., & Reynolds, T. (2003). Differentiating instruction in response to student readiness, interest, and learning profile in academically diverse classrooms: A review of literature. *Journal for the Education of the Gifted, 27*(2,3), 119–145.

Valencia. R. (Ed.). (1997). *The evolution of deficit thinking.* Washington D.C.: The Falmer Press.

Williamson, P., Bondy, E., Langley, L., Mayne, D. (2005). Meeting the challenges of high-stakes testing while remaining child-centered: The representations of two urban teachers. *Childhood Education, 81*(4), 190–195.

Witziers, B., Bosker, R. J., & Krüger, M. L. (2003). Educational leadership and student achievement: The elusive search for an association. *Educational Administration Quarterly, 39*(3), 398–425.

Wong, H. K., & Wong, R. T. (2004). *The first days of school.* Mountain View, CA: Harry K. Wong.

Yair, G. (2000). Not just about time: Instructional practices and productive time in school. *Educational Administration Quarterly, 36*(4), 485–512.

✠ CHAPTER 4

Building Leadership Capacity to Improve Student Learning: The Power and Practice of Reflection

Bruce G. Barnett and Gary R. O'Mahony

Education, perhaps more so than most professions, is subject to trends and fads affected by local, national, and even global factors and contexts. Policy makers clamor for raising test scores, producing high-school graduates, and supplying an educated workforce in the school, while the media rushes to report when schools are failing to achieve these outcomes, especially in comparison to school systems around the world. Consequently, school leaders not only are expected to improve student achievement while raising learning standards for PK-12 students, but also advance school improvement through teacher and leader capacity-building to assist students in achieving rigorous learning standards. Coupled with these school improvement reforms is the importance of professional development geared to allow educators to increase their knowledge and skills in delivering instruction and assessing learning outcomes. Oftentimes, professional development is touted as means for stimulating reflective practice, or the ability to merge thinking and action (Osterman & Kottkamp, 2004). Enter the phrase "reflective practice and professional development" in the Google search engine and over 500,000 entries appear.

Despite claims that reflection has become one of the most often-mentioned ways of helping practitioners think about and revise their practices, the real power of reflection as a means for affecting school leaders and teachers as they strive to improve student performance may not have been realized.

Therefore, this chapter examines the value of reflection as a viable means for improved instructional leadership that impacts classroom practices and ultimately student performance. To set the stage, we begin by summarizing what is known about instructional leadership, focusing on the most promising pathways for understanding how school leaders impact student learning. We then examine how reflection has been conceptualized and how it is being used for preparing and developing school leader capabilities to affect teaching and learning. The chapter concludes with implications for strengthening reflective pathways educators can use to improve student learning in their schools.

School Leadership for Student Learning

The responsibility to help students obtain the skills and attitudes required in the twenty-first century falls heavily on the shoulders of schools, particularly teachers and principals. In weighing the contextual factors affecting teaching and learning, Townsend (2008) argues that third-millennium leaders need to think and act locally and globally, similar to Friedman's (2005) concept of "globalization of the local" (p. 506). As future leaders balance global trends with local decisions about curriculum, pedagogy, and assessment, not only must they distribute leadership throughout the organization, but also they must attend to developing future leaders in the organization (Townsend, 2008). At the same time, school leaders are being held accountable for student performance, a pattern that is likely to escalate given the expanding set of skills students will be expected to master. Therefore, the present-day focus on understanding the instructional leadership role of principals is bound to be a driving force in research and professional development.

At the same time, the whirlwind of activities and expectations that principals face in managing the school and influencing instructional practices requires them to process incredible amounts of information in relatively short amounts of time. One way of assisting principals to cope with these realities is to help them develop the habit of reflection (e.g., Barnett, O'Mahony, & Matthews, 2004). We will examine the power and benefits of reflection after examining how instructional leadership has been defined and reviewing findings and models that capture the effects school leaders have on student learning. Particular attention is devoted to the four pathways of school leadership influence proposed by Leithwood and his colleagues (2009).

What Makes an Effective Instructional Leader?

The principal's role has gained prominence because "school leadership is second only to classroom teaching as an influence on pupil learning" (Leithwood & Day, 2008, p. 2). Hallinger (2005) attests that the lasting legacy of the effective schools movement is the institutionalization of the term "instructional leadership" into the vocabulary and practice of school leaders. While this role is acknowledged as both necessary and sufficient for affecting changes in teaching and learning, Leithwood, Seashore-Louis, Anderson, and Walstrom (2004) note that its survival rests upon finding a suitable operational definition that can be understood and applied by school principals.

As distinct from other managerial tasks, instructional leadership include, "those actions that a principal takes, or delegates to others, to promote growth in student learning" (DeBevoise, 1984, p.15). Hart and Bredeson (1996) indicate the literature has attempted to *describe* (Duke, 1987), *measure* (Hallinger & Murphy, 1986), *explain* (Bossert, Dwyer, Rowan & Lee, 1982) and *predict* (Heck, Larsen, & Marcoulides, 1990) specific instructional leadership behaviors of principals associated with high levels of student achievement with limited degree of success. Overall, the research on instructional leadership is somewhat narrow, and relies heavily on standardized achievement scores, typically in mathematics and reading, as the measures of desired educational outcomes in schools. Furthermore, Leithwood et al. (2004) suggest that what constitutes successful leadership can be shrouded and often confused by the exploding mass of current evidence about instructional leadership.

Despite the multitude of labels found in the literature and mixed findings about how instructional leaders behave, there is some light that has helped clear up this fog of confusion. Research indicates successful school leaders indirectly affect student learning by influencing other people, the organization, and school processes (e.g., Darling-Hammond, La Pointe, Meyerson, Orr, & Cohen, 2007; Davis, Darling-Hammond, LaPointe, & Meyerson, 2005). Specific examples include the following:

- Influencing other people—developing their talents (Leithwood, et al., 2004), supporting teachers (Waters, Marzano, & McNulty, 2003), promoting and participating in teacher learning and development (Robinson, Lloyd, & Rowe, 2008), and providing feedback on classroom instruction (Hallinger & Heck, 1996a, 1996b).
- Affecting the school organization—setting direction and shaping the school's mission (Bamburg & Andrews, 1990; Goldring & Pasternak,

1994; Leithwood, et al., 2004; Marks & Printy, 2003), redesigning the organization and instructional programs (Hallinger, 2005; Leithwood, et al., 2004), establishing goals and expectations (Robinson, Lloyd, & Rowe, 2008), resourcing strategically (Robinson, Lloyd, & Rowe, 2008), creating an orderly and supportive environment (Robinson, Lloyd, & Rowe, 2008), and creating a positive school climate (Hallinger, 2005).

- Altering school processes—restructuring the curriculum (Waters, Marzano, & McNulty, 2003); planning, coordinating, and evaluating teaching practices (Robinson, Lloyd, & Rowe, 2008), improving school management procedures (Hallinger, 2005); and setting academic standards and reallocating time (Barth, 2003; Hallinger & Heck, 1996a, 1996b; Southworth, 2002).

How Do Principals Influence Student and School Outcomes?

Whether or not principals influence student and school outcomes is a question posed by many in the field. We agree with those who posit that principals have an important role in affecting school outcomes; however, research indicates that while their direct influence may be limited, their indirect role is vital in establishing the conditions in which improved student learning can flourish. A useful synthesis of research on instructional leadership has been advanced by Kenneth Leithwood and his colleagues (2009), identifying four distinct, yet interrelated, pathways for influencing teaching and learning. Leithwood contends failure to take such interaction into account severely limits school leaders' influence.

Rational pathway. According to Leithwood et al. (2009), the variables associated with the rational path are grounded in knowledge and skills about curriculum, teaching, and learning. Following the rational pathway provides sense-making and meaning to any school improvement initiative, as people need to know what and why changes are needed and what the benefits will be for the students and the school. Therefore, for principals to be strong and effective instructional leaders, they must clearly articulate what constitutes effective schools and practices and then provide ways for this to be explored and embedded into the existing culture. Matthews and Crow (2003) suggest that successful instructional leadership involves the harnessing and promoting of three crucial leadership factors in building a rational pathway:

1. Understanding and shaping school culture so it is able to respond, renew, change, and maintain a cultural press towards better teaching and learning

2. Developing a personal vision of quality teaching and learning that can be incorporated into a shared and understood vision that can be embraced by the school as a learning community

3. Using leadership tools such as communication and collaboration to implement the shared vision in the school to improve teaching and learning for all students.

Leithwood et al. (2009) argue that the rational path includes both classroom- and school-level variables. Determining the variables of influence in the rational pathway is crucial. Because there is considerable evidence available about factors affecting student learning, school leaders must focus everyone's attention on those factors known to have the greatest chance of improving student learning. On one hand, they can work with teachers in order that they provide students with immediate and informative feedback, use differentiated teaching strategies, maintain positive teacher–student relations, and effectively manage their classrooms (Hattie, 2009). On the other hand, Matthews and Crow (2003) maintain that instructional leaders attend to the rational approach when they want to ensure teachers view school improvement as a continuing process, rather than a one-time effort.

Collecting and examining data on present teaching and assessment practices prepares the way for educators to acknowledge there is a need for improvement in teaching and learning for all students. Cuban (1988) suggested labeling the difference between superficial and substantial change as first-order and second-order changes. First-order changes seek to refine current practices, making them more efficient; however, teachers and students continue their work in much the same way as they have done in the past. Second-order changes, however, entail fundamental shifts in values, beliefs, and practices where underlying assumptions and sacred cows are challenged and debated, resulting in new practices and procedures.

Emotional pathway. Considerable evidence indicates that emotions direct cognition: they structure perceptions, direct attention, give preferential access to certain memories, and bias judgment in ways that shape how individuals respond to their environments (Oatley, Keltner, & Jenkins, 2006). Exercising influence on variables located on the emotional path depends on leaders' emotional and social intelligence, which accounts for up to 80% of what leaders say and do (Goleman, Boyatzis, & McKee, 2002). Cooper and Sawaf (1997) emphasize that instructional leaders need to develop:

1. **Emotional literacy**—being authentic and displaying personal power which engenders emotional honesty, energy, feedback and, connection with intuition and wisdom
2. **Emotional fitness**—building inspiration and clarity with others that results in authentic presence, trust, constructive debate and inquiry, resulting in development of resilience and renewal
3. **Emotional depth**—building integrity and purpose, which brings hope, faith, integrity, and trust when working with others.

Emotional and social intelligence, recently popularized by Goleman, Boyatzis, and McKee (2002), is critical for leaders because they not only motivate themselves and others, but also are excellent team players (Kets de Vries, 2004). Goleman, Boyatzis, and McKee (2002) conceptualize emotional and social intelligence as being comprised of four areas: self-awareness, self-management, social awareness, and relationship management. *Self-awareness* is the ability to understand emotions and be clear about one's purpose, which leads to *self-management*, or a type of internal conversation that "allows the mental clarity and concentrated energy that leadership demands, and what keeps disruptive emotions from throwing us off track" (Goleman, Boyatzis, & McKee, 2002, p. 46). Leaders with *social awareness* possess empathy for others' feeling and perspectives or "the ability to stand in others' shoes, to see with their eyes, and to feel with their hearts" (Pink, 2005, p. 159). Finally, *relationship management* is the ability of leaders to move people in the right direction by serving as change agents capable of managing conflict while building teamwork and collaborative action.

An important aspect of the emotional pathway is the leaders' ability to build trust with and among people in the organization. Leithwood et al. (2009) suggest that the development of trust with colleagues, students, and parents is essential for achieving the schools' goals for student learning. Transparency, competence, benevolence, and reliability are among the qualities persuading others that a person is trustworthy. Teacher trust is critical to the success of schools, and nurturing trusting relationships with students and parents is a key element in improving student learning (Bryk & Schneider, 2003, 2005; Lee, Smith, & Croninger, 1997). Principals engender trust with and among staff and with parents and students when they:

- recognize and acknowledge their own and their staff's vulnerabilities,
- listen to the personal needs of staff members and reconcile those needs with a clear vision for the school,

- create a space for parents in the school and demonstrate to parents they are reliable, open, and scrupulously honest in their interactions,
- buffer teachers from unreasonable policy, parental, and community demands,
- treat teachers in a friendly, supportive, and open manner, and
- set high standards for students and then follow through with support for teachers.

Organizational pathway. The organizational path deals with how teachers respond to their conditions as they work with students, taking into consideration school structures, culture, policies, and operating procedures (Leithwood et al., 2009). The role of the instructional leader is to set in place the conditions for effective learning for all students and provide ways for all teachers to meet them so as to ensure that no child is short-changed and failure does not become an option. Hattie's (2009) synthesis of research identifies more than a dozen variables located on the organizational path. Some can be found in the classroom (e.g., class size, ability groupings), some are school-wide (e.g., school size, multigrade or age classes, retention policies), and others are typically controlled by agencies outside the school (e.g., school funding, summer school).

One of the more powerful and researched variables associated with the organizational path is instructional time. Early research on time for learning captured four distinct ways in which it could be conceptualized and measured: (1) total amount of time available for learning (e.g., number of days of schooling per year, number of hours of instruction per day), (2) time devoted to instruction is the potential time left for learning once unplanned events, recesses, transitions, interruptions are subtracted from the total amount of time, (3) academically engaged time is the time students actually spend on their own learning within the time devoted to instruction. Leithwood et al. (2009) maintain that there has been little direct evidence reported about leadership practices for optimizing instructional time in schools, with the major exception of research on leadership "buffering." The value of buffering as a contribution to organizational goals is justified by evidence collected in schools and many other different types of organizations as supporting the protection of teacher and classroom time to allow more direct teaching and learning (Yukl, 1994). In schools, buffering aims to protect the efforts of teachers from the many distractions they face from both inside and outside their organizations. Principals buffer external forces by running interference with unreasonable parents, supporting teachers in the discipline of students, and aligning government and district policy initiatives with the school's improvement efforts.

Family pathway. Increased involvement of parents and families often is cited as one of the most important ways to improve public schools. A variety of studies confirm parental involvement impacts students' attitude, attendance, and academic achievement (e.g., Henderson & Berla, 1994). Leithwood and Jantzi's (2006) summary of 40 studies points to the important influence of family work habits, academic guidance and support provided to children, stimulation to think about issues in the larger environment, provision of adequate health and nutritional conditions, and physical settings in the home. Not only are the academic and occupational aspirations and expectations parents hold for their children important (e.g., Hong & Ho, 2005), but also the family's involvement in helping young children learn to read. A recent synthesis of reading in the home environment found that if parents or their child were relatively passive, then minimal effects on reading performance resulted (Senechal & Young, 2008).

Traditionally, parent involvement in education has included home-based activities (e.g., helping with homework, promoting school attendance) and school-based activities (e.g., attending school functions, volunteering at school) (Hattie, 2009). Although most parents care about their children, want them to succeed, and are eager to obtain better information from schools, some families have far more resources than others to be involved in productive ways. Families living in poverty, struggling to speak the dominant language, dealing with unemployment, and facing unstable housing have considerable difficulty in providing home-based resources to support their children's education. As families strive to reinforce the school's goals and programs, school leaders may need to intervene; however, many educators may not know how to go about building positive and productive parental programs. Epstein (1995) provides guidance for school leaders by suggesting an array of ways parental involvement can be encouraged:

1. Parenting—help families establish home environments that support children's learning (e.g., parent education workshops, home visits, family health care support programs)

2. Communicating—design various forms of communication regarding school programs (e.g., language translators, weekly folders of student work, telephone trees)

3. Volunteering—recruit parents to assist during school day (e.g., parent center for volunteers, parent patrols for school safety, surveys of parent talents and availability)

4. Learning at home—provide information on ways to reinforce classroom learning (e.g., homework policies, summer learning packages, calendar of activities)

5. Decision-making—develop parent leaders and involve them in decision-making (e.g., parent advisory committees, network of family representatives, independent lobby groups)

6. Collaborating with the community—integrate community resources into school programs (e.g., information on community health agencies, alumni participation, service-learning projects by students).

The Power and Practice of Reflection

As mentioned earlier, developing the habit of reflection has been touted as assisting principals to improve their decision-making processes (e.g., Barnett, O'Mahony, & Matthews, 2004; Osterman & Kottkamp, 2004; Short & Rinehart, 1993). The merits of reflection have been suggested for centuries. One of the earliest references to reflection is the "Socratic method," a form of questioning and dialogue developed in ancient Greek times. Over 75 years ago, John Dewey (1933), a prominent educational psychologist and progressive educator, noted the importance of reflection as a means for understanding knowledge and beliefs and making future decisions. In recent years, reflection has gained momentum as an important way for teachers and principals to process vast amounts of information to make well-informed decisions (e.g., Mohlman Sparks-Langer & Berstein, 1991; York-Barr, Sommers, Ghere, & Montie, 2001). As a means for improving leadership practice, Osterman (1990) asserts:

> Reflective practice enhances professional practice in several ways. It leads to greater self-awareness, to development of new knowledge about professional practice, and to a broader understanding of problems which confront practitioners. Because it enhances professional growth, and thereby responds to the needs of individual practitioners, it also influences the environment of the workplace in ways that support organizational change and effectiveness. (p. 134)

Recently, attempts to link reflection, school improvement, and professional development with improved student learning outcomes have surfaced (e.g., Leithwood, Riedlinger, Bauer, & Jantzi, 2003; Osterman & Kottkamp,

2004; Wright, 2009); however, empirical evidence demonstrating the effects of reflection on student achievement is scant (Wilson, 2008). Despite the unproven premise that reflective practitioners are more likely to think and behave in ways that ultimately affect student learning, many professional learning programs for practicing school administrators are attempting to connect reflection with student performance outcomes. Before examining these types of programs, we briefly review how reflection has been defined and conceptualized in education.

Overview of Reflection

Reflection and reflective practice have been defined in a variety of ways. Valverde (1982) indicates the reflective process allows individuals to examine their actions, practices, and outcomes by addressing the question: What am I doing and why? He also maintains reflection is not an idle process, but one that must be practiced repeatedly, deliberately, and constructively.

Defining reflection. Typically viewed as a rational problem-solving process, reflection occurs when: (1) a problem is identified, (2) the problem is analyzed, (3) a tentative theory for solving the problem is tested, and (4) a decision is made about how to resolve the problem (Daudelin, 1996). Confucius, the Chinese social philosopher, concurs by stating, "The first rule in being a wise leader is that you must first define the problem." Descriptions of reflection are abundant, most of which depict this decision-making process as occurring in various phases or stages (e.g., King & Kitchener, 1994; Ross, 1989; Sparks-Langer, Simmons, Pasch, Colton, & Stark, 1990). According to Brookfield (1987), critical reflection consists of five phases: (1) experiencing a trigger event, (2) appraising the event, (3) exploring possible solutions, (4) identifying alternative perspectives, and (5) reaching a conclusion or decision. Taking these phases into account, Kottkamp (1990) defines reflection as "a cycle of paying deliberate attention to one's own actions and making decisions about improved ways of acting in the future, or in the midst of the action itself" (p. 182).

The reflective cycle, therefore, consists of an awareness of a problem or event, consideration of possible ways to address the problem, and a preferred course of action. Experiential learning theory (Kolb, 1984) is one of the most often cited conceptualizations describing the reflective cycle. Basically, this four-phase theory indicates learning occurs as individuals experience or recall an event (concrete experience), recount the details of the event (reflective observation), make sense of the event (abstract conceptualization), and take action based on their insights. Similar to York-Barr et al. (2001), Barnett et al. (2004) have abbreviated these phases into three questions representing the phases of reflection: (1) *What* happened? (2) *So what* does this mean? and (3) *Now what* should happen? They contend that reflection is "the ability to examine current or past practices, behaviours or thoughts and to make conscious choices about our future actions... [and] when combining hindsight, insight, and foresight people make the most of their reflective powers" (p. 6).

Types of reflection. Various types or levels of reflection have been identified. Schön (1983, 1987), for instance, maintains individuals reflect *on* action by recalling past events and making sense of them as well as reflect *in* action by processing information and making decisions as events are unfolding. A third type of reflection, reflecting *before* action, is the ability "to speculate or reflect on what the future might bring and, importantly, be influenced" (Wilson, 2008, p. 179). Another popular categorization indicates three hierarchical levels of reflection exist: technical, practical, and critical (Van Manen, 1977). Using Sergiovanni's (1992) mindscapes of hand, head, and heart, Schuttloffel (n.d.) suggests technical reflection is performed by the hand (our actions and responses), practical reflection occurs through the head (our view of the world), and critical reflection comes from the heart (our beliefs and values).

In summarizing the literature on reflective typologies, Larrivee (2008) indicates there are four levels, particularly related to teachers' thought processes: (1) *prereflection* occurs when no conscious thought process is used when taking action, (2) *surface reflection* arises when goals are pursued without consideration of their value, (3) *pedagogical reflection* takes place when individuals apply their knowledge about what constitutes quality practice, and (4) *critical reflection* surfaces when a commitment to social justice is acknowledged as the moral and ethical consequences of actions are considered. Finally, Eraut (1994) claims reflective practice allows principals to uncover various knowledge bases driving their actions: (1) personnel—understanding the staff based on personal interactions, (2) situational—responding to events based on previous experiences and existing knowledge, (3) educational—understanding the range of possible policies and practice available, (4) conceptual—solving problems based on personal ideas, theories, and concepts, and (5) control—knowing one's personal strengths and weaknesses in determining tasks to complete or delegate.

Reflection for practicing school leaders. School administrators are being encouraged to develop habits of reflection and critical analysis allowing them to improve practice. Within leadership preparation programs and professional development programs, an abundance of learning activities aimed at helping participants reflect on their practice have been suggested (e.g., Barnett & O'Mahony, 2002, 2006, 2008; Cordeiro & Sloan, 1996; Daresh, 2001; Darling-Hammond et al, 2007; Murphy, 2001). Not only should the curriculum embed essential questions for reflection (Wasley, 1991), but principals must be adept at applying solutions to problems of practice, especially to gauge their influence on student learning (Hallinger & McCary, 1990). Illustrations of prominent ways in which reflective practice is incorporated for developing the knowledge and skills of aspiring and practicing school leaders are described below.

Because of the frantic pace of the job and the increasing responsibilities school leaders encounter, they must process large amounts of information and make rapid-fire decisions. Consequently, many principals must react as events occur (reflection *in* action [Schön, 1983]), rather than standing back and reflecting on alternative courses of action (reflection *on* action [Schön, 1983]). Therefore, many professional development programs for school leaders attempt to assist them to learn productive ways of reflecting on their thoughts and actions, presumably to improve school processes and student outcomes (e.g., Barnett & O'Mahony, 2002, 2006, 2008; Larrivee, 2008). One of the most convincing studies of the how professional development affects school leaders' internal thought processes and leadership practices that ultimately are associated with school and classroom conditions leading to increased student achievement was conducted by Leithwood et al. (2003).

Although it is beyond the scope of this chapter to describe the array of programs in which practicing school leaders are being taught to build habits of reflection, two of the most prominent approaches for stimulating reflection are mentoring and coaching programs. Often, these terms are confused; however, many authors contend that mentoring is an ongoing process for career development while coaching is short-term focusing on skill development (e.g., Danielson & McGreal, 2000; Hobson, 2003; Male, 2006; Mertz, 2004). Mentoring programs, particularly for novice school leaders, have proliferated in recent years around the world (e.g., Weindling, 2004). Many states in America now require new principals to be assigned a mentor to socialize them to a new school system; build their professional networks; and understand how their actions are affecting staff, students, and community members (Daresh, 2004; Vallani, 2006). Reflection has been touted as an important aspect of mentoring programs (e.g., Matthews & Crow, 2003). For example, Weindling's

(2004) synthesis of 43 principal induction programs operating in 14 countries revealed that effective mentoring programs carefully select and train mentors and that "the use of reflection was highlighted as a fundamental component in most (induction) programmes, whereby the new headteacher or principal would be encouraged to be a reflective practitioner" (p. 16).

In addition, coaching programs for school leaders also have become more prevalent lately. Typically, coaching is viewed as a reciprocal process meant to encourage reflection without evaluation or judgment (Calabrese & Tucker-Ladd, 1991; Robertson, 2005). Therefore, the coaching relationship is meant to facilitate learning, takes time to develop, requires strong interpersonal communication between partners, and is guided by the person being coached (O'Mahony, Matthews, & Barnett, 2009; Robertson, 2005). The features of effective coaching programs include: (1) clear outcomes, (2) support from the organization, (3) careful selection, training, and matching of coaches, (4) attention to the learner's needs, and (5) ongoing monitoring and evaluation (Hopkins-Thompson, 2000). Many coaching programs are designed for beginning school leaders (e.g., Bloom, Castagna, Moir, & Warren, 2005); however, a recently developed coaching program in Australia (Coaching for Enhancing the Capabilities of Experienced Principals [CEP]) provides support for experienced principals as they are implementing school improvement initiatives (O'Mahony & Barnett, 2008). Important benefits reported by CEP principals included a greater awareness of their leadership tendencies, a better appreciation for the skills and talents of their staff members, and an improved sense of strategic direction for the school improvement initiatives they were implementing.

A host of reflective activities are embedded in these mentoring and coaching programs for school leaders (e.g., Brown, 2005; Conyers, 2004; Hibert, 2000; Zellner, Ward, McNamara, Gideon, Camacho, & Edgewood, 2002). Robertson (2005), for example, maintains that coaching programs encourage reflective practice as school leaders complete self-assessments, develop specific goals based on these assessments, and observe and describe their own and others' leadership practices. In their overview of reflection for school leaders, Barnett et al. (2004) advocate reflective practice can be promoted during coaching and mentoring by

- recounting our own experiences (e.g., autobiographies, self inventories, journals),
- reviewing other peoples' experiences (e.g., shadowing, case studies),

- practicing skills (e.g., action research, supervised practicum), and

- integrating theory and practice (e.g., leadership style inventories, reflective writing exercises)

Regardless of the type of reflective activities being implemented, assisting others to become more reflective about their practice occurs by focusing on the learner's needs, listening rather than talking, asking guiding questions, providing alternative approaches when asked, and respecting the learner's need for independence (O'Mahony et al., 2009).

Conclusions and Implications

Earlier in this chapter, we summarized various ways for principals to infuse reflection into their practice. Our work in assisting educators to become more reflective about their thoughts and actions has taught us valuable lessons about the relevance of reflection as a professional development tool:

- Use self-assessment inventories to personalize learning

- Focus reflective activities on relevant issues, particularly ways of affecting student learning

- Blend opportunities for individual and group reflection

- Encourage school teams to examine their development and accomplishments

- Provide follow-up activities to debrief experiences and determine how practices are affecting the organization and student learning (Barnett & O'Mahony, 2002).

A potentially powerful way for school leaders to reflect on their instructional leadership practices would be to use Leithwood and his colleagues' (2009) four pathways: rational, emotional, organizational, and family. Brief illustrations of activities aimed at each of these paths are provided below.

Rational

This pathway deals with the core technology of schools, namely how curriculum and instruction affect student learning. Collecting and analyzing information on classroom instructional practices is at the heart of this path. Many peer mentoring and coaching programs include opportunities for classroom observation and feedback, as do instructional supervision strategies, including clinical supervision (Sullivan & Glanz, 2000), developmental supervision (Glickman & Gordon, 1987), and cognitive coaching (Costa & Garmston,

1994). Teachers are required to gather assessment data on their students, which is an important area where individual and collective reflection can occur. For instance, teachers can begin by describing their classroom assessment practices using reflective questions: (1) What are my purposes for assessment? (2) What targets do I set for assessments? (3) What elements of a sound assessment design do I use? (4) How do I communicate to students my expectations for assessment? and (5) How are students involved in assessing their learning? (Stiggins, 2002). After sharing their descriptions, teachers can identify particular strengths and areas for improving student assessment approaches. Teachers with particular strengths can share their practices with colleagues and be observed. As common areas of growth emerge, principals can ensure appropriate professional development is provided. Over time, teachers can re-examine their assessment practices, noting how changes are affecting students' engagement and learning.

Emotional

Attending to values, attitudes, and feelings as they relate to teaching and student learning is the focus of this pathway. The use of self-assessment inventories allows teachers and principals to uncover their tendencies and the emotions associated with these practices. For example, work teams often flounder because they lack clear mechanisms for examining personal expectations and team performance. Responses to inventories and/or reflective questions can be shared among team members that address their initial expectations and assumptions about working together (Beach & Reinhartz, 2000; Wigtil & Kelsey, 1978), reactions to team meetings (York-Barr et al., 2001), and team dynamics (Larson & LaFasto, 1989; Lencioni, 2002). A particular effective activity is for a facilitator to ask individual team members to complete the Five Dysfunctions of a Team Inventory (Lencioni, 2002) and compare responses. Based on their ratings, team members reveal what pleases them about the team's performance and frustrations. When these emotions arise, the facilitator records strengths of the team and areas for growth. As teams become more comfortable addressing their shortcomings, they can begin to address how their accomplishments are affecting school and student performance.

Organizational

Examining policies, structures, and processes that affect student learning are the center of this pathway. Once again, principals can facilitate teachers' reflections about how the school's infrastructure is supporting and/or impeding their instruction. For example, teachers can reflect on ways they are maximizing instructional time as well as factors that are impeding their teaching time (e.g., Guskey, 2000). Time-maximizing ideas can be shared and/or observed in practice; common factors that are interfering with teachers' instructional time can be identified and potential solutions raised. The most promising solutions can be administered and monitored for their impact on teachers. In addition, teachers can identify differentiated instruction strategies they are using in the classroom. Peers can observe their lessons, noting student engagement rates as various instructional strategies are used. As this information is collated across classrooms, instructional strategies with high engagement rates can be shared among staff. Similarly, those strategies where student engagement is not at the level expected will emerge, which can inform professional development strategies for the school.

Family

This final pathway deals with how parental and community involvement affects teaching and student learning. A particular effective way to ensure if the school is involving community stakeholders is to use Epstein's (1995) typology as a reflective exercise. For instance, surveys and/or interviews can be completed by teachers and parents regarding how the school: (a) assists families in establishing supportive home environments for student learning, (b) communicates information about events and programs, (c) recruits parents as volunteers, (d) informs parents on ways of reinforcing classroom learning, (e) involves parents in decisions, and (f) integrates community resources. A team of teachers and parents can review these results to ascertain strengths and areas needing attention. Strengths can be shared with the staff and community; task forces can be formed to address deficiencies and the types of information needed to determine how planned changes are affecting teachers and students.

Clearly, linking teaching and learning improvements to the reflective practices of school leaders and teachers makes intuitive sense. On one hand, schools and their leaders will continue to be held accountable for overseeing school conditions that improve student performance. Comparisons of school performance locally, regionally, nationally, and internationally will put mounting pressure on leaders to find the most effective ways of helping students matriculate through the school system, learn essential academic and social skills, and become contributing members of society. At the same time, leaders must balance the climate and culture of the school with community expectations. On the other hand, the increasing complexity of schools will require school leaders to access and process large amounts of information in order to make accurate, thoughtful decisions. Hence, the importance of reflection as a means for analyzing information and making informed decisions to improve school and student performance. Despite the logical relationship between reflection and school improvement, our analysis suggests little empirical evidence exists to demonstrate a causal connection. Therefore, the challenge for researchers and practitioners is to clearly articulate the intersection between instructional leadership, school improvement, and reflection. If future studies and practical approaches document this relationship, not only will the educational leadership field benefit, but there is also a greater chance students will receive the education they deserve.

References

Bamberg, J. D., & Andrews, R. L (1990). Instructional leadership, school goals, and student achievement. Paper presented at the annual meeting of the American Educational Research Association, Boston, MA.

Barnett, B. G., & O'Mahony, G. (2002). One for the to-do list: Slow down and think. *Journal of Staff Development, 23*(3), 54–58.

Barnett, B. G., & O'Mahony, G. R. (2006). Developing a culture of reflection: Implications for school improvement. *Reflective Practice, 7*(4), 499–523.

Barnett, B. G., & O'Mahony, G. R. (2008). Mentoring and coaching programs for the development of school leaders. In J. Lumby, G. Crow, & P. Pashiardis (Eds.), *International handbook on the preparation and development of school leaders* (pp. 232–262). New York: Routledge.

Barnett, B. G., O'Mahony. G. R., & Matthews, R. J. (2004). *Reflective practice: The cornerstone for school improvement*. Moorabbin, Victoria: Hawker Brownlow Education.

Barth, R., (2003) *Lessons learned: Shaping relationships and the culture of the workplace*. Thousand Oaks, CA: Corwin Press.

Beach, D. M., & Reinhartz, J. (2000). *Supervisory leadership: Focus on instruction*. Boston, MA: Allyn & Bacon.

Bloom G., Castagna, C., Moir, E., & Warren, B. (2005). *Blended coaching: Skills and strategies to support principal development*. Thousand Oaks, CA: Corwin Press.

Bossert, S., Dwyer, D., Rowan, B., & Lee, G. (1982). The instructional management role of the principal. *Educational Administration Quarterly, 18*(3), 34–64.

Brookfield, S. D. (1987). *Developing critical thinkers: Challenging adults to explore alternative ways of thinking and acting*. San Francisco, CA: Jossey-Bass.

Brown, F. (2005). Leveling the playing field for new principals. *Principal, 84*(5), 22–24.

Bryk, A. S., & Schneider, B. (2003). Trust in schools: A core resource for school reform. *Educational Leadership, 60*(6), 40–44.

Bryk, A. S., & Schneider, B. (2005). *Trust in schools: A core resource for improvement.* New York: Russell Sage Foundation.

Calabrese, R. L., & Tucker-Ladd, P. R. (1991). The principal and assistant principal: A mentoring relationship. *NASSP Bulletin, 75*(533), 67–74.

Conyers, J. G. (2004). Thinking outside to support newcomers. *School Administrator, 61*(6), 18–21.

Cooper, R. K., & Sawaf, A., (1997). *Executive EQ: Emotional intelligence in business.* London: Orion Publishing Co.

Cordeiro, P., & Sloan, E. S. (1996). Administrative interns as legitimate participants in the community of practice. *Journal of School Leadership, 6*(1), 4–29.

Costa, A. L., & Garmston, R. J. (1994). *Cognitive coaching: A foundation for renaissance schools.* Norwood, MA: Christopher-Gordon Publishers.

Cuban, L. (1988). *The managerial imperative and the practice of leadership in schools.* Albany, NY: SUNY Press.

Danielson, C., & McGreal, T. L. (2000). *Teacher evaluation to enhance professional practice.* Princeton, NJ: Educational Testing Service.

Daresh, J. C. (2001). *Leaders helping leaders: A practical guide to administrative mentoring.* Thousand Oaks, CA: Corwin Press.

Daresh, J. (2004). Mentoring school leaders: Professional promise or predictable problems? *Educational Administration Quarterly, 40*(4), 495–517.

Darling-Hammond, L., La Pointe, M., Meyerson, D., Orr, M. T., & Cohen, C. (2007). *Preparing school leaders for a changing world: Lessons from exemplary leadership development programs.* Palo Alto, CA: Stanford University, Stanford Educational Leadership Institute.

Daudelin, M. W. (1996). Learning from experience through reflection. *Organizational Dynamics, 24*(3), 36–48.

Davis, S., Darling-Hammond, L., La Pointe, M., & Meyerson, D. (2005). *Review of research: School leadership study. Developing successful principals.* Palo Alto, CA: Stanford University, Stanford Educational Leadership Institute.

DeBevoise, W. (1984). Synthesis of research on the principal as instructional leader. *Educational Leadership, 41*(5), 14–20.

Dewey, J. (1933). *How we think: A restatement of the relation of reflective thinking to the educative process.* Boston, MA: D. C. Heath.

Duke, D. L. (1987) *School leadership and instructional improvement.* New York: Random House.

Epstein, J. L. (1995). School/family/community partnerships: Caring for the children we share. *Phi Delta Kappan, 76*(9), 701–712.

Eraut, M. (1994). *Developing professional knowledge and competence.* London: Falmer Press.

Friedman, T. L. (2005). *The world is flat: A brief history of the twenty-first century.* New York: Farrar, Straus and Giroux.

Glickman, C. D., & Gordon, S. P. (1987). Clarifying developmental supervision. *Educational Leadership, 44*, 64–68.

Goldring E., & Pasternak, R. (1994). Principals' coordinating strategies and school effective-ness. *School Effectiveness and School Improvement, 5*(3), 239–253.

Goleman, D., Boyatzis, R., & McKee, A. (2002). *Primal leadership: Learning to lead with emotional intelligence.* Boston, MA: Harvard Business School Press.

Guskey, T. R. (2000). *Evaluating professional development.* Thousand Oaks, CA: Corwin Press.

Hallinger, P. (2005) *Instructional leadership: How has the model evolved and what have we learned?* Paper presented at the annual meeting of American Educational Research Association, Montreal, Canada.

Hallinger, P., & Heck, R. (1996a). Reassessing the principal's role in school effectiveness: A review of empirical research, 1980–1995. *Educational Administration Quarterly, 32*(1), 5–44.

Hallinger, P., & Heck, R. (1996b). The principal's role in school effectiveness: A review of methodological issues, 1980–95. In K. Leithwood (Ed.), *The international handbook of educational leadership and administration* (pp. 723–784). Dordrecht, Netherlands: Kluwer.

Hallinger, P., & McCary, C. E. (1990). Developing the strategic thinking of instructional lead-ers. *The Elementary School Journal, 91*(2), 89–105.

Hallinger, P., & Murphy, J. (1986). The social context of effective schools. *American Journal of Education, 94*(3), 328–355.

Hart, A. W., & Bredeson, P. V. (1996). *The principalship: A theory of professional learning and prac-tice.* New York: McGraw-Hill, Inc.

Hattie, J. (2009). *Visible learning: A synthesis of over 800 meta-analyses relating to achievement.* London: Routledge.

Heck, R. H., Larsen, T. J., & Marcoulides, G. A. (1990). Instructional leadership and school achievement: Validation of a causal model. *Educational Administration Quarterly, 26*(2), 94–125.

Henderson, A. T., & Berla, N. (1994). *A new generation of evidence: The family is critical to student achievement.* Washington, D.C.: National Committee for Citizens in Education.

Hibert, K. M. (2000). Mentoring leadership. *Phi Delta Kappan, 82*(1), 16–18.

Hobson, A. (2003). *Mentoring and coaching for new leaders.* Nottingham, UK: National College for School Leadership

Hong, S., & Ho, H. (2005). Direct and indirect longitudinal effects of parental involvement on student achievement: Second-order latent growth modeling across ethnic groups. *Journal of Education Psychology, 97*(1), 32–42.

Hopkins-Thompson, P. A. (2000). Colleagues helping colleagues: Mentoring and coaching. *NASSP Bulletin, 84,* 29–36.

Kets de Vries, M. R. (2004). Putting leaders on the couch. *Harvard Business Review.* Retrieved January 23, 2009, from: http://harvardbusinessonline.hbsp.harvard.edu/b01/en/hbr/hbrsa/current/0401/article/r0401F.

King, P. M., & Kitchener, K. S. (1994). *Developing reflective judgment.* San Francisco, CA: Jossey-Bass.

Kolb, D. (1984). *Experiential learning: Experience as the source of learning and development.* Engle-wood Cliffs, NJ: Prentice-Hall.

Kottkamp, R. (1990). Means of facilitating reflection. *Education and Urban Society, 22*(2), 182–203.

Larrivee, B. (2008). Development of a tool to assess teachers' level of reflective practice. *Reflective Practice, 9*(3), 341–360.

Larson, C. E., & LaFasto, F. M. J. (1989). *Teamwork: What must go right/what can go wrong.* Newbury Park, CA: Sage Publications.

Lee, V. E., Smith, J. B., & Croninger, R. G. (1997). How high school organization influences the equitable distribution of learning in mathematics and science. *Sociology of Education, 70,* 128–150.

Leithwood, K., Anderson, S. E., Mascall, B., & Strauss, T. (2009). School leaders' influences on student learning: The four paths. In T. Bush, L. Bell, & D. Middlewood (Eds.), *The principles of educational leadership and management.* London: Sage Publishers.

Leithwood, K., & Day, C. (2008). The impact of school leadership on pupil outcomes. *School Leadership and Management, 28*(1), 1–4.

Leithwood, K., & Jantzi, D. (2006). *A critical review of the parent engagement literature.* Toronto, ON: Ontario Ministry of Education.

Leithwood, K., Riedlinger, B., Bauer, S., & Jantzi, D. (2003). Leadership program effects on student learning: The case of the Greater New Orleans School Leadership Center, *Journal of School Leadership, 13*(6), 707–738.

Leithwood, K., Seashore Louis, K., Anderson, S., & Wahlstrom, K. (2004). *How leadership influences student learning: A review of research for the Learning from Leadership Project.* New York: The Wallace Foundation.

Lencioni, P. (2002). *The five dysfunctions of a team: A leadership fable.* San Francisco, CA: Jossey-Bass.

Male, T. (2006). *Being an effective headteacher.* London: Paul Chapman Publishing.

Marks, H. M., & Printy, S. M. (2003). Principal leadership and school performance: An integration of transformational and instructional leadership. *Educational Administration Quarterly, 39*(3), 370–397.

Matthews, L. J., & Crow, G. M. (2003) *Being and becoming a principal: Role conceptions of contemporary principals and assistant principals.* Boston, MA: Allyn & Bacon.

Mertz, N. T. (2004). What's a mentor, anyway? *Educational Administration Quarterly, 40*(4), 541–560.

Mohlman Sparks-Langer, G., & Berstein, C. A. (1991). Synthesis of research on teachers' reflective thinking. *Educational Leadership, 48*(6), 37–44.

Murphy, J. (2001). The changing face of leadership preparation. *The School Administrator, 58*(10), 14–18.

Oatley, K., Keltner, D., & Jenkins, J. M. (2006). *Understanding emotions.* Hoboken, NJ: Wiley-Blackwell.

O'Mahony, G., & Barnett, B. (2008). Coaching relationships that influence how experienced principals think and act. *Leading & Managing, 14*(1), 16–37.

O'Mahony, G. R., Matthews, R. J., & Barnett, B. G. (2009). *The power of coaching for school improvement: Nurturing talent and building capacity.* Moorabbin, Victoria: Hawker Brownlow Education.

Osterman, K. F. (1990). Reflective practice: A new agenda for education. *Education and Urban Society, 22*(2), 133–152.

Osterman, K. F., & Kottkamp, R. B. (2004). *Reflective practice for educators: Professional develop-ment to improve student learning* (2nd ed.). Thousand Oaks, CA: Corwin Press.

Pink, D. (2005). *A whole new mind.* New York: Penguin Books.

Robertson, J. (2005). *Coaching leadership.* Wellington, New Zealand: New Zealand Council for Educational Research.

Robinson, V. M. J., Lloyd, C. A., & Rowe, K. J. (2008). The impact of leadership on student outcomes: An analysis of the differential effects on leadership types. *Educational Administra-tion Quarterly, 44*(5), 635–674.

Ross, D. D. (1989). First steps in developing a reflective approach. *Journal of Teacher Education, 40*(2), 22–30.

Schön, D. A. (1987). *Educating the reflective practitioner.* San Francisco, CA: Jossey-Bass.

Schön, D. A. (1983). *The reflective practitioner: How professionals think in action.* New York: Basic Books.

Schuttloffel, M. J. (n.d.) *The principle of coherence: The coherent principal.* Unpublished manuscript.

Senechal, M., & Young, L. (2008). The effects of family literacy interventions on children's acquisition of reading from kindergarten to grade 3: A meta-analytic review, *Review of Edu-cational Research, 78,* 880–907.

Sergiovanni, T. (1992) *Moral leadership.* San Francisco, CA: Jossey-Bass.

Short, P. M., & Rinehart, J. S. (1993). Reflection as a means of developing expertise. *Educa-tional Administration Quarterly, 29*(4), 501-521.

Southworth, G. (2002). Instructional leadership in schools: Reflections and empirical evidence. *School Leadership & Management, 22*(1), 73–92.

Sparks-Langer, G. M., Simmons, J. M., Pasch, M., Colton, A., & Starko, A. (1990). Reflective pedagogical thinking: How can we promote it and measure it? *Journal of Teacher Education, 41*(4), 23–32.

Stiggins, R. J. (2002). Assessment crisis: The absence of assessment for learning. *Phi Delta Kap-pan, 83*(10), 758–765.

Sullivan, S., & Glanz, J. (2000). *Supervision that improves teaching: Strategies and techniques.* Thou-sand Oaks, CA: Corwin Press.

Townsend, T. (2008). Third millennium leaders: Thinking AND acting BOTH locally and globally. Paper presented at the Commonwealth Council for Educational Administration and Management Conference, Durban, South Africa.

Vallani, S. (2006). *Mentoring and induction programs that support new principals.* Thousand Oaks, CA: Corwin Press.

Valverde, L. (1982). The self-evolving supervisor. In T. Sergiovanni (Ed.), *Supervision of teaching* (pp. 81–89). Alexandria, VA: Association for Supervision and Curriculum Development.

Van Manen, M. (1977). Linking ways of knowing with ways of being practical. *Curriculum In-quiry, 6*(3), 205–228.

Wasley, P. A. (1991). Stirring the chalk dust: Changing practices in essential schools. *Teachers College Record, 93*(1), 28–58.

Waters, J. T., Marzano, R. J., & McNulty, B. A. (2003). *Balanced leadership: What 30 years of research tells us about the effect of leadership on student achievement.* Aurora, CO: Mid-continent Research for Education and Learning.

Weindling, D. (2004). *Innovation in headteacher induction.* Retrieved March 2, 2009 from: http://www.ncsl.org.uk/index.cfm?pageID=randd-research-publications

Wigtil, J. V., & Kelsey, R. C. (1978). Team building as a consulting intervention for influencing learning environments. *Personnel and Guidance Journal, 56*(7), 412–416.

Wilson, J. P. (2008). Reflecting-on-the-future: A chronological consideration of reflective practice. *Reflective Practice, 9*(2), 177–184.

Wright, L. L. (2009). Leadership in the swamp: Seeking the potentiality of school improvement through principal reflection. *Reflective Practice, 10*(2), 259–272.

York-Barr, J., Sommers, W. A., Ghere, G. S., & Montie, J. (2001). *Reflective practice to improve schools: An action guide for educators.* Thousand Oaks, CA: Corwin Press.

Yukl, G. (1994). *Leadership in organizations* (3rd ed.). Englewood Cliffs, NJ: Prentice-Hall.

Zellner, L., Ward, S. M., McNamara, P., Gideon, B., Camacho, S., & Edgewood, S. D. (2002). The loneliest job in town: Sculpting the recruitment and retention of the principal. Paper presented at the annual meeting of the Southwest Educational Research Association, Austin, TX.

✠ CHAPTER 5

Toward Critical Servant Leadership in Graduate Schools of Education: From Theoretical Construct to Social Justice Praxis

Patrice A. McClellan

The integrity of educational leadership preparation programs has been under attack at the state and national levels (Achilles & Price, 2001; Grogran & Andrews, 2002; Levine, 2005; Schmidt, 2007). Critics have expressed grave concerns about their lack of relevance and ability to successfully prepare school leaders to address the crisis conditions facing many children in the United States (Cambron-McCabe & McCarthy, 2005). While far too many children face difficult circumstances even prior to the start of the school day, these harsh realities are compounded and become a further hindrance to their learning once they enter the school building. Student alienation via culturally irrelevant curricula, culturally insensitive teaching practices, and/or culturally precompetent leadership perceptions of student identity and ability coupled with deficit perspectives that blame students, parents, and teachers further establish the need to prepare leaders committed to inclusive and socially just practices.

These complex educational contexts, increasing scrutiny of leadership preparation, and the increase in private, for-profit organizations vying for top position in leadership preparation as an alternative to traditional models of training and professional development call immediate attention to whether or not these programs are equipped to address the barriers to quality education for all children. They also serve as a clarion call for leadership faculty to interrogate and examine their commitment or lack of commitment to social justice and to reassess the purpose, approach, and functionality of their leadership preparation programs in addressing aspirant leader needs to address social justice issues within schools as well as those in surrounding communities.

The Changing Contexts of Schools and Leadership Preparation

Educational leadership faculty members are in prime position to address concerns about leadership preparations' relevance to social justice issues that face administrators in schools today. Demographics of schooling have been changing for some time at a significant rate.

Changing Demographics in Public Schools

According to the National Center for Education Statistics (Planty et al., 2009), 20% of school age children speak a language other than English, approximately 5% of those children speak English with difficulty; in 2005–06 academic school year, approximately 33% of black students and 33% of Hispanic students attended high-poverty schools compared with 4% of white students; and it is projected that by 2017, public school enrollment is expected to reach 54.1 million. Aside from school administrator and teacher reaction to these demographic changes and the effects of these changes on instruction and cultural dynamics in schools, educational leadership faculty have constant interface with these issues due to their interactions with administrators and teachers enrolled in graduate-level leadership preparation programs across the country. Given these weekly interchanges with faculty, administrators, and aspirant school leaders, there remains a wall of silence in graduate classrooms that fails to dissect, analyze, interface with, or challenge notions of difference in graduate education. Such interactions inherently have the possibility to transform daily interactions with difference and privilege in schools. The silence in the graduate classroom pertaining to difference and privilege are compounded by the isolation felt by students whose identity deviates from the norm.

Conversely, what is found by aspirant school leaders, especially those from diverse backgrounds, is a faculty that is less interested in or committed to social justice, cultural competent leadership, or education of black and/or brown children (Delpit, 1995; Parker & Hood, 1995; Riehl, 2000; Rusch, 2004). Rusch's (2004) study of faculty perceptions of discourses about gender and race in educational leadership programs, departments, and classrooms hails important findings about changes necessary in the professoriate as we prepare school leaders to deal with equity and social justice issues in public education. Rusch identified fault lines in professional practice, leadership preparation programs, and research that have adverse consequences for those willing to learn new approaches to make schooling just and equitable.

According to her study, fault lines were defined as points of rupture between socially organized practices and daily lived experiences (Smith, 1987). These fault lines as they operate in graduate educational leadership programs inhibit courageous conversations about difference and privilege that have the propensity to promote a deeper understanding of such issues while acquiring skills to tackle injustice in school policy and practices. The lack of intentional conversations impedes progress and hinders sustainable change in schools. Therefore, it is pertinent that faculty in educational leadership programs takes a critical examination of the inclusiveness of their teaching practices, their personal stance on issues of difference (i.e., race, sexual orientation, social class, linguistic, ability, etc), and how their teaching, research, and personal stance on difference may hinder or promote commitment to equal education for all children. In essence, what faculty do in the classroom transfers to words and actions in schools (Foster, 1986; Mabokela & Madsen, 2003; Rusch, 2004; Rusch & Horsford, 2008, 2009).

Changing Demographics in Graduate Schools of Education

Just as we have seen the changes in demographics in public schools, so to are demographics changing at the graduate level. Those students who pursue graduate degrees in education are more diverse than previous years. For example, NCES projects that by 2017, graduate enrollment will exceed 2.6 million and first professional enrollment will reach 418,000. Women represented 60% of graduate enrollment in 2006. Students from traditionally underrepresented groups represented 23% of total enrollment in 2006. Enrollment in graduate programs increased for traditionally underrepresented groups from 359,000 to 519,000 between during 2000 and 2006. The greatest relative growth in graduate enrollment was seen by blacks who comprised 57%, Hispanics/Latinos who comprised 42% and American/Alaskan Natives who comprised 40% of the respective increase from 359,000 to 519,000 of graduate enrollment. In essence, graduate enrollment from traditionally underrepresented groups has increased and is projected by NCES to continue increasing.

Therefore, it is very important that we take all of these issues into consideration as educational leadership programs address the status of public schools via our role as faculty.

This chapter offers an alternative of leadership preparation by focusing on faculty development, using critical servant leadership as a catalyst to address, change, and tackle social justice issues in graduate education that adversely affect leadership practice(s) in schools. For the sake of this chapter, faculty development is defined as the resources and/or programs to foster learning that contribute to growth of faculty in areas such as teaching, scholarly productivity, and individual and interpersonal well-being. In the following section, I will review literature that addresses social justice and leadership preparation. Next, I will introduce and define critical servant leadership and its role in faculty development. I conclude with a discussion of future research and implications for educational leadership programs and faculty development.

Leadership Preparation and Social Justice in Education

The role of faculty in knowledge construction and education of school leader aspirants is vital to transforming schools for the better. Unfortunately, there is a discrepancy between what is taught, understood, and valued as important in educational leadership programs versus what aspirant school leaders need to know and learn while in graduate school that prepares them to analyze, challenge, and change unjust practices in schools. This is not to say that all graduate educational leadership programs are not tackling social justice issues, but there needs to be a sense of urgency and a critical mass at the faculty level that focuses on faculty preparation to deal with such issues professionally (teaching, research, and service) and personally (reflection, self-study, and critical consciousness). It would be naïve and egregious for us to think that our perceptions of race, class, gender, sexual orientation, linguistic, and/or ability differences do not impact delivery of course material(s), affect interaction with students from traditionally underrepresented groups (TURG), and/or affect the future research of leadership and leadership praxis of graduate students we teach.

The need for change in leadership preparation is not contested (Cambron-McCabe & Cunningham, 2002). The approaches, suggestions, and proposals for accomplishing change in leadership preparation toward a social justice end are often the subject of theoretical conversations. The literature on leadership preparation reflects the multiple perspectives regarding strengthening educational leadership programs by focusing on social justice. A significant body of work from preeminent scholars focuses on leadership preparation and social justice are separated into following themes:

- *Curriculum Development and Instructional Leadership* (Capper, Theoharis, & Sebastian, 2006; McClellan & Dominguez, 2006; McKenzie et al., 2008)
- *Democratic and Moral Imperative of Educational Leadership* (Dantley, 2003; Dantley & Tillman, 2009; Foster, 1986; Marshall, 2004; Shields, 2005)
- *Social Justice Praxis* (Cambron-McCabe & McCarthy, 2005; Dantley & Tillman, 2009; Evans, 2007; Marshall & Oliva, 2009; Theoharis, 2007)
- *Faculty & Systems of Support and Inclusion* (race, class, gender, sexual orientation, linguistic, ability, etc.) (Rusch, 2004; Sanders-Lawson, Smith-Campbell, & Benham, 2009; Shakeshaft, 1995; Shields, 2004; Taylor, 1995)

Curriculum Development and Instructional Leadership

Scholars have posed serious concerns about instructional leadership and curriculum development that aid in identifying instructional behaviors that foster learning (Delpit, 1995; Garcia, 2005; Ladson-Billings, 1995a; Larson & Murtadha-Watts, 2002; López, 2003; McKenzie et al., 2008; McKenzie, Skrla, & Scheurich, 2006). More specifically, Ladson-Billings (1994, 1995b) states, "what does good instruction look like for the student whose culture or race is different from the White culture that is privileged in most schools." López and Vàzquez (2006) raise the same question while focusing on non-English-speaking students, and Koschorek and Slattery (2009) address similar concerns in regards to LGBTQ (lesbian, gay, bisexual, transgender, and queer) issues in schools. Even though the aforementioned scholars are referring to curriculum development and instructional leadership practices in K-12 education, these questions should be intentionally probed and considered by faculty as leadership preparation programs are developed and altered.

Democratic and Moral Imperative

In this vein, Dantley and Tillman (2009) have noted that leadership for social justice interrogates policies and procedures that shape schools and perpetuate social inequalities and marginalization. They propose moral transformative leadership as a way to link principles of democracy and equity in schools. According to Dantley and Tillman, three distinct characteristics of moral transformative leadership are (1) viewing education and educational leadership using progressive or critical theoretical perspectives by focusing on the use and abuse of power in institutional settings, (2) deconstructing the work of school administration in an effort to unearth how leadership practices generate and perpetuate inequality and marginalization, and (3) viewing schools as sites that engage in academic pursuits and help to create activists to bring about the de-mocratic reconstruction of society. Dantley and Tillman are not stand-alone scholars in addressing the moral imperative of schooling. Shields (2005) as well as Capper, Keyes, and Theoharis (2000) also address and interrogate edu-cational leadership as a moral endeavor linked to social justice praxis.

Social Justice Praxis

In addition to curriculum development, instructional leadership, and moral imperatives of schooling as avenues to enhance the operation of schools, Cambron-McCabe and McCarthy (2005) suggest that leadership preparation's focus go beyond effectiveness and efficiency of schools. According to Cam-bron-McCabe and McCarthy, in order to promote a social justice orientation, preparation programs must prepare administrators and leader aspirants to en-gage in difficult work that requires a shift in values, attitudes, and behaviors within the school community (p. 214).

Failure to prepare administrators and leader aspirants to engage in such work severely limits their ability to address fundamental social justice issues (Cambron-McCabe & McCarthy, 2005). Therefore, leadership preparation programs must encourage and prepare administrators and leader aspirants to think critically and differently about organizational structures, leadership roles, power and privilege, and empirical data regarding racism in schools, and examine policies and procedures that promote homophobia, sexism, and clas-sism (Cambron-McCabe & McCarthy, 2005; Marshall, 2004; Marshall & Oliva, 2009; McClellan & Dominguez, 2006; McKenzie et al., 2008; Pounder, Reitzug, & Young, 2002). The aforementioned strategies are vital to trans-forming schools to focus on equity and social justice issues. However, the strategies mentioned above are not all inclusive of the discourse on leadership preparation and social justice. This is a brief synopsis of theoretical conversa-tions and action plans for improving leadership preparation by focusing on what administrators and leader aspirants need to know in order to improve schools.

As mentioned, a focal point of the majority of the literature on leadership preparation and social justice is student-centered. At the heart of the literature is the focus on content knowledge, reflexive skills, and incorporation of social justice ideas for administrator and aspirant application. This focus is much needed and required. However, a critical gap exists in the literature on social justice and leadership preparation. There has been less attention paid to the content knowledge of faculty, the practiced reflexivity (McKenzie & Scheurich, 2004) of faculty and the incorporation of professional and personal social justice activism by educational leadership faculty.

Systems of Support and Inclusion

Marshall (2004) challenged the field of educational administration and leadership to take an active and prosocial justice stance, stating that professors and leadership preparation programs are inadequately attuned to equity concerns. According to Marshall, traditional training for educational leadership reflects a culture that has marginalized issues and concerns for social justice (p. 4). Similarly, Rusch and Horsford (2008, 2009) examined faculty perceptions of discourse about race and gender in leadership preparation and found that there is a culture of fear and lack of openness to learning about race and gender issues. She further posits that to understand the praxis of creating equal opportunity in school communities, educational leadership faculty must move beyond program rhetoric and experience the complex and challenging practices of learning how to enact equity (p. 14). Marshall (2004) and Rusch (2004) are among many scholars who have issued a clarion call for faculty to critically examine and dissect notions of power, privilege, and silence around equity and social justice issues in leadership preparation. The constrained discourse in leadership preparation is similarly mirrored in school settings. Therefore, critical servant leadership is offered as a theoretical construct to foster dialogue about equity and social justice, interrogate faculty's professional commitment to equity and social justice, and aid in developing professional development for faculty that interrogate and examine individual responses and deeply held beliefs about equity and social justice.

Critical Servant Leadership—Defined and Explored

Critical servant leadership is a theoretical construct originated from a research study on servant leadership and spiritual practices of black leaders using portraiture as the qualitative methodology (McClellan, 2006). Although, critical servant leadership is birthed from a perspective grounded in the African American experience, I posit that much can be gained by incorporating different voices to the leadership preparation discourse that can result in transformation and sustained change. Through critical servant leadership, I suggest that the servant leadership theory be broadened by combining it with critical spirituality (Dantley, 2003).

Critical Spirituality

Critical spirituality is the by-product of the infusion of two radical perspectives, which are critical theory and Cornel West's notion of prophetic spirituality. Critical spirituality has three major components. The first component is a prophetic spirituality, which is a combative spirituality and frames the urgency for institutional and personal transformation. The second component is the impact of reflection on the leader(s). The third and final component is a spirit-filled resistance that proposes a project or praxis for self- and institutional change. The overarching goal of critical spirituality is to critique and destroy undemocratic power relations blended with a spiritual reflection grounded in an African American sense of moralism and prophetic resistance (Dantley, 2003). According to Dantley, this goal is in agreement with Capper's (1993) perspective on power in practice because it considers how school administrators promote conflict, dissensus, control, domination, and resistance, and how this resistance is used in the process of restructuring schools. In this vain, critical spirituality coupled with a servant leadership orientation provides new opportunities and conversations on how to restructure schools, change leadership preparation programs, and reenvision a future committed to equity and social justice. But prior to restructuring schools and leadership preparation programs, we must address the issues with faculty perceptions about equity and social justice and their willingness to confront issues related to equity and social justice.

Servant Leadership

The term *servant leadership* was coined by Robert K. Greenleaf in his essay "The Servant as Leader" (1977). In it, he defines servant leadership as a way to serve and lead as a way of expanding service to individuals and institutions. Similarly, leaders such as Dr. Martin Luther King, Jr., Mrs. Fannie Lou Hamer, and Septima Clark embodied the concept of leadership as service. Furthermore, the notion of servant leadership or leadership as service is not germane to those who promote social change.

The key elements of servant leadership are to encourage collaboration, trust, and foresight, and provide the foundation of the ethical use of power (Spears, 1995) via a leadership role. In theory, servant leadership thrives on the concept of reciprocity. In this regard, the servant as leader is to enlist others in an effort to build a community of practice that motivates members to create shared knowledge and shared ways of knowing (Drath & Palus, 1994). This type of leader is committed to serving others through a cause, a crusade, a movement, and a campaign with humanitarian, not materialistic goals (Williams, 1998).

The servant leader is willing to take risks to achieve a higher good. He or she is guided by an overarching, prophetic, transforming vision that is carefully conceived and simply articulated (Williams, 1998) similar to the tenets as described by Dantley's critical spirituality (2003). Servant leadership is not only about "doing" the acts of service, but also "being" a steward, entrusted with responsibility, and accountable to a larger community. By precept and example, a servant leader is to co-create a shared vision, sharing learned knowledge, and build upon the skills and abilities that foster co-creating of processes that sustain the vision.

The servant model of leadership has nine functional attributes (vision, honesty, integrity, trust, service, modeling, pioneering, appreciation of others, and empowerment) (Russell & Stone, 2002) and 11 accompanying attributes (communication, credibility, competence, stewardship, visibility, influence, listening, encouragement, teaching, delegation, and persuasion), which provide direction for practical implementation (p. 153). Servant leadership as a researchable and applicable leadership phenomenon is scarce in that the very notion of "servant leader" may appear to be an oxymoron (Sendjaya & Sarros, 2002). To some, it may be difficult to think and act as a leader and servant at the same time. Nevertheless, for others, the relationship between service and leadership are compatible and intertwined. Therefore, after reviewing the functional and accompanying attributes as well as the philosophical foundations on servant leadership such as reciprocity and stewardship, I posit in conjunction with Wallace (2007) that servant leadership may be more than a leadership theory as leadership theories have been presented.

Typically, leadership theories are presented in leadership preparation programs as styles or techniques open to choosing based upon preference or situation and in a manner that often neglects the social context of institutions or communities and rarely considers individual philosophical foundation or values orientation. As English (2008) states, "leadership has been cast largely in structural hues almost devoid of any consideration of human interiority" (p. xx). Servant leadership is more a personal orientation toward life, which grows as an individual's worldview grows or changes. As such, a key implication is that servant leadership is not merely a tool to use; rather it is an ego ideal that governs daily interactions (Wallace, 2007).

Critical Servant Leadership

As stated, critical servant leadership is an amalgamation of critical spirituality and servant leadership. This construct is an extension of both servant leadership and critical spirituality. It is all encompassing of the underlying foundations of servant leadership and the overarching goal of critical spirituality. In this regard, critical servant leadership is more than a leadership theory; it is a way of being, a connection to communities and people who are marginalized, frowned upon, and separated by the mainstreams of society. A critical servant leader is guided by a willingness and commitment to promote and sustain equity and social justice. One does not merely practice critical servant leadership; one is a critical servant leader. Those who commit themselves to becoming a critical servant leader must begin a journey of personal reflection and a recommitment to social justice by incorporating the characteristics of critical servant leadership into his or her daily life.

1. A "Way of being." The first and most important characteristic of a critical servant leader is a "way of being," which is a culmination of ego identity, reciprocity, and reflection based on one's worldview. Worldview is defined as a person's assumptions about the makeup of reality, how the world works, conceptual schemes or patterns of ideas or values used to organize, interpret, and interact with people, communities, and organizations within the world (Wallace, 2007). One's ego identity is shaped by his or her worldview and constructed through ongoing narratives and relationships with others. Ego is the necessary evil a leader must contend with and keep in perspective. Whether one identifies as a critical servant leader or not, one must not allow ego to override genuine concern for others, jeopardize collegiality, and cloud judgment to new ways of being, learning, and leading. Ego is the tolerable part of a leader that has the ability to clog reception, but also has the propensity to encourage individual and collective achievement. The critical servant leader seeks to minimize ego through commitment to equity and social justice, acting on a spirit-filled resistance that proposes individual and institutional change, and addressing what is moral, democratic, and equitable in communities, schools, and organizations.

2. Capacity for reciprocity. A second characteristic of a critical servant leader is the capacity for reciprocity. *I AM BECAUSE WE ARE* is a well-known mantra used by Dr. Khaula Murtadha-Watts in opening ceremonies at national conventions and mentoring sessions that permeates the meaning of reciprocity through interaction with others. The premise of reciprocity is grounded in accountability and responsibility for one another and the communities of practice we seek to build. Reciprocity is the result of an exemplary relationship between faculty and students, the haves and have-nots, and between the powerful and the powerless.

There is nothing more demoralizing than to be powerless (Buchen, 1998). For reciprocity to be empowering as it is intended, critical servant leadership urges a transfer of power and a transfer of resources. Power is defined by scarcity (Buchen, 1998; Greenleaf, 1978). Only a few hold on to it, they are in charge and oftentimes they are called leaders, administrators, and faculty. A paradox and revolutionary idea espoused by Greenleaf (1978) is that scarce power becomes more power when distributed. A multiplier effect presides over the transfer of power and knowledge (Buchen, 1998). The teacher becomes the student and the student becomes the teacher. The relationship is reciprocal and built on mutual respect for one another. The leader and/or faculty member who never learns from students is a failure (Buchen, 1998).

Reciprocity and relationship are intertwined and interlinked. Unchecked ego promotes relationships that are self-serving, manipulative, and political (Buchen, 1998). However, a critical servant leader understands that his or her function is to build a community of practice that enables others to grow professionally, personally, and spiritually. Allowing others to grow fosters reciprocity in that the critical servant leader learns from others' transformation. Learning from others allows us to learn about ourselves and aids in reflecting upon personal convictions, behaviors, and worldviews. Critical servant leadership as a theory promotes the notion of self-reflection, which is a deep probing of one's inner essence as opposed to externalities and actions (Lumby & English, 2009).

3. Transforming vision. The final characteristic of a critical servant leader is preoccupation with the future through a prophetic transforming vision. This transforming vision is grounded in a prophetic resistance, sense of moralism, and democratic and equitable practices (Dantley, 2003). The critical servant

leader is to be way ahead and has acquired the discipline of learning and listening to the future. They see the writing on the wall, but seek to differentiate
fads from substantive frameworks. A critical servant leader also seeks to understand and analyze historical contexts and power structures and articulate a
plan for radical reconstruction of communities, schools, and/or organizations.

Critical servant leaders are receptive to the burdens of communities,
schools, and/or organizations in distress. They actively pursue ways to transform and effect future outcomes by resisting the status quo, introducing oppo-
sition to unfair policies and procedures, and ultimately conveying a message
and action plan for revolution to communities, schools, and/or organizations.
Those who identify as critical servant leaders must be open and willing to
learn about themselves in relation to others, be willing to take risks and accept
the consequences for what they feel is right, moral, and democratic, and help
build a community of practice that allows others to learn and grow and ultimately subscribe to tenets of critical servant leadership.

Critical servant leadership is not just another leadership theory; it is a way
of life, an opportunity to interrogate professional and personal ego that heavily
impacts individual and institutional change. In essence, critical servant leadership is a theory and a way of being. It is a radical commitment to fighting injustice in schools, leadership preparation, communities, and/or organizations
through a critical spiritual worldview and seeking solutions to complex problems.

Critical Servant Leadership and Faculty Development—
the War from Within

Nationally, our schools are in disarray and many are overwhelmed when trying
to find solutions to complex problems. Greenleaf (1978) described a "leadership crisis," by which he argued that colleges and universities have failed in the
responsibility to prepare aspirant leaders for leadership roles in society (p. 77).
What does critical servant leadership offer current and future faculty when
seeking to address the complexities facing schools? I posit that in order to
tackle these complexities, unjust and unfair policies in schools, that faculty
needs to take a long hard look at the underlying assumptions that drive our
teaching and research; examine our personal convictions about privilege, difference, and social justice; analyze how our leadership preparation programs
are a hybrid of our assumptions, convictions, and deeply held beliefs about
schooling; and scrutinize our commitment to equitable, just, and fair school-

ing for all children. Critical servant leadership as a framework in faculty professional development offers communal space to interrogate the silences of privilege in curriculum and the perceived lack of commitment of faculty by diverse groups of students to address social justice concerns in leadership preparation.

Critical servant leadership also provides an opportunity for faculty to examine their individual convictions about privilege, power, equity and social justice through a self-reflective process called *ME-Search*. *ME-Search* is defined as a reflective process used in conjunction with faculty self-study (Allan, 2003; Cochran-Smith et al., 1999) and cultural immersion projects (Landreman, King, Rasmussen, & Xinquan-Jiang, 2007) that critically examine faculty position(s) on issues of difference and privilege, reassess commitment to the education of all children, re-evaluate how actions promote or hinder socially just practices in graduate education and public education, and develop an action plan accountable to others that seeks out resources and opportunities to promote professional and personal growth in the area of social justice leadership. This form of faculty professional development includes, but is not limited to structured conversations on individuals' biographical and ideological underpinnings on equity and social justice; individual writing and journaling, expert led discussion groups; and exploring the impact of these conversations, writings, and ideological stances on faculty teaching, research, and service (Lindsey & Terrell, 2009).

In this sense, critical servant leadership as a professional development framework agrees with Theoharis' (2007) definition of social justice leadership which states that "leaders make issues of race, class, gender, disability, sexual orientation, and other historically and currently marginalizing conditions in the U.S. central to their advocacy, leadership practices, and vision" (p. 223). In this vain, the same can be said for faculty. Critical servant leadership as faculty professional development seeks incorporation into faculty roles.

In order for schools to be transformed, faculty as individuals and departments as a whole need to centralize issues of race, class, gender, disability, sexual orientation and other marginalizing conditions in teaching practices, in leadership preparation standards and yes, in our daily lives. Rhetoric can no longer be the standard for equity and social justice conversations in leadership preparation. Rhetoric can no longer take the place of cultural immersion and visiting struggling schools, nor can only consulting with "effective" leaders and schools. Given the current condition of public education and the national scrutiny of leadership preparation programs, it is an urgent matter for faculty to make issues of difference central to our leadership identities and practices, central in our advocacy for radically transforming schools, and central in how we envision leadership preparation for social justice.

Most people outside of the academy are oblivious to academic politics, and most inside shun away from admitting how manipulative, controlling, and discordant academic politics are. The academy is incredibly competitive (Buchen, 1998). There is individual as well as departmental competition fueled by ego that fosters superiority/inferiority, supports credentialed pedigrees from Ivy League colleges versus second-tier or teaching institutions, and promotes an "us-versus-them" mentality in our interactions with students and with other faculty who deviate from the "norm" or "status quo" in terms of identity, orientation, and ethnicity, etc.

This competition between and among faculty is useless and ineffective. However, it does serve a need to keep the faculty gatekeepers in control of what is valued in leadership preparation while focusing faculty attention on competing loyalties of the professoriate. The focus on competing loyalties prevents a galvanizing of efforts that aim to overhaul leadership preparation programs to focus on diverse perspectives, equity, and social justice. Therefore, critical servant leadership as a framework for faculty professional development aims to re-focus attention on what is important in leadership preparation: faculty who are willing to be vulnerable to learn something new, admit shortcomings, be radical in their approach, and recommit themselves to a socially just orientation for the betterment of schooling for all children. There needs to be a critical mass of faculty in leadership preparation that are willing to debunk political agendas in terms of social justice and fight for what is right, moral, and democratic.

As stated, a critical servant leader is preoccupied with the future. Faculty members need to ask similar questions: What does the future of schooling look like if leadership preparation fails to address social justice commitment within faculty? What message are we sending to the future generation of leaders? How can we change our roles as faculty to improve schooling for the future? Commentaries and research studies have supported that what faculty do in the classroom transfers to words and actions in schools (Foster, 1986; Mabokela & Madsen, 2003; Rusch, 2004). Therefore, a very important question must be asked: What have we not done as faculty inside the academy to prepare aspirants once they leave the academy?

Future Directions—Where Do We Go from Here?

The goal of teachers is to help others become teachers. And the goal of leaders is to help others become leaders (Buchen, 1998). How is this accomplished if faculty and department heads have not acknowledged that there is something wrong with the way we teach, lead, and model efforts to advance equity and social justice within leadership preparation? How can we expect administrators and aspirant school leaders to teach, lead, and model in this area, if they haven't been given the necessary skill set to investigate, analyze, or interrogate these issues?

These questions among many others need to be addressed in faculty professional development. In my opinion, critical servant leadership offers a critical position, prodding our sense of justice and fairness, a genuine concern and commitment to the betterment of others, schooling, and leadership preparation as well providing an opportunity to build community while proposing unique and radical solutions to positively transforming schools through leadership preparation. However, we must proceed with caution when seeking to develop faculty professional development programs centered on honest talk, conversations about faculty ideological positions, and revealing personal information in professional programs. Honest talk and building community to address equity and social justice is complicated (Cochran-Smith et al., 1999).

Professional development work geared toward social justice aims brings with it spoken and unspoken tensions that could possibly thwart progress. Most likely, there will be considerable disagreement around every aspect of social justice based on theoretical, ideological, personal, and professional position(s) of each faculty member involved. Extended and repeated conversations about social justice changes the boundaries of what is included in the discourse of leadership preparation. Our socially constructed identities, personal and professional experiences cause us all to have significantly different worldviews and understandings of equity and social justice (Calderwood, 2002). But these are not the only tensions faced within professional development. Depending on the faculty group involved, issues of rank, job security, and departmental politics may impact who feels free to speak versus those who may choose to remain silent.

Faculty as a whole must address issues of vulnerability and academic politics if professional development is to be successful. There will always be tension between commitments to speak openly and honestly address equity and social justice, collaboration between those who see no need for dialogue versus those who hold deep convictions, and those who want to learn more, but don't know where to start versus those who don't want to deal. Nevertheless, the goal of critical servant leadership as faculty professional development is not to relentlessly push others to change their minds and shift to more "enlightened" perspectives (Cochran-Smith et al., 1999), but to move forward while validating different perspectives, respecting individual rights to hold them, and acknowledging that if we don't make the necessary changes inside, external entities governing bodies, and policy makers will make decisions for us. Therefore, critical servant leadership as faculty professional development should be used as a way to interrogate faculty understandings of equity and social justice vis-à-vis relationships with colleagues, with diversity in graduate education, and diverse school settings in coordination with developing an action plan to produce sustainable democratic change for K-12 schools.

In the context of leadership preparation and social justice, there are many suggestions, critiques, and explorations of what administrators and aspirant school leaders need to know to improve schools. There has been less attention paid to the content knowledge and/or skills faculty need to know in order to prepare administrators and aspirant school leaders to be successful in schools. Critical servant leadership as faculty professional development seeks to fill this void. I suggest that this concept be further explored using qualitative methodologies such as portraiture (Lawrence-Lightfoot & Davis, 1997), narrative inquiry (Lincoln & Guba, 1985, 2000), case study (Creswell, 1998, 2002, 2003; Patton, 1990), and/or duoethnography (Sawyer & Norris, 2005, 2009) to gain deeper understanding of faculty roles and their commitment to social justice. In addition to researching critical servant leadership as faculty development using qualitative methodology, I propose in conjunction with Lumby and English (2009) that the complex nature of identity and multiple identity construction be explored in its relationship to leadership, leadership development, and leadership preparation.

In conclusion, critical servant leadership as faculty development offers new possibilities to engage in dialogue, reflections, and a recommitment to equity and social justice, resulting in changes in leadership preparation. Therefore, instead of faculty development centered on consensus and simplistic notions of identity, equity, and social justice, I suggest a greater concentration on complex notions of the aforementioned, the discrepancy between rhetoric and action, and the models of faculty development that are congruent with new realities gained in a community of practice geared toward equity and social justice.

References

Achilles, C. M., & Price, W. J. (2001). What is missing in the current debate about Education Administration standards? *AASA Professor, 24*(2), 8–13.

Allan, E. J. (2003). *Bringing voice to the silences of privilege: Strategies for faculty development and curricular change.* Paper presented at the Annual Meeting of the American Educational Research Association, Chicago, IL.

Buchen, I. H. (1998). Servant leadership: A model for future faculty and future institutions. *The Journal of Leadership Studies, 5*(1), 125–134.

Calderwood, P. (2002). *Toward a professional community for social justice.* Paper presented at the Annual conference of the National Association for Women in Catholic Higher Education, Santa Clara, CA.

Cambron-McCabe, N., & Cunningham, L. (2002). National commission for the advancement of educational leadership: Opportunity for transformation. *Educational Administration Quarterly, 38*(2), 289–299.

Cambron-McCabe, N., & McCarthy, M. M. (2005). Educating school leaders for social justice. *Educational Policy, 19*(1), 201–222.

Capper, C. (Ed.). (1993). *Educational administration in a pluralistic society.* Albany: State University of New York Press.

Capper, C., Keyes, M. W., & Theoharis, G. (2000). Spirituality in leadership: Implications for inclusive schooling. In J. Thousand & R. Villa (Eds.), *Restructuring for caring and effective education: Piecing the puzzle together.* Baltimore, MD: Brookes Publishing.

Capper, C., Theoharis, G., & Sebastian, J. (2006). Toward a framework for preparing leaders for social justice. *Journal of Educational Administration, 44*(3), 209–224.

Cochran-Smith, M., Albert, L., Dimattia, P., Freedman, S., Jackson, R., Mooney, J., et al. (1999). Seeking social justice: A teacher education faculty's self-study. *International Journal of Leadership in Education, 2*(3), 229–253.

Creswell, J. W. (1998). *Qualitative inquiry and research design: Choosing among the five traditions.* Thousand Oaks, CA: Sage Publications.

Creswell, J. W. (2002). *Educational research: Planning, conducting, and evaluating quantitative and qualitative research.* Upper Saddle River, NJ: Merrill Prentice Hall.

Creswell, J. W. (2003). *Research design: Qualitative, quantitative, and mixed methods approaches* (2 ed.). Thousand Oaks, CA: Sage Publications.

Dantley, M. E. (2003). Critical spirituality: Enhancing transformative leadership through critical theory and African American prophetic spirituality. *International Journal of Leadership in Education, 6*(3), 3–17.

Dantley, M. E., & Tillman, L. C. (2009). Social justice and moral transformative leadership. In C. Marshall & M. Oliva (Eds.), *Leadership for social justice: Making revolutions in education* (2nd ed., pp. 19-31). Boston, MA: Allyn & Bacon.

Delpit, L. (1995). *Other people's children: Cultural conflict in the classroom.* New York: The New Press.

Drath, W. H., & Palus, C. J. (1994). *Making common sense: Leadership as meaning-making in a community of practice.* Greensboro, NC: Center for Creative Leadership.

English, F. (2008). *Anatomy of professional practice: Promising research perspective on educational leadership*. Lanham, MD: Rowman and Littlefield Education.

Evans, A. (2007). Horton, Highlander, and leadership education: Lessons for preparing educational leaders for social justice. *Journal of School Leadership, 17*(3), 250–275.

Foster, W. (1986). *Paradigms and promises*. Buffalo, NY: Prometheus Books.

Garcia, E. (2005). *Teaching and learning in two languages: Bilingualism and schooling in the United States*. New York: Teachers College Press.

Greenleaf, R. K. (1977). *Servant leadership: A journey into the nature of legitimate power and greatness*. Ramsey, NJ: Paulist Press.

Greenleaf, R. K. (1978). The leadership crisis. In L. C. Spears (Ed.), *The power of servant leadership* (pp. 17–60). San Francisco: Berrett-Koehler.

Grogran, M., & Andrews, R. (2002). Defining preparation and professional development for the future. *Educational Administration Quarterly, 38*(2), 233–256.

Koschoreck, J. W., & Slattery, P. (2009). Meeting all students' needs: Transforming the unjust normativity of heterosexism. In C. Marshall & M. Oliva (Eds.), *Leadership for social justice: Making revolutions in education*. Boston, MA: Allyn & Bacon.

Ladson-Billings, G. (1994). *The dreamkeepers: Successful teachers of African American children*. San Francisco, CA: Jossey-Bass.

Ladson-Billings, G. (1995a). But that's just good teaching! The case for culturally relevant pedagogy. *Theory Into Practice, 34*(3), 465–491.

Ladson-Billings, G. (1995b). Toward a theory of culturally relevant pedagogy. *American Educational Research Journal, 32*(3), 465–491.

Landreman, L., King, P. M., Rasmussen, C. J., & Xinquan-Jiang, C. (2007). A phenomenological study of the development of university educators' critical consciousness. *Journal of College Student Development, 48*(3), 274–296.

Larson, C., & Murtadha-Watts, K. (2002). Leadership for social justice. In J. Murphy (Ed.), *The educational leadership challenge: Redefining leadership for the 21st century* (pp. 134–161). Chicago, IL: University of Chicago Press.

Lawrence-Lightfoot, S., & Davis, J. H. (1997). *The art and science of portraiture*. San Francisco, CA: Jossey-Bass Publishers.

Levine, A. (2005). Educating school leaders. Retrieved April 15, 2009, from http://www.edschools.org/

Lincoln, Y. S., & Guba, E. G. (1985). *Naturalistic inquiry*. Beverly Hills, CA: Sage Publications.

Lincoln, Y. S., & Guba, E. G. (2000). Paradigmatic controversies, contradictions, and emerging confluences. In N. K. Denzin & Y. S. Lincoln (Eds.), *Handbook of qualitative research* (2nd ed., pp. 163–188). Thousand Oaks: Sage.

Lindsey, R. B., & Terrell, R. D. (2009). *Culturally proficiant leadership: The personal journey begins within*. Thousand Oaks, CA: Corwin Press.

López, G. (2003). The (racially neutral) politics of education: A critical race theory perspective. *Educational Administration Quarterly, 39*(1), 68–94.

López, G. R., Gonzalez, M. L., & Fierro, E. (2010). Educational leadership along the US/Mexico border: Embracing hybridity/crossing borders/building bridges. In C. Marshall & M. Oliva (Eds.), *Leadership for social justice: Making revolutions in education* (2nd ed.). New York: Allyn & Bacon.

López, G. R., & Vàzquez, V. A. (2006). "They don't speak English": Interrogating (racist) ideologies and perceptions of school personnel in a Midwestern state. *International Electronic Journal for Leadership in Learning, 10(29).* Retrieved January 24, 2010, from http://www.ucalgary.ca/iejll/vol10/vazquez

Lumby, J., & English, F. (2009). From simplicism to complexity in leadership identity and preparation: Exploring the lineage and dark secrets. *International Journal of Leadership in Education, 12(2),* 95–114.

Mabokela, R. O., & Madsen, J. A. (2003). "Color-blind" leadership and intergroup conflict. *Journal of School Leadership, 13(2),* 130–158.

Marshall, C. (2004). Social Justice challenges to educational administration: Introduction to a special issue. *Educational Administration Quarterly, 40(1),* 3–13.

Marshall, C., & Oliva, M. (Eds.). (2009). *Leadership for social justice: Making revolutions in Education* (2nd ed.). Boston, MA: Allyn & Bacon.

McClellan, P. (2006). *Wearing the mantle: Spirited Black male servant leaders reflect on their leadership journey.* Unpublished Dissertation, Bowling Green State University, Bowling Green.

McClellan, R., & Dominguez, R. (2006). The uneven march toward social justice: Diversity, conflict, and complexity in educational administration programs. *Journal of Educational Administration, 44(3),* 225–238.

McKenzie, K. B., Christman, D. E., Hernandez, F., Fierro, E., Colleen A. C., Dantley, M. E., et al. (2008). Educating leaders for social justice: A design for a comprehensive, social justice leadership preparation program. *Educational Administration Quarterly, 4(1),* 111–138.

McKenzie, K.B., & Scheurich, J. (2004). Equity traps: A construct for departments of educational administration. *Education Administration Quarterly, 40(5),* 601–632.

McKenzie, K. B., Skrla, L., & Scheurich, J. (2006). Preparing instuctional leaders for social justice. *Journal of School Leadership, 16(2),* 158–170.

Parker, L., & Hood, S. (1995). Minority students vs minority faculty and administrators in teacher education. *Urban Review, 27(2),* 159–174.

Patton, M. Q. (1990). *Qualitative evaluation and research methods.* Beverly Hills, CA: Sage Publications.

Planty, M., Hussar, W., Snyder, T., Provasnik, S., Kena, G., Dinkes, R., et al. (2009). *The condition of education 2008 (NCES 2008-31).* Washington, DC: U.S. Department of Educationo. Document Number)

Pounder, D., Reitzug, U., & Young, M. D. (2002). Preparing school leaders for school improvement, social justice, and community. In J. Murphy (Ed.), *The educational leadership challenge: Redefining leadership for the 21st century* (pp. 261–288). Chicago: University of Chicago Press.

Riehl, C. (2000). The principal's role in creating inclusive schools for diverse students: A review of normative, empirical, and critical literature on the practice of educational administration. *Review of Educational Research, 70(1),* 55–81.

Rusch, E. (2004). Gender and race in leadership preparation: A constrained discourse. *Educational Administration Quarterly, 40(1),* 14–46.

Rusch, E. A., & Horsford, S. D. (2008). Unifying messy communities: Learning social justice in educational leadership classrooms. *Teacher Development, 12(4),* 353–367.

Rusch, E. A., & Horsford, S. D. (2009). Changing hearts and minds: The quest for open talk about race in educational leadership. *International Journal of Leadership In Educational Management, 23*(4), 302–313.

Russell, R., & Stone, A. G. (2002). A review of servant leadership attributes: Developing a practical model. *Leadership & Organizational Development Journal, 23*(3), 145–157.

Sanders-Lawson, E. R., Smith-Campbell, S., & Benham, M. K. P. (2009). Wholistic visioning for social justice: Black women theorizing practice. In C. Marshall & M. Oliva (Eds.), *Leadership for social justice: Making revolutions in education.* Boston, MA: Allyn & Bacon.

Sawyer, R. D., & Norris, J. (2005, October). *Towards the dialogic and critical engagement of duoethnography for transformative curriculum: An interactive discussion of methodology.* Paper presented at the Sixth Annual Conference on Curriculum and Pedagogy, Miami, OH.

Sawyer, R. D., & Norris, J. (2009). Duoethnography: Articulations, (re)creation of meaning in the making. In W. S. Gershon (Ed.), *In the collaborative turn: Working together in qualitative research* (pp. 127-141). Rotterdam, Netherlands: Sense Publishers.

Schmidt, P. (2007). Southern reginonal education board faults university programs that prepare school prinicipals [Electronic Version]. *The Chronicle of Higher Education.* Retrieved May 15, 2009, from www.chronicle.com

Sendjaya, S., & Sarros, J. C. (2002). Servant leadership: Its origin, development, and application in organizations. *Journal of Leadership and Organization Studies, 9*(2), 57–64.

Shakeshaft, C. (1995). A cup half full: A gender critique of the knowledge base in educational administration. In R. Donmoyer, M. Imber & J. J. Scheurich (Eds.), *The knowledge base in educational administration: Multiple perspectives* (pp. 139–157). Albany: State University Press of New York.

Shields, C. M. (2004). Dialogic leadership for social justice: Overcoming pathologies of silence. *Educational Administration Quarterly, 40*(1), 109–132.

Shields, C. M. (2005). Liberating discourses: Spirituality and educational leadership. *Journal of School Leadership, 15*(6), 608–623.

Smith, D. (1987). *The everyday word as problematic: A feminist sociology.* Boston: Northeastern University Press.

Spears, L. C. (Ed.). (1995). *Reflections on servant leadership.* New York: John Wiley & Sons, Inc.

Taylor, E. (1995). Talking race in concrete: Leadership, diversity, and praxis. *Journal of Professional Studies, 3*(1), 61–68.

Theoharis, G. (2007). Social justice educational leaders and resistance: Toward a theory of social justice leadership. *Educational Administration Quarterly, 43*(2), 221–258.

Wallace, J. R. (2007). Servant leadership: A worldview perspective. *International Journal of Leadership Studies, 2*(2), 114–132.

Williams, L. E. (1998). *Servants of the people: The 1960s legacy of African American Leadership.* New York: St. Martin's Press.

✠ PART TWO

Contextual and Cultural Considerations

✠ CHAPTER 6

Leading Schools in an Era of Change: Toward a "New" Culture of Accountability?

Wayne D. Lewis and Lance D. Fusarelli

For the last three decades, public education has undergone a major shift from input-based accountability toward performance-based and market-based systems of accountability. This shift, begun during the Reagan Administration and supported by free-market conservatives, new Democrats such as former President Clinton, and generally accepted by the public writ large, has had a significant impact on schooling and school leadership in the United States. Given the current economic crisis, amidst the demand to do more with less, calls for increased accountability in all sectors are not surprising and are taking on ever-more serious tones, particularly in education, which represents the single largest state expenditure.

The adoption of performance-based accountability systems signaled a substantial shift in leadership, bringing the values and processes of the private sphere (measurement, commodification, merit pay, contracting out, school report cards, and high-stakes testing, among others) into the public sphere. Lubienski (2000) asserts that the ascendancy and expansion of free market ideology in education during the Reagan, Bush, Clinton, and Bush administrations was part of an overall "trend of elevating private goods over public goods" (p. 207). This movement, celebrated by conservatives who view the private sphere as "good" and the public (or government) sphere as "bad," privileged the private over the public, resulting in school leaders' performance being linked primarily to test scores. Accordingly, school personnel evaluation systems became more tightly linked to such accountability systems.

In this chapter, we trace the development and evolution of accountability systems in education; assess the strengths and weaknesses of each type, including the dominant models now in use; forecast the future of school accountability and the implications for school leaders in light of the deepening economic crisis, the renewed questioning of market-based accountability, and new leadership in Washington (principally President Obama and U.S. Secretary of Education Arne Duncan); and recommend a hybrid model of accountability that combines elements of strong external and internal accountability systems.

Input-Based Accountability and Educational Effectiveness

In education, accountability means different things to different people, and that meaning has changed significantly over the past century. For most of the twentieth century (until roughly the 1980s), input-based models of evaluation were utilized to hold schools and school personnel accountable to the public. Input-based or bureaucratic models of accountability utilized extensive checklists in which lots of things were counted and principals dutifully evaluated teachers annually based upon the organization of their lesson plans, their coverage of the subjects taught, their classroom management, the look and organization of their classrooms, etc. Principals were evaluated on inputs such as whether the school was well-organized and staffed, had sufficient supplies, had an efficient class and bus schedule, and a sound budget.

Often, a successful teacher was one who seldom sent disruptive students to the principal's office. A successful principal was one whom the superintendent or school board never received complaints from or about. If the students got to and from school safely, and if no one complained much or too loudly about anything, then the teachers and principal were deemed to be doing a good job. The basic idea was that quality inputs would produce quality outcomes. While input-based accountability was the dominant model for much of the history of education in the United States, whether or not students were actually learning anything, or to what degree, was never discussed. The virtue of input-based accountability models was that they were easy (and inexpensive) to implement and execute. The major limitation was that they were woefully ineffective at assessing performance at the student, teacher, school, and school-system levels.

Performance-Based Accountability

In contrast to an input-based model of accountability, a performance-based accountability model has very little concern with inputs. Instead, it emphasizes rigorous performance standards and outcomes (Kanter, 1989). The enactment of the No Child Left Behind Act of 2001 (NCLB) marks a distinct shift in federal education policy from a focus on education inputs and resources to an emphasis on performance objectives. NCLB requires each state to implement its own school accountability system, which includes mandatory annual testing of all students in grades three through eight, and the disaggregation of data on student performance for all schools. Further, NCLB requires that states intervene in schools that continually fail to meet performance targets (Hanushek & Raymond, 2005; Kane & Staiger, 2002).

Prior to the enactment of NCLB, states were making strides toward implementing performance-based accountability policies (Kane & Staiger, 2002; Leithwood, Steinbach, & Jantzi, 2002). By 2000, 40 states were using standardized test scores to rate student and school academic performance, and 20 states had attached monetary rewards and sanctions to performance (Kane & Staiger, 2002); but NCLB greatly reinforced movement toward systems based on measured student achievement (Hanushek & Raymond, 2005).

Performance-based accountability systems are based on various empirical indicators used to assess the attainment of education goals. Such indicators can include the percentage of students taking college-admissions tests, the percentage of students taking advanced-placement courses or International Baccalaureate tests, the percentage of students going on to college, or student success rates in college (Bracey, 2000; Lashway, 2001). But the most common and controversial of these indicators, of course, has been student standardized test scores. While testing students has been routine in schools for many years, using student test scores to measure schools' progress toward achieving goals and as a basis for school-level rewards and sanctions is a relatively new phenomenon (Lashway, 2001).

Research evidence from several states including Texas, California, Tennessee, Kentucky, Florida, North Carolina, and Maryland, and cities, including Chicago and Charlotte-Mecklenburg, suggest that performance-based accountability systems, when properly implemented, positively increase student achievement, including reducing the achievement gaps between subgroups of students (Fusarelli & Fusarelli, 2003; National Governors Association, 2002; O'Day, 2004; Scheurich, Skrla, & Johnson, 2001; U.S. Department of Education, 2007). In Texas, "the gaps between the performances of different racial/ethnic/socioeconomic groups of students have diminished over time" in reading, math, and writing, which Fuller and Johnson (2001) attribute to the state's well-developed accountability system (p. 261). A recent report by the Center on Education Policy found that, contrary to criticism that NCLB encourages school leaders to ignore the highest- and lowest-achieving students, test scores "for both 'advanced' and 'basic' students rose in nearly three-quarters of assessments studies across [50] states and grade levels, a level of progress only slightly lower than that of students reaching proficiency" (Cavanagh, 2009, p. 1). Furthermore, while current performance-based accountability systems are inadequate for real-time use in specific classrooms, they "can be extremely valuable for identifying schools and subject areas that may need additional attention, resources, or possibly changes in strategies . . . [and can shine] the spotlight at failing parts of the system that then can be given additional assistance" (O'Day, 2004, p. 27).

While performance-based accountability has been touted widely as an effective solution to problems of unresponsiveness and ineffectiveness in public education, it also has its criticisms. First, schools usually pursue multiple goals, with very few of those goals amenable to precise measurement (Cullen & Reback, 2006). Because NCLB mandates that performance incentives and consequences be tied to measurable goals, a diversion of resources away from pursuing immeasurable, but nonetheless important, goals may result. For example, teachers and administrators have reported that pressure to increase student performance on standardized exams in core content areas has resulted in decreased time for elective courses.

Further, an overreliance on performance outcomes may result in school leaders "exploit[ing] loopholes" that allow for exemptions for academically disadvantaged students (Cullen & Reback, 2006, p. 30). Cullen and Reback (2006), Figlio and Getzler (2002), and Hanushek and Raymond (2005) found evidence of school leaders engaging in performance "gaming" tactics to reshape the pool of students that are tested. These tactics included the targeting of exemptions for low-performing black and Hispanic students, classifying an expanding number of students as special needs, and encouraging absences for students whose test scores administrators believed would weaken school results. There was controversy surrounding revelations of performance gaming tactics during Rod Paige's tenure as superintendent of the Houston Independent School District (HISD) that led to his resignation as U.S. Education Secretary. These cases show that an unintended consequence of performance-based accountability can be a shift away from student learning toward avoiding school-level (and adult) sanctions for low performance (O'Day, 2004).

Scholars have also expressed methodological concerns regarding performance accountability systems that are based primarily on standardized testing. Kane and Staiger (2002) cautioned that standardized test scores are far more volatile than the general public realizes, and the implications of their volatility may be profound. They asserted that there are two key sources of test score imprecision: sampling variation stemming from idiosyncrasies of particular samples of students being tested, and "one-time factors that are not sensitive to the size of the sampling" (p. 235). Such factors could include police or fire sirens nearby on the morning of the test, disruptive students in the testing room, or the effects of chemistry between a group of students and their teacher.

Scholars concerned with the isomorphic effects of high-stakes accountability on schooling practices and values, particularly democracy and inclusion, argue that high-stakes accountability systems encourage the use of neo-Tayloristic, centralized management approaches that emphasize control and tight coupling (Black, 2008). Drawing on an ethnographic study of one school, Black (2008) found that school leaders committed to democratic, pluralistic, and inclusive leadership felt constrained and limited by an accountability system that legitimized and privileged a top-down, command-and-control style of leadership. Related studies have criticized high-stakes accountability reforms including NCLB for narrowing the curriculum, encouraging teachers to teach to the test, and inhibiting innovation in schools (Jones, Jones, & Hargrove, 2003; Schoen & Fusarelli, 2008).[1] In schools suffering from poor, ineffective leadership, "High-stakes environments [can] create a single-minded focus on avoiding sanctions, accompanied by a fear to attempt anything new or untried . . . [and] can dictate where educators are willing to invest their time and attention" (Schoen & Fusarelli, 2008, p. 192).

Furthermore, Deming (1986) observed that fear induced by the pressure to demonstrate success can cause dishonesty and competition in employees, creating perverse incentives to game the system. According to Jennings (2009), one recent example may be the Saturday Scholars program, an intensive tutoring program for elementary school students in Washington, D.C. who failed the city's standardized examinations. While approximately 20,000 students were eligible to participate, only about 2,500 did so, and critics charge that educators targeted the "bubble kids"—those on the cusp who barely failed the exams. Jennings argues that the system encourages educators to focus their time and attention on such children and ignore those whom they deem incapable of passing the exams.

However, such criticisms miss two critical points. First, well-structured performance-based accountability systems leave the "how you get there is up to you" question to local school leaders and teachers (Fusarelli & Fusarelli, 2003, p. 170). While school leaders may feel more constrained than in the past, even high-stakes accountability systems give local school leaders the flexibility to implement research-based best practices. The belief that more tightly coupled policies will preclude bottom-up reform reflects a fundamental misunderstanding of such systems, "treating tighter coupling policies synonymously with top-down management" (Fusarelli, 2002, p. 572). It is not impossible to create workable effective accountability systems that contain both top-down and bottom-up elements. Indeed, "Successful systemic reform initiatives combine elements of both top-down and bottom-up strategies" (Fusarelli, 2002, p. 572). The either-or dichotomy presented by both top-down and bottom-up advocates is false and runs contrary to the growing consensus on effective policy implementation. Second, the growing body of research evidence cited earlier in this article demonstrates fairly conclusively that effective, performance-based accountability systems can improve student achievement across all ethnic groups and narrow the achievement gap.

This is where leadership is critical. In schools with poor leadership and a dysfunctional, constrained culture in which bad teachers simply teach to the test or leaders "game the system," the performance-based or high-stakes accountability system is often blamed, when in reality the problem may well lie in poor leadership and poor teaching. In their ten-year study of school effectiveness, Teddlie and Stringfield (1993) found that school leaders and teachers in less effective schools tend to focus on superficial activities and gimmicks, such as teaching test-taking skills, whereas in high-performing schools, teachers and school leaders focus on deeper changes in the teaching and learning process, even in states with high-stakes accountability systems.

Some research suggests that the shift toward performance-based accountability systems over the last two decades has done little if anything to ameliorate the persistent achievement gap between white and minority students. Harris and Herrington (2006) asserted that performance-based accountability policy has thus far been unsuccessful in improving equity because it is based on flawed assumptions. Of particular significance, they alleged that performance-based systems are based on the assumptions that "school capacity is sufficient, that the lack of success for many students is due to a lack of choices and competition, and that students will demand more rigorous content if given the opportunity" (Harris & Herrington, 2006, p. 227). However, none of these assumptions has been empirically verified.

Market-Based Accountability

The third type of accountability discussed in this chapter is market-based accountability, which along with performance-based accountability has occupied a central place in educational reforms since the 1980s. The goal of market-based accountability is to improve student achievement by increasing the level of competition between schools (Darling-Hammond, 1991; Garn, 2001; Leithwood, 2001; Miron, 2008). In this context, "good schools" demonstrate their worth by attracting students and maintaining sizeable enrollments, while "bad schools" are held accountable by parents who remove their children from the school (Garn, 2001; Lashway, 2001).

Chubb and Moe (1988) likened the operation of public schools in market-based systems to the operation of private schools. Private schools, they maintained, determine their own goals, standards, and methods, reflecting the values of owners and patrons; unless they are subsidized from external sources, they must satisfy their consumers if they are to stay open. Correspondingly, in a market-based system of public schools, consumers unhappy with the type or quality of services provided may leave, "give[ing] schools incentives to please their clientele, as well as to set up voice mechanisms—committees, associations—that build a capacity for responsiveness into organizational structure" (Chubb & Moe, 1988, p. 1068).

Market-based accountability systems require a markedly different approach to school leadership than input-based or even performance-based accountability systems. Market-based accountability is based on the assumption that school leaders will "recreate their schools as marketable products" (Leithwood, 2001, p. 227). These school leaders, not unlike managers in the private sector, must continually redesign their organizations to meet the ever-changing demands of educational consumers (parents and students); effectively market their products/services; and deliver their products as efficiently as possible; all while staying abreast of their competitors' products, services, and prices (Garn, 2001; Leithwood, 2001).

Only recently, in this period characterized by skepticism of everything governmental and limitless optimism in the free market, has the market-based accountability concept in education taken root, with the idea of schools competing like businesses, becoming both "intellectually appealing and emotionally satisfying" (Lashway, 2001, p. 6). The market concept in education has seen an increase in support from both state and federal levels. In 1986, the National Governors' Association agreed on the goal of providing choice among public schools; and in 1989, during the nation's first Education Summit, President George H. W. Bush and the National Governors' Association endorsed school choice as a major component of the national education policy agenda (Lee, 1993).

Currently, states are employing tools for increasing school competition including the creation of private school voucher systems, the creation of magnet schools, and allowing school choice among traditional public schools by removing school attendance boundaries both within and across school districts (Darling-Hammond, 1991; Leithwood, 2001). In 1987, Minnesota passed legislation creating the nation's first public school open enrollment program (Wong & Langevin, 2007). In *Zelman v. Simmons-Harris* (2002), the U.S. Supreme Court upheld the constitutionality of a school voucher program in Cleveland, ruling that the program did not violate the Establishment Clause of the 1st Amendment to the U.S Constitution, and removing any foreseeable constitutional barriers for voucher programs in other jurisdictions (DeBray-Pelot, Lubienski, & Scott, 2007). And following *Zelman*, in 2004 Congress approved the nation's first federally funded school voucher program, the D.C. Opportunity Scholarship Program which currently provides approximately 1,700 private school vouchers valued at up to $7,500 per year for low-income students.

But it has been the creation and expansion of charter schools that represents the most widespread manifestation of the market-based concept in public education. As of 2008, 40 states and the District of Columbia had adopted some variant of charter school legislation, with roughly 3,600 charter schools in operation, and over one million students attending charter schools nationally (Wong & Langevin, 2007). The first charter school legislation was passed in Minnesota in 1991 during the George H. W. Bush administration, and shortly thereafter the federal government's financial support of charter schools began. In 1993, as part of the Clinton administration's Improving America's Schools Act, Congress authorized $15 million to support a program of grants to states with charter school legislation (Murphy & Shiffman, 2002). In 1998, Congress passed the Charter Schools Expansion Act, increasing federal funding of public charter schools from $15 million to $100 million (Murphy & Shiffman, 2002). And in 2000, President Clinton announced $16 million in new funding for charter schools and another $121 million in charter school continuation grants (Bracey, 2002).

However, just as with inputs-based and performance-based accountability, market-based accountability has its critics. First, because the concept of market-based accountability is relatively new, there may be role confusion among stakeholders responsible for administering such a system in the early stages of implementation. For example, after the creation of a "thriving charter school market" (Garn, 2001, p. 574) in Arizona, politicians failed to clearly outline the details of the market-based system. Their failure resulted in role confusion at implementing agencies such as the State Board of Education, the Arizona Department of Education, and State Board for Charter Schools; and misinformation for education consumers (parents and students).

Further, market-based accountability systems are based on the assumption that all consumers have adequate information to make informed choices on school alternatives, but we argue that this is rarely if ever possible. For example, Garn (2001) found in the Arizona charter market system that the availability and trustworthiness of school performance information was not as complete, accessible, or valid as market-based advocates believed. But even in circumstances where reliable school information is available, research has shown that the parents of academically and socially disadvantaged students are less likely to seek out information about the consequences of school choices, "magnifying the social stratification of educational outcomes" (Lee, 1993, p. 125).

The Future of Accountability and Implications for School Leadership

Even with the political lightning rod that NCLB has been, President Obama has given no indication that he plans to scrap the legislation or its controversial performance-based accountability mechanisms. In fact, he has repeatedly called for a "new culture of accountability" (Dinan, 2009, ¶ 2) with higher standards for schools and teachers. Obama has said that he "reject[s] a system that rewards failure and protects a person from its consequences" (Dinan, 2009, ¶ 3).

Under the leadership of Secretary Arne Duncan, the U.S. Department of Education is challenging states to improve the quality of the assessments used to measure student progress. President Obama said in a March 2009 speech to the Hispanic Chamber of Commerce: "I'm calling on our nation's governors and state education chiefs to develop standards and assessments that don't simply measure whether students can fill in a bubble on a test, but whether they possess 21st-century skills like problem-solving and critical thinking and entrepreneurship and creativity" (Obama, 2009, ¶ 21). Toward that goal, Secretary Duncan announced in June 2009 that the Obama administration would dedicate up to $350 million dollars to help with the development of new state assessments aligned with new national standards.

Also, the Obama administration has announced the U.S. Department of Education's new "Race to the Top" contest, giving states the opportunity to compete for $4.35 billion in federal education funding. In order to compete for funds, states are required to submit plans for overhauling their education systems with suggested components including linking teacher pay to student achievement, easing restrictions on charter schools, improving the tracking of student performance data, signing on to national academic standards, and developing action plans for turning around failing schools. Given the economic crisis in most states, it is unlikely state policy makers would be willing or able to invest the state resources necessary to make such reforms, but the opportunity to win substantial federal funding may persuade states to make an attempt.

However, state implementation of the Obama administration's suggested reforms will not be easy. Teachers unions have historically fought against giving merit pay to teachers based on standardized test scores, and fewer restrictions on charter schools. For states that attempt to make these reforms in order to compete for federal funds, political battles could be intense, particularly in states with strong teachers unions. Additionally, given that state education departments face sharply reduced budgets and staffing (with some states such as North Carolina considering laying off 30–50% of their employees), states lack sufficient capacity to utilize their accountability systems to provide assistance or aggressively monitor and sanction low-performing schools and school systems. Fuhrman, Goertz, and Duffy (2008) found that few schools receive comprehensive assistance or intervention from the state due to low performance. This finding is remarkably consistent with research on charter schools, which finds that schools are seldom closed due to poor student performance (Fusarelli, 2001). This is partly attributable to politics but also attributable to the fact that few states, particularly now, have the personnel and fiscal resources to intervene in low-performing schools, which makes accountability itself something of a political construction (Elmore, 2008; Fusarelli, 2001).

Consistent with the theme of the political construction of accountability (or at least the political dimension of such policies), President Obama's handling of D.C.'s school voucher program gives some indication of future federal support for market-based accountability in education. Facing considerable pressure from Congressional liberal Democrats and professional education organizations, in March 2009 President Obama approved a budget eliminating funding for the program after the 2009–10 school year unless the program was reapproved by the Congress. This move was not a surprise given Obama's admission during the 2008 presidential campaign of his skepticism about school vouchers. In a subsequent compromise proposal, however, President Obama proposed eliminating the D.C. voucher program through attrition; allowing students already receiving vouchers to continue to receive them until they graduate from high school, but not allowing new students to apply for or receive vouchers.

While President Obama's compromise proposal falls far short of a monumental ideological shift, two conclusions may be drawn from this gesture. First, it indicates that he does not wish to put ideological differences ahead of the welfare of the children already receiving vouchers and attending private schools. U.S. Secretary of Education Duncan reasoned, "It didn't make sense to take kids out of a school where they're happy and safe and satisfied and learning" (Turque & Murray, 2007, ¶ 9). Second, it sends a message to the right that while he may not be willing to make an about-face on education policy, he is at least willing to play ball.

Given the deepening economic crisis and increasing skepticism of market-based accountability as the "magic bullet" to improve education for all children, it appears that while market-based accountability will continue to play a role in school reform, the focus of policy makers will be on refining performance-based accountability systems in education. Elmore (2008) notes that, "Performance-based accountability systems are, to say the least, works in progress" whose "designs [even in the best cases] are still schematic and, in many respects, underspecified" (p. 278). Policy makers will continue to tinker, revise, modify, and hopefully improve such systems, but it is clear they are here to stay. For example, it is expected that reauthorization of NCLB will incorporate a growth model into the determination of adequate yearly progress (AYP), similar to the longitudinal, performance-based accountability systems currently used by states such as North Carolina (the "School-Based Management and Accountability Program") that "holds schools accountable for the educational growth of the same groups of students (cohorts) over time" (Linn, 2008, p. 86).

Some researchers have suggested combining performance-based accountability with "professional accountability"—which views teaching and learning as "too complex an activity to be governed by bureaucratically defined rules and routines" (O'Day, 2004, p. 33). Professional accountability focuses on "the process of instruction—that is, on the work of teachers as they interact with students around instructional content" (p. 33). Professional accountability emphasizes the development and application of the knowledge and skills essential for effective practice and "norms of professional interchange" that place "the needs of the client (students) at the center of professional work" (pp. 33–34). Combining performance-based accountability with professional accountability would facilitate teacher professionalism and provide "strong internal accountability coupled with existing external accountability" (Schoen & Fusarelli, 2008, p. 197).

This approach goes hand-in-hand with leadership efforts to create professional learning communities in schools (DuFour, DuFour, & Eaker, 2008), which seek to create communities of adult learners (teachers, administrators, parents, and other stakeholders, including students) together to create knowledge and improve practice through data-based, evidence-based research coupled with professional norms and habits of inquiry. Citing research from Baltimore, New York City, and Boston, O'Day suggests that the combination of performance-based and professional accountability, in which areas of low performance are identified (performance-based) and professional based interventions are implemented ("to foster school adaptation to address these problems" – professional accountability) may "be most useful for establishing the conditions [necessary] to foster long-term school improvement" (p. 37).

We agree with this assessment. Effective school leaders and effective teachers do not fear well-designed performance-based accountability; they welcome it. If school leaders (at both the district and building levels) work in concert with state policymakers and other key stakeholders, and if these key stakeholders are willing to invest the time, resources, and energy to implement performance-based and professional accountability in schools and school systems, we may finally be able to get beyond isolated cases of individual school improvement and begin to make substantive progress toward widespread systemic educational reform. But it will take key leadership on multiple levels to make this happen.

Note

1   Institutional theorists argue that the normative, coercive, and mimetic isomorphic effects of high-stakes accountability systems encourage "greater institutional conformity" and create an environment in which "significant departures from the norm are unlikely" (Fusarelli, 2004, p. 84). However, unlikely is different from impossible. For example, high-performing schools with high concentrations of students in poverty are not common, but ample research evidence demonstrates that effective leaders and teachers can create such schools.

References

Black, W. R. (2008). The contradictions of high-stakes accountability "success": A case study of focused leadership and performance agency. *International Journal of Leadership in Education,* *11*(1), 1–22.

Bracey, G. W. (2000). *Bail me out: Handling difficult data and tough questions about schools.* Thousand Oaks, CA: Corwin Press.

Bracey, G. W. (2002). *The war against America's public schools: Privatizing schools, commercializing education.* Boston, MA: Allyn and Bacon.

Cavanagh, S. (2009, June 17). NCLB found to raise scores across spectrum. *Education Week.* Retrieved June 24, 2009 from http://www.educationweek.com

Chubb, J. E., & Moe, T. M. (1988). Politics, markets, and the organization of schools. *American Political Science Review, 82*(4), 1065–1087.

Cullen, J. B., & Reback, R. (2006, June). *Tinkering toward accolades: School gaming under a performance accountability system.* NBER Working Paper. Retrieved May 28, 2009, from http://ssrn.com/abstract=908525.

Darling-Hammond, L. (1991). Accountability mechanisms in big city school systems. *ERIC/CU Digest, 17.* Retrieved May 28, 2009, from http://www.eric.ed.gov.

DeBray-Pelot, E. H., Lubienski, C. A., & Scott, J. T. (2007). The institutional landscape of interest group politics and school choice. *Peabody Journal of Education, 82*(2–3), 204–230.

Deming, W. E. (1986). *Out of the crisis.* Cambridge, MA: MIT Press.

Diamond, J. B., & Spillane, J. (2004). High-stakes accountability in urban elementary schools: Challenging or reproducing inequality? *Teachers College Record, 106*(6), 1145–1176.

Dinan, S. (2009, March 10). Obama wants teacher "accountability." *The Washington Times* (online). Retrieved May 26, 2009, from http://www.washingtontimes.com/

DuFour, R., DuFour, R., & Eaker, R. (2008). *Revisiting professional learning communities at work: New insights for improving schools.* Bloomington, IN: Solution Tree.

Elmore, R. F. (2008). Conclusion: The problem of stakes in performance-based accountability systems. In S. H. Fuhrman & R. F. Elmore (Eds.), *Redesigning accountability systems for education* (pp. 274–296). New York: Teachers College Press.

Figlio, D. N., & Getzler, L. S. (2002). *Accountability, ability and disability: Gaming the system.* National Bureau of Economic Research Working Paper 9307. Retrieved May 28, 2009, from http://bear.cba.ufl.edu/figlio/w9307.pdf .

124 New Perspectives in Educational Leadership

Fuhrman, S. H., Goertz, M. E., & Duffy, M. C. (2008). "Slow down, you move too fast": The politics of making changes in high-stakes accountability policies for students. In S. H. Fuhrman & R. F. Elmore (Eds.), Redesigning accountability systems for education (pp. 245–273). New York: Teachers College Press.

Fuller, E. J., & Johnson, J. F. (2001). Can state accountability systems drive improvements in school performance for children of color and children from low-income homes? Education and Urban Society, 33(3), 260–283.

Fusarelli, B. C., & Fusarelli, L. D. (2003). Systemic reform and organizational change. Planning and Changing, 34(3&4), 169–177.

Fusarelli, L. D. (2001). The political construction of accountability: When rhetoric meets reality. Education and Urban Society, 33(2), 157–169.

Fusarelli, L. D. (2002). Tightly coupled policy in loosely coupled systems: Institutional capacity and organizational change. Journal of Educational Administration, 40(6), 561–575.

Fusarelli, L. D. (2004). The potential impact of the No Child Left Behind Act on equity and diversity in American education. Educational Policy, 18(1), 71–94.

Garn, G. (2001). Moving from bureaucratic to market accountability: The problem of imperfect information. Educational Administration Quarterly, 37(4), 571–599.

Harris, D. N., & Herrington, C. D. (2006). Accountability, standards, and the growing achievement gap: Lessons from the past. American Journal of Education, 112(2), 209–238.

Hanushek, E. A., & Raymond, M. E. (2005). Does school accountability lead to improved performance? Journal of Policy Analysis and Management, 24(2), 297–327.

Jennings, J. L. (2009, June 12). Educational triage in D. C. Education Week [on-line]. Retrieved June 26, 2009, from www.edweek.org/ew/articles/2009/06/17/35jennings.h28.html

Jones, M. G., Jones, B. D., & Hargrove, T. Y. (2003). The unintended consequences of high-stakes testing. Lanham, MD: Rowman & Littlefield.

Kane, T. J., & Staiger, D. O. (2002). Volatility in school test scores: Implications for test-based accountability systems. Brookings Papers on Education Policy, 5, 235–283. Retrieved May 26, 2009, from http://www.jstor.org

Kanter, R. M. (1989). When giants learn to dance. New York: Simon & Schuster.

Lashway, L. (2001). The new standards and accountability: Will rewards and sanctions motivate America's schools to peak performance? Eric Clearinghouse on Educational Management, University of Oregon. Retrieved May 28, 2009, from http://www.erid.ed.gov

Lee, V. (1993). Educational choice: The stratifying effects of selecting schools and courses. Educational Policy, 7(2), 125–148.

Leithwood, K. (2001). School leadership in the context of accountability policies. International Journal of Leadership in Education, 4(3), 217–235.

Leithwood, K., Steinbach, R., & Jantzi, D. (2002). School leadership and teachers' motivation to implement accountability policies. Educational Administration Quarterly, 38(1), 94–119.

Linn, R. L. (2008). Accountability models. In S. H. Fuhrman & R. F. Elmore (Eds.), Redesigning accountability systems for education (pp. 73–95). New York: Teachers College Press.

Lubienski, C. (2000). Whither the common good? A critique of home schooling. Peabody Journal of Education, 75(1&2), 207–232.

Miron, G. J. (2008). The shifting notion of "publicness" in public education. In B. S. Cooper, J. G. Cibulka, & L. D. Fusarelli (Eds.), *Handbook of education politics and policy* (pp. 338–349). New York: Routledge.

Murphy, J., & Shiffman, C. D. (2002). *Understanding and assessing the charter school movement.* New York: Teachers College Press.

National Governors Association. (2002). *Maintaining progress through systemic education reform* [online]. Retrieved June 16, 2009 from www.nga.org

Obama, B. (2009, May, 10). *Remarks by the president to the Hispanic Chamber of Commerce on a complete and competitive American education.* The White House: Office of the Press Secretary. Retrieved June 1, 2009, from http://www.whitehouse.gov/the_press_office/

O'Day, J. A. (2004). Complexity, accountability, and school improvement. In S. H. Fuhrman & R. F. Elmore (Eds.), *Redesigning accountability systems for education* (pp. 15–43). New York: Teachers College Press.

Scheurich, J. J., Skrla, L., & Johnson, J. F. (2001, April). *State accountability policy systems and educational equity.* Paper presented at the Annual Meeting of the American Educational Research Association, Seattle, WA.

Schoen, L., & Fusarelli, L. D. (2008). Innovation, NCLB, and the fear factor: The challenge of leading 21st-century schools in an era of accountability. *Educational Policy, 22*(1), 181–203.

Teddlie, C., & Stringfield, S. (1993). *Schools make a difference: Lessons learned from a ten-year study of school effects.* New York: Teachers College Press.

Turque, B., & Murray, S. (2007, May 7). Obama offers D.C. voucher compromise. *Washington Post.* Retrieved May 26, 2009, from http://www.washingtonpost.com/

U.S. Department of Education. (2007). *No Child Left Behind: Performance and accountability report, fiscal year 2007.* Washington, DC: U.S. Government Printing Office.

Wong, K. K., & Langevin, W. E. (2007). Policy expansion of school choice in the American states. *Peabody Journal of Education, 82*(2–3), 440–472.

✠ CHAPTER 7

The Politics of Equity, Adequacy, and Educational Leadership in a (Post)Racial America

Enrique Alemán, Jr.

> Well I'll tell you one thing it [the election of President Obama] means, as the former Secretary of Education, you don't take excuses anymore from anybody who says, "the deck is stacked, I can't do anything, there is so much in-built this and that." There are always problems in a big society but what we have just—if this turns out to be...President Obama — we have just achieved an incredible milestone for which the world has to have more respect for the United States than it sometimes does.
>
> —William Bennett,
> (CNN commentator and former U.S. Secretary of Education
> in the George H.W. Bush administration)

> The politics of racial grievance died tonight. No longer can people use the excuse of being blocked by other people. This former slave holding republic has demonstrated to the world—beyond question—its commitment to democracy and inclusion.
>
> —Reverend Eugene Rivers[1]
> (Azusa Christian Community Church, MSNBC commentator)

Although a watershed moment in the nation's history, it was not long after the major networks called the November 4, 2008, election and declared Barack Obama the winner of the U.S. presidential race that some began to make the argument that an end to racism was upon the United States of America. Claiming that the pervasive discrimination and racism that had historically infused institutional settings like schools could now be deemed irrelevant, many pointed to the nation's first African American president as "proof" of a postracial society and argued that U.S. historical precedence was above critique, "beyond question."[2]

Claims such as these are not uncommon. Too often, any debate about race, inequity, or the historical legacy of oppression in the United States begins and ends with examples of individual-level racism or with the citing of industrious people of color. Extraordinary public figures such as Tiger Woods, or one of the most powerful people on television, Oprah Winfrey, and now the election of the 44th president of the United States, are tokenized as reinforcing examples of racial progression. The majoritarian story silences racial critique, employing neutral language and political power to institutionalize racial hierarchy vis-à-vis structures such as school systems.

Purpose and Overview of the Chapter

In an effort to decelerate the uncritical, de-contextualized, and de-raced understanding of social phenomena in the age of Obama, this chapter focuses its attention on public school funding as a racialized, systemic problem and contends that claims of a so-called postracial society further ingratiate the status quo and buttress the colorblind ideologies that already dominate everyday life in the United States. By presenting an analysis of the politics of equity and adequacy of school funding, I seek to extend the scholarship of Ladson-Billings (1998) and to reinforce López' (2003) call for the field of educational leadership to improve in its preparation of critical scholars and school leadership. In utilizing a critical race theoretical (CRT) perspective on policy, funding, and educational leadership, I attempt to supplement the debate on equity and adequacy by overtly challenging the inequity and inadequacy that exists in today's public schools. I also present practical applications for teaching and learning in the field.

In my approximately five years of work in academia and in teaching graduate-level courses on school finance, human resources and budgets, and the politics of education, students have often asked me what I thought the role of educational leaders should be in advocating for change in school funding, raising questions about intradistrict equity, and preparing leaders to argue for adequacy at the state level. In a state like Utah—where I currently reside, teach, and conduct my research—litigation has yet to be introduced as part of the educational narrative, therefore, inquiring students have asked why and how a political strategy via the courts could be implemented. Although the state has consistently ranked last in per pupil funding (Carey, 2004), continues to have the highest class sizes in the nation (Perlich, 2004), and produced some of the largest achievement gaps among public school systems (Alemán & Rorrer, 2006; Education Trust, 2001, 2003, 2004), many educators and policy makers still consider the school funding system to be performing adequately and equitably (Lynn, 2005; Schencker & Stewart, 2008). After being introduced to concepts such as the socialization of conflict, the power of consciousness-raising, and the role of leadership in the political process, my students have consistently challenged me to respond to the question, "What do we need to do to change this?" Therefore, this chapter also seeks to make an argument for preparing educational leaders to become active political players in this process and to bolster López' (2003) call for social justice progression in the field of educational leadership.

I begin by first providing an overview of critical race theory, its central tenets, and its potential for application in the practice and study of educational leadership. After discussing the key elements in the study of the politics of education, I then delineate key questions considered in the funding of schools and the power, conflict and values that are wrestled with in the process. Finally, I make an argument for a more engaged political role for social-justice-minded educational leaders. I utilize critical race theory in proposing a framework which scholars and leaders in the field of educational leadership may consider in the preparation of school and district leadership.

Critical Race Theory: A Framework for Leadership Preparation

Having emerged formally in the 1980s and articulated by legal scholars seeking to center discussions and scholarship on race and racism, critical race theory (CRT) posits that racism and white privilege dominate and permeate institutions and systems, social norms, and daily practice. From this perspective, institutions—such as criminal justice, health care, and most notably in this case, educational systems—represent and inculcate practices, policies, and programs that disadvantage people and communities of color (Crenshaw, 2002; Crenshaw, Gotanda, Peller, & Thomas, 1995; Delgado & Stefancic, 2001). Based on the experiences of people of color, the framework de-centers white normative experience, traditions, and notions of history (Bell, 1992; Delgado, 2003). Described as a movement by those who hope to study and transform the relationship among race, racism, and power, critical race epistemologies and methodologies strive for empowerment of oppressed peoples (Delgado Bernal, 2002; Delgado & Stefancic, 2001; Solórzano & Yosso, 2001a). Including activ-

ists and scholars in legal studies, sociology, ethnic studies, and women's studies, educational researchers have also published scholarship that challenges
dominant education theory, discourse, policy, and practice by inserting the
voices of students and communities of color and centering their experiential
knowledge (Alemán, 2009; Delgado Bernal & Villalpando, 2002; Ladson-
Billings & Tate, 1997; Solórzano, 1998; Yosso, 2006).

Background and Tenets

Professor Derrick Bell, known by many as CRT's intellectual founding father
(Crenshaw, 2002; Delgado & Stefancic, 2001), was a law professor at Harvard
Law School until the early 1990s when his departure and the refusal of the
school's administration to hire another professor of color to teach his class on
race and constitutional law led some students to question hiring practices.
This controversy led to the convening of a student and scholar conference
where CRT's theoretical framework was outlined and research strategies were
defined (Crenshaw, 2002).

Scholars of critical race theory hold that racism is endemic and ingrained
in U.S. society and that the civil rights movement and subsequent laws require
reinterpretation (Bell, 1992; Delgado, 2006). Like Bell and Delgado, Delgado
and Stefancic (2001) stated that racism is the normal routine and the everyday
experience of most people of color. Lawrence (1987) developed this tenet by
introducing "unconscious racism" to the discourse. He noted that racism is
part of U.S. history and the nation's cultural heritage and influences everyone
influenced by that belief system—even if they are not aware of it. CRT challenges concepts of neutrality, objectivity, color-blindness, and meritocracy and
seeks to create a space for the voices of marginalized people to be heard for
purposes of social transformation (Crenshaw, Gotanda, Peller, & Thomas,
1995; Delgado & Stefancic, 2001; Valdés, Culp, & Harris, 2002). Whiteness,
constructed as the "ultimate property" (Harris, 1993), is analyzed as the reifica-
tion of power and privilege while its maintenance, it is argued, further exacer-
bates disadvantage in structures like finance systems in both public and higher
education (Alemán, 2009; Parker, 2003). Finally, commitment to social justice
and an interdisciplinary perspective is a central feature of critical race theory
(Alemán, 2007a; Ladson-Billings & Donner, 2005; Solórzano & Yosso, 2002)
as scholars seek to remedy the historical nature of racism by proposing new
methods and strategies for bringing about change.

Also essential to an understanding of CRT, Bell's (1980) concept of "interest convergence" aids in expanding upon traditional interpretations of the *Brown v. Board of Education* (1954) landmark court case. Arguing that African Americans' demands for racial equality cannot be met until white interests are satisfied, Bell contends that the *Brown* decision was not based on moral or human rights. Rather, the decision was made in the context of a perceived communist threat, which worried U.S. leaders about its standing in the international community; the end of World War II, which meant that returning soldiers of color would demand an improvement in civil rights and educational opportunities; and the need to promote economic growth or industrialization, which even in the South meant that segregationists had to consider changing the economic structure in ways that would maintain U.S. superiority (Bell, 1980, 2004). Bell further argues that a civil rights strategy seeking change *solely* on moral grounds may not be the best way to advance the interests of people of color (Bell, 1995, 2004).

Influence in Education

Gloria Ladson-Billings and William Tate (1997) were the first to consider the usefulness of critical race theory frameworks in the study of educational issues as they simultaneously cautioned researchers about embracing the new theoretical framework without finding practical applications in education. Scholars soon began to tell the stories of students and communities of color in higher and public education, integrating critical race theory with their research agendas while promoting social change (Solórzano, 1998; Solórzano & Delgado Bernal, 2001; Solórzano & Yosso, 2001b). Utilizing critical race theory methodologies to provide a space for the voices of marginalized communities and students to emerge was an important addition to the educational literature (Dixson & Rousseau, 2005; Yosso, 2006). Others situated their research in educational policy and politics (Alemán, 2007b; Brady, Eatman, & Parker, 2000; López, 2003; Morfin, Perez, Parker, Lynn, & Arrona, 2006). Parker (2003) proposed a framework for analyzing policy decisions by scrutinizing them and the conditions they create for students of color. After ten years of scholarship, critical race theory has emerged as a powerful tool and one that remains to be fully explored.

The Politics of Education

From a critical race perspective, educational practice, programs, and systems are political *and* raced. For example, the nature of schooling and the opportunities afforded to students identified as persons of color are markedly different than the experiences of those who benefit from white privilege (Darling-Hammond, 2007; Delpit, 1995; Kozol, 1991, 2005; Valenzuela, 1999). These experiential differences are facilitated by power, conflict, and the values centered by society's majority population. And although educators and policy makers have historically cited their desire to avoid or remove the "dirty politics" from educational settings (Marshall & Scribner, 1991; Scribner, Alemán, & Maxcy, 2003)—a sentiment that no doubt still exists today—scholars argue that it is in utilizing politics and actively and critically engaging in the political process that leaders become more effective (López, 2003; Marshall & Gerstl-Pepin, 2005).

Political Values

Eliot (1959) is most often credited with having been the first to introduce the politics of education as a field of study. Calling for an examination of the effects that political decisions made by administrators and elected officials had on schooling, his seminal article "Toward an Understanding of Public School Politics" posed questions such as: Who should pay for schools? Who should lead schools? And, what should be taught in schools? Utilizing Easton's (1965) "authoritative allocation of values" definition of a political system, Scribner and Englert (1977) attempted to define the field of the politics of education within educational administration research by categorizing and framing their discussion around the concepts of government, power, conflict and policy. As Easton described it, the political process includes an "interaction through which values are allocated for a society" (p. 57), values that are then used to inform the policy formation process.

Scribner, Englert, and other scholars, propose that an understanding of how a community's values are manifested as policy and examining how such policy is advocated for, debated, and opposed prior to implementation becomes vital to understanding the politics of education and the democratic process. Stout, Tallerico, and Scribner (1995) later discussed similar questions while pointing to the inherent conflict of values at play. Discussing how values continually shift, the authors state that tensions are brought about by definitions of choice, equity, efficiency, and quality or excellence. Inherently political, these tensions continue to drive the policy debate around school effectiveness, teaching, curriculum, and in particular, funding.

Historical Perspective

While Eliot (1959), Scribner and Englert (1977), and Stout et al.'s (1995) inquiries provide useful concepts and parameters from which to understand politics, they exemplify what has become apparent in much of the politics of education scholarship—a lack of historical context. For example, in his article, Eliot (1959) failed to acknowledge the political turmoil, overt discrimination, and in some cases, state-sanctioned violence that was being waged against African Americans at that particular time in U.S. history (Takaki, 2002; Williams, 1987). Contrary to Eliot, Bell (2004) demonstrates the importance of historical perspective with his re-telling of the *Brown v. Board of Education* Supreme Court case. He explains that one could view it as good intentions gone awry and critiques how the case has taken on an almost mythical quality, stating that *Brown* "served to reinforce the fiction that, by the decision's rejection of racial barriers posed by segregation, the path of progress would be clear. Everyone can and should make it through individual ability and effort" (p. 7).

Employing Bell's (1980) interest convergence principle as an analytical lens from which to understand the court's ruling, Ladson-Billings (2004) argues that the justices had no other choice but to rule in favor of the plaintiffs given the "larger sociopolitical context of the post war era" (p. 3). Both she and Dudziak (1988) provide supporting evidence that President Eisenhower refused to lead on the issue of desegregation, cite the concern of high-level U.S. State Department officials' and describe their desire to prevent the spread of communism, and explain that the transformation of the Southern plantation economy to a post-war industrial one were reasons why the state-sanctioned segregation was struck down. In utilizing Bell's (1980) interest convergence theory, Ladson-Billings (2004) gives a fuller, more nuanced, and critical historical understanding of the politics of education of the 1950s. However, it is Bell's (2004) recounting of the case from his first-person perspective as a civil rights, desegregation attorney that melds the history and politics of this era in ways that diverge critically from traditional politics of education scholarship.

Similarly, the educational historian, Joel Spring (2005), traces the history of politics in schools from 1958 and the development of the National Defense Education Act to the 2001 re-authorization of the Elementary and Secondary

Education Act (ESEA), commonly known as the No Child Left Behind (NCLB) Act. He delineates how educational policy and politics have influenced the effectiveness, fairness, and equity in schools. In identifying key political players, Spring asks how they may have influenced the schooling experience. How did civil rights lawyers and leaders at the heels of the *Brown v. Board of Education* landmark case frame the political debate? How did Chicano rights activists spur the development of bilingual education programs across the nation that culminated in the federal bilingual education legislation in 1968? And, how are current advocates of multiple-criteria accountability legislation attempting to combat high-stakes testing systems or organizing and mobilizing their efforts? By centering discussions of power and conflict, these questions are at the heart of understanding the political nature of educational reform and law.

Conflict and Power

Schattschneider (1960) argued that the essence of politics is in the privatizing or nationalizing of conflict. As he stated, "Nothing attracts a crowd as quickly as a fight. Nothing is so contagious" (p. 1). Without a public or nationalizing effect of conflict, the multiple sides or competing interests cannot air their differences. It is for this reason that those in power may attempt to suppress debate by privatizing the conflict, "for one way to restrict the scope of the conflict is to localize it, while one way to expand it is to nationalize it" (p. 10). López (2003), however, contends that conflict must be considered while also understanding how power can be used to institute racial hierarchies. While understanding how educational conflict influences, for example, the adoption of history textbooks; the method of teaching science, evolution, and/or creationism; or the ability for students to meet in gay-straight alliances is essential and informs educational research. López argues that the inherently and institutionally racist nature of educational policy, politics, and practices coupled with unequal power dynamics also influences political phenomena.

Fowler (2008) develops several definitions of power while stressing that although "power relations are institutionalized in school systems, school administrators have power through their organizational positions" (p. 24). She develops her working definition by noting how power is wielded over a community or in conjunction with certain constituencies, is relational, and may take the form of resistance.[3] But it is in her use and further development of Bachrach and Baratz' (1962) dimensions of power that a discussion of its uses becomes instructive. Someone who exercises the first dimension of power is using it explicitly while the second dimension is implicit. One is able to see the exercise of first-dimension power, such as the case when a principal has the authority to direct a teacher or staff member to complete a task or to dole out punishment to students.

With the second dimension, "few or none of the actors may realize that power is being exercised" because power brokers "usually limit the meaningful participation of certain groups or restrict the issues that can be raised for debate" (p. 35). Scholars have called this instance in which power is wielded implicitly, the mobilization of bias. Finally, the third dimension of power that Fowler (2008) describes is the power to shape consciousness. Citing schools and churches as institutions that change the way students or people "see" the world, Fowler describes the role that educational leaders play in facilitating certain messages, discourses, and behaviors in pervading their school's environs, which serve to shape the conscious of the students that attend. It is in identifying the values, conflict, and power dynamics that the politics of school funding becomes more useful to educational scholars and school leaders.

Framing the Political Debate on Public School Funding

The funding of schools and the debate over equity and adequacy in the United States is ongoing and consistently spirited. Despite the fact that the United States has the highest poverty rate among children of any advanced, industrialized nation and U.S. public schools remain inequitably funded within and among states (Biddle & Berliner, 2002), there are those who still believe that too much money is being spent on public schools (Hanushek, 1981; Spring, 2005). Although "only about 17% of African American young people between the ages of 25 and 29—and only 11% of Hispanic youth—had earned a college degree in 2005, as compared with 34% of White youth in same age bracket" (Darling-Hammond, 2007, p. 318 citing U.S. Census data), some continue to argue that money does not impact student achievement (Hanushek 1981, 1991, 1996).

Others unabashedly advocate for additional equity measures, supporting the equalization of wealth among school districts and systems. In all but a handful of states, the courts have been utilized to rule on school finance systems and policies (Dayton, 2000; McUsic, 1991), sometimes over several decades and, most times, after grassroots political mobilization and prodding from parents and civil rights activists (Valencia, 2008). In fact Anyon (1997) notes that between 1975 and 1990, during the post–Civil Rights time period when a retrenchment of segregation and "white flight" from the urban centers was occurring, forty-two states faced challenges to their school finance systems. This section addresses some of the most prevalent questions at the center of the politics of school funding and begins to identify the inherent conflicts that arise when value judgments are made in regards to who pays for schools, how revenue is generated, and how conceptions of equity and adequacy are built into educational finance systems.

Is Public School Funding a Cost or an Investment?

Prior to addressing questions of the significance of funding or conceptions of equity and adequacy, it is important to first discuss how language is used in framing the debate on educational spending. As Odden and Picus (2008) note, "education is an enormous enterprise in the United States" (p. 3). They cite statistics demonstrating the continued growth in enrollment, historical data on educational revenue, and the impact that school funding has on the economy. On the latter issue, they state, "in 2003, public school revenues totaled $440.2 billion, an increase of $232 billion—more than double the 1990 total of $208 billion" (p. 5). When compared to the $339.9 billion in total sales of Exxon Mobil during this same time period, one is able to gauge how the "educational enterprise" measures up against the top-rated company on the 2006 *Fortune* 500 list (Odden & Picus, 2008).

Schools and school districts are often the largest employer in a community, and because the local property tax valuations directly impact school budgets (Owings & Kaplan, 2004), additional property taxes needed to raise teacher salaries or upgrade technology is sometimes seen as a "cost" to taxpayers or as a detriment to citizen purchasing power rather than as an investment capable of bettering the community. Key to this debate are those with roles in the policy-making process. Arguing for "productivity," "efficiencies," and "outcomes," legislators utilize terminology and arguments taken straight from the business sector (Apple, 2001; Valenzuela, 2005).

Whichever argument is made, however, the fact remains that the youngest and most vulnerable children—those who attend public schools—suffer the highest poverty rates of any age group in the United States. Nearly one in five children under age six lives in poverty, totaling 19.8% of all children in that age group (Lynch, 2004). Lynch finds that these children have inadequate access to food, clothing, shelter, health care, and clean, safe, crime-free living environments. He argues that with "high-quality investments" in the education and health care of young children, there would be huge long-term economic payoffs, both to children and to society. Citing research on early childhood development programs, Lynch states that those afforded access to such programs are less likely to become teenage parents, experience less child abuse and neglect, have higher rates of immunization and lower rates of drug use, and are better prepared to enter school ready to learn.

Since the 1960s, research on the effectiveness of these programs has found that students with access to high-quality, early educational programs have scored at higher levels of verbal, math, and intellectual achievement; greater success at school (i.e., less grade retention, higher graduation rates); higher earnings in their employment; better health outcomes and less welfare dependency; generated greater government revenue; and needed lower government expenditures (Lynch, 2004). Owings and Kaplan (2004) also make a strong argument for thinking of educational spending as a long-term investment rather than a cost to the taxpayer. They state "education is a significant investment in human capital that has clear benefits for the individual, the economy, and society at large" (p. 95).

Demonstrating how increased levels of education also generate higher incomes, an increase in tax revenues, a decrease in social services needed, decreased crime rates, and lower levels of complications of childbirth, the authors employ language that recognizes the contributions to society that a well-educated citizenry makes. However, it is the assumptions that are made by "pundits, policy makers, and everyday people [that] typically blame children and their families for lack of effort, poor child rearing, a 'culture of poverty,' or inadequate genes" (Darling-Hammond, 2007, p. 320) that drives the debate on cost versus investment. The question remains, would society still view these children as a cost if they were not predominantly children of color?

What is the Nature of School Funding?

Similar to language describing educational funding as a "cost" rather than an "investment," perceptions that funding is relatively equal are still prevalent. Yet, scholars argue and demonstrate that stark funding differences exist both within and between states and between white students and students of color (Alemán, 2007b; Anyon, 1997; Biddle & Berliner, 2002; Carey, 2004; Darling-Hammond, 2007). For example, an Education Trust (2005) report states that the differences in funding are so stark that the authors state, "Instead of organizing our educational systems to make things better for these children [students of color and those classified as low socioeconomic status], we organize our systems of public education in ways that make things worse. One way we do that is by simply spending less in schools serving high concentrations of low-income and minority children than we do on schools serving more affluent and White children" (p. 1).

While the Education Trust report cites state-level data disaggregated by race, other scholars discuss similar disparities between states in general. Biddle and Berliner (2002) demonstrate state inequities by citing New Jersey as having the highest per-pupil expenditure ($8,801) and Utah the lowest ($3,804). Presenting updated 2005 data, Odden and Picus (2008) find that New York has the highest per-pupil expenditure ($13,211) of any state, while Utah continues to expend the least ($5,247). Citing Education Testing Service statistics, Darling-Hammond (2007) notes, "The wealthiest 10% of school districts in the United States spend nearly 10 times more than the poorest 10%, and spending ratios of 3 to 1 are common within states" (p. 319).

Similar to the Education Trust report, Biddle and Berliner (2002) found that the differences in funding were greater within the state systems than between states. Scholars such as Anyon (1997) delineate how inequities within states and among racial groups persist. In her book, *Ghetto Schooling*, Anyon contextualized state funding in New Jersey in the early 1990s and explains that at the time, New Jersey was the wealthiest and "most suburban" state in the nation. Controlled by representatives from suburban districts, the state legislature was almost entirely white. Indicative of the political and economic trends that contributed to the unequal state of funding for public schools in New Jersey during the 1970s and 1980s, Anyon's study demonstrates how a "national polarization between African Americans and Whites" (p. 131) was a leading factor in inequity. She found that the racial urban-suburban split became more pronounced as suburban voting power, urban poverty, and levels of "hypersegregation" (p. 132) rose. These factors together with the Reagan administration's removal of federal housing supports led to the doubling of homelessness from 1986 to 1988 in the city of Newark, and as Anyon (1997) stated, "The national isolation of minority poor in central cities would have substantial impact on educational funding remedies proposed by white suburban-dominated state legislatures throughout the period" (p. 132).

As demonstrated, the concentration of African Americans and Latinos in urban areas leads to their attendance in urban, poor schools. The electoral dominance gained by suburban districts skews the political power to predominantly White representatives. Spring (2005) states that this phenomenon is an example of how unequal funding resulted from suburban power and notes that decisions to fund schools using property value as the primary variable in revenue generation was a decision made by state legislatures. Questioning whether funding formulas that rely so heavily on property value can ever be equitable, Alemán (2007b) found that even among a so-called "equalized" Texas school finance system, court-affirmed inequity was allowed. Brimley and Garfield (2005) state that "even though the property tax has served the schools well for many years . . . It is not the fair or equitable measure of taxpaying ability that it was years ago" (p. 130).

Structural inequities codified in law, the defunding of support of urban centers coupled with the flight of employment and wealth to the suburbs, and an overreliance on property values as the central component in generating revenue and paying for school funding (Alemán, 2007b; Anyon, 1997; Biddle & Berliner, 2002; Kozol, 1991, 2005) all contribute to the state of inequity. In addition to these structural barriers and similar to Darling-Hammond's (2007) argument, Biddle and Berliner (2002) also claim that deep-rooted societal beliefs regarding the causes of poverty stymie any progress toward the equitable funding of schools. On the basis of individualism and blaming underachievement on genetic characteristics, the authors explain that legislators rely on deficit-based arguments to explain away the lack of achievement by students of color.

Does Money Matter in the Achievement of Students?

For decades, policy makers, parents, and community activists called for funding equity, pointing to egregious examples of inequity in areas such as access to rigorous academic programs, the inability to modernize facilities, and excessive class size. This debate continues today and has been engaged much more directly by academics. The question of whether "money matters," first posed as a political question with the release of the Coleman Report in 1966, found that a student's background and individual motivation had more bearing on underachievement than that of the school itself, educational practice or policy, or disadvantaging structures and institutions (Rebell & Wardenski, 2004).

Odden and Picus (2008) state there has been "disagreement among researchers as to whether a statistical link can be found between student outcomes and money (or, what money buys, such as class size, teacher experience and degrees, etc.)" (p. 52). However, some, such as Hanushek (1981), stated that a "review of a wide range of sophisticated and comprehensive studies shows that there is not a consistent relationship between expenditures and achievement despite the increased funding for teachers salaries, reduced class sizes" (p. 20). He suggested that although expenditures had increased, and student-teacher ratios had declined from 26.5 to 19.9, there had been little improvement in student achievement and possibly declines in student performance. Hanushek's (1981) premise was that better schools cost more money. However, he claimed that schools with higher expenditures should, other things being equal, have higher student performance. Thus, he considered whether expenditure differences were positively related to achievement differences and concluded, "what we currently 'know' about student performance" is that there is "overwhelming evidence that a student's performance is strongly affected by the student's family background" and that "higher school expenditures per pupil bear no visible relationship to higher student performance" (p. 30). He argued that the "educational equity arguments" lie on the assumption that more money will improve achievement, and this "assumption is untenable" (p. 31).

Analyzing some of the same data used by Hanushek, other scholars found the opposite. Hedges, Laine, and Greenwald (1994) provided evidence that money does matter and can make a difference in student achievement. They refuted some of Hanushek's conclusions after re-analyzing some of his original data, finding that the data showed correlations between funding and performance. Pointing to weaknesses with the data set, including a failure to include certain studies in the meta-analysis and problems with selection bias, they concluded that Hanushek's (1981) analysis and conclusions were flawed. In the end, they did not argue with "throwing money at schools" (p. 13), but did contend that money does matter.

Grissmer, Flanagan, and Williamson (1998) also provided evidence challenging both Hanushek's (1981) and Hedges et al.'s (1994) assumptions, stating that additional money does matter for students of color and from less advantaged backgrounds, but may not for students from more highly advantaged backgrounds. Their data showed that disadvantaged students that received the largest resource gains also had the largest gains in scores.

Finally, Rebell and Wardenski (2004) argue that "sufficient funding" and "meaningful accountability devices" are needed to ensure equal opportunity and achievement (p. 32). While opponents argue that "money doesn't matter" and that students, teachers, and communities should be motivated to succeed and that allocating more funds may be wasteful, they instead stated unequivocally, "Of course money matters, but it matters most when its spent well" (p. 6). The authors stated that the "basic fact is that consistent large-scale correlations between increases in spending on public education and student outcomes cannot be expected unless states have provided sufficient funding to supply qualified teachers, [and] lower class sizes" (pp. 32–33) and concluded by advocating for an adequately funded system where funding can be determined in a way that will assure funds are spent effectively.

How are Concepts of Equity and Adequacy Defined?

Whether one believes that money matters or not, most states and school districts do not provide equal access to funding, rigorous academic programs, or highly experienced teachers (Alemán, 2007b; Biddle & Berliner, 2002; Carey, 2004; Darling-Hammond, 2007; Odden & Picus, 2008; Owings & Kaplan, 2004). Reviewing data at the macrolevel, Owings and Kaplan (2004) declare that education spending in the United States "may be so variable as to insufficiently support many of the neediest students, leaving them less prepared to perform well on rigorous tests" (p. 24). Peske and Haycock (2006) state that although some students enter or attend school with various challenges, "the very children who most need strong teachers are assigned, on average, to teachers with less experience, less education, and less skill than those who teach other children" (p. 2). They document how students of color and poor students are most affected by these findings.

Although definitions of equity and adequacy are complex and can be technical (Alexander, 1982; Odden & Picus, 2008), educators, taxpayers, and policy makers may find "neutral" definitions of them to be helpful in articulating standards by which funding can be distributed. Yet the tendency in the politics of funding is to debate definitions of equity and adequacy, and to argue over accepted levels of inequality. Owings and Kaplan (2004) state definitions of equity and adequacy are not neutral and are instead highly contested, value-laden concepts that are generated through the political process. They state: "School financing often depends on values and other subjective factors that are determined in the political process of state government. Increasingly, these ambiguous issues are leading to legal challenges" (p. 223). It is in defining the concepts and establishing the parameters for discussion that the politics of school funding holds the most weight.

Horizontal equity, vertical equity, and fiscal neutrality. The most debated, misunderstood, and misapplied concept is equity. Equity encompasses three elements—*horizontal equity*, *vertical equity*, and *fiscal neutrality* (Brimley & Garfield, 2005; Odden & Picus, 2008). Owings and Kaplan (2004) explain that the term *horizontal equity* is sometimes conflated with equality and holds that "students who are alike should receive equal shares (of funding)" (p. 203).

Those who argue for horizontal equity believe that every student is entitled to the same funding and dismiss the need for additional funding that accounts for the structural societal barriers that some may face. *Vertical equity*, on the other hand, requires that unequal students be treated as unequals, meaning that an application of this concept takes into account that not all children learn the same way or have access to equal opportunity. Vertical equity demands that these differences be taken into account and would allow for more funding to go to those who may require it so that equal opportunity is provided.

Finally, *fiscal neutrality* states "equity is achieved when the taxpayers' preference for education—not the locality or state's fiscal capacity—determines the distribution of services" (Owings & Kaplan, p. 205). In other words, fiscal neutrality would guarantee that school districts not able to generate a certain amount of funding due to their low property valuation would be compensated, usually by a weighted funding formula and a minimum or basic state allotment. This aspect of the equity debate led to many of the school finance court cases of the 1970s and 1980s (Odden & Picus, 2008).

It is in considering all three elements that one has a more complete picture of the concept of equity. Although it is clear that many states continue to operate with a horizontal perspective of equity (Odden & Picus, 2008), scholars have found that horizontal equity or equality of funding has not been achieved and has disproportionately affected poor students and students of color (Alemán, 2007b; Carey, 2004; Darling-Hammond, 2007).

Equity and equality. Despite these definitions of equity, confusion or misappropriation of terms exists in the politics of funding. Equality or horizontal equity—meaning treating every student the same, is a concept that is sometimes confused with the three-pronged definition of equity. Brimley and Garfield (2005) state that the "principle of equity, or fairness...should not be considered synonymous with equality in this context" (p. 61). Scholars argue that public systems should be designed to produce equity and equality, but when policy makers aspire to produce a system based solely on equality, the varying abilities and needs of students are disregarded. For example, Odden and Picus (2008) state "when horizontal equity is used, one assumes that all students are alike. While it is a crude assumption at best, it is implied when it is argued that spending should be equal across school districts or schools" (p. 66). One can see why relying on this one standard of equity has generated unequal results for decades.

Equity and adequacy. While equity is defined as "giving people what they need," adequacy is defined as "providing sufficient resources to accomplish the job of educating our children" (Owings & Kaplan, p. 201). But the question remains, who gets to decide what is "needed" or how "sufficiency" is decided? Legislators may determine funding on available funds, competing constituent needs, or public perception. Owings and Kaplan (2004) contend that "adequacy as a fiscal concept is value driven" (p. 218), therefore, neutral language serves to mask the value-laden competition of scarce resources that can occur during state legislative sessions. They state that, "people define adequacy subjectively according to their own priorities and opinions.

Attempts have been made to quantify how much a state or school district needs to spend for its students, but the actual figure remains ambiguous" (p. 218). Odden and Picus (2008) describe the adequacy framework as having emerged in the 1990s after a slew of state court cases were filed. Tied to the accountability-standards movement that was sweeping the states, scholars and lawyers interested in increasing funds to poor school districts attempted to circumvent equity and "money matters" arguments by arguing for a method built on a calculation of sufficient inputs that would generate desired outputs. Odden and Picus (2008) describe adequacy as the "provision of a set of strategies, programs, curriculum, and instruction, with appropriate adjustments for special-needs students, districts, and schools, and their full financing, that is sufficient to provide all students an equal opportunity to learn to higher performance standards" (p. 75).

Preparing Educational Leaders for the Politics of (In)Equity and (In)Adequacy

Because of heroic grassroots organizing, legal maneuvering, and community activism, the struggle against Jim Crow policies and state-sanctioned racial barriers was successful in many ways (Cardenas, 1997; Williams, 1987). However, despite progress being made, the state of education, and of school funding in particular, is discouraging. Students of color are still more likely to attend schools that are inequitably and inadequately funded (Carey, 2004; Darling-Hammond, 2007), highly segregated (Horsford, 2010; Orfield, 2001), and lacking highly experienced teachers (Peske & Haycock, 2006). These schooling conditions not only continue today (Alemán, 2007b; Carey, 2004; Darling-Hammond, 2007), but viewed in historical context have always existed (Anyon, 1997; Kozol, 1991; Takaki, 2000; Valencia, 2008).

While decrepit school finance systems are not the sole culprit in instituting inequity, it is important to recognize the disadvantaging impact these mechanisms have had. Discussing educational inequity and inadequacy in schools, Darling-Hammond (2007) provides a vivid example of how school finance policies and practices have impacted the educational experiences of students of color, and African Americans specifically. Citing data from a 2005 Justice Policy Institute report, Darling-Hammond states "in 2000, there were an estimated 791,000 African American men in prison or jail, and 603,000 in higher education" (p. 318).

In this section, I reconsider the question posed by several of my students. What role can educational leaders play in transforming this reality? Recognizing that I approach this discussion from a critical race perspective—adhering to the notion that institutionalized racism is pervasive, common, and real (Crenshaw, Gotanda, Peller, & Thomas, 1995; Delgado & Stefancic, 2001)— my response to this query commences not with whether racism exists and is pervasive, but with how educational leadership programs and myself as an educational leadership scholar, should proceed in preparing students to become social justice leaders in this context.

Understanding social phenomenon as I do, it is not surprising that institutionalized racism exists and majoritarian perspectives attempt to silence counter-understandings of reality (Yosso, 2006). This is in fact the way that U.S. society and the dominant power structure have operated since the "founding" of the United States (Acuña, 1988; Blauner, 2001; Omi & Winant, 1994; Takaki, 2000; Zinn, 2005). So while the work of Anyon (1997), Kozol (1991, 2005), and Darling-Hammond (2007) demonstrates one view of educational inequity and inadequacy, others like Hanushek (1981) are cited as providing evidence that money does not matter in the achievement of students. Much of the work that educational leaders must do politically encompasses the retelling of school finance realities, the challenging of majoritarian perspectives of equity, and the reframing of the significance of funding in the achievement of students.

Also cognizant of the centrality of race and racism in society, my understanding is that inequity and inadequacy are by-products of social norms and expectations. In this way, school finance systems are similar to other institutions like the juvenile justice system, which incarcerates a disproportionate number of African American and Latino males, and the higher educational system, which exhibits an underrepresentation of students of color at four-year universities (Darling-Hammond, 2007). There exist clearly demarcated views and strongly held beliefs regarding the need for educational opportunity. Evaluating the long history of educational oppression and discrimination, it is clear that the current state of educational inequity and inadequacy is acceptable to some. Educational politics and policy play a vital role in maintaining racial hierarchy. By not preparing students to be more overtly critical *and* activist—without disregarding roles such as that of the instructional leader—the field is abdicating its professional and moral responsibility and forgoing an opportunity to impact social transformation.

Like Bell (1980), I approach this problem from a "racial realist" stance, meaning that I conclude that change will occur only when the interests of whites are benefited. Although this interest convergence perspective may appear to be pessimistic, naïve, or simplistic, it is in maintaining this "racial realist" view that I argue that a critically prepared, historically grounded, and community-engaged leadership will be engendered. Responding to challenges from those attempting to maintain the status quo should begin by posing the following questions. What would occur politically if white students were experiencing the same schooling conditions and academic underachievement levels as African American or Latino students? How would school funding be reformed if white students experienced similar drop-out rates, lack of access to higher education, or disproportionate placement in special education classes, as do students of color? In pondering these questions, I call on educational leadership scholars and students to consider the following principles in advocating for equity and adequacy in school funding.

Embracing the Socialization of Conflict

Schattschneider (1960) stated conflict is central to the existence of politics. Without conflict, tension, or discomfort, there is no change. It is therefore essential for educational leaders seeking to challenge status quo funding to lead with this foundationally. One must think of this as "fanning the flames" or socializing conflict so that an issue is engaged. Those in power often attempt to localize the problem by silencing critique, arguing that money doesn't matter, or "blaming the victim" by pointing to culture, student motivation, or lack of parental involvement as reasons for student underachievement.

Whether it is by raising issues as an expert witness in legislative testimony or in speaking out on intra-district inequities at school board meetings, conflict may be socialized in multiple ways.

Centering Institutionalized Racism as the Primary Culprit to Inequity and Inadequacy

As stated in the introduction of this chapter, majoritarian responses to questions of racial disparity usually center individual cases of success as a way of silencing race talk. Attempting to discredit understandings of institutionalized racism or historical perspectives on racial discrimination and state-sanctioned inequities, critics rely on misunderstood and misappropriated definitions of race and racism. Educational leaders seeking to play a role in the debate over funding must rely on long-established conceptualizations of institutionalized racism. Citing data such as that provided by Carey (2004), Biddle and Berliner (2002), or Darling-Hammond (2007).

Focusing on Property Values as the Maintenance of Racial Hierarchy

While stressing a definition of institutionalized racism, educational leaders must also focus analysis and discussion on the disparate impact that property values play in maintaining racial hierarchies. As Alemán (2007b) found, school finance systems' overreliance on property values in determining state school funding further disadvantages poor school districts. Property values acting as a central variable in most school funding formulas make it likely that low-wealth districts can never generate equal funds to those in property-wealthy school districts. However, the common perception is that poor school districts have more money, not less. Reliant on conservative state legislators and mindful of more pronounced inequities in the past, poor school districts are left having to be appreciative of what they have.

De-"Neutralizing" Concepts of Equity and Adequacy

As stated by Owings and Kaplan (2004), the concepts of equity and adequacy are value-laden. Although their use is accepted as "neutral" in educational vernacular among many educational policy makers, researchers, and practitioners, social justice educational leadership must challenge this notion by speaking to alternative perspectives. Equity in its broadest sense does not mean funding everyone equally and should in fact generate more money for property-poor school districts or students identified as low socioeconomic status, English-language learners, or special education (Odden & Picus, 2008). Funding formulas are technical and complex, however, what is simple to understand is that even though many states have put in so-called equity provisions into their school finance policy, many still provide less funding to poor students and students of color (Alemán, 2007b; Carey, 2004). Social justice educational leaders must combat the perception that funding formulas are neutral.

Privileging Counterstories of Inequity and Inadequacy

Finally, critical race scholarship centers the experiences of people and communities of color because majoritarian stories do not recognize them as legitimate knowledge (DeCuir & Dixson, 2004; Delgado Bernal, 2002). The silencing of these voices can lead to public perception that schools are funded equitably. In fact, many believe that poor schools are overfunded or the schools with a majority of students of color have an advantage. Scholarship like that of Kozol (1991, 2005) is therefore crucial because it paints a vivid portrait of inequity, oppression, and quite literally, the "shame of the nation." Educational leaders know the stories of struggle, especially those who work with communities of color. Engaging in the political arena, testifying to legislative committees, and utilizing the media are methods that can work to counter the majoritarian and mainstream narratives, which are often taken as fact.

Concluding Thoughts

Television pundits and hired commentators such as former U.S. Secretary of Education, William Bennett, are typical majoritarian storytellers. Refusing to critically understand the historical and contextual nature of issues such as inequity and inadequacy of school funding, they instead rely on milestone events or exceptional individuals as they attempt to refute research, stories, and experiences that in fact demonstrate that the "deck may be stacked." It has been over fifty years since the *Brown* decision and total school funding has increased dramatically since that time. However, school finance systems not only continue to generate inequity and inadequacy, but fail to produce equal funding for students of color. Conflict, power, and values will always play a role in the politics of funding. Multiple constituencies including taxpayers, the business sector, and members of the major political parties contest definitions of equity and adequacy. It is my contention, however, that the time for educational leaders to be engaged, critical, and activist on this issue is here. What would funding levels be if white students were forced to attend inequitably and inadequately funded schools? Would equity and adequacy be defined differently? Fostering discomfort and tension with the status quo by posing questions such as these is the first step in engaging in the politics of public school funding. Educational leaders seeking to engage in this political role must not relent to arguments that claim that we live in a post-racial society if they are to aid in the transformation of educational opportunity, particularly in regards to the age-old question of "who gets what."

Notes

1. See http://www.youtube.com/watch?v=NTixCXmrezY for the news clips and commentary by Dr. Dominique Apollon, Research Director of the Applied Research Center, a racial justice think tank (http://www.arc.org/component/option,com_frontpage/Itemid,1/). Retrieved May, 30, 2009.

2. I contend that it was not necessarily that the U.S. electorate was so much "ready" to make this a historical election, but rather, that the interests of *some* whites were better served by the election of Barack Obama. For example, despite being in the throes of the worst economic situation since the Great Depression, bogged down in unpopular wars in Iraq and Afghanistan, and running an almost flawless and innovative campaign, if it were not for the support of a young, college-educated and an overwhelming majority of Black and Latino voters, Obama would not have won. See www.cnn.com/ELECTION/2008/results/president/ for full results of the 2008 election. They indicate that in every demographic category, except the overall whites group, Obama won convincingly. When disaggregated, the results indicate that only young white voters (those 18–29 years) voted for Obama. These results demonstrate the wide racial divide among Americans voting in the presidential election.

3. For further discussion of Fowler's (2008) concepts of power see her Chapter 2 in which she delineates how power is "contested," discourse as power, the three dimensions of power, ethical uses of power, and how power is manifested in educational settings.

References

Acuña, R. (1988). *Occupied America: A history of Chicanos* (3rd ed.). New York: Harper Collins.

Alemán, E., Jr. (2007a). Critical race theory and human capital theory: Framing the discourse on the nexus between social justice and education finance. In G. M. Rodriguez & R. A. Rolle (Eds.), *To what ends and by what means: The social justice implications of contemporary school finance theory and policy* (pp. 35–57). New York: Routledge.

Alemán, E., Jr. (2007b). Situating Texas school finance policy in a CRT framework: How "substantially equal" yields racial inequity. *Educational Administration Quarterly, 43*(5), 525–558.

Alemán, E., Jr. (2009). LatCrit educational leadership and advocacy: Struggling over whiteness as property in Texas school finance. *Equity & Excellence in Education, 42*(2), 183–201.

Alemán, E., Jr., & Rorrer, A. K. (2006). *Closing educational achievement gaps for Latino students in Utah: Initiating a policy discourse and framework.* Salt Lake City: Utah Education Policy Center.

Alexander, K. (1982). Concepts of equity. In W. W. McMahon & T. G. Geske (Eds.), *Financing education: Overcoming inefficiency and inequity* (pp. 193–214). Urbana: University of Illinois Press.

Anyon, J. (1997). *Ghetto schooling: A political economy of urban educational reform.* New York: Teacher's College Press.

Apple, M. W. (2001). *Educating the "right" way.* New York: RoutledgeFalmer.

Bachrach, P., & Baratz, M. (1962). Two faces of power. *American Political Science Review, 56,* 947–952.

Bell, D. A. (1980). Brown v. Board of Education and the interest-convergence dilemma. *Harvard Law Review, 93,* 518–533.

Bell, D. A. (1992). *Faces at the bottom of the well.* New York: Basic Books.

Bell, D. A. (1995). Racial realism. In K. Crenshaw, N. Gotanda, G. Peller & K. Thomas (Eds.), *Critical race theory: The key writings that formed the movement* (pp. 302–312). New York: The New Press.

Bell, D. A. (2004). *Silent covenants: Brown v. Board of Education and the unfulfilled hopes for racial reform.* Oxford: Oxford University Press.

Biddle, B. J., & Berliner, D. C. (2002). *What the research says about small classes and their effects.* San Francisco: WesEd.

Blauner, R. (2001). *Still the big news: Racial oppression in America.* Philadelphia: Temple University Press.

Brady, K., Eatman, T., & Parker, L. (2000). To have or not to have? A preliminary analysis of higher education funding disparities in the post-*Ayers v. Fordice* era: Evidence from critical race theory. *Journal of Education Finance, 25*(3), 297–322.

Brimley, V., & Garfield, R. R. (2005). *Financing education in a climate of change* (9th ed.). Boston, MA: Pearson Education.

Cardenas, J. A. (1997). *Texas school finance reform: An IDRA perspective.* San Antonio, TX: Intercultural Development Research Association.

Carey, K. (2004). *The funding gap 2004: Many states still shortchange low-income and minority students.* Washington, DC: Education Trust.

Crenshaw, K. W. (2002). Critical race studies: The first decade—critical reflections, or "a foot in the closing door". *UCLA Law Review, 49,* 1343–1372.

Crenshaw, K. W., Gotanda, N., Peller, G., & Thomas, K. (Eds.). (1995). *Critical race theory: The key writings that formed the movement.* New York: The New Press.

Darling-Hammond, L. (2007). The flat earth and education: How America's committment to equity will determine our future. *Educational Researcher, 36*(6), 318–334.

Dayton, J. (2000). Recent litigation and its impact on the state-local power balance: Liberty and equity in governance, litigation, and the school finance policy debate. In N. D. Theobald & B. Malen (Eds.), *Balancing local control and state responsiblity for K-12 education: AEFA 2000 Yearbook* (pp. 93–117). Larchmont, NY: Eye on Education, Inc.

DeCuir, J. T., & Dixson, A. D. (2004). "So when it comes out, they aren't that surprised that it is there": Using critical race theory as a tool of analysis or race and racism in education. *Educational Researcher, 33*(5), 26–31.

Delgado Bernal, D. (2002). Critical race theory, Latino critical theory, and critical raced-gendered epistemologies: Recognizing students of color as holders and creators of knowledge. *Qualitative Inquiry, 8*(1), 105–126.

Delgado Bernal, D., & Villalpando, O. (2002). An apartheid of knowledge in academia: The struggle over the "legitimate" knowledge of faculty of color. *Equity & Excellence in Education, 35*(2), 169–180.

Delgado, R. (2003). White interests and civil rights realism: Rodrigo's bittersweet epiphany. *Michigan Law Review, 101,* 1201–1224.

Delgado, R. (2006). Rodrigo's roundelay: *Hernandez v. Texas* and the interest-convergence dilemma. *Harvard Civil Rights - Civil Liberties Law Review, 41,* 23–65.

Delgado, R., & Stefancic, J. (2001). *Critical Race Theory: An introduction.* New York: New York University Press.

Delpit, L. (1995). *Other people's children: Cultural conflict in the classroom.* New York: The New Press.

Dixson, A. D., & Rousseau, C. K. (2005). And we are still not saved: Critical race theory in education ten years later. *Race ethnicity and education, 8*(1), 7–27.

Dudziak, M. L. (1988). Desegregation as a Cold War imperative. *Stanford Law Review, 41*(1), 61–120.

Easton, D. (1965). *A framework for political analysis.* Englewood Cliffs, NJ: Prentice-Hall.

Education Trust. (2001). *State summary of Utah.* Washington, DC: Education Trust.

Education Trust. (2003). *Engaged institutions: Impacting the lives of vulnerable youth through place-based learning.* Washington, DC: W.K. Kellogg Foundation.

Education Trust. (2004). *Education Watch Utah: Key education facts and figures.* Washington, DC: Education Trust, Inc.

Eliot, T. H. (1959). Toward an understanding of public school politics. *American Political Science Review, 53*(4), 1032–1051.

Fowler, F. C. (2008). *Policy studies for educational leaders: An introduction* (3rd ed.). Boston, MA: Pearson.

Grissmer, D., Flanagan, A., & Williamson, S. (1998). Does money matter for minority and disadvantaged students? Assessing the new empirical evidence. In W. J. Fowler (Ed.), *Developments in school finance, 1997* (pp. 15–30). Washington, DC: National Center for Education Statistics.

Hanushek, E. A. (1981). Throwing money at schools. *Journal of Policy Analysis and Management, 1*(1), 19–41.

Hanushek, E. A. (1991). When school finance "reform" may not be good policy. *Harvard Journal on Legislation, 28*(2), 423–455.

Hanushek, E. A. (1996). A more complete picture of school resources on student achievement. *Review of Educational Research, 66*(3), 397–410.

Harris, C. I. (1993). Whiteness as property. *Harvard Law Review, 106,* 1707–1791.

Hedges, L. V., Laine, R. D., & Greenwald, R. (1994). Does money matter? A meta-analysis of studies of the effects of differential school inputs on student outcomes. *Educational Researcher, 23*(3), 5–14.

Horsford, S. D. (2010). Black superintendents on educating Black students in separate and unequal contexts. *Urban Review, 42*(1). (Published Online April 8, 2009). doi: 10.1007/s11256-009-0119-0

Kozol, J. (1991). *Savage Inequalities.* New York: Harper Perrenial.

Kozol, J. (2005). *The shame of the nation: The restoration of apartheid schooling in America.* New York: Crown Publishers.

Ladson-Billings, G. (1998). Just what is critical race theory and what's it doing in a nice field like education. *Qualitative Studies in Education, 11*(1), 7–24.

Ladson-Billings, G. (2004). Landing on the wrong note: The price we paid for Brown. *Educational Researcher, 33*(7), 3-13.

Ladson-Billings, G., & Donner, J. (2005). The moral activist role of critical race theory scholarship. In N. K. Denzin & Y. S. Lincoln (Eds.), *Sage handbook on qualitative research* (3rd ed., pp. 279-301). Thousand Oaks, CA: Sage Publications.

Ladson-Billings, G., & Tate, W. (1997). Toward a critical race theory in education. *Teachers College Record, 97*(1), 47.

Lawrence, C. R. (1987). The id, the ego, and equal protection: Reckoning with unconscious racism. *Stanford Law Review, 39*, 317-388.

López, G. R. (2003). The (racially neutral) politics of education: A critical race theory perspective. *Educational Administration Quarterly, 39*(1), 69-94.

Lynch, R. G. (2004). *Exceptional returns: Economic, fiscal, and social benefits of investment in early childhood developement.* Washington, DC: Economic Policy Institute.

Lynn, R. (2005, April 20). Utah bucks feds on schools. *Salt Lake Tribune.*

Marshall, C., & Gerstl-Pepin, C. (2005). *Re-framing educational politics for social justice.* Boston, MA: Pearson.

Marshall, C., & Scribner, J. D. (1991). 'It''s all political': Inquiry into micropolitics. *Education and Urban Society, 23*(4), 347-355.

McUsic, M. (1991). The use of education clauses in school finance reform litigation. *Harvard Journal on Legislation, 28*(2), 307-340.

Morfin, O. J., Perez, V. H., Parker, L., Lynn, M., & Arrona, J. (2006). Hiding the politically obvious: A critical race theory preview of diversity as racial neutrality in higher education. *Educational Policy, 20*(1), 249-270.

Odden, A. R., & Picus, L. O. (2008). *School finance: A policy perspective* (4th ed.). New York: McGraw Hill.

Omi, M., & Winant, H. (1994). *Racial formation in the United States: From the 1960s to the 1990s* (2nd ed.). New York: Routledge.

Orfield, G. (2001). *Schools more separate: Consequences of a decade of resegregation.* Cambridge, MA: Harvard University.

Owings, W. A., & Kaplan, L. S. (2004). School finance as investment in human capital. *NASSP Bulletin, 88*(640), 12-28.

Parker, L. (2003). Critical race theory and its implications for methodology and policy analysis in higher education desegregation. In G. R. López & L. Parker (Eds.), *Interrogating racism in qualitative research methodology* (pp. 145-180). New York: Peter Lang.

Perlich, P. (2004). Immigrants transform Utah: Entering a new era of diversity. *Utah Economic and Business Review, 64*(5 and 6), 1-16.

Peske, H. G., & Haycock, K. (2006). *Teaching inequality: How poor and minority students are short-changed on teacher quality.* Washington, DC: The Education Trust.

Rebell, M. A., & Wardenski, J. J. (2004). *Of course money matters: Why the arguements to the contrary never added up.* New York: The Campaign for Fiscal Equity, Inc.

Schattschneider, E. E. (1960). *The semi-sovereign people.* New York: Holt, Rinehart and Winston.

Schencker, L., & Stewart, K. (2008, January 13). Legislature eyes education budgets for more funding cuts. *Salt Lake Tribune.*

Scribner, J. D., Alemán, E., & Maxcy, B. (2003). Emergence of the politics of education field: Making sense of the messy center. *Educational Administration Quarterly, 39*(1), 10-40.

Scribner, J. D., & Englert, R. M. (1977). The politics of education: An introduction. In J. D. Scribner (Ed.), *The politics of education: The seventy-sixth yearbook of the National Society for the Study of Education* (pp. 1-29). Chicago, IL: University of Chicago Press.

Solórzano, D. G. (1998). Critical race theory, racial and gender microagressions, and the experiences of Chicana and Chicano scholars. *International Journal of Qualitative Studies in Education*, *11*, 121–136.

Solórzano, D. G., & Delgado Bernal, D. (2001). Examining transformational resistance through a critical race and LatCrit theory framework: Chicana and Chicano students in an urban context. *Urban Education*, *36*(3), 308–342.

Solórzano, D. G., & Yosso, T. J. (2001a). Critical race and LatCrit theory and method: Counter-storytelling. *Qualitative Studies in Education*, *14*(4), 471–495.

Solórzano, D. G., & Yosso, T. J. (2001b). From racial stereotyping and deficit discourse: Toward a critical race theory in teacher education. *Multicultural Education*, *9*(1), 2–8.

Solórzano, D. G., & Yosso, T. J. (2002). Critical race methodology: Counter-storytelling as an analytical framework for education research. *Qualitative Inquiry*, *8*(1), 23–44.

Spring, J. (2005). *Conflict of Interests: The politics of American education* (5th ed.). New York: McGraw-Hill.

Stout, R. T., Tallerico, M., & Scribner, K. P. (1995). Values: The "what?" of the politics of education. In J. D. Scribner & D. H. Layton (Eds.), *The study of educational politics* (pp. 5–20). Washington, DC: The Falmer Press.

Takaki, R. (2000). *Iron cages: Race and culture in 19th century America* (Revised edition ed.). New York: Oxford University Press.

Takaki, R. (Ed.). (2002). *Debating diversity: Clashing perspectives on race and ethnicity in America*. New York: Oxford University Press.

Valdés, F., Culp, J. M., & Harris, A. P. (Eds.). (2002). *Crossroads, directions, and a new Critical Race Theory*. Philadelphia: Temple University Press.

Valencia, R. (2008). *Chicano students and the courts: The Mexican American legal struggle for educational equity*. New York: New York University Press.

Valenzuela, A. (1999). *Subtractive schooling: U.S.-Mexican youth and the politics of caring*. Albany: State University of New York Press.

Valenzuela, A. (2005). Accountability and the privatization agenda. In A. Valenzuela (Ed.), *Leaving children behind: How "Texas-style" accountability fails Latino youth* (pp. 263–294). Albany: State University of New York Press.

Williams, J. (1987). *Eyes on the prize: America's civil rights years, 1954–1965*. New York: Penguin Books.

Yosso, T. J. (2006). *Critial race counterstories along the Chicana/Chicano educational pipeline*. New York: Routledge.

Zinn, H. (2005). *A people's history of the United States: 1492–present* (2nd ed.). New York: Harper-Perennial.

✠ CHAPTER 8

Considering the Social Context of School and Campus Communities: The Importance of Culturally Proficient Leadership

T. Elon Dancy II and Sonya Douglass Horsford

Across primary, secondary, and postsecondary educational institutions in the U.S., educators implement curriculum, leadership, and policy initiatives that not only inform student learning opportunities and outcomes, but also impact student worldviews. As students representing diverse backgrounds and experiences progress along the P-20 education pipeline, they often become aware of the irrational and unjust aspects of society as demonstrated by their schooling experiences. And while we believe that most teachers and professors endeavor to present ideas in the classroom to equip students to think critically and become productive citizens, a lack of attention to cultural influences and dynamics in educational settings can lay an instructional foundation resulting in negative and culturally destructive implications for students, schools, and society.

Seminal research in sociology has long documented the presence of status groups and cultural reproduction (Bourdieu & Passerson, 1977) in education, which maintain educational institutions as exclusive enclaves of superiority and opportunity for the privileged few. While European-American ideologies and perspectives continue to dominate the work of schools and universities (Brown, 2005); institutional cultures, and the workers therein, are under pressure to mine sources and develop practices that advance equity and inclusion for increasingly diverse constituencies. Given the changing cultural landscape of school and campus communities, the social and professional identities of education workers and students become increasingly significant given the "cultural mismatch" that occurs between these two groups (Delpit, 1995; Hilliard, 1967). For instance, while student populations are becoming more and more racially, ethnically, economically, and linguistically diverse, the majority of teachers and school leaders remain overwhelmingly white (Brown, 2005). Similarly, in U.S. colleges and universities, the student demographic in most four-year colleges (i.e., predominantly white institutions) is increasingly diverse while faculty and senior-level administrators are less likely to reflect that diversity.

While a large body of conceptual and empirical work engages topics of school leadership (Lindsey, Robins, & Terrell, 2003; Terrell & Lindsey, 2009) and collegiate leadership (Bensimon & Neumann; 1992; Pope, Reynolds, & Mueller, 2004; Tierney, 1990; Rhoads & Tierney, 1991) from cultural perspectives, literature that engages the intersections of culture, education, and leadership, more broadly is limited and misses critical moments to speak across P-20 contexts about leadership competencies for education workers. Additional attention to culturally proficient leadership is needed in scholarship concerning the education pipeline, organizational effectiveness, student access, equity, and gains.

In this chapter, we explore, discuss, and present the possibilities of culturally proficient leadership in ways that serve and benefit students and stakeholders in both PK-12 and higher education settings. Through a review and analysis of the existing research on culturally proficient leadership in both K-12 educational administration and higher education administration, this chapter offers strategic ways to improve student learning and achievement using Terrell and Lindsey's (2009) framework of cultural proficiency. In this effort, we also consider schoolteacher and collegiate faculty positionality in education classrooms and consider how issues of educational equity and access serve as both pitfalls and possibilities for student engagement, support, and success.

Why Culturally Proficient Leadership?

Cultural pluralism in the U.S. presents schools and colleges with unique challenges and opportunities, which are quite naturally reflected within the sociocultural contexts of these institutions. Social and community contexts frame educational institutions as spaces in which individuals with diverse characteristics and experiences are distributed, engaged, or disengaged. Barriers to educational access, opportunities, and achievement are widely correlated to student background factors like family income, parent education levels, and family structure, while race, class, and culture often shape student experiences across the educational pipeline. In this section, we illustrate how contemporary contexts and conditions in education generate a compelling interest in culturally proficient leadership through a selection of scholarly and empirical literature on the following areas important to learning and leading contexts: (1) cultural reproduction in education; (2) trends and conditions in urban schools, colleges and communities; and (3) educational experiences of students of color. We then move our discussion to a review of cultural proficiency as a framework for P-20 educational leadership.

Cultural Reproduction in Education

Schooling processes function in America as sorting devices (Brown, Dancy, & Norfles, 2006; Spring, 1976). Economic, cultural, and social differences combine to shape differential privilege in schools. For instance, resources that contribute to educational success, such as supplies, books, computers, a place to study, and tutors, are available to children whose families have greater income and wealth (Alexander, 2004; Coleman et al., 1966). To maintain advantage, persons in positions of power use schooling to preserve vantage points of themselves and their progeny. For example, higher socioeconomic status (SES) families are afforded opportunities to choose neighborhoods with high-quality schools in the interest of their children's educational outcomes and can afford tuition for private schools, which often purport to provide positive short-term outcomes (i.e., test scores) that lead to positive long-term outcomes (i.e. entry into elite and competitive colleges). Conversely, children whose parents received lower levels of education are disadvantaged in the school system (Alexander, 2004; Bourdieu & Passeron, 1977; Coleman et al., 1966).

Research indicates that students who own more books, subscribe to newspapers and magazines, visit libraries, and engage in other compatible enrichment opportunities perform better on cognitive tests, receive higher grades, and stay in school longer than do students from families who lack these resources (Alexander, 2004; DiMaggio & Mohr, 1985). Differences in habits, tastes, attitudes, preferences, and linguistics are among the many cultural conditions that make it more difficult for students from disadvantaged families to succeed in school (Alexander, 2004; Bernstein, 1974), while pressuring these same families to compromise their cultural norms and values to those of the school (Payne, 1996). Because schools are largely predisposed to middle-class values (Alexander, 2004), middle-class students often respond more readily to the requirements of schooling than those students who come from low-income communities (Alexander, 2004). This mismatch between home and school culture is further compounded by differential access to social networks, reproducing inequality in educational opportunities and outcomes (Coleman et al., 1966; Coleman & Hoffer, 1987). For example, the social capital and networks of middle-class parents provide them with insights and information that help them manage their children's educational careers successfully and navigate the complexities of educational opportunities more effectively than their working-class counterparts (Lareau, 2000, Useem, 1992). Economic, social, and cultural resources therefore become a potent combination in the reproduction of privilege and disadvantage in educational access and achievement.

The belief that privileged students matter more in schools is consistent with reproduction theories that maintain that dominant social groups use educational credentials to preserve their positions of privilege (Alexander, 2004; Bourdieu & Passeron, 1977; Collins, 1971). Reproduction theorists recognize that subordinate groups often strive for greater educational opportunities. In tandem, a society that expands mass education benefits concomitant groups by broadening the socialization of persons from lower-status origins into a common value system and prepares them for the workforce (Alexander, 2004). Further, society perpetuates *maximally maintained inequality* in schools (Raftery & Hout, 1993 as cited in Alexander, 2004). Maximally maintained inequality suggests that students from lower socioeconomic families can stay in school longer but their relative position compared to their higher-status peers remains constant albeit educational opportunities have improved for all members of society. For example, little social inequality exists in relation to the completion of lower secondary education in this country. When saturation is reached, however, inequality shifts upward to preserve relative differences (Alexander, 2004).

Despite growing diversity within America's schools, signs of change in economic inequalities affecting schooling are modest at best (Alexander, 2004). States increasingly recognize that unequal school financing across school districts is unfair. The steps taken, however, are reticent to close the advantage gap between high socioeconomic status families and low socioeconomic families. Alexander (2004) maintains that, despite interventions, society can expect inequality in educational achievement and attainment by social background to persist throughout the twenty-first century. Disturbing trends across school, college, and community contexts bear out the causes and consequences of inequities in education.

Trends and Conditions in Urban Schools, Colleges, and Communities

Urban schools, unlike their suburban counterparts, serve a disproportionate number of students of color and poverty, representing ethnically and linguistically diverse populations. As middle-class families continue to flee to the suburbs, a trend that has continued since the conceptualization of mandatory and voluntary school desegregation plans; poor, students of color are now more than twice as likely to attend high-poverty schools (schools in which more than half the students qualify for free or reduced price lunch) (Legters et al., 2004). In fact, urban school districts enroll half of all minority students, one-third of poor students, and only one-quarter of all public school students (Legters et al., 2004), requiring them to serve high-need student populations with eroding tax bases. Although states increasingly recognize that unequal school financing across school districts is unfair, steps taken to close the disparities of funding in public education are inadequate. According to Legters and colleagues (2004), additional challenges facing urban high schools are: (1) fewer resources, (2) poor prior preparation among students, (3) school climate, (4) diversity and segregation, and (5) politics.

Fewer resources. Central city schools serve students with greater educational needs and face the challenges of aging facilities that often require expensive maintenance and renovation, competition with wealthier districts for teachers, and a tax base that has dwindled in recent decades as residents have moved out of the city. These conditions arguably make urban education costlier than in other more advantaged settings (Legters et al., 2004). Data is scant that shows updated findings in the past ten years, although data shows that urban districts spent $500 less per pupil than their suburban counterparts from 1993 to 1994 (Legters et al., 2004). Disparate spending implies that urban students become predisposed to academically deficient outcomes in school.

Poor prior preparation. Many students are entering urban high schools with extremely poor prior preparation. Urban students consistently score below nonurban students in math, science, and reading according to national data obtained from various achievement tests (Legters et al., 2004). In Baltimore for example, in the 1999–2000 school year, 60% of ninth graders passed the basic Maryland functional test in math and 76% passed the functional writing test, compared with statewide averages of 85% and 92%, respectively (Legters et al., 2004). Even worse performance was reported across eight nonselective urban high schools vis-à-vis suburban selective magnet high schools. Less than half (47%) of ninth graders passed the math test and two-thirds (67%) passed the writing test in the eight urban schools (Maryland State Department of Education, 2001 as cited in Legters et al., 2004).

School climate. High concentrations of poverty among students in urban schools and surrounding neighborhoods have implications for their health, safety, and early transitions into adulthood as well as for the daily operation of urban high schools (Legters et al., 2004). Physical conflicts are also viable concerns in urban schooling environments. Nearly half of the teachers in urban districts characterize physical conflicts among students as moderate or serious problems versus less than a third in nonurban districts (Legters et al., 2004).

Diversity and segregation. Students enrolled in urban high schools are exposed to higher levels of academic, linguistic, and cultural diversity than those enrolled in nonurban high schools (Legters et al., 2004). Increased diversity among urban learners is often attributed to larger numbers of students who require special or individualized services. The typical nonselective high school in Baltimore that Letgers and colleagues (2004) discuss, for example, must provide special education services to 20% of its students versus 12% statewide and less than 1% in the suburban magnet high schools. Diversity within minority-stratified student populations is also a consideration. The predominance of students of color in urban high schools (in some cases reaching over 90%) has led scholars to argue that increasing racial segregation has completely supplanted the democratizing ideal of comprehensive high schools (Legters et al., 2004; Orfield & Eaton, 1996).

Politics. Many urban city school systems become susceptible to bureaucratic inertia, complicated politics, and short-term leadership as side effects to their large size (Legters et al., 2004). High schools are left both unsupported and ignored in the aggregate. The average urban superintendent serves fewer than 3 years (Legters et al., 2004). In the majority (51) urban districts, superintendents have served between 1 and 5 years, and nearly a third are led by superintendents who have served for 1 year or less. New superintendents feel compelled to introduce new reforms to show constituents that they are effective, but policy is rarely changed during the short tenure of the superintendent (Legters et al., 2004). On the surface, these reforms appear to most benefit the image of the leader, while urban school system troubles persist. In fact, continually unfulfilled expectations for improvement leave teachers disillusioned and resistant to further change (Legters et al., 2004).

Educational Experiences of Students of Color

While trends among students of color are often tied to multiple factors, a key contributing factor in school and collegiate classrooms found to affect the educational experiences of students of color across the P-20 education pipeline are their classroom experiences. Stovall (2005) gathered information over a ten-week period from a group of low-income, academically "middle-tier" students at a school in Chicago's south side. The school selected largely serves students of color, most of whom are "low-income" or "at-risk." Students in the class were required to complete a video project and writing assignment based on questions concerning their lives. Findings suggest that how these students portrayed themselves (i.e., drug dealers, gang members, pregnant mothers on welfare) indicated how they perceive their place in the larger society. When multicultural or urban education was included into the academic experience, both self-identity and likelihood of retention increased among students of color.

In addition, scholars argue that faculty produce and reproduce a hidden curriculum of hegemony in the university setting that affects experiences of students of color negatively (Solórzano & Villalpondo, 1998; Solórzano & Yosso, 2000). Hegemony describes how ruling groups normalize patriarchal ideologies and marginalize others' ideologies to maintain power and dominance (Gramsci, 1971). Consequently, cultural perspectives are skewed to favor the dominant group. As a result of hegemony, people of color are excluded. Solórzano and Villalpondo (1998) insist that while most colleges endorse the importance of multiculturalism and provide educational opportunities to students of color, colleges still remain racially stratified with differential access, opportunity, and experiences. Using qualitative approaches to study the experiences of Chicana college students and their interactions with college faculty, Solórzano and Villalpondo (1998) reported the following experience:

> I argued almost as frequently with professors who couldn't understand how they were also insulting me or might just be plain wrong. I couldn't study for those classes be-

cause I felt totally alienated. It was like I was studying and being tested on some things that I knew were wrong. Yet, I was expected to repeat these incorrect "facts" or fail the class. (p. 218)

Solórzano and Villalpondo (1998) found that colleges and universities encourage dissenting ideologies that skew the meaning, purposes and function of society. The experience of the Chicana student suggests that these ideologies reveal themselves in faculty pedagogies and subsequently expose hidden curricula of hegemony. The extensive research documenting the classroom experiences of students of color and its correlation to teacher expectations and, subsequently, student performance have resulted in much more work on cultural proficiency in teacher education and the preparation of classroom teachers as compared to that of PK-12 and higher education administrators. In the next section, we review the work that has been done by teacher education researchers and consider the ways in which the value for and practice of cultural relevance and responsiveness in the classroom can inform the work of educational leaders across the P-20 pipeline.

Culture in the Classroom: Culturally Relevant, Culturally Responsive, and Multicultural Education

For more than a decade, culturally relevant pedagogy (Ladson-Billings, 1994, 2000a, 2000b), culturally responsive teaching (Gay, 2000), and similar approaches to multicultural education (Banks, 1993, 2005; Banks & Banks, 1988; Grant, 1992; Nieto, 1999; Sleeter & Grant; 1996; Sleeter & McLaren, 1996) have been examined and advanced in teacher education. In her study of the successful teachers of African American children, Ladson-Billings (1994) argues that learning can be improved through the use of culturally relevant pedagogy, which she defines as "a pedagogy that empowers students intellectually, socially, emotionally, and politically by using cultural referents to impart knowledge, skills, and attitudes" (p. 18). By examining the dominant culture and student's own culture through cultural referents that are embedded in the curriculum, culturally relevant pedagogy establishes the student's ability to develop a skill necessary for school and life success. Geneva Gay's work defines culturally responsive teaching as "using the cultural knowledge, prior experiences, and performance styles of diverse students to make learning more appropriate and effective for them" in ways that teach "to and through the strengths of these students." These examples reflect the larger and seminal body of work of scholars in multicultural education, such as James Banks, Sonia Nieto, Carl Grant, and Christine Sleeter.

Conversely, theoretical and practical considerations of culture remain underexamined and underexplored in the field of educational leadership. Although the study of higher education includes a large body of scholarly and empirical work that both engages topics of collegiate leadership from cultural perspectives (Bensimon & Neumann, 1992; Pope, Reynolds, & Mueller, 2004; Tierney, 1990; Rhodes & Tierney, 1991) and connects the importance of organizational and individual culture to implications for college student outcomes and collegiate leadership, literature that engages the intersections of culture, leadership, and education more broadly remain limited. Further, it misses critical moments to speak across educational contexts about required leadership competencies for higher education faculty and administrators, particularly the knowledge, skills, and dispositions of the collegiate faculty who prepare them for leadership.

Branch (2005) details the ways in which multicultural education is a more suitable and effective framework to guide the pedagogies of teachers of diverse classrooms. Specifically, Branch discusses the implications of white teachers of students of color who fail to identify the race/gender of an assigned book's author or who hesitate to discuss race relations in class. Branch's discussion builds on his previous work, which found white teachers avoiding certain discourses that created "uncomfortable moods (Branch, 2005)." Scholars argue that these moods are uncomfortable for dominant cultures and groups (whites) across schools and universities (Gay, 2000; Giroux, 1998). These assertions are additionally located in studies of white teachers and white preservice teachers in multicultural classroom contexts.

Marx and Pennington (2003) investigated white preservice teachers' negotiation of race in the classroom. The authors individually conducted studies to understand these future teachers' attitudes toward and interactions with students of color. Pennington weaved her own experience with the experiences of white preservice teachers in two neighboring predominantly Hispanic schools. Pennington found that the teachers felt positioned as outsiders in the classroom communities dominated by students of color. Her participants also expressed feelings of confrontation in situations in which they felt un-included or rejected (i.e., student whispering, meeting with parents of students of color) albeit they agreed that including conversations about the white race would benefit classrooms subjugated by students of color. Ironically, the teachers in this study experienced what marginalized groups of color have felt for decades—exclusion from discourses that appear to disregard them. Recent work encourages teachers to develop authentic caring dispositions to connect with students.

For example, Rolòn-Dow explored the interface between race/ethnicity and caring in the educational experiences of middle school Puerto Rican girls. Through participant narratives, Rolòn-Dow finds gaps betweens teachers' concern for students' academic work and their concern for students' personal lives. Rolòn-Dow also describes how inauthentic caring may mask white privilege. For example, she interviewed a teacher who never mentioned race in the interview, yet would distinguish herself from her students through using language such as "these kids" and "our values" (Rolòn-Dow, 2005, p. 94) in ways exclusionist of students of color. In contrast, Rolòn-Dow also presents the story of a teacher who was found to negotiate the importance of race differently from other teachers by using a racial lens to guide his interactions with students. As a result, students identified him as a caring teacher. Rolòn-Dow bifurcates caring in two ways—(a) aesthetic/technical caring and (b) authentic/relational caring (Noddings, 1984; Valenzuela, 1999). Aesthetic caring focuses attention to the technical aspects of teaching and learning such as curricula, academic goals, and teaching strategies. Authentic caring describes attention to the personal aspects related to student background and experiences.

The students in Rolòn-Dow's study also linked race and care by arguing that the racial/ethnic differences between them and their teachers affected the amount and type of care teachers offered to them. Rolòn-Dow notes the following:

> As the girls spoke of the differences between their community and the communities of their teachers, they brought up race/ethnicity as a topic that influenced the perceptions that teachers held of their community and of them as members of that community. What was troubling about this dynamic was not that the teachers did not live in the same community but that, as the girls ascertained, their race and class positions influenced the assumptions they formed of the girls' community and of the girls as members of that community. These perceptions, in turn, influenced the way caring was distributed and perceived within the context of the teacher-student relationship (p. 101).

Rolòn-Dow's (2005) clarion call for a critical care schema requires that teachers in multicultural classrooms have a historical understanding of students' lives, translate ideological and political orientations into pedagogical approaches that benefit Latino and Latina students, and use intimate, caring approaches. The most effective teachers of multicultural classrooms in this study were those who demonstrated both aesthetic and authentic caring in their classrooms while also paying attention to the community context in which education took place.

In our attempt to address the existing concerns facing educational leaders as it relates to issues of educational inequality and inequity; complex urban contexts; and the disconcerting experiences of students of color along every point of the P-20 pipeline, we consider the ways in which research on cultural awareness and relevance has enhanced teaching and learning in the classroom and its possible application to educational administration. Because we believe the teacher education research data and findings have important implications for educational leaders who also serve diverse student populations and communities, we extend this discussion with a review of cultural proficiency as a useful framework and set of tools by which educational leaders can better meet the needs of their educational constituencies.

From the Classroom to the Boardroom: Cultural Proficiency as a Framework for Educational Leaders and Administrators

As a theoretical framework, cultural proficiency is designed to assist educational leaders in their efforts to measure and assess their effectiveness in working with student, family, and community populations that may reflect values, beliefs, and assumptions different from their own. In their book, *Culturally Proficient Leadership: The Personal Journey Begins Within* (2009), Terrell and Lindsey put forth a theory of cultural proficiency that demonstrates a commitment by educational leaders to "educat[e] all students to high levels through knowing, valuing, and using the student's cultural backgrounds, language, and learning styles within the selected curricular and instructional contexts." They also describe cultural proficiency as "a worldview that carries explicit values, language, and standards for effective personal interactions and professional practices" (p. 21), and they provide the following four interrelated personal and professional development tools to support leaders in engaging in practices that foster culturally relevant and meaningful educational experiences for all children. While the authors are former K-12 administrators and provide many examples that are particularly pertinent to K-12 school administration and leadership, we believe the concepts offered would also prove valuable in postsecondary and higher education contexts.

Guiding Principles

These principles serve as guide for educational leaders to interrogate and acknowledge their deeply held beliefs and assumptions concerning students who
represent a racial, ethnic, economic, or linguistic background or life experience different from that of the school or institutional leader. They provide a
foundation for establishing "an ethical and professional frame for effective
cross-cultural communication and problem solving" and include the following:

- Culture is a predominant force in people's and school's lives.
- People are served in varying degrees by the dominant culture.
- People have group identities and individual identities.
- Diversity within cultures is vast and significant.
- Each cultural group has unique cultural needs.
- The best of both worlds enhances the capacity of all (p. 24).

As the authors conclude, "either you believe students can learn and be taught
or you don't" (p. 101). These principles, therefore, not only promote individual reflection concerning whether or not the culture of underrepresented students is viewed as a deficit or asset to educational organizations, but also
compel these organizations to acknowledge the intent, processes, and practices
of the dominant culture that construct barriers, limit opportunities, and create
hostile conditions for students of color in school and campus contexts (p.
101).

Cultural Proficiency Continuum

The second tool designed to promote individual reflection and moral responsibility concerning matters of cultural understanding and respect is the cultural proficiency continuum, which consists of six points: cultural
destructiveness, cultural incapacity, cultural blindness, cultural precompetence, cultural competence, and cultural proficiency. It "provides language for
describing healthy and unhealthy values, behaviors, policies, and practices existing in schools" and for the purposes of this chapter, institution of higher
education (p. 103). These leaders dispositions are summarized as follows:

- Cultural destructiveness—Seeking to eliminate the cultures of others in all
  aspects of the schools and communities served
- Cultural incapacity—Trivializing and problematizing other cultures
- Cultural blindness—Failing to acknowledge and ignoring the cultures and
  experiences of others

- Cultural precompetence—Leading with awareness of what you and the organization don't know about working in diverse settings
- Cultural competence—Leading with your personal values and behaviors and the organization's polices and practices aligned in ways that are inclusive with cultures new or different from yours and the organizations
- Cultural proficiency—Leading as an advocate for life-long learning with the purpose of being increasingly effective in serving the educational needs of cultural groups.

The first three points (cultural destructiveness, cultural incapacity, and cultural blindness) reflect a deficit-oriented leadership perspective that views students and families representing cultural backgrounds and values different from one's own as deficient or "at-risk." The following points (cultural precompetence, cultural competence, and cultural proficiency) represent an engagement of "transformational" leadership practice that focuses on the ways educational leaders can improve their work using an "inside-out" approach that effectively serves diverse school and campus communities (p. 25).

Essential Elements

This inside-out approach toward leadership development and practice, which Terrell and Lindsey (2009) describe as "the personal journey within" is facilitated through essential elements of cultural proficiency, which serve as standards for organizational values and behaviors, to include the administrative policies, processes, and practices that occur within schools and on college campuses on a daily basis. The first is *assessing cultural knowledge* and requires leaders to explore and understand other cultures and develop the skills and dispositions necessary for effective cross-cultural communication and relationships. The second element is *valuing diversity* or engaging small groups and teams of people who represent diverse lived experiences, cultural backgrounds, and perspectives to facilitate conversations, make decisions, and solve problems collaboratively to improve the organization. To demonstrate the third element, *managing the dynamics of difference*, leaders are responsible for "modeling problem solving and conflict resolution strategies as a natural and normal process within the organizational culture of the schools and the cultural contexts of the communities of your school" (p. 26). Integrating and incorporating the cultural capital and wealth that is represented in the sociocultural context of the school or campus community in ways that benefit and strengthen the organization represents the work of the fourth element, *adapting to diversity*.

Finally, the fifth element, *institutionalizing cultural knowledge*, exemplifies the culturally proficient educational leader's efforts to make "learning about cultural groups and their experiences and perspectives an integral part of the [organization's] professional development (p. 26).

Possible Barriers

As with any form of organizational change, efforts to demonstrate and engage culturally proficient leadership in schools and universities will face challenge and resistance from those who prefer to keep things the way they are (Theoharis, 2009). Therefore, educational leaders must become familiar not only with the guiding principles, continuum, and essential elements of cultural proficiency, but also the obstacles and resistance they will face as they seek to dismantle oppression and reveal privilege and entitlement within their respective organizations and communities. As Terrell and Lindsey (2009) explain, "Knowledge of the barriers helps you to see the extent to which the status quo serves selected groups of students and/or educators" (p. 103). They identify these barriers as *resistance to change, systems of oppression* (i.e., racism, sexism, heterosexism, ableism, and classism), and *a sense of privilege and entitlement*, which Terrell and Lindsey describe as the phenomenon where "those who benefit from historical and current practices are oblivious to the negative effects of systemic oppression on others because they can choose not to see" (p. 27). As a result, the path to cultural proficiency requires resilience and authentic commitment to educational justice on the part of educational leaders who honor their moral and professional obligations to leading equitable and excellent schools and institutions.

Toward Culturally Proficient Leadership across School and Campus Communities: From Theory to Practice

As mentioned at the start of this chapter, school and campus community leaders who demonstrate competence and proficiency in leading and serving culturally diverse populations are essential to the successful educational experiences and outcomes of all students. These considerations translate into the following actions: (a) Study historical and sociocultural contexts of school and campus communities, (b) Resist cultural reproduction of educational inequality and inequity, (c) Value experiences and perspectives of students of color, and (d) Monitor and mediate cultural conflict through cross-cultural communication.

Study Historical and Sociocultural Contexts of School and Campus Communities

For educational leaders to successfully lead and serve their school and campus communities, they must have a keen awareness and understanding of the historical and sociocultural contexts of their school and campus communities (Horsford, 2009). It is critical for them to be familiar with histories of discrimination, systems of oppression, and contemporary manifestations of marginalization, which may contribute to mistrust, skepticism, and cynicism by communities and cultural groups that may have been excluded or devalued by an institution and its leaders. This information can be gained through historical research and artifacts to include newspaper reports; governmental data; school, district, and university performance reports; and informal interviews that capture the experiential knowledge of people who have been marginalized, underserved, or silenced in a particular community.

Resist Cultural Reproduction of Educational Inequality and Inequity

To effectively recognize and resist the cultural reproduction of educational inequality and inequity in school organizations and institutions of higher education, and the P-20 pipeline, educational leaders must be able to discern patterns of exclusion and segregation as perpetuated through administrative policies and practices that continue to grant privilege and a sense of entitlement to one group while only offering disadvantage and limited access and opportunity to others. This also requires reticence toward supporting diversity and inclusion programs and initiatives that fail to recognize how inequality and inequity are reproduced by failing to address issues concerning decision-making, allocation of resources, and power distribution. For example, many U.S. teacher preparation programs require the study of whiteness as it impacts teacher and learner epistemology and teacher pedagogy, and we believe this practice should be extended to the field of educational leadership. The work of scholars like Giroux (1998), Marx and Pennington (2003), Delgado and Stefancic (1997), and Leonardo (2009) provide excellent starting points for familiarizing future educational leaders to research on white privilege and Whiteness studies.

Value Experiences and Perspectives of Students of Color

Just as teachers must understand how culture operates daily in the classroom, foster learning environments that value cultural and ethnic diversity, and understand how these environments inform student achievement, educational leaders must also gain this awareness to assist them in establishing a school or institutional culture and climate that advances student learning, engagement, and success. In the context of teaching and learning, Gay (2000) explains: "Opportunities must be provided for students from different ethnic backgrounds to have free personal and cultural expression so that their voices and experiences can be incorporated into teaching and learning processes on a regular basis" (p. 43). We agree, and believe that the experiences and perspectives of students of color should also be considered and embraced by educational leaders in their efforts to lead organizations that meaningfully educate and serve all students.

Monitor and Mediate Cultural Conflict through Cross-Cultural Communication

According to Beverly Daniel Tatum (2007), "we are confronted by the loss of civility in increasingly diverse communities" at the same time we are in desperate need of "balance, integrity, vision; a clear sense of collective responsibility and ethical leadership—in order to prepare our students for wise stewardship of their world and active participation in a democracy" (pp. 105–106). Our commitment to preparing students educationally along the P-20 pipeline requires school, college, and university leaders who can successfully monitor and mediate cultural conflict by modeling cross-cultural communication effectively and proficiently. Therefore, educational leaders and administrators must be trained and experienced in assuming the role of "mediators in diverse contexts" (Ryan, 2007) and able to navigate and negotiate opposing cultural perspectives and conflict through dialogue and mediation. These lessons can be learned and guided by the research on teachers and faculty as cultural mediators (Diamond & Moore, 1995; Gay, 2000). This work demonstrates how educators must provide opportunities for students to engage in critical dialogue about conflicts among cultures and analyze inconsistencies between mainstream cultural ideals/realities and those across cultures. Just as teachers and faculty are required to do, educational administrators must assume the lead in clarifying cultural misunderstanding and fostering positive cross-cultural relationships.

Conclusion

Educators, whether justly or unjustly, are often the decisive element in the classroom, school, and campus experience. The messages they consciously or subconsciously send their students, particularly historically excluded or marginalized students, have important educational and social implications for schools and society. While learning institutions are often blamed for the educational inequities perpetuated therein, school and university leaders can improve student learning experiences and outcomes through culturally proficient approaches and practices along with the commitment to actively locate, hire, mentor, and support culturally proficient leaders at every point along the P-20 educational pipeline. By considering the sociocultural environments of school and campus communities, educational researchers and leaders can begin the important work of improving student engagement, support, and success in no matter the cultural or educational context.

References

Alexander, K. L. (2004). Public schools and the public good. In J. H. Ballantine and J. Z. Spade (Eds.) *Schools and society: A sociological approach to education* (2nd ed). pp. 234–249. Belmont, CA: Thomson Wadsworth.

Banks, J. A. (1993). *An introduction to multicultural education*. Boston: Allyn & Bacon.

Banks, J. A. (2005). *Cultural diversity and education: Foundations, curriculum, and teaching*. (5th ed.). Boston: Allyn & Bacon.

Banks, J. A., & Banks, C. A. (Eds.) (1988). *Multicultural education: Issues and perspectives*. Boston: Allyn & Bacon.

Bensimon, E., & Neumann, A. (1992). *Redesigning collegiate leadership: Teams and teamwork in higher education*. Baltimore: Johns Hopkins University Press.

Bernstein, B. (1974). Sociology and the sociology of education: A brief account. In J. Rex (Ed.), *Approaches to sociology*. London: Routledge & Kegan

Bourdieu, P., & Passeron, J. (1977). *Reproduction in education, society, and culture*. Beverly Hills, CA: Sage.

Branch, A. J. (2005). Practicing multicultural education: Answering recurring questions about what it is (not). In M. C. Brown & R. Land (Eds.), *The politics of curricular change: Race, hegemony, and power in education*. New York: Peter Lang.

Brown, M. C. (2005). Telling the truth, again: Another introduction. In M. C. Brown & R. Land (Eds.), *The politics of curricular change: Race, power, and hegemony in education*. New York: Peter Lang.

Brown, M. C., Dancy, T. E., and Norfles, N. (2006). A nation still at risk: No child left behind and the salvation of disadvantaged students. In F. Brown (Ed.) *No child left behind and other special programs in urban school districts*. pp. 341–364. Oxford: Elsevier.

Coleman, J. S., et al. (1996). *Equality of educational opportunity*. Washington, DC:GPO.

Coleman, J. S., & Hoffer, T. (1987). *Public and private high schools: The impact of communities.* New York: Basic Books.

Collins, R. (1971). Functional and conflict theories of educational stratification. *American Sociological Review. 36,* 1000–1019.

Delgado, R., & Stefancic, J. (1997). Imposition. In R. Delgado & J. Stefancic (Eds.), *Critical white studies: Looking behind the mirror.* Philadelphia: Temple University Press.

Delpit, L. (1995). *Other people's children: Cultural conflict in the classroom.* New York: The New Press.

Diamond, B. J., & Moore, M. A. (1995). *Multicultural literacy: Mirroring the reality of the classroom.* New York: Longman.

Dimaggio, P. & Mohr, J. (1985). Cultural capital, educational attainment, and marital selection. *American Journal of Sociology, 90,* 1231–1261.

Gay, G. (2000). *Culturally responsive teaching: Theory, research, and practice. Multicultural Education Series.* New York: Teachers College Press.

Giroux, H. A. (1998). Critical pedagogy as performative practice: Memories of whiteness. In C. A. Torres & T. R. Mitchell (Eds.), *Sociology of education: Emerging perspectives.* New York: SUNY Press.

Gramsci, A. (1971). *Selections from the Prison Notebooks* (Q. Hoare & G. Nowell-Smith, Trans.). New York: International Press.

Grant, C. A. (1992). Research and multicultural education: From the margins to the mainstreatm. Bristol, PA: The Falmer Press.

Hilliard, A. G. (1967). Cross-cultural teaching. *Journal of Teacher Education, 18*(1), 32–35.

Horsford, S. D. (2009, Summer). The case for racial literacy in educational leadership: Lessons learned from superintendent reflections on desegregation. *UCEA Review, 50*(2), 5–7.

Jay, M. (2003). Critical race theory, multicultural education, and the hidden curriculum of hegemony. *Multicultural Perspectives, 5*(4), 3-9.

Ladson-Billings, G. (1994). *The dreamkeepers: Successful teachers of African American children.* San Francisco, CA: Jossey-Bass Publishers.

Ladson-Billings, G. (2000a). Culturally relevant pedagogy in African-centered schools: Possibilities for progressive educational reform. In D. S. Pollard & C. S. Ajirotutu (Eds.), *African-centered schooling in theory and practice* (pp. 223). Westport, CT: Bergin & Garvey.

Ladson-Billings, G. (2000b). Fighting for our lives: Preparing teachers to teach African American students. *Journal of Teacher Education, 51*(3), 206–214.

Lareau, A. (2000). *Home Advantage* (2nd ed.) Lanham, MD: Rowman & Littlefield.

Legters, N. E., Balfanz, R., Jordan, W. J., and McPartland, J. M. (2004). Comprehensive Reform for Urban High Schools. In J. H. Ballantine and J. Z. Spade (Eds.) *Schools and society: A sociological approach to education (2nd ed).* pp. 220–227. Belmont, CA: Thomson Wadsworth.

Leonardo, Z. (2009). *Race, whiteness, and education.* London: Taylor and Francis.

Lindsey, R. B., Robins, K. N., & Terrell, R. D. (2003). *Cultural proficiency: A manual for school leaders* (2nd ed.). Thousand Oaks, CA: Corwin Press.

Marx, S., & Pennington, J. (2003). Pedagogies of critical race theory: Experimentations with white preservice teachers. *International Journal of Qualitative Studies in Education, 16*(1), 91-110.

Nieto, S. (1999). *The light in their eyes: Creating multicultural learning communities*. New York: Teachers College Press.

Noddings, N. (1984). *Caring: A feminine approach to ethics and moral education*. Berkeley: University of California Press.

Orfield, G., and Eaton, S. (1997). *Dismantling desegregation: The quiet reversal of Brown v. Board of Education*. New York: The New Press.

Payne, R. (1996). *A framework for understanding poverty*. Highlands TX: aha! Process, Inc.

Pope, R. L., Reynolds, A. L., & Mueller, J. (2004). *Multicultural competence in student affairs*. San Francisco: Jossey Bass.

Rhoads, R. A., and Tierney, W. G. (1991). *Cultural leadership in higher education*. University Park, PA: National Center on Postsecondary Learning, Teaching, and Assessment.

Rolòn-Dow, R. (2005). Critical care: A color(full) analysis of care narratives in the schooling experiences of Puerto Rican girls. *American Educational Research Journal, 42*(1), 77-111.

Ryan, J. (2007). Dialogue, identity and inclusion: Administrators as mediators in diverse school contexts. *Journal of School Leadership, 17*(3), 340–369.

Sleeter, C. E., & Grant, C. A. (1996). *Multicultural education as social activism*. Albany: State University of New York Press.

Sleeter, C. E., & McClaren, P. L. (Eds.) (1996). *Multicultural education, critical pedagogy, and the politics of difference*. Albany: State University of New York Press.

Solórzano, D. G., & Villalpando, O. (1998). Critical race theory, marginality, and experience of students of color in higher education. In C. A. Torres & T. R. Mitchell (Eds.), *The sociology of education: Emerging perspectives*. Albany: SUNY Press.

Solórzano, D. G., & Yosso, T. J. (2000). Critical race theory, LatCrit theory and method: Counterstorytelling Chicana and Chicano graduate school experiences. *International Journal of Qualitative Studies in Education, 14*(4), 471-495.

Spring, J. (1976). *The sorting machine: National educational policy since 1945*. New York: David McKay Company.

Stovall, D. M. (2005). A sociological treatise on the racialized context of American education. In M. C. Brown & R. Land (Eds.), *The politics of curricular change: Race, hegemony, and power in education*. New York: Peter Lang Publishing.

Tatum, B. D. (2007). *Can we talk about race? And other conversations in an era of school resegregation*. Boston: Beacon Press.

Terrell, R. D., & Lindsey, R. B. (2009). *Culturally proficient leadership: The personal journey begins within*. Thousand Oaks, CA: Corwin Press.

Theoharis, G. (2009). *The school leaders our children deserve: 7 keys to equity, social justice, and school reform*. New York: Teachers College Press.

Tierney, W. G. (1990). Assessing academic climates and cultures. *New Directions for Institutional Research*, (68). San Francisco: Jossey-Bass.

Useem, E. L. (1992). Middle schools and math groups: Parents' involvement in children's placement. *Sociology of Education*. 65, 263-279.

Valenzuela, A. (1999). *Subtractive schooling: U.S. Mexican youth and the politics of caring*. Albany: State University of New York Press.

✠ CHAPTER 9

Educational Leaders as Cultural Workers: Engaging Families and School Communities through Transformative Leadership

Camille Wilson Cooper

In an educational era where tremendous emphasis is placed on the academic achievement gap that separates many students along racial, ethnic, class, and linguistic lines, educational leaders often regard parents as needed allies in their battle to raise achievement scores. Leaders typically look to parents and families for assistance when it comes to ensuring students' school readiness, fostering student's learning and positive behavior, and participating in school events. Consequently, many leaders adopt a top-down approach to soliciting site-based parent involvement. A collaborative approach to engaging families that seeks to build community, bridge cultural differences between families and schools, foster dialogue, and share power is rare. Developing collaborative, culturally relevant and empowering school-family partnerships, however, can aid educational leaders in co-creating culturally affirming and responsive environments in which diverse families can contribute to school improvement. Indeed, true school-family partnerships have the potential to not only empower families to help ensure their children's academic success, they can also enhance educational leaders' efforts to promote student learning and transform the culture of school communities.

In this chapter, I consider how both theoretical models and practical approaches to transformative leadership, which often overlook the importance of school-family relations, can better encompass critical family engagement strategies. I explain how the discontinuities between schools and families contribute to the marginalization of many families and lessen the effectiveness of educational leaders. Moreover, I discuss the tendency of educators to privilege the values, voices, knowledge and norms of white, middle-class families, thereby enabling this group to influence the educational process more than other families. I assert a notion of transformative educational leadership that calls for educators to embrace, engage, and empower diverse families by countering deficit-thinking, developing collaborative structures, and proactively addressing cultural conflicts. My discussion includes a review of parent involvement studies that address the engagement of white, Latino, and African American families, including my study of cultural change in North Carolina elementary schools. Theories related to the "new cultural politics of difference" and "cultural workers" (West, 1999, p. 119) influence my discussion. I conclude the chapter by recommending strategies and resources that can assist educational leaders in better engaging cultural diverse families in schools.

Notions of Transformative Leadership

Notions of transformative educational leadership describe the practice as being collaborative, culturally responsive, inclusive of all students, infused with a democratic ethos, and/or socially just. For instance, Murphy (2000) suggests this kind of leadership entails leaders "depending on others" and "letting go" of some power and authority to "provide a scaffolding for collaboration" so that all school community members have a sense of shared responsibility for improving schools (pp. 116–117). Johnson (2007) emphasizes the importance of leaders trying to diminish the cultural discontinuities between students of color and educators by acting out a sociopolitical consciousness, redressing social inequities, and implementing curriculum and policies that affirm multiculturalism and diversity. A variety of scholars further stress the need for transformative leadership that is inclusive overall, whether it means better integrating children with special needs, developing governing structures that involve a variety of educational stakeholders, or developing school environments where all students and families feel welcomed (Frattura & Capper, 2007; Cooper & Gause, 2007; Larson & Ovando, 2001). Critical scholars particularly call on educational leaders to be transformative for the sake of working toward social justice, which means striving to counteract biased and marginalizing forces that reproduce social and political inequality (Dantley &

Tillman, 2006; Marshall & Oliva, 2006; Pounder, Reitzug, & Young, 2002; Theoharis, 2007). Transformative leaders, therefore, are mindful of the democratic aims of schooling and do not regard themselves as needing to hold too much power and authority because they know they cannot lead alone.

Altogether, leading for transformation requires a collaborative effort between school administrators, teachers, staff, students, families, and partners from the broader community. As a result, educational leaders guide school reform efforts with a sense of clarity about their commitments and goals, a desire to build trusting relationships with school community members, a willingness to share leadership and power, and an ability to exit their comfort zone and take risks as they confront politically charged issues for the sake of building equitable learning environments that serve all children well (Cooper, 2009a; Cooper, Allen, & Bettez, 2009; Evans, 2000; Brown, 2004; Theoharis, 2007).

Despite the plethora of scholarship that stresses the value of transformative leadership that is collaborative and shared, school administrators and teachers are most commonly named as the key collaborators. The roles of parents, families and other community members are rarely considered. As discussed in later sections, scholarship that meaningfully integrates school-family-community relations into leadership frameworks is emerging (Auerbach, 2007; Cooper, 2009a; López, Gonzalez, & Fierro, 2006; López, Scribner, & Mahitivanichcha, 2001), as are practical discussions of how to integrate school-family partnership building into leadership practice (FINE, 2009; Henderson, Mapp, Johnson, & Davies, 2009). Still, the school-family relations literature remains largely untapped in educational leadership, though it offers important insight about how to develop successful, strong and inclusive school communities.

Considering the Roles of Families in School Communities

Parents and families have long been recognized as pivotal stakeholders in and contributors to student learning within the school-family relations literature (Constantino, 2003; Cooper, 2009b; Cooper & Christie, 2005; Epstein, 2001; Fine, 1993; Tutwiler, 2005). Likewise, educators and policy makers generally accept that when families feel welcomed in schools, have positive relationships with educators, and promote children's academic success, they also help increase students' motivation and learning (Constantino, 2003; Tutwiler, 2005). This acknowledgement is reflected in a variety of federal legislation and national and standards, such as No Child Left Behind Act mandates that call for educators to partner with parents, and, the Interstate Leadership Licensure Consortium's urging for educational leaders to "build and sustain positive relationships with families and caregivers" to improve student learning (Council of Chief State School Officers, 2008, p. 15; U.S. Department of Education, 2008). Still, as Constantino (2003) contends, "before there is achievement, there needs to be engagement," which requires educators to take an active role in getting to know and reaching out to families (p. 5).

Whereas the term parent "involvement" has traditionally referred to parents participating in specific school- and home-based activities to assist teachers and boost their children's academic achievement and school readiness, the term "engagement" pertains to broader and more inclusive ways that educators can help connect parents and other family members to learning, governing, and social and community-building processes that aim to not only increase their children's learning but to also enhance the life and climate of school communities (Auerbach, 2007; Cooper & Christie, 2005; Constantino, 2003; Henderson et al., 2009). Altogether, critical scholars and educators consider engagement as having a more collaborative and democratic aim that involves educators and families working together and participating in dialogue, negotiation, and a range of substantive educational activities.

Though outreach approaches that seek to engage families as true partners in the educational lives of children are greatly needed, many educational leaders still desire and expect parents and families to assume traditional parent involvement roles. Such roles include classroom volunteering, attending parent meetings and extracurricular programs, and participating in parent councils, offering homework help, reading, and encouraging children to adopt a strong work ethic and a love of learning (Cooper & Christie, 2005; Delgado-Gaitan, 1994; Epstein, 2001; Jackson & Cooper, 1989; Lareau, 1999; Smalley & Reyes-Blanes, 2001). All of these involvement activities are important, yet I also emphasize (Cooper, 2009b) the importance of acknowledging that parents and other family caregivers involve themselves in children's education in additional ways that are important but undervalued. Indeed, some families participate in advocacy, political activism and social resistance that fall outside traditional parent involvement models.

Educational involvement, particularly among marginalized families, can include:

advocating for the interests and needs of children before inequity arises; confronting educators to speak out against perceived inequities; engaging in organized protests to

bring about educational reform; and choosing alternative schools when traditional
public schools lack satisfactory teachers, resources and fair policies. (Cooper, 2009b)

These are all significant, action-oriented steps family caregivers take to engage
the educational arena on a higher level, but educators often dismiss or criticize
such action as combative and nonproductive (Cooper, 2007). Nevertheless,
when families take these steps they are exuding their own sense of leadership
because they feel they and their children have been overlooked and excluded
by educators. Consequently, educational leaders who make a proactive effort
to solicit all families' feedback, include them in decision-making, respond to
their needs, and value the contribution they make to their children's lives have
a better chance of cultivating alliances with families instead fueling adversarial
relationships. Such proactive efforts can also decrease the amount of conflicts
that emerge. To date, however, this type of transformative practice is uncommon; and thus, the structure, power and culture of schools continue to greatly
clash with the structure, culture and lack of power that many families possess.[1]

Structure, Culture, and Power Clashes between Families and Schools

Educators and scholars have highlighted the need for schools to better understand, engage, and communicate with parents and families of all racial, ethnic,
and class backgrounds while being sensitive to cultural differences (Epstein,
2001; Noguera, 2001; Tutwiler, 2005). Nevertheless, many studies that shed
light on educators' responsiveness to African American, Asian, Latino, and
white families show that schools are not doing enough to seriously consider
the distinct experiences, challenges, and assets of culturally and linguistically
diverse families, nor are they recognizing how the structure, culture, and
power of schools can clash with those of families (Cooper, 2007; Evans, 2007;
Lareau, 2003; Hidalgo, Sui, & Epstein, 2004; Moll, 2005; Valenzuela, 1999;
Lareau, 2003).

According to the typical power structure in schools, administrators are
situated at the top, with teachers in the middle, and students and families at
the bottom. The few structures and forums open to family participation, most
notably parent teacher organizations (e.g., parent–teacher organization [PTO]
and parent–teacher association [PTA]), grant very limited power to parents,
leaving them to organize social and fundraising events versus influence curricular, instructional, or organizational decisions (Henderson et al., 2009;
Henry, 1996). Indeed, research continues to supports Fine's (1993) conclusion

that parents "are usually not welcomed, by schools, to the critical and serious work of rethinking educational structures and practices" (p. 683). The dichotomy that positions educators as experts and parents as helpers is upheld as well; therefore, little is done to reexamine the traditional power structure of schools or the participatory role of families (Abrams & Gibbs, 2002; Cooper & Christie, 2005; Gonzalez, 2005; Henry, 1996). This is complicated by the tendency of public schools to privilege the values, voices, knowledge and norms of white middle-class families thereby empowering this group to influence the educational process more than others (Cooper, 2007, 2009b; Tutwiler, 2005). As a result, not all families are held in the same esteem, nor are they equally equipped with the understanding, status, and ability to navigate the public education system to adequately support their children (Abrams & Gibbs, 2002; Cooper, 2009b; Evans, 2007; Gonzalez, 2005; Henry, 1996).

Several scholars have drawn upon Bourdieu's cultural capital theory to assert that low-income families and families of color lack the "languages, customs, styles, and behaviors" that educators value; thus, many educators consciously exclude or unwittingly marginalize them (Abrams & Gibbs, 2002, p. 385; Lareau & Horvat, 1999; Henry, 1996). Social capital theorists explain that this type of exclusion hinders culturally and linguistically diverse families from cultivating important social networks and accessing school power structures (Noguera, 2001).

Indeed, too often deficit-based notions of difference cause educators to uphold stereotypes that are associated with particular racial, class, linguistic, and family backgrounds and then view poor students and families of color as inferior. Educational discourse and ideologies that automatically cast certain families as "uninvolved" or inadequate are therefore perpetuated along with exclusionary and segregating schooling practices (Cooper, 2007, 2009b; DeGaetano, 2007; Lightfoot, 2004; López, Scribner, & Mahitivanichcha, 2001). As a result, the same families that educators deem as inactive become alienated in an educational system they wish to contribute to and inform.

In a study of parent education programs, Lightfoot (2004) compared discourse and texts geared towards upper-middle class, U.S.-born parents and those geared towards immigrant parents. She found that even well-meaning educators (and equity-oriented scholars collaborating in such work) can perpetuate a deficit-based discourse that projects an "empty" versus "full" binary (p. 97). This binary contrasts low-income parents of color who are framed as "at-risk" and having little to contribute to schools against upper- and middle-class parents—many of whom are white—who are perceived as having desirable resources or "giving too much" (p. 97, 98). In addition, research involving culturally and linguistically diverse families shows they are usually aware of and disturbed by educators' bias (Abrams & Gibbs, 2002; Cooper, 2009b; Delgado-Gaitan, 2001). These families painfully perceive educators as discounting them and therefore underserving their children. Moreover, Abrams and Gibbs (2002) studied the educational perceptions and experiences of African American, Latino, and White parents and found that parents often view schools as being "available only to white parents who participate in the PTA" while being "closed" to other parents and families (p. 397). They further conclude that the power inequities between educators and parents and the power inequities among parents affect both groups' status and influence within schools.

Other studies, some of which draw upon critical race analyses, have shown that well-intentioned educators who have wanted to promote equity in schools claim to maintain colorblind beliefs and practices (Cooper, 2009a; Evans, 2007). Such educators assert that racial and ethnic differences are not salient and that all people are the same, so all families should be engaged in the same way. The colorblind approach to engaging culturally and linguistically diverse families proves problematic because it reduces educators' ability to be culturally responsive to students and families. It prompts educators to overlook or minimize valid cultural differences that affect how families view the role of schools, how they socially construct their educational involvement role, and how they interact with educators. Moreover, the colorblind approach often leads educators to avoid understanding white privilege, deny the affects of systemic bias, and perpetuate inequities (Cooper, 2009a; Evans, 2007; Tutwiler, 2005; Rosenburg, 2004; Sheilds, 2000).

The so-called "colorblind" educators who strive to leave difference unacknowledged in the name of equity end up maintaining the status quo they wish to disrupt. For instance, in her study of educators' response to rising African American populations in suburban schools, Evans (2007) found that these educators become complicit in socially reproducing a schooling culture that normalizes whiteness in the face of growing cultural diversity. Similarly, I found in my research that schools tend to reinforce a system of racialized parental privilege as well as class and language-based biases (Cooper, 2009a,b).

Linking Family Engagement and Educational Leadership

Research on school-family relations reveals a myriad of educational issues that warrant greater attention from educational leaders, yet these studies are not widely targeted to educational leadership audiences, nor do educational leadership journals and curriculum commonly incorporate such important material. As Auerbach (2007) found after completing a comprehensive literature review, "There is a perplexing disconnect between the literature on parent involvement, including leadership for parent involvement, and the literature on collaborative leadership," (p. 704). Nevertheless, scholarship that offers such linkage is slowly growing. In the following section, I highlight three varied studies that explicitly connect family engagement and educational leadership to offer important findings and innovative conceptual schemes that can advance efforts to make family engagement part of transformative educational practice. Together, the studies suggest that educational leaders tend to view family engagement as a symbolic role they must fulfill and/or one that narrowly pertains to raising student achievement. They also seek to "manage" and assess culturally and socially diverse families according to middle-class, white norms, and they can fail to adequately address the cultural biases and tensions affecting families that undermine learning communities.

Engagement as Symbolic and Limited to Student Achievement Goals

In a detailed study that links family engagement issues with educational leadership frameworks, Auerbach (2007) examined school and district officials' leadership vision, role, capacity, constraints, and tools as they pertain to fostering parent engagement in urban, culturally diverse, Title I schools. The twelve leaders she discusses are based in the Los Angeles Unified School District. They lead schools and subdistricts that serve immigrant families from numerous ethnic backgrounds and the families are linguistically diverse. Auerbach, in part, found that educational leaders often deem cultivating positive family relations as an important part of their job; yet, they regard doing so as being essential only because parents and families can help boost student achievement. Other educational leaders view family engagement as being an add-on duty that has less importance than their achievement-oriented responsibilities. Moreover, she found that many administrators approach parent involvement and family engagement as a "mostly symbolic" gesture that entails making community appearances, welcoming families to schools, and meeting with them to hear their grievances, rather than involving them in decision-making and school-improvement initiatives.

Auerbach (2007) explains that the tendency to separate family engagement out from a broader focus on learning, relationship building, and the "moral of leadership of democratic schools" is reinforced by federal, state, and district politics that attach high stakes to student test score performance and by leadership preparation programs that do little to teach educators how to develop good family partnerships (p. 711).

Drawing upon Honig's theories of school-community connections, Auerbach analyzes the leaders' approach to parents and families and identifies several categories that capture how leaders construct their role, including those who are (a) "visionaries and modelers" who engage families in substantive dialogue, interactions and decision-making, (b) "resource mobilizers" who work to gather funding and organization tools to sponsor parent involvement activities, (c) "listeners and facilitators" who are accessible to parents and try to respond to their concerns and needs, often in a reactive versus proactive way; and (d) "responsive managers" who invite families to schools but are relatively hands off, endorse traditional parent activities and are managerial in their approach (pp. 725-726). Auerbach applauds the few leaders she studied who view "parent engagement as integral to the broader mission of leading urban schools for social justice and community uplift" and who understand that engaging families is needed "not only for student achievement but for family life-long learning, health, and development, as well as for expanded access to educational opportunity and equity-oriented school reform," (pp. 727-728).

Engagement Managed and Assessed by White Middle-Class Norms

Henry (1996) identifies several ways educational leaders are hesitant to embrace families as partners in her older, but very insightful, study of family-school collaboration in a predominantly white, well-resourced school district in the Rocky Mountain region of the United States. She notes a range of equity-oriented tensions that involve district and school leaders: vying to hold on to their power and authority; being resistant to alter traditional school structures in order to involve parents in governing; imposing middle-class, white school involvement norms on all families, regardless of race, ethnicity or class; and doing little to address the cultural discontinuity between school culture and students' home culture. Instead, she found the superintendent and principals to be more influenced by "traditional administrative practices for school-community relations" that are "aimed at disarming critics, 'selling' the school through public relations such as newsletters, activities," and "teaching parents and others how they should relate to school" (p. 138). Henry found that leaders most widely used managerial approaches in governing schools, particularly when interacting with low-income families and students and parents of color, as opposed to shared leadership approaches that promote collaborative structures and norms.

With regard to what Henry (1996) calls the imposition of a "White middle class culture of school," (p. 109) she asserts:

> The language, rituals, and symbolism of schooling is no one's first language, but it is more closely synonymous with, for instance, white rather than black culture, middle class rather than working class. In addition, if "minority" students have to learn to use a "majority" cultural code, the cultural cards are stacked against them in terms of ease of access and knowledge and self-esteem, which is linked to school success. (p. 110)

Henry emphasizes the value and contribution of culturally diverse families and importance of their knowledge and caring, yet she associates the Westernized, rational-technical, and efficiency-based model of schooling that has become so prevalent in the United States with white, middle class culture that is different from—not inferior to—other cultural models. Furthermore, she appeals to educational leaders to embrace a more collaborative, inclusive and culturally responsive approach to engaging families. This approach stems from Henry's conceptualization of school-family collaboration that is grounded in feminist theory and in "an ethic of care and connectedness" (p. 19). She explains how employing feminist frameworks can benefit both men and women, and states, "instead of autonomy, separation, distance, and a mechanistic view of the world, feminism values nurturing, empathy, a caring perspective," (p. 20). Henry then interweaves consideration of such values into her analysis of school-family relations.

Engagement Thwarted by Cultural Bias and Tensions

Some of the themes related to cultural marginalization that Henry (1996) and others found in prior studies have proven to be salient to more recent research. For instance, I examined the structural, cultural, and political clashes between educators and families in North Carolina elementary schools experiencing rapid demographic change, and data from my comparative case study indicated that brooding tensions were emerging between educators—both white and African American—and African American and Latino families (Cooper, 2009a; Cooper, Allen, & Bettez, 2009). These tensions relate to the fast growth of Latinos in the region and the ways that biased and fear-based notions of cultural difference influence teacher ideology, educators' approach to family engagement, families' perceptions of each other, and educational leadership overall.

Data from the two schools I studied also indicated that patterns of social and academic segregation were occurring in the schools, particularly at one of the schools whose leadership team decided to start holding separate meetings for English-speaking and Spanish-speaking parents to be more efficient and make everyone feel "more comfortable" (Cooper, 2009a). A Spanish-speaking parent, however, was not on the leadership team to inform this decision. The principal framed the decision as an attempt for the leadership team to be culturally responsive, but it was unclear how that choice ultimately affected families. It was evident that the separate meetings decreased opportunities for various families to interact, and I question whether that their separation will increase the social and cultural divides between families.

Indeed, various school community members expressed biases about culturally diverse, Spanish-speaking and low-income families inside the schools. Some white parents emphasized their concern that Latinos "outnumber us," and a few parents were more severe in voicing alarm because "you cannot go anywhere without seeing a Mexican." Such xenophobic comments relate to the alarmist views of some of the long-term residents of the school community who fear diversification and feel threatened as they observe their conservative, Southern towns moving beyond the narrow, black–white racial dynamics that have characterized the town's and school's history. The African American principal in the study noted that she thinks accommodating Latinos in North Carolina schools is a challenge as well. African American parents, on the other hand, expressed little concern about this. They, instead, focused on their educational concerns and experiences with inequity. Some suggested that educators overlooked or devalued parents who were not formally educated.

Latino parents also focused on equity issues. They spoke highly of the principals' friendliness and responsiveness, yet said they wished teachers were more friendly, acknowledging of the fact that Latino parents care about their kids, and not quick to underestimate their children's intelligence or potential because of their immigrant status and "the language barrier" that educators were so quick to pinpoint. The Latino parent coordinator at one of the schools was very concerned about the deficit-based thinking of teachers. She said she wished teachers would visit students' home to get a better understanding of them, their family, their culture, and their financial struggles to see "why they dress the way they do" and "why they may not come to school with all the things the other kids have." The coordinator noted teachers' tendency to equate Latino families' limited financial resources with cultural-based disadvantages. Indeed, numerous teachers and parents asserted biased remarks or reported hearing prejudiced comments from their peers in the schools; still, other teachers, staff members and parents emphasized their disdain for the prejudiced and xenophobic reactions of others.

In addition, biases were described as affecting the reputations of the schools in their broader communities. For instance, a white, parent-staff member at one of the schools stated that that the demographic change occurring at the school caused others to regard it as a place in which it was "dirty to work or go to school" (Cooper, Allen, & Bettez, 2009).

One of the most remarkable findings from the study was that, compared to teachers, staff and parents, data indicated that the principals were not as aware or distressed by the cultural biases and tensions affecting their schools. In fact, it was a school counselor (white female) who was most frank in describing cultural tensions. She simply stated, "Racism is here." Though, the principals voiced a commitment to cultural inclusion and equity in their schools, they stopped short of fully enacting transformative leadership. For example, the principals took positive steps to promote family engagement and to develop a school environment that was welcoming to all on the surface such as: hiring the full-time, bilingual parent coordinator; partnering with a local senior citizen home to enhance their grandparent–student mentoring program; providing health and literacy resources to low-income and non-English-speaking families; and scheduling regular parent meetings and family-friendly social events. According to the principals, they also assisted their staff in considering the racial balance of students' classroom assignments and they stood a strong moral ground in emphasizing to teachers, staff, and parents their expectations that all students and families be treated with respect and equality. The principals further held their ground in the face of some white parents' threat to exit and flee to more predominantly white schools (Cooper, 2009a; Cooper, Allen, & Bettez, 2009).

The principals, on the other hand, did not pinpoint cultural bias or tension as a major problem in their schools, nor did they indicate any intention of addressing their schools' emerging tensions at a systems level. Instead, they commented that "things are getting better," explained their efforts to counsel intolerant teachers and communicate to them that "maybe you need to go." The principals said they planned to continue to support positive efforts like teachers forming a multicultural committee and increasing the resources and use of interpreters so Spanish-speaking families could be more included at events. The principals, however, did not seize important opportunities to ex-amine bias; learn how such bias was affecting teaching, learning, and relation-ships; resolve conflict; and further build community.

In a 2009 discussion of my study, I draw upon Cornel West's (1999) criti-cal philosophies of the new cultural politics of difference to consider the im-plications of the study's findings. I extend West's notion of cultural work so that it encompasses transformative leadership, and I propose how educational leaders can perform cultural work in demographically changing schools to "in-spire and mobilize others to cross or deconstruct borders that keep school community members divided" (Cooper, 2009a). I overview the concept of cul-tural work in the next section of this chapter to more specifically consider how performing cultural work can help educators better integrate family engage-ment practices with transformative leadership strategies.

Performing Cultural Work to Embrace and Engage Families

Families and educators could potentially form strong, powerful allegiances that benefit children because they are the most influential people in children's lives, they care deeply about children's social, emotional, physical and educa-tional welfare, and they typically work extremely hard to teach and nurture children. Nevertheless, as Lightfoot (1978) asserted decades ago, traditional school management hierarchies, the lack of trust between educators and fami-lies, and discontinuities between home and school cultures too often keep educators and families "worlds apart."

Both educators' and families' notions of difference and perceptions of each other as the nonunderstanding "other" deepens that chasm that separates them, causing them to be adversaries at times instead of allies, especially when they differ along racial, ethnic, class, and linguistic lines. The groups can find themselves at odds when they perceive each others' differences as detrimental barriers rather than as an asset or resource. West (1999) provides a critical and comprehensive conceptual framework regarding the "new cultural politics of difference" that cautions against one conceptualizing cultural difference along dominant, Anglocentric dimensions that negate the knowledge, values, norms, and cultures of people of color—relegating them to a position of perceived in-feriority within institutions and in society-at-large. The framework also calls for one to: gain and value multicultural and interdisciplinary sources of knowl-edge; engage in critical self-reflection; explore the social and cultural contexts and identities of people, communities, institutions, and norms; systematically critique inequities; denounce separatist politics that reify social, cultural and political divisions among people; and, collaborate with others to combat injustice. Engaging in these practices constitutes one performing "cultural work." Performing cultural work can be an essential part of enacting transformative leadership for social justice. Indeed, West's description of cultural work complements the transformative aspects of leadership that various critical education scholars describe (Cooper, Allen & Bettez, 2009; Dantley & Tillman, 2006; Johnson, 2007; López, Gonzalez, & Fierro, 2006; Shields, 2000; Shields & Sayani, 2005). Still, the cultural work concept is not often linked to K-12 school leadership contexts. I believe connecting the notion of cultural work, which West applies to social critics and artists, can broaden our vision of transformative possibilities. I have asserted that:

> Within the context of educational leadership, a cultural worker is an educator who validates and draws upon knowledge that is critical, multicultural and interdisciplinary. She or he recognizes and cultivates cultural capital among culturally and linguistically diverse students and families; forges collaborative relationships with school community members; and shares leadership while forming alliances with those who hold a similar vision of equity and inclusiveness. A cultural worker is also a transformative educational leader who maintains political clarity, demonstrates courage, and takes risks to advance social justice. Accomplishing these objectives is essential when leading culturally diverse and demographically changing schools. (Cooper, 2009a)

Performing cultural work as a transformative educational leader has specific implications given the need for inclusive, collaborative, and culturally responsive family partnerships. These implications go beyond the importance of raising test scores and more deeply pertain to changing the culture of school communities. The implications indicate the need for educational leaders to guide their school community members in countering deficit thinking, developing collaborative decision-making structures, and seeking to resolve equity-oriented conflicts and cultural tensions.

Implications for Transformative Leadership

For educational leaders to be transformative, they must address the divergences between educators, students, and families that threaten to hinder student learning and the life of schools. The research on school-family-leadership relations specifically reveals three overarching trends that pose challenges that educational leaders should tackle.

Countering Deficit Thinking and Cultural Bias

The first trend is that families of color and those from urban or low-income backgrounds are too often unwelcomed and/or criticized in school settings. These families are critiqued for not being sufficiently involved in their children's schooling; and, at worst, they are deemed as uncaring and/or detrimental to their children's education (Cooper, 2009b; De Gaetano, 2007; Henderson et al., 2009). Some educators judge these families as having values and culture that undermine academic achievement, or, as simply being unpleasant and hard to "manage" (Auerbach, 2007; Cooper, 2007; Noguera, 2001). Consequently, educational leaders must tackle the deficit-based thinking of teachers, parents, staff, students, and themselves. An important first step can be examining one's conceptualization of "difference" and guiding others in examining all the assumptions, biases, and stereotypes that stem from their conceptualization (Cooper, Allen, & Bettez, 2009). As Shields (2000) states:

> . . . if we are to use differences as resources, we will need to overcome stereotypes and focus on understanding the interplay of richness and complexity which individuals and groups contribute to the development of community norms. (p. 282)

Developing this type of understanding embodies cultural work that rejects essentialized views of personal identities and appreciates how, if inequitable power structures are left unchecked, educational inequalities, and tense relationships between educators and families will be reified (West, 1999).

Many written and online resources by critical multicultural educators describe instructional, curricular, professional-development, and community-building strategies that educators can use to guide school communities in critical self-reflection, dialogue, and reform. Some of these resources can be found on the Web sites of the National Association for Multicultural Education (http://www.nameorg.org/) and the EDCHANGE organization (http://www.edchange.org/) and in guidebooks such as and *Beyond Heroes and Holidays: A Practical Guide to K-12 Anti-Racist, Multicultural Education and Staff Development*, which provide critical readings, lessons plans, and relationship building activities for educators' use (Lee, Menkart & Okinawa-Rey, 2008).

Developing Collaborative Decision-Making Structures

Second, research suggests that even when families are present in schools their participation is constrained due to the limited involvement roles that educators invite them to fulfill. Many schools lack collaborative and democratic decision-making structures that solicit and respond to families in a substantive way. Families are instead ushered into assistance-oriented roles where they can provide "helping hands" in classrooms, fundraisers, and social events (Cooper & Christie, 2005; Henderson et al., 2009). Moreover, as Henry (1996) found, educational leaders can feel that "loss of control over the policies and operations of the school is threatening"; thus, educators' sense of control is "jealously guarded" (p. 55). This struggle to retain control does not necessarily mean leaders are merely power hungry, but rather they do not trust the insight and capabilities of families to be sensitive to broader reform needs and to the political pressures that compel educators to be so achievement oriented. This trend may be fueled by some good intentions, but it is still paternalistic and problematic.

Based on my own research, teaching, and involvement in school-family programs, I sense that many times educational leaders do not deliberately restrict the roles of families in schools out of a desire to be exclusive. Instead, educators can lack vision about how to engage families in meaningful ways because they have not been taught how to develop inclusive partnerships in leadership preparation programs, nor has inclusive partnership building been modeled to them in practice. Some educators also feel they have to take "baby steps" to just get parents "through the door," and they believe that such steps mean creating a friendly school environment and hosting social events. In the words of a principal from my North Carolina study, "If you make them feel wanted, they will come."

While an incremental approach to partnership building is sometimes needed, educators should be careful to not stifle family engagement by resigning themselves to only acknowledge, request and expect minimal site-based participation. Valuing and engaging families in a range of activities and roles is essential—including those that are practical, festive, learning based, and governance related. In addition, the advocacy and activist-oriented activities of families constitute important forms of engagement that, while not always pleasant to confront, promote democratic schooling, and can serve as needed wake-up calls to educators who are unaware or irresponsive to students and families' needs.

Creating more meaningful ways to engage families requires transformative educational leaders to do more to establish collaborative, decision-making structures and offer opportunities for all school community members to engage in dialogue, planning, and negotiation. This can mean soliciting diverse family representation on leadership teams, holding town hall–type of forums where families also participate in small interactive group activities, and involving students and families in professional learning communities (Cooper, 2009b; Cooper, Allen, & Bettez, 2009). Special effort should be made to engage low-income families of color and other marginalized families. Fostering collaboration among various community members who are vested with disparate amounts of power is another vital element of cultural work. Indeed, performing cultural work entails taking up the new cultural politics of difference that West (1999) describes to counteract cultural separatism and racial segregation. Cultural work further consists of "forging solid and reliable alliances of people of color and white progressives guided by a moral and political vision of greater democracy and individual freedom in communities, . . ." (West, 1999, p. 136). This is work that transformative leaders in culturally diverse settings who are committed to social justice routinely strive to do.

Online resources such as the Web site for the Family Involvement Network of Educators (FINE) (http://www.hfrp.org/family-involvement/fine-family-involvement-network-of-educators) based at Harvard University provide examples of successful strategies, programs, and research related to developing inclusive school partnerships with families and communities. This site also provides information about workshops and conferences that are geared toward educational practitioners and it distributes online newsletters that educational leaders may find very helpful. Furthermore, several educators involved in the FINE network recently published a thoughtful guide that offers a range of practical tips and resources for developing collaborative partnerships that engage culturally diverse populations (Henderson et al., 2009).

Resolving Equity-Oriented Conflicts and Culture Clashes

The third trend evident in the school-family-leadership studies is that educational leaders often strive to be colorblind and/or fail to address racial/ethnic tensions in schools. Educational leaders, however, must be prepared to address the conflicts that naturally arise in schools, especially when families are actively engaged. Maintaining colorblind stances and not acknowledging the social and cultural differences among educators, students and families is counterproductive to developing schools that are culturally responsive. Avoiding conflict and uncomfortable dialogue related to equity and diversity can also mean avoiding the social and educational growth of school community members and missing opportunities to help prepare children to thrive in a multicultural society where difference is the norm (Shields, 2000; Shields & Sayani,

2005; Theoharis, 2007). In fact, West (1999) reviews a plethora of political, social, and artistic movements to remind us that transformation without tension is impossible and agitation is typically the catalyst for change. Hence, transformative educational leaders who serve as cultural workers accept that without conflict, and occasionally crises, "transformation degenerates into more accommodation or sheer stagnation" (West, p. 120). Ignoring conflict, therefore, leaves educators in a place of complacency that eventually undermines their reform efforts and credibility.

Of course, developing effective family engagement practices can be challenging, complex and very time-consuming. It involves learning, valuing, and interacting with knowledge, culture, and people in new and different ways, which educational leaders need assistance and support to do. Thus, it is imperative that higher education play a larger role in preparing educational leaders to better engage families. Curriculum that addresses family and community engagement should be incorporated into leadership programs along with field-based activities that require educators to visit student homes, spend time in culturally and economically diverse communities, and identify potential community-based partners. I have found educators especially learn from participating in activities such as community walks that require students to map the assets of students' communities and home visits in which they identity families' strengths and funds of knowledge (Gonzalez, 2005). Henderson et al. (2009) describe versions of such activities in their book *Beyond the Bake Sale: The Essential Guide to Family-School Partnerships*.

Incorporating family and community engagement activities into administrative internship requirements could also help to better prepare educational leaders, as could the development of school-university partnerships through which K-12 educators, university faculty members, families, students, and community organizations collaborate to strengthen schools. In their book *Learning Power*, Oakes, Rogers, and Lipton (2006) document the development and implementation of a successful school-university partnership spearheaded by University of California, Los Angeles researchers. Educational leaders would likely gain from also exploring the information about Pepperdine University's Urban Parent/Teacher Education Collaborative (UPTEC) that is coordinated by Professor Tony Collatos and greatly influenced by parent activist Mary Johnson (https://gsep.pepperdine.edu/urban-initiative/initiatives-with-community-partners/urban-parent-teacher-education-collaborative-uptec/).

Last, it would be advantageous for scholars to research successful school-family-community partnerships at the school, district, community and state level, analyze the policies that help support this work, and document the narratives and practices of educational leaders who have successfully guided their schools in developing the partnerships through transformative leadership.

Conclusion

Families are not engaged as collaborators or educational partners nearly enough despite popular policy rhetoric and calls for shared leadership from both traditional and critical educational scholars and reformers. Indeed, integrating an inclusive, culturally responsive, and collaborative approach to building school-family partnerships is a challenge for educators not only because their professional preparation does not typically train them to do so, but because collaborations that are grounded in democratic and social justice ideals counter the culture of U.S. schooling.

Public education in the United States remains driven by an accountability system that is steeped in rational-technical and efficiency norms and narrowly focused on producing achievement outcomes. Embracing and engaging families as partners in schools, however, requires educational leaders to perform cultural work that also emphasizes inputs. Indeed, both the new cultural politics of difference framework and critical conceptions of transformative leadership stress vital elements of transformation that standardized tests cannot measure, such as trust, dialogue, power sharing, relationships, risk-taking, and crossing social and cultural borders to break down biases and build alliances (Cooper, 2009b; Cooper & Gause, 2007; López, Gonzalez, & Fierro, 2006; Shields & Sayani, 2005; Theoharis, 2007; West, 1999).

Transformative educational leadership is not the domain of school administrators alone; families, teachers, students, and other school community members can and should be part of the process. Since administrators remain situated at the top of the educational hierarchy, it is particularly important that they begin to reconceptualize their roles in more equity-oriented ways, while broadening their vision of collaboration, taking action to redress inequities, and being prepared by higher education leaders and educational mentors to do so. The conceptual frames, strategies, and resources I have discussed in this chapter are aimed at bringing those of us vested in transformative educational leadership together to assist educators in performing this essential cultural work.

Note

1. I call (Cooper, 2007) for scholars to address how "the structure, culture and power of schools can sharply counter" that of families (p. 507). The discussion in this chapter represents my efforts to answer that call and explain how clashes between schools and families occur in light of the parent involvement and leadership research.

References

Abrams, L. S., and Gibbs, J. T. (2002). Disrupting the logic of home-school relations: Parent involvement strategies and practices of inclusion and exclusion. *Urban Education, 37*(3), 384–407.

Auerbach, S. (2007). Visioning parent engagement in urban schools. *Journal of School Leadership, 17*(6), 699–734.

Brown, K. M. (2004). Leadership for social justice and equity: Weaving a transformative framework and pedagogy. *Education Administration Quarterly, 40*(1), 77–108.

Constantino, S. M. (2003). *Engaging all families: Creating a positive school culture by putting research into practice.* Lanham, MD: Scarecrow Education.

Cooper, C. W. (2007). School choice as "motherwork": Valuing African American women's educational advocacy and resistance. *International Journal of Qualitative Studies in Education, 20*(5), 491–512.

Cooper, C. W. (2009a). Performing cultural work in demographically changing schools: Implications for expanding transformative leadership frameworks. *Educational Administration Quarterly, 45* (5), 694–724 .

Cooper, C. W. (2009b). Parent involvement, African American mothers, and the politics of educational care. *Equity and Excellence in Education, 42*(4), 379–394.

Cooper, C. W., Allen, R., & Bettez, S. (2009). Forming culturally responsive learning communities in demographically changing schools. In C. A. Mullen (Ed.), *The handbook of leadership and professional learning communities.* (pp. 103–114). London: Palgrave Macmillan.

Cooper, C. W., & Christie, C. A. (2005). Evaluating parent empowerment: A look at the potential of social justice evaluation in education. *Teachers College Record, 107*(10), 2248–2271.

Cooper, C. W., & Gause, C. P. (2007). Who's afraid of the big bad wolf? Confronting identity politics and student resistance when teaching for social justice. In D. Carlson and C. P. Gause (Eds.), *Keeping the promise: Essays on leadership, democracy and education* (pp. 197–216). New York: Peter Lang.

Council of Chief State School Officers (2008). *Educational Leadership Policy Standards: ISLLC 2008 as Adopted by the National Policy Board for Educational Administration.* Online access at http://www.ccsso.org/publications/details.cfm?PublicationID=365. Accessed January 11, 2010.

Dantley, M., & Tillman, L. C. (2006). Social justice and moral transformative leadership. In C. Marshall and M. Oliva (Eds.), *Leadership for Social Justice: Making Revolutions in Education* (pp. 16–30). Boston, MA: Pearson Education.

De Gaetano, Y. (2007). The role of culture in engaging Latino parents' involvement in school. *Urban Education, 42*(2), 145–162.

Delgado-Gaitan, C. (2001). *The power of community: Mobilizing for family and schooling.* Lanham, MD: Rowman & Littlefield.

EDCHANGE http://www.edchange.org/ Accessed June 13, 2009.

Epstein, J. (2001). Toward a theory of family-school connections: Teacher practices and parent involvement. In J. L. Epstein (Ed.), *School, family, and community partnerships" Preparing educators and improving schools.* Boulder, CO: Westview Press.

Evans, A. E. (2007). Changing faces: Suburban school responses to demographic change. *Education and Urban Society, 39*(3) 315-348.

Evans, R. (2000). The authentic leader. In *The Jossey-Bass reader on educational leadership.* San Francisco, CA: John Wiley & Sons, Inc.

Family Involvement Network of Educators (FINE). http://www.hfrp.org/family-involvement/fine-family-involvement-network-of-educators. Accessed June 13, 2009.

Fine, M. (1993). [Ap]parent involvement: Reflections on parents, power, and urban public schools. *Teachers College Record, 94*(4), 682-708.

Frattura, E. M., & Capper, C. A. (2007). *Leading for social justice: Transforming schools for all learners.* Thousand Oaks, CA: Corwin Press.

Gonzalez, N. (2005). Beyond culture: The hybridity of funds of knowledge. In N. Gonzalez, L. C. Moll, & C. Amanti (Eds.), *Funds of Knowledge: Theorizing practices in households, communities, and classrooms.* Mahwah, NJ: Lawrence Erlbaum.

Henderson, A. T., Mapp, K. L., Johnson, V. R., & Davies, D. (2009). *Beyond the bake sale: The essential guide to family–school partnerships.* New York: The New Press.

Henry, M. (1996). *Parent-school collaboration: Feminist organizational structures and school leadership.* Albany: State University of New York Press.

Hidalgo, N. M., Sui, S-F., & Epstein, J. L. (2004). Research on families, schools, and communities: A multicultural perspective. In J. A. Banks & C. A. M. Banks (Eds.), *Handbook of research on multicultural education* (pp 631-655). San Francisco, CA: Jossey-Bass.

Jackson, B. L.,& Cooper, B. S. (1989). Parent choice and empowerment: New role for parents. *Urban Education, 24*(3), 263-286.

Johnson, L. (2007). Making her community a better place to live: Lessons from history for culturally responsive urban school leadership. In D. Carlson and C. P. Gause (Eds.), *Keeping the promise: Essays on leadership, democracy and education* (pp. 269-285). New York: Peter Lang.

Lareau, A. (2003). *Unequal Childhoods: Class, race, and family life.* Berkeley, CA: University of California Press.

Lareau, A., & Horvat, E. M. (1999). Moments of social inclusion and exclusion race, class, and cultural capital in family-like relationships. *Sociology of Education, 72,* 37-53.

Larson, C., & Ovando, C. (2001). *The color of bureaucracy: The politics of equity in multicultural school communities.* Belmont, CA: Wadsworth/Thomas Learning.

Lawrence-Lightfoot, S. (1978). *Worlds apart: Relationships between families and schools.* New York: Basic Books.

Lee, E., Menkart, D., & Rey-Okazawa, M. (2008). (Eds.) *Beyond heroes and holidays: A practical guide to K-12 anti-racist, multicultural education and staff development.* Washington, DC: Network of Educators on the Americas.

Lightfoot, D. (2004). "Some parents just don't care": Decoding the meanings of parental involvement in urban schools. *Urban Education, 39*(1), 91-107.

López, G. R., Gonzalez, M. L., & Fierro, E. (2006). Educational leadership along the U.S.-Mexico border: Crossing borders/embracing hybridity/ building bridges. In C. Marshall and M. Oliva (Eds.), *Leadership for Social Justice: Making Revolutions in Education.* Boston, MA: Pearson.

López, G. R., Scribner, J. D., & Mahitivanichcha, K. (2001). Redefining parental involvement: Lessons from high-performing migrant-impacted schools. *American Educational Research Journal,* 38(2), 253-288.

Marshall, C. & Oliva, M. (2006). Building the capacities of social justice leaders. In C. Marshall and M. Oliva (Eds.), *Leadership for social justice: Making revolutions in education* (pp. 1-15). Boston: Pearson Education.

Moll, L. (2005). Reflections and possibilities. In N. Gonzalez, L. C. Moll, & C. Amanti. (Eds.), *Funds of Knowledge: Theorizing practices in households, communities, and classrooms.* Lawrence Erlbaum Associates: Mahwah, NJ.

Murphy, J. T. (2000). The unheroic side of leadership. In *The Jossey-Bass reader on educational leadership.* New York: John Wiley & Sons, Inc.

National Association for Multicultural Education. http://www.nameorg.org/ Accessed June 13, 2009.

Noguera, P. A. (2001). Transforming urban schools through investments in the social capital of parents. In S. Saegart, J. P., Thompson, and M. Warren (Eds.), *Social capital and poor communities.* New York: Russell Sage Foundation.

Oakes, J., Rogers, J., & Lipton, M. (2006). *Learning Power: Organizing for education and justice.* New York: Teachers College Press.

Pounder, D., Reitzug, U., & Young, M. D. (2002). Preparing school leaders for school improvement, social justice and community. In J. Murphy (Ed.), *The educational leadership challenge: Redefining leadership for the 21st century* (pp. 261-288). Chicago, IL: University of Chicago Press.

Rosenburg, P. M. (2004). Color blindness in teacher education: An optical delusion. In M. Fine, L. Weis, L. P. Pruitt, & A. Burns (Eds.) *Off White: Readings on power, privilege, and resistance.* Second edition. New York and London: Routledge.

Shields, C. M. (2000). Learning from difference: Considerations for schools as communities. *Curriculum Inquiry,* 30(3), 275-294.

Shields, C. M., & Sayani, A. (2005). Leading in the midst of diversity: The challenge of our times. In F. W. English (Ed.), *The Sage handbook of educational leadership: Advances in theory, research, and practice.* Thousand Oaks, CA: Sage.

Smalley, S. Y., & Reyes-Blanes, M. E. (2001). Reaching out to African American parents in an urban community: A community-university partnership. *Urban Education,* 36 (4), 518-533.

Theoharis, G. (2007). Navigating rough waters: A synthesis of the countervailing pressures against leading for social justice. *Journal of School Leadership, 17*(1), 4-27.

Tutwiler, S. W. (2005). Teachers as collaborative partners: Working with diverse families and communities. Mahwah, NJ: Lawrence Erlbaum Associates.

United States Department of Education. Work with parents & the community: The Partnership (No Child Left Behind Information Page). http://www.ed.gov/parents/academic/help/partnership. html Accessed Oct 2, 2008.

Urban Parent/Teacher Education Collaborative (UPTEC). https://gsep.pepperdine.edu/urban-initiative/initiatives-with-community-partners/urban-parent-teacher-educationcollaborative-uptec/). Accessed June 13, 2009.

Valenzuela, A. (1999). *Subtractive schooling: U.S.–Mexican youth and the politics of caring.* Albany: State University of New York Press.

West, C. (1999). The new cultural politics of difference. In C. West (ed.) *The Cornel West Reader.* New York: Basic Civitas Books.

✠ CHAPTER 10

Educational Leadership in a Changing World: Preparing Students for Internationalization and Globalization through Advocacy Leadership

Elizabeth Murakami-Ramalho

In the first decade of the twenty-first century, the United States experienced adverse events that threatened the safety of its society. As a consequence of September 11, 2001, terrorist attacks, discussions concerning globalization and internationalization in schools have been limited to protecting U.S. borders and insulating our nation from others (Apple, 2002; Giroux, 2002). With the Obama administration, however, comes the possibility for renewed talks on international relations, which may spark interest in preparing students for civic engagement through internationalization and globalization. A critical understanding of our nation's role in building relations and familiarity with countries around the globe is paramount in education, especially in preparing students for a changing world.

Knowledge of international relations begins with a local preparation of multicultural education. As a foundation, multicultural education provides the fundamental basis from which we begin to understand differences and similarities at home before moving our understanding of diverse cultures beyond our borders. Addressing racism and discrimination is the first step, but not enough to prepare students for the complexity of international relations. International education expands on multicultural education as it prepares students for immersion in contemporary sociopolitical, cultural, and economic contexts and conversations. While it is important to understand how we in-fluence and are influenced by other countries, opportunities to prepare stu-dents for these changing international and global realities remain underexamined and untapped. In this chapter, I seek to explore these possi-bilities and discuss the importance of continuing conversations concerning globalization and internationalization in K-12 schools in the twenty-first cen-tury.

Internationalization, Globalization, and Critical Educational Studies

Common to multicultural education and conducive to international educa-tion is the push to invite educational leaders and teachers to engage in critical educational studies as part of their leadership and pedagogical practices. By exposing students to critical educational studies, educational leaders and teachers help students process public information, analyze facts, and under-stand world events. According to Apple (2009), "Critical educational studies turn to issues of the global, of the colonial imagination, and to postcolonial approaches in order to come to grips with the complex . . . relations between knowledge and power, between the state and education, and between civil so-ciety and the political imaginary" (p. x). Informed educators and educational leaders can inspire students to become engaged global citizens through critical studies that include international issues.

Knight (2004) defined internationalization as the "process of integrating an international, intercultural or global dimension into the purpose, functions or delivery of education" (p. 11). Guided by the work of interdisciplinary scholars focused in internationalization, globalization, and critical educational studies, I revisit their scholarship in the next section in order to examine the complexities of sociopolitical issues related to internationalism that affect edu-cators and educational leaders, students, and their families. These scholars bring up interesting points in relation to how we are constrained by local per-spectives, and why we need to provide more opportunities for critical pedago-gies in order to prepare our students and ourselves for world realities.

Understanding International and Global Contexts through Linguistics, Curriculum, and Leadership

In many years of working and researching among U.S. educational leaders and educators immersed in American international schools (Murakami-Ramalho,

2008a, 2008b), I experienced the transformation of teachers and administrators while they prepared students through multicultural and international curriculum and pedagogy. Development of all-inclusive perspectives and skills takes practice, as educators and leaders immerse themselves in schools with highly diverse populations in different countries. However, their in-depth experience and preparation, especially to prepare students of diverse backgrounds, are less recognized when they return to the United States. Why are teachers and administrators with experience in international education not valued for their expertise upon returning to their home country?

Concurrently, in America, especially in the last two decades, we were focused on the competitive world market, especially by improving student performance in the basics of K-12 curriculum. However, efforts to enhance the preparation of students in the different disciplines should not result in losing sight of the changes taking place around the world. If we focus too much on the trees, soon we lose sight of the forest. For example, I am not certain that students understand that high-stakes testing was imposed in response to low-academic-performance indicators as demonstrated by reports like the National Center for Education Statistics' Third International Mathematics and Science Study (TIMSS), in 1999, and the Programme for International Student Assessment (PISA), a triennial worldwide test of 15-year-old school children's scholastic performance, coordinated by the Organization for Economic Cooperation and Development (OECD). In both reports, the United States lagged behind several other countries in terms of mean average academic performance. Nevertheless, student cognition must still be developed as a "social activity distributed with mediational tools and artifacts connected to historical and situated culture" (Lee & Smagorinsky, 2000, p. 2). Providing students with an understanding of the disciplines is essential, embedded in informed knowledge and applied to a global context.

Internationalism vs. Nationalism

In previous research reports, I argued that even though internationalization initially is defined by using ideas of agreement, support, and cooperation (Liebeck & Pollard, 1994), in America, we may have used *internationalism* as an antonym of *nationalism*. When we are prompted to contrast the word *internationalism* against *nationalism*, we feel threatened. Social reality as cognitive frames occurs through parallelisms, according to Burbules and Torres (2000): "in things and in minds, in fields and in habitus, outside and inside of agents"

(p. 5). Internationalism, then, ceases to have a supportive and collaborative tone, and begins to revolve around a political or nation-state tension (Murakami-Ramalho, 2008b). This tension separates *us* from the *others*, preventing us from learning more about our roles and relationships in relation to other countries and continents around the globe.

Although we may consider what is foreign as threatening our national boundaries, we are daily consumers of international goods, like clothing, fuel, and technology. It seems that we place higher importance on things rather than people when it comes to understanding the word *international*. In addition, there is a difference between internationalism and globalization, even though these expressions are used interchangeably. Internationalism, I believe, is more focused on being informed about globalization movements.

Globalization, Universalization, and Commodification of Knowledge

Globalization is a phenomenon that scholars have defined in two different ways. Some scholars have focused on globalization as a universalization and commodification of knowledge, studying issues such as caring for natural resources, the progress of technologies, communication enhancement, culture, world health care, heritages, and genetic codes across civilization (Barlow & Clarke, 2002; Basiga, 2004; Scholte, 2000; Smith, 2000). Others have believed that globalization relates to political and economic processes (Burbules & Torres, 2000; Carnoy, 1999; Gabbard, 2003) that oppress people for profitable gains.

These scholars have agreed that knowledge related to globalization involves people and things. As consumers, however, we tend to pay more attention to things, whether they are products or services, instead of analyzing how these things are organized and by whom. It is important to develop knowledge about these supportive systems, especially when we are continuously leading the preparation of individuals to merge into increasingly globalized negotiations. In schools, knowledge development also involves people, and as a result, exploring the knowledge about what roles people play in facilitating the process of producing goods and services is essential, in particular regarding how this knowledge is used to benefit or hasten the demise of present and future societies.

Walker and Dimmock (2002), for example, stressed the importance of understanding the societal culture when guiding students. Our culture is strongly influenced by the societal culture, which shapes our minds and language. Bruner (1996), in addition, explained that "culture shapes the mind and provides us with the toolkit by which we construct not only our worlds but our very conceptions of our selves and our powers" (p. x). Especially in education, school learning is situated in a cultural context, and we exercise this culture through a language that defines our work and us.

Three interesting arenas can be considered in the pedagogical approach of enhancing students' understanding of international contexts and the meaning of globalization: (a) linguistics, (b) curriculum, and (c) leadership. The scholars in language and linguistics (Gee, 2004; Lakoff, 2004, 2006), culturally relevant curriculum (Apple, 2004, 2009; Giroux, 1988, 2005; Sleeter, 1996; Sleeter & McLaren, 1999), and leadership for advocacy, social justice, diversity, and globalization (Anderson, 2009; Banks, 2008; Bottery, 2004; Theoharis, 2008, 2009), among many others cited here, add to this chapter's critical analysis of deterrents to people's developing knowledge and skills necessary to become engaged, critical global citizens.

Conceptualizing Internationalism in Education: How Language Defines Our Work

Language plays a powerful role in students' lives (Gee, 2004) and a significant role in how we construct the world in which we live. By way of language, we also define education and who is served by it (Bruner, 1996; Gee, 2004). Linguistics and cognitive scientists like Lakoff (2004) and Gee (2004) explained that when we hear a word (like *international*, for example), we build a mental structure or frame that guides the "way we reason and consider what *counts* as common sense" (Lakoff, 2004, p. xv). According to Lakoff, a concept can make sense only when it is instantiated in the synapses of our brains, referring to how we "connect facts to long-term concepts that structure how we think" (p. 17). This means that if the concept *international* can be connected only to an individual's mental model of war images or catastrophes, the concept of internationalism as collaboration among countries will make no sense. Cognitive frames, Lakoff attested, also shape the way we act; and when we act within the collective frames of sociopolitical protectionism, we may define our culture as one of fear, moving into a re-action, which prevents us from exercising our beliefs on broader societal levels.

A lived experience of this idea is in the U.S. teachers I met working in international schools in Europe. The school administrator reported:

> Educators may walk into an American international school with a set assumption of
> what international means. When you ask a U.S. educator new to living overseas what
> international means, the perception is of "anything else but us." So, in a short session
> with the faculty, we got into this whole discussion of American vs. International, and
> one American teacher asked, "Are you saying that because I am an American I can be
> an international, too?" —that's the dilemma we get in here.

Not clear about the definition of *international* as a new teacher overseas, this teacher asked whether, as an American, she was considered international. This candid but powerful example of defining representation of self speaks of societal constructions. Because in the United States cognitive frames are constructed through color and ethnic divisions, these cognitive frames challenged this educator now that she was a member of an international community. Historical colonization movements may have originated the idea that *international* is "everyone but us."

Most interesting in Lakoff's examples is that cognitive frames carry two opposing and contrasting metaphors of *family*: one of a *nurturant parent*, and another of a *strict father* image. He explained that we use "both models regularly in different parts of [our] lives" (p. 21). No Child Left Behind (NCLB), for example, is a language metaphor that appeals to our nurturant values. However, "the real policies are *strict father* policies" (p. 21), affirmed Lakoff. At the same time that the federal act meant to address every child, the policies punished children and schools with financial restrictions. The author cautioned that this phenomenon is recognized as "Orwellian language—language that means the opposite of what it says" (p. 22). Another example is the term *school testing*. When we define that schools are the ones being tested, we are positioning the public to use a strict father image. Lakoff explained, "Once the testing frame applies not just to *students* but also to *schools* (emphasis added), then schools can, metaphorically, fail—and be punished for failing by having their allowance cut" (p. 32). Indeed, several scholars have raised concerns about the dissonance resulting from these cognitive frames and resulting paradoxes related to NCLB (Nichols & Berliner, 2007; Nichols, Glass, & Berliner, 2006; E. Smith, 2005; Sunderman, Kim, & Orfield, 2005). Even those scholars who are helping us understand policy inconsistencies may use the term *failing schools*.

The images created by words are powerful, and scholars like Lakoff have shown that the terms we use may further define our educational system. The Obama/Biden education plan conveys that "tests should not come at the expense of a well-rounded education—they should help complete that well-rounded education" (Editorial Projects in Education, 2009, p. 26). What, then, can educational leaders do in terms of defining a well-rounded education?

We can begin by recognizing that the terms used to describe the schools and our work accurately communicate their purpose to constituents and stakeholders. How we define schools and education may compromise the intention to secure learning environments vital for students. The way we define our profession is important—instead of letting others define our work. Similarly, giving in to mind frames that define internationalism as opposed to nationalism is not helping students learn about what they need to know to become active members in society.

Leaders Supporting Critical Pedagogies in the Curriculum

Educational leaders can support critical pedagogies that prepare students to discuss world issues. Such leaders have the advantage of informing and inspiring schoolteachers, students, parents, and community members to understand and minimize powerful structures that prevent students from being well informed about schools and their place in society. Before understanding how education plays a role internationally, it is also important to understand the role of schools themselves. In the United States, the bureaucratization of schooling began in the nineteenth century as an urban social and economic necessity. The *grammar of schooling* was the term that defined the structures, the rules, and the practices. A template of a "real school" was created to establish public educational institutions. The template defined how the system would be free and would accommodate the wave of immigrant workers and their children, supplying the society with operational workers in an urban-industrial modernized order (Tyack, 1974). In this context, "educational leaders have tried to transform immigrant newcomers and 'outsiders' into individuals who matched an idealized image of what an 'American' should be" (p. 235).

The "Americanization" rhetoric often was messianic, according to Tyack, "a mixture of fear outweighed by hope, of a desire for social control accompanied by a quest for equality of opportunity for the newcomers" (p. 232). The Americanization ideology was less than idyllic, however, as the new pluralistic society concurrently developed a culture of ethnocentrism and bigotry inside and outside the schools. Scholars in multicultural education then challenged old grammars of schooling, especially when schools were not suppressing ethnocentrism and bigotry, but were replicating these behaviors with students.

These scholars stressed the importance of being attentive to practices that en-force unequal structures in schools (Apple, 2004, 2009; Giroux, 1988, 2005; Sleeter, 1996; Sleeter & MacLaren, 1969).

In a study of transforming teachers in international American schools from monocultural to intercultural educators, Murakami-Ramalho and Sper-andio (2009) considered two important steps in teachers' multicultural devel-opment: (a) a first stage, when educators living abroad learn to be more internationally minded and multiculturally competent and (b) a second stage, in which the educators' experience and personal transformation translate into professional practice, with educators focused on helping students become in-ternational thinkers and global citizens. These educators are cognizant of themselves as immersed in an international environment and as such help students understand this context. I believe it is possible to prepare educators for multicultural practices without having to travel abroad.

In a country with a flourishing economy, with a world-renowned enter-tainment industry and a highly respected educational system that receives many students and visitors from other countries, we may still be coming to terms with issues of domestic diversity and overlooking the opportunity to learn from visitors and immigrants. Multicultural competence and the practice of internationalizing the curriculum can be developed within our country's borders when we recognize that a political context of power exists in the eve-ryday practices of teachers and in the academic lives of students.

Apple (2004) has been a long-time advocate of the connections among knowledge, teaching, and power in education. Apple affirmed that schools are indeed sites of political conflict in questions about what kind of knowledge is delivered, about "whose knowledge is 'official,'" and about who has the right to decide both what is to be taught and how teaching and learning are to be evaluated" (Apple, as cited in Anderson, 2009, p. vii). Beyond discussions of curricular implications, Apple questioned whether we are paying enough at-tention to the global restructuring of markets:

> Of paid and unpaid labor, of housing and health care, of communities large and small and so much more—all of this is having a differential effect in terms of race, and class, and gender. And all of this has had profound effects on the financing and gov-ernance of schools, on what is to count as "official knowledge" and "good teaching." (p. x)

The author cautioned about the century's first decade and the "reductive models of accountability, standardization, and strict control over pedagogy and curricula, especially in urban schools" (p. x). He contended that it is important to observe educational pushes as linked to political economies, especially in urban centers, where students will emerge as workers into a society that values an affluent lifestyle, which can exist only when served by a large pool of low-wage workers.

Are educators really neutral about societal values, or are educators contributing to an intended replication of a neutrality of values? Political, economic, or educational debates about people in society are currently replaced by the development of technical skills in schools. Apple thought of this as an equation:

> Considerations of the *justice* of social life are progressively depoliticized and made into supposedly neutral puzzles that can be solved by the accumulation of neutral empirical facts, which when fed back into neutral institutions like schools can be guided by the neutral instrumentation of its educators. (p. 7)

Scholars like Apple have argued that even by being apolitical in schools, we are being political. In other words, he suggested that neutral conversations in schools, using neutral facts, in fact neutralize educators and students in schools and society. As educators we were prepared to believe that education is a neutral activity. It has been suggested that, by not taking a political stance, those in education can better focus on school subjects. However, schools play a significant role in economic and cultural stratification, and by being apolitical we may be perpetuating existing biases from those who designed curricula. Zimmerman (2005), who extensively researched the history of American education, affirms that education is shaped by politicized decisions of what and who should be included in school offerings. All the aforementioned scholars agree about the role of political power and planned narratives that reduce the agency of schools and its educators.

Teachers as neutral agents are not regarded respectfully when the nature and process of educational reform were critically examined in the late 1980s. Giroux (1988) indicated that, due to power control in schools, teachers are expected to deliver the content with expertise, but without questioning the curriculum. In this century, the influence of teachers on educational reform seems to have been devalued even further. Teachers have little time to devote to intellectual discussions when they are busy focusing on high-stakes testing procedures. Giroux, following Dewey's ideas, warned, "the standardization of school knowledge in the interest of managing and controlling it is a disservice to the nature of teaching and the students" (p. 123).

Teachers lose enthusiasm in preparing students to engage in connections between academics and real life, be it local or international, when they are not regarded as transformative intellectuals. Teachers as transformative intellectuals can educate students to be active, critical citizens. Giroux expanded on this idea:

> Central to the category of transformative intellectual is the necessity of making the pedagogical more political and the political more pedagogical. . . . Making the political more pedagogical means utilizing forms of pedagogy that embody political interests that are emancipatory in nature; that is, using forms of pedagogy that treat students as critical agents; make knowledge problematic; utilize critical and affirming dialogue; and make the case for struggling for a qualitatively better world for all people. (p. 127)

Providing spaces for critical dialogue and inquiry among students might not be a top priority in the educational agenda these days. Providing students with a voice, especially before college, is highly relevant, in order to engage students who see no connection between their studies and their lives. Such disengagement may, in fact, be one of the elements that contribute to student dropout. Gewertz (2008), in reflecting on the state of affairs and the upcoming new government as influencing education, indeed considered the importance of student-led engagement in Chicago schools in reducing dropout rates and making high school more relevant and responsive to students' needs. Teachers and educational leaders continuously are at the crossroads between socioeconomic and cultural changes. By being open to new trends, constantly examining the local and international landscape and how the information can be translated into best practices and programs, teachers and educational leaders may be better prepared to make decisions that will empower students to become global citizens.

Empowering Students to Become Global Citizens: Advocacy Leadership and Policy Analysis in a "Neutral Enterprise"

Apple (2009), in the foreword to Anderson's (2009) call to establish a new agenda for advocacy leadership, reiterated the importance of inviting educational leaders to consider three post-reform questions: (a) What does it mean to be a public school leader in the current political, social, and economic climate? (b) What mind shift must occur so that educational leaders see themselves as advocates, especially when focusing on urban and segregated suburban schools with educational inequality? and (c) How can school leaders be informed simultaneously about educational leadership and policy analysis? Anderson reinforced Apple's point that providing apolitical and ahistorical examples to emerging educational leaders does not, in fact, prepare these leaders to be advocates for schools and students. Advocacy leaders may want to prepare themselves and their teachers to critically analyze local, national, and international landscape of sociopolitical and economic implications, and encourage both teachers and students to create spaces for dialogue about civic participation in society.

In turn, if teachers are not prepared to interpret the national and international landscape of sociopolitical and economic implications, leaving critical discussions to students' own investigations (or only available at the college level), we may be guaranteeing that those who are unable to move on to college have limited chances to make critical and informed decisions. This would confirm Apple's premise that "the institution of schooling is not a neutral enterprise in terms of its economic outcomes" (p. 7). Sleeter and McLaren (1999), scholars who largely contributed to an understanding of critical pedagogy added: "The dominant culture of schooling mirrors that of the larger culture insofar as teachers and students willingly and unwittingly situate themselves within a highly politicized field of power relations that partake of unjust race, class, and gender affiliations" (p. 6). When teachers are constrained in discussing relevant world events, they also constrain students to develop higher critical thinking.

Interestingly, students similarly are not empowered to take part in planning their own preparation in schools. Anderson (2009), talking about the importance of advocacy leaders, called for a reorientation of leadership as intrinsic to the promotion of the school's most important clients—the students. Teachers and administrators advocating for students can then lead students, not as "mere performers professionally equipped to realize effectively any goals that were set for them" (Giroux, 1988, p. 125), but as informed and critical transformative intellectuals examining curriculum, structures, rules, and regulations as enhancing students' knowledge.

In relation to the curriculum, respected scholars such as Gutierrez (1995) have indicated that remedying educational structures and social injustices through the use of "token inclusions in the curricula" (p. 440) is not enough. Sleeter (1996), who dedicated her career to the preparation of teachers, suggested that the commitment to inform students involves critical pedagogy, with educators asking important "why" questions when examining unequal relations and privileges among people, especially in terms of institutional and social discrimination. When institutional and social discrimination exists within borders, these will be replicated and expanded into discrimination across countries. Discrimination relates to diversity issues in students of all races and nationalities, and in these students' future relations with people around the world.

Teachers can empower students only through critical pedagogy, and when supported by advocacy leaders. In preparing to become informed citizens in society, teachers and students benefit from courageous conversations infused with discussions of race, ethnicity, culture, religion, and social class (Banks, 2008; Singleton & Linton, 2005). Until now, much of our effort has been spent analyzing each other's differences within the country. Moving students to reconcile these differences through their contributions in transforming this society prepares them for leadership at the international level. Nieto (1996) added that we can practice critical pedagogy only when "we are convinced that all our students deserve a better, more complete, and more challenging education" (p. 214).

Shaping a School Culture that Supports Global Citizenship: Applying the Eight Characteristics of a Multicultural School

School leaders have the latitude to set the tone for school operations, establish a school culture, situate the school in the contemporary context of district, state, and nation, and help stakeholders set goals and objectives conducive to the highest opportunities for student learning. To achieve this mission, leadership for social justice seems to be the suggested modus operandi in educational leadership (see Theoharis, 2009, and other chapters in this book). Theoharis, along with other scholars, defined social justice for school administrators as including advocacy and leadership centered in the practice and vision that includes "race, class, gender, disability, sexual orientation, and other historically and currently marginalizing conditions in the United States" (Theoharis, 2008, p. 5). Advocacy is the core of leadership for social justice, which might not have been the main priority in the past. Through social justice, works such as Banks' (2008) emerge as significant, especially as he argued about the importance of unifying "a deeply divided nation" (p. 11).

It is interesting that Banks' work is rarely connected to the preparation of school leaders, even though he is highly regarded by educators and scholars around the globe. The absence of discussions related to multicultural education among school administrators is troublesome, especially when scholars like

Apple and Banks have suggested "schools and classrooms must become micro-cosms and exemplars of democracy and social justice in order for students to develop democratic attitudes and learn how to practice democracy" (Banks, 2008, p. 26). How can educational leaders exercise advocacy and social justice, strengthening teachers' and students' understanding of citizenship education based on diversity and multiculturalism at the local and international levels?

At the local level, "diversity enriches a nation by providing all citizens with rich opportunities to experience other cultures, and thus to become more ful-filled as human beings" affirmed Banks (2008, p. 1). An empowering school culture and structure, in this case, begins with the observation of characteris-tics that enable students to experience educational equality and empower-ment. Banks' eight characteristics of a multicultural school seem to include tenets that apply directly to educational leaders' empowering students to be-come global citizens through social justice (Table 8.1):

Table 8.1. Eight Characteristics of a Multicultural School*

1. The teachers and school administrators have high expectations for all students and positive attitudes toward them. They also respond to them in positive and caring ways.
2. The formalized curriculum reflects the experiences, cultures, and perspectives of a range of cultural and ethnic groups as well as of both genders.
3. The teaching styles used by the teachers match the learning, culture, and motivational characteristics of the students.
4. The teachers and administrators show respect for the students' first languages and dialects.
5. The instructional materials used in the school show events, situations, and concepts from the perspectives of a range of cultural, ethnic, and racial groups.
6. The assessment and testing procedures used in the school are culturally sensitive and result in students of color being represented proportionately in classes for the gifted and tal-ented.
7. The school culture and the hidden curriculum reflect cultural and ethnic diversity.
8. The school counselors have high expectations for students from different racial, ethnic, and language groups and help these students to set and realize positive career goals.

*Excerpted from Banks (2008, p. 36).

These characteristics align with the desired practices of leaders practicing ad-vocacy and social justice, as suggested by Anderson (2009) and Theoharis (2008, 2009).

The foregoing characteristics of a multicultural school also align with the recently revised Interstate School Leaders Licensure Consortium (ISLLC), cre-ated to provide guidelines for the preparation of educational leaders through the Educational Leadership Policy Standards: ISLLC 2008 (National Policy Board for Educational Administration, 2007). Banks' aforementioned characteristics then provide ways in which school leaders can exercise several of the standards established by the National Policy Board for Educational Administration, especially in relation to meeting the needs of students.

Most relevant to this discussion is ISSLC Standard 6, which states, "An education leader promotes the success of every student by understanding, responding to, and influencing the political, social, economic, legal, and cultural context" (NPBEA, 2007 p. 3). Standard 6 further considers that the desirable leader has the following functions:

A.　Advocate for children, families, and caregivers

B.　Act to influence local, district, state, and national decisions affecting student learning

C.　Assess, analyze, and anticipate emerging trends and initiatives in order to adapt leadership strategies

Acting to influence in decisions affecting student learning does not directly relate to a call for the internationalization of education. However, globalization may be considered as part of the trends and initiatives that may influence students and their preparation. Advocating for students in this sense may directly relate to fulfilling the expectations for a well-rounded education.

Significant to the work of leaders empowering teachers and students to become global citizens begins with the responsibility of discontinuing the perpetuation and pervasiveness of practices that are not conducive to the preparation of children to merge into a healthy and productive society. It involves leaders' problem posing, in addition to problem-solving (Bottery, 2004). Empowering teachers and students to become global citizens is a challenging process that begins with the critical examination of established blueprints of practices. Reframing academic and cultural givens, as well as the language of use created around notions of supremacy and oppression, are subjects worthy of critical examination.

Conclusion

> Now is the time to finally meet our moral obligation to provide every child a world-class education, because it will take nothing less to compete in the global economy.
> —Barack Obama

It is too early in the new administration's tenure to talk about the ways in which President Obama's aspirations of improving education in the United

States might be realized. The first decade of this century recognizably left international education and world relations on the back burner. United Nations representatives' recommendations for developing world relations between the United States and other countries were not regarded as relevant. Changes are occurring at the national and international levels, and rationales driving internationalization and globalization are occurring at the political, economic, and institutional levels (Knight, 2004). Ignoring the globalization movement no longer is an option if freedom to determine domestic policies is being reduced. The freedom to determine local policies is subject to the country's involvement in favoring economic exchanges at the global level and the country's influence in economic and political negotiations.

Studies of the consequences of globalization and its effects on school-age children, however, continue to be critical; the topic still is understudied and undertheorized. In the last decade, educational experts and scholars voiced polarized opinions related to ignoring students' sociopolitical conditions at the expense of performance indicators. In response to this state of affairs, the Department of Education shared the president's position that

> Our nation's economic competitiveness and the path to the American Dream depend on providing every child with an education that will enable them to succeed in a global economy that is predicated on knowledge and innovation. President Obama is committed to providing every child access to a complete and competitive education, from cradle through career. (White House, 2009)

I agree with several scholars who have asserted that high-stakes testing and accountability procedures were necessary in order to evaluate student learning across individual states, especially in a decentralized educational system, as compared to countries with centralized educational systems. Standardized tests were efficient instruments that allowed for performance evaluation and cross-comparison with other countries (Burbules & Torres, 2000; Carnoy, 1999; Valverde, Bianchi, Wolfe, Schmidt, & Houang, 2002). The improvement of students can be effectively evaluated only through national measurements. However, I question whether we have lost sight of improving students' civic capacities—through a divide-and-conquer pattern that has kept us focused on the skill and drill of student performance rather than the adequate preparation of students to merge fully into society and exercise their freedoms.

"Schools are one of the few places in which students have the freedom to exercise sociopolitical ideas," attested Apple (2009). I hope that we have developed a mechanism to empower students in order to empower the nation—

and not empower the nation at the expense of its students. Suárez-Orozco (2001) added that schools can "profoundly shape the current and future well-being of children, as well as their chances and opportunities" (p. 345). Educational leaders as advocates for social justice therefore have the chance to bring international context and meaning to education. Educational leaders can shape the future of students by revealing the *cognitive unconscious* (Piaget, 1973), that is, providing students with understanding related to the tools needed in order to be engaged as civic participants in society—not only through philosophical discussions, but also through a well-developed language that defines education and authentic social justice practices modeled by educational leaders and teachers in schools.

References

Anderson, G. L. (2009). *Advocacy leadership: Toward a post-reform agenda in education*. New York: Routledge.

Apple, M. W. (2002). Patriotism, pedagogy, and freedom: On the educational meanings of September 11. *Teachers College Record, 104*(8), 1760–1772.

Apple, M. W. (2004). *Ideology and curriculum*. New York: Taylor & Francis.

Apple, M. W. (2009). Foreword. In C. A. Torres (Ed.), *Globalizations and education: Collected essays on class, race, gender, and the state* (pp. ix-xix). New York: Teachers College Press.

Banks, J. A. (2008). *An introduction to multicultural education (4th ed.)*. Boston: Pearson.

Barlow, M., & Clarke, T. (2002). *Blue gold: The fight to stop the corporate theft of the world's water*. New York: New York Press.

Basiga, B. (2004). Globalization and peace education. *Canadian Social Studies, 38*(3), Accessed May 30, 2009 at www.quasar.ualberta.ca/css/.

Bottery, M. (2004). *The challenges of educational leadership: Values in a globalised age*. London: Paul Chapman.

Bruner, J. (1996). *The culture of education*. Cambridge, MA: Harvard University Press.

Burbules, N. C., & Torres, C. A. (2000). *Globalization and education: Critical perspectives*. London: Routledge.

Carnoy, M. (1999). *Globalization and educational reform: What planners need to know*. Paris: UNESCO, International Institute for Educational Planning.

Editorial Projects in Education. (2009). *The Obama education plan: An Education Week guide*. San Francisco, CA: Wiley.

Gabbard, D. (2003). A nation at risk—Reloaded, part I. *Journal for Critical Education Policy Studies, 1*(2). Available: http://www.jceps.com

Gee, J. O. (2004). *Situated language and learning: A critique of traditional schooling*. New York: Routledge.

Gewertz, C. (2008). Chicago students to play lead role in dropout project. *Education Week, 28*(13), 7.

Giroux, H. A. (1988). *Teachers as intellectuals: Toward a critical pedagogy of learning.* Gramby, MA: Begin & Garvey.

Giroux, H. A. (2002). Terrorism and the fate of democracy after September 11. *Cultural Studies, Critical Methodologies, 2*(1), 9–14.

Giroux, H. A. (2005). *Schooling and the struggle for public life: Democracy's promise and education's challenge.* Herndon, VA: Paradigm Publishers.

Gutiérrez, K. (1995). Afterword. In C. Sleeter & P. McLaren (Eds.), *Multicultural education, critical pedagogy, and the politics of difference* (pp. 439–442). Albany: State University of New York Press.

Knight, J. (2004). Internationalization remodeled: Definitions, approaches, and rationales. *Journal of Studies in International Education, 8*(1), 5–31.

Lakoff, G. (2004). *Don't think of an elephant: Know your values and frame the debate.* White River Junction, VT: Chelsea Green Publishing.

Lakoff, G. (2006). *Whose freedom? The battle over America's most important idea.* New York: Macmillan.

Lee, C. D., & Smagorinsky, P. (Eds.) (2000). *Vygotskian perspectives on literacy research: Constructing meaning through collaborative inquiry.* New York: Cambridge University Press.

Liebeck, H., & Pollard, E. (1994). *The Oxford dictionary.* Oxford: Oxford University Press.

Murakami-Ramalho, E. (2008a). Domestic practices in foreign lands: Lessons on leadership for diversity in American international schools. *Journal of Studies in International Education, 12*(1), 76–95.

Murakami-Ramalho, E. (2008b). On what side of "international" are we? Using cognitive frames to explore educational leaders. *International Journal of Urban Educational Leadership, 2*(1), 16–29.

Murakami-Ramalho, E., & Sperandio, J. (2009). Riding the wave: Educational leaders developing intercultural practices in international schools. In J. Collard, A. Normore, & B. Merchant (Eds.), *Leadership and intercultural dynamics* (pp. 281–298). Charlotte, NC: Information Age Publishers.

National Policy Board for Educational Administration (NPBEA). (2007). Educational Leadership Policy Standards: ISLLC 2008. Retrieved May, 31, 2009, from http://www.npbea.org/projects.php.

Nichols, S. L., & Berliner, D. C. (2007). *Collateral damage: How high-stakes testing corrupts America's schools.* New York: Harvard Education Press.

Nichols, S. L., Glass, G. V., & Berliner, D. C. (2006). High-stakes testing and student achievement: Does accountability pressure increase student learning? *Education Policy Analysis Archives, 14*(1). Retrieved May 5, 2009, from http://epaa.asu.edu/ epaa/v14n1/.

Nieto, S. (1996). From brown heroes and holidays to assimilationist agendas: Reconsidering the critiques of multicultural education. In C. Sleeter (Ed.), *Multicultural education as social activism* (pp. 191–220). Albany: State University of New York Press.

Piaget, J. (1973). The affective unconscious and the cognitive unconscious. *Journal of the American Psychoanalysis Association, 21,* 249–261.

Scholte, J. (2000). *Globalization: A critical introduction.* New York: St. Martin's Press.

Singleton, G., & Linton, C. (2005). *Courageous conversations about race: A field guide for achieving equity in schools.* Thousand Oaks, CA: Corwin Press.

Sleeter, C. (1996). *Multicultural education as social activism.* Albany: State University of New York Press.

Sleeter, C. E., & McLaren, P. L. (1999). *Multicultural education, critical pedagogy, and the politics of difference.* Albany: State University of New York Press.

Smith, D. G. (2000). A few modest prophecies: The WTO, globalization and the future of public education. *Canadian Social Studies, 35*(1). Accessed online June 1, 2009, at http://www.quasar.ualberta.ca/css/CSS_35_1/modest_prophecies.htm

Smith, E. (2005). Raising standards in American schools: The case of No Child Left Behind. *Journal of Education Policy, 20*(4), 507–524. http://www.informaworld.com/smpp/title%7Econtent=t713693402%7Edb=all%7Etab=issueslist%7Ebranches=20 - v20

Suárez-Orozco, M. M. (2001). Globalization, immigration, and education: The research agenda. *Harvard Educational Review, 71*(3), 345–365.

Sunderman, G. L., Kim, J. S., & Orfield, G. (2005). *NCLB meets school realities: Lessons from the field.* Thousand Oaks, CA: Corwin Press.

Theoharis, G. (2008). *Woven in deeply: Identity and leadership of urban social justice principals.* Education and Urban Society, 41(1), 3–25.

Theoharis, G. (2009). *The school leaders our children deserve: Seven keys to equity, social justice, and school reform.* New York: Teachers College Press.

Tyack, D. B. (1974). *The one best system: A history of American urban education.* Cambridge, MA: Harvard University Press.

Valverde, G. A., Bianchi, L. J., Wolfe, R., Schmidt, W. H., & Houang, R. (2002). *According to the book: Using TIMSS to investigate the translation of policy into practice through the world of textbooks.* Dordrecht: Kluwer.

Walker, A., & Dimmock, C. (2002). Moving school leadership beyond its narrow boundaries: Developing a cross-cultural approach. In K. Leithwood & P. Hallinger (Eds.), *Second international handbook of educational leadership and administration* (pp. 167–207). Dordrecht, Netherlands: Kluwer.

White House. (2009). Obama Education Plan. Accessed May 30, 2009, at http://www.white house.gov/issues/education.

Zimmerman, J. (2005). *Whose America? Culture wars in the public schools.* Boston, MA: Harvard University Press.

✠ PART THREE

Looking to the Future

✣ CHAPTER 11

Leading across Boundaries: The Role of Community Schools and Cross-Boundary Leadership in School Reform

Gaetane Jean-Marie, Verna Ruffin, and Kevin Burr

Historically, educational reform efforts have consisted of complex undertakings associated with design, implementation, and systematic impact. A common attribute of educational reforms, regardless of their scope or intended target, is to improve student learning (Goertz, Floden, & O'Day, 1995; Hannaway & Kimball, 1998; Pechman, 1994; Samberg & Sheeran, 2000). Reform efforts are often ambitious and seek to eradicate the extenuating circumstances that impact the developmental dimensions of young people—social, emotional, physical, cognitive, civic, moral, and academic (Coalition for Community Schools, 2006, n.d.). However, the complex needs of our diverse American families challenge the moral imperative of schools to educate all learners to their fullest potential (Rothstein, 2004).

Sustaining reform efforts in schools is increasingly difficult because educational organizations have to contend with paradoxes and dilemmas associated with the shifting educational landscape, that is, increased standards, teacher retention and attrition, student demographic shift (Jean-Marie, 2008; Marshall & Oliva, 2009). Achieving long-range success under such pressures can be insurmountable; however, the proliferation of community schools across the nation suggests a restructuring of school governance, policies, leadership, and mobilization of resources to support improved achievement, respond to the increased needs of families and children, and effectively reform public schools.

With the increasing emphasis on accountability and developmental needs of students, the purpose of school continues to expand. Education Secretary Arne Duncan (2009), in a recent speech outlining his education reform goals, argued that schools need to become centers of communities where schools extend the hours to provide programs and services to children and families. The community school approach as a reform of urban schooling seeks to implement systematic educational change in which partners come together to offer a range of support and opportunities for children, youth, families, and communities during and after school (Coalition for Community Schools, 2006). While the concept of community schools is not new to school reform, it has taken on different meaning over the years. For the purpose of our discussion, the authors draw from the Coalition for Community Schools' (2006) typology of a community school in which "leaders (e.g., principals) in our nation's schools and communities are working together across the boundaries of education, government, and public" (p. v.).

The philosophy that undergirds community schools is an "integrative focus on academics and family support, health and social services, and youth and community development that leads to improved student learning, stronger families and healthier communities (CSC, 2006, p. v)." To fully capture this conceptualization of community schools, we explore the emergence of urban regime theory in education in which governmental and nongovernmental, and private and public sector develop collaborative partnerships to bring together resources and opportunities to scale up and sustain community schools. As examined in this chapter, urban regime theory (Burns, 2003; Mossberger & Stoker, 2001; Stone, 1989) offers a new way of thinking about community schools in relation to cross-boundary leadership.

Chapter Overview

This chapter is conceptual in nature. As a framework, the authors summarize the definition of urban regime theory, the core attributes and application to urban educational reform. In particular, we apply urban regime theory to the examination of community schools with a focus on the evolving role of the principal as cross-boundary leader and spanning boundaries for systemic education reform. The chapter concludes with implications for future research on the normative and structural elements of cross-boundary leadership that are necessary to transform public schools to meet the holistic needs of students, and improve the quality of life for families and communities.

School Reform and Urban Regime Theory

Spurred by Clarence Stone's 1989 study of Atlanta, urban regime theory came to prominence and has since been extensively used to examine urban politics both inside North America and beyond (Mossberger & Stoker, 2001). Stone (1989) defines urban regime as "the informal arrangements by which public bodies and private parties function together in order to be able to make and carry out governing decisions (p. 6). In local city governance, the structural coordination of local government authority involves nuances hindering processes to effectively address problems and issues impacting urban communities. Similar to urban city reform, the political context of public schools as it exists currently often hinders system-wide education reform because of diverse and conflicting agendas, which inhibits the deployment of public and private assets that may alter structural and positional power (Shipps, 2006; 2008; Stone, 1998a).

Governance, Power, and Leadership

The core attributes of urban regime theory lend themselves to a political analysis framework involving *governance, power,* and *leadership* (Shipps, 2008; Stone, 1998a, 1998b). First, a premise of regime theory is that *governance* through the establishment of shared goals creates coordination between private and shared assets (Shipps, 2008). Both the private and public sector have resources and assets that can provide solutions to societal problems but efforts often are disjointed and not well coordinated with these entities to identify and address issues impacting communities. In public schools, there are many essential services that are carried out by nonpublic-school sectors (e.g., businesses, civic and religious organizations, neighborhood groups) and schools increasingly are in need of assistance to address high-risk circumstances (Fusarelli, 2008).

Second, in urban regime theory, political *power* plays a central role but is a deviation from hierarchical authority. Recognizing that private and public agencies specialize in a variety of services, political power involves the manifestation of both systemic and social production of power. Systemic power is the impersonal power that is structured into economic, political, or socially advantaged roles (Shipps, 2008, p. 91). It serves as a resource to form a regime—local actors from both the public and private sector. Social production of power involves the collaborative efforts of local actors to address and develop creative solutions of societal problems through coalition building (Shipps, 2008; Stone, 2004, 2005). According to Mossberger and Stoker (2001), regime analysis views power as fragmented and regimes as the collaborative arrangements through which local governments and private actors assemble the capacity to govern.

A third component of urban regime theory is *leadership*. In order for cities to effectively be governed, multiplayers across a broad spectrum are instrumental in providing leverage to sustain resources that communities need to thrive. The coalition surrounding multiplayers is one that has to be developed; urban regime does not emerge without such coalition building. However, because each player from the private and public sector is involved in decision-making, cooperation among the players based on trust and loyalty enables them to advance a common agenda. Leadership is fluid because all the potential players have the capacity to use their personal influence and organizational resources to bring about change for those in need (Shipps, 2008; Stone, 1998b). The use of personal power to inspire others and collaborate with them rather than hierarchical power becomes the locus operandi. Although schools have explored the ways in which to extend child, family and community services to tackle a series of social problems (poor parenting, low skills, poor health, etc.) and help drive up standards of educational attainment, the lack of capacity and mobilization of resources hinders such efforts.

The Politics of Urban Regime Theory and Community Schools

From a political perspective, urban regime theory emphasizes local actors, coalition building, resources, and power (Shipps, 2003, p. 824). Local actors include government agencies, interest groups, and nongovernmental organizations, and political leaders, and have a common reform initiative in which each actor brings its resources (i.e., political, organizational, or economic) to manifest reform (Hannaway & Kimball, 1998; Mossberger & Stoker, 2001; Shipps, 2003). In local governance, urban governing regime theory holds that cities are governed by ongoing coalitions of local economic and political actors who, in processes more complex than once thought, work to achieve particular ends, particularly but not exclusively economic (Hula, Jackson, Orr, & Marion, 1997; Mossberger & Stoker, 2001).

As urban communities have experienced change, urban regime analysis has been applied to examine and understand the complexities of issues and problems urban communities confront. For example, urban communities have undergone the reduction of affordable houses for the working class, inadequate resources and services, and lack of infrastructures and health provisions that impact the quality of life for families and communities. In contrast, urban developments in numerous localities have also resulted in improved neighborhoods, employment opportunities and healthy communities. Through an urban regime analysis, scholars have studied the impact of stable and long-lasting partnerships among resource providers (i.e., regimes cities) that have built alliances to effectively target resources for disadvantaged families and communities (Orr, 1996; Shipps, 2008). A regime analysis also considers the impact of nonregimes in urban cities and how a crisis may potentially exacerbate the negative effects of these environments. In considering the application of urban regime theory to school, this is an important consideration.

In large cities across the United States, the call for fundamental change to improve the nation's urban schools persists (Hula, Jackson, Orr, & Marion, 1997; Orr, 1996). Through civic capacity, local educational stakeholders form alliances with public and private sectors to shape and carry out meaningful systemic school reform. Such attempts have unfolded in school districts in Atlanta (Stone, 2001), Baltimore (Orr, 1996), Chicago (Shipps, 2003), and Philadelphia (Bulkley, 2007). The application of urban regime theory to schooling focuses on the relationship of school system governance to the political authority structure of the city and to the resources of local civic groups (Shipps, 2003; Stone, 2005, 2004, 1989; Stone, Henig, Jones, & Pierannunzi, 2001). In exploring this further, the authors synthesize the literature on community schools to expound on urban regime theory.

Comprehensive School-Wide Reform in Urban Communities

Urban public schools face a range of issues such as overcrowding, deteriorating facilities, inadequate funding, high turnover of staff, lack of up-to-date textbooks, and children who perform below grade level (Fusarelli, 2008; Jean-Marie, 2008; Trevillion, 1991). To tackle these issues requires comprehensive school-wide reform (CSR) that hinges on civic capacity and obligates partners from the public and private sector to develop collaborative relationships, networks and strategic alliances, and take action to improve schools, families, and communities (Hannaway & Kimball, 1998; Shipps, 2008, 2003; Stone, 2005, 2004).

A growing body of research suggests that comprehensive school-wide reform is more effective than reactionary reform or implementation of several decentralized efforts within a single building (Goertz, Floden, & O'Day, 1995; Hannaway & Kimball, 1998; Pechman, 1994). This approach to reform is defined as "programs that are intended to work across grades and disciplines, and that incorporate elements such as teacher leadership and parental involvement" (Education Research Service, 1998, p. 1). As such, effective school reform is comprehensive (Education Research Service, 1998). In response to early success in the 1980s and the potential of emerging CSR models, the federal government funded a program designed to increase academic achievement for all students through the promotion of reform models based on CSR principles.

Among CSR programs (e.g., Roots and Wings, Accelerated Schools, Paideia Project, etc.), one model that has integrated these principles and evolved into a holistic approach to connect schools and communities is the Coalition for Community Schools. The Coalition for Community Schools is an alliance of national, state, and local organizations that represents community development and community building with an emphasis on improving student learning by connecting community resources to students' education in a meaningful and powerful way (Samberg & Sheeran, 2000). Importantly, community schools are not solutions to problems based on deficit thinking, but rather are a strength-based approach that celebrates and channels a community and a school's strengths toward student support structures (Blank, Berg, & Melaville, 2006; Blank, Melaville, & Shah, 2003). Community schools are based on common principles, but are idiosyncratic, as they are based on community strengths, values, and needs. They are schools combining rigorous academics, which would be a requirement of quality schools, while offering a wide range of in-house services, supports, and opportunities for the purpose of promoting children's learning and development (Hannaway & Kimball, 1998).

In the context of community schools, schools are the hubs that knit together inventive and enduring relationships among educators, families, volunteers, and community partners (Blank, Melaville, & Shah, 2003, p. 2). Additionally, health and social agencies, family support groups, youth development organizations, institutions of higher education, community organizations, businesses, and civic and faith-based groups play a vital role in working closely together for the benefit of every child (Fusarelli, 2008). These governmental and nongovernmental agencies share expertise and resources with schools and schools value the resources and involvement of such partnerships to improve the educational attainment of students and the quality of life for families (Blank, Melaville, & Shah, 2003).

We argue that community schools have the capacity to ameliorate educational disparities in urban communities. Alongside community schools' efforts at systemic reform in public schools, they also have a particular focus on social problems disadvantaged children and families encounter. Community schools seek to address educational and wider social problems by aligning policy interventions in different domains to address the complex problems of the most disadvantaged urban schools and communities (Blank, Melaville, & Shah, 2003). As applied to urban regime theory to address educational change (Shipps, 2003), the Coalition for Community Schools brings together civic actors with a strong, shared identity to create the conditions necessary for every child to learn at high levels (Blank, Melaville, & Shah, 2003).

The proliferation of educational partnerships across the United States was developed in response to legislation and created to reform the educational system and improve student outcomes (Brunner, Kunesh, & Knuth, 1992; Dryfoos, 1995; 2002; Fusarelli, 2008). For advocates of community schools, improving education and increasing student achievement require the procurement of services and programs that schools in general do not have. Drawing from urban regime theory, public schools serve as hubs to mobilize and develop coalition of partners to pull together resources to improve the quality of life for children and families. As Fusarelli (2008) contends, "by building stronger communities (and families) the hope is that students will be less at risk of academic failure and social problems . . . and the logical place to address the needs of at-risk children is at the place where so many of society's problem intersect—the public school" (p. 380).

Coalition for Community Schools: A Framework for School Reform

There are five conditions for learning that guide the framework of the Coalition for Community Schools for comprehensive school reform in school districts in the United States. These five conditions create an environment in which all children can achieve success:

Condition #1: The school has a core instructional program with qualified teachers, a challenging curriculum, and high standards and expectations for students.

Condition #2: Students are motivated and engaged in learning—both in school and in community settings, during and after school.

Condition #3: The basic physical, mental, and emotional health needs of young people and their families are recognized and addressed.

Condition #4: There is mutual respect and effective collaboration among parents, families, and school staff.

Condition #5: Community engagement, together with school efforts, promotes a school climate that is safe, supportive, and respectful and connects students to a broader learning community (Blank, Melaville, & Shah, 2003, p. 15).

Creating these conditions in community schools is a process and context specific. The emergence of community schools is unique to the specific needs of the community; yet, each community school reflects a common set of principles (i.e., conditions for learning) that characterizes national models and local implementations (Blank, Melaville, & Shah, 2003). Although systemic education reform is a focus of the Coalition for Community Schools, the type of reform varies among the community schools across the United States.

Stone (1998b) argues that although many cities may have education regimes (e.g., comprehensive school-wide reform) few have the kind of regime that leads to sustainable improvements in education for all children. Such a regime, which he labels a performance regime, incorporates both public and private (both for-profit and nonprofit) entities with a shared purpose of school improvement. He also argues that changes in leadership in a district are insufficient to build and sustain a performance regime; rather, other kinds of changes and supports are needed, including resources and widespread support. However, leading these collaborative efforts requires a new understanding of leadership. Hence, the role of the principal is not simply to lead within internal boundaries (i.e., school building) but across multiple boundaries to work collaboratively with groups in and outside of the school. Within the Coalition for Community Schools, this approach to leadership is called cross-boundary leadership.

Principals as Cross-Boundary Leaders in Community Schools

Cross-boundary leadership operates on multiple levels. It involves community leaders, leaders on the ground, and leaders in the middle collaborating in unconventional ways (Blank, Berg, & Melaville, 2006). These leaders from schools, businesses and government, and local organizations work in concert and across boundaries to create a network of engaging partnerships collaboratively working together to influence the lives of all children (Adams, 2008; Blank, Berg, & Melaville, 2006). Ira Harkavy and Marty Blank (2003), experts of Coalition for Community Schools identify leadership as one of four keys to creating community schools. According to Melaville (1998), leadership provides "fuel and direction and community school initiatives that last are led by people committed to the well-being of poor children and families, and who know where they want to go and have the position, personality, and power to make others want to come along" (p. 96).

Four Realms of Leadership: Distributed, Instructional, Democratic, and Boundary-Spanning

Given the layers of leadership in community schools, governance functions are distributed within a wide variety of systems that provide general oversight, day-to-day management, and site-level decision-making (Harkavy & Blank, 2000). Governance is an umbrella term that refers to the policy making, administering, fiscal, and operational systems necessary to run an enterprise in the public interest (Melaville, 1998, p. 27). Improving the quality of education for all learners is a public interest beneficial to the public and private sector. To govern, community schools' principals as cross-boundary leaders provide leadership through four realms: *distributed, instructional, democratic,* and *boundary spanning.*

Distributed leadership. Distributed leadership is a move away from positional authority and is viewed as leadership practice that is distributed across an organization and constitutes the interaction of formal leaders, teachers, and activity being undertaken (Spillane, Halverson, & Diamond, 2001). Within *distributed leadership,* the principal works with teachers and staff to improve teaching and learning, identify factors that impact academic performance and organizational climate, foster parent relationships, etc. (Camburn, Rowan, & Taylor, 2003). Within this scope, informal leaders (e.g., such as teacher leaders or leadership teams) emerge and are developed.

Three leadership arrangements operate within distributed leadership: division of labor, co-performance, and parallel performance (Spillane, 2006). A division of labor involves leaders in different positions who perform various leadership functions with considerable overlap among positions (Heller & Firestone, 1995; Spillane, 2006). Co-performance involves two or more leaders performing a leadership function or routine in a collaborated fashion (Spillane, 2006). Parallel performance refers to situations where people perform the same functions or routines but without any coordination among them (Spillane, 2006). There are various leadership responsibilities a community school principal has to attend to inside the school. Whether it is teacher and curriculum development or school improvement plan, a principal working with formal (assistant principals) or informal leaders (teacher leader, leadership team) provides assistance with the execution of leadership functions. For principals of community schools, leadership is distributed not only within schools but also outside the school.

Instructional leadership. Instructional leadership clarifies the relationship between leadership and student outcomes. It refers to the work of principals to improve their schools by setting high expectations for all children, instituting a regular testing program, and focusing on basic academic learning (Prestine & Nelson, 2005, p. 49). At the center of improving the quality of education is effective leadership, which has a profound influence on successful school reforms to impact student success and learning (Goertz, Floden & O'Day, 1995; Mangin, 2007; Murphy, 2005; Pechman, 1994). However, many children's basic needs are unmet, which hinders schools from focusing only on the instructional program in the absence of health and social services that are needed to promote resiliency among children and adolescents (Children's Aid Society, 2001.)

Within the community school framework, cross-boundary leadership facilitates processes that enable school leaders to identify student needs, and mobilize school and community resources to address those needs. In this realm, the scope of instructional leadership broadens. Accordingly, the role of the principal further evolves into one of collaborator characterized by the ability to bring diverse groups often with diverse needs together as they work across multiple, sometimes conflicting, accountabilities (Firestone & Shipps, 2005; Mangin, 2007; Murphy, 2005). While a community schools leader (i.e., the principal) attempts to improve student learning, the political, bureaucratic, market, professional, and moral accountability often become conflicting demands on the job of the leader (Firestone & Shipps, 2005).

Democratic leadership. Democratic leadership in a broad sense focuses on the collective actions within the purview of the organization (e.g., community schools). In its simplest form, it involves a trialectic of social dynamics—structure, people, and engagement (Woods, 2003, 2005). Within this context, democratic leadership becomes a part of governance drawing from varying systems that coordinate social life (Blasé & Blasé, 1999; Woods, 2003). Democratic leadership empowers everyone to work in concert and is inclusive (Woods, 2003). It opens the boundaries of leadership and respectfully accepts that all beings have an ethical right to participate in decision-making processes (Woods, 2004).

Unlike distributed and instructional leadership, democratic leadership is transformational in tackling difficult challenges through the creation of collaborative networks dedicated to re-creating schools that service the whole child, families, neighborhood, and community. Democratic leaders have the capacity to form coalitions with community-based organizations, family support agencies, faith-based institutions, and youth development groups while creating an environment of shared decision-making.

Boundary-spanning leadership. Beyond instructional, distributed, and democratic leadership, the work of community school leaders also involves boundary spanning to engage local actors (private and public sector) to meaningfully impact the well-being of children and families in urban regimes. *Boundary-spanning leadership*, which has been studied in business and management, involves individuals who link the organization to external sources of information for the efficient and effective operation of an organization (Tushman & Scanlan, 1981). Boundary spanners are characterized by their ability to engage others and deploy effective relational and interpersonal competencies (Williams, 2002). The cross-boundary leader in community schools takes stock of what individual contributors (i.e., partners from the private and public sector) have by leveraging their collective strength, bringing them together in strategy sessions, partnerships, collaborations, and united efforts.

In particular, spanning boundaries elevates the principal's role as a political actor who initiates collaborative partnerships—noneducation government agencies and not-for-profit organizations including foundations, universities, and religious organizations. As a political actor, the principal maintains collaborative relationships to help garner resources and expertise that are necessary to improve learning and enhance the well-being of children, families, and communities. The political activism of the cross-boundary leader is beyond the scope of the school, district, or local community. It includes developing stronger relations with local and state level governance, civic organizations, as well as businesses. Developing the competent skills to effectively work across a broad spectrum of partners from the private and public sector is paramount.

Often, the private and public sector will bring a high degree of credibility and organizational capacity to the creation of community schools, but they may have conflicting or multiple expectations that create tension among the partners. Effective community schools require resources and assets beyond the scope of public schools. The principal plays a central role in providing leadership to connect vested partners around a common agenda and bring balance to the level of influence each partner possesses (i.e., power with vs. power over). While different partners want expedient results to assess outcomes, the principal strikes a balance of maintaining enthusiasm and communicating progress because the challenge to educate and provide for the basic needs of children remains and will take time to eradicate.

Developing Networks and Engaging Stakeholders across Boundaries

As educators continue to face challenges when seeking to educate all children, there is growing recognition that schools must work in tandem with communities to maximize their collective educational potential (Murphy, Beck, Crawford, Hodges, & McGauphy, 2001). Growing numbers of students live in poverty, violence, fragmented, or nonexistent families, and/or substance abuse (Panasonic Foundation, 2007). For today's school leaders, out-of-school factors (e.g., unsafe neighborhoods, dysfunctional life circumstances, generational poverty) pervade in-school factors such as high-stakes testing, and college and workforce readiness. Though not all collaborative partners agree on how or what to change, change is inevitable in order to make a significant difference in the quality of life of children and families.

Leading across boundaries involves the development of networks (e.g., school and community) to build coalitions. Coalitions are based on shared vision with clear understanding of the goals to provide guidance and support (Shipps, 2008; Stone, 1998a). A common vision enjoins coalitions to work collaboratively to help students achieve academically and socially. Involving out-of-school resource agencies; businesses; faith-based, political, and governmental agencies helps meet the needs of the whole family, thereby connecting those services, previously unavailable to families, within the school and the school community (Fusarelli, 2008). Schools are limited in their capacity to meet all the developmental needs of learners; yet, society's expectation is that every child will be developmentally competent. In order to accomplish this, the role of the principal must be redefined to include developing skills pertinent to encompass a broader coalition of people and resources to meet the needs of families, which impacts the quality of life for the whole child.

Within cross-boundary leadership, the leadership in community schools extends beyond the school in a more democratic fashion to within and outside the school community to include government agencies, businesses, and a different set of providers to best meet the needs of families within and outside the school community. Spanning boundaries links to the community school philosophy, which encompasses the development of the whole child beyond the development of cognitive skills (Blank, Melaville, & Shah, 2003; Blank, Berg, & Melaville, 2006; Coalition for Community Schools, 2002). Emotional, physical, and social needs require attention, and while community schools address these needs they also focus on family support, out-of-school time and developing the professional capacity of staff to meet the needs of the entire family. Dryfoos (1995) notes that school facilities are used for delivering services in partnership with other agencies (Muijs, 2007, p. 348).

According to Shipps (2008), regime analysis emphasizes leaders' personal power to inspire others and collaborate with them rather than the hierarchical power they may have over government functionaries, or the inherent power of their being in a systemic position of economic or political advantage. This normative stance highlights leaders' abilities to inspire trust within disadvantaged communities and has implications for our understanding of leadership succession in times of reform (Stone, 1998a). Cross-boundary leadership is important in the work of multiagency work, which is a component of community schools. It is the principal's ability to bring all stakeholders to the table to determine what is best for the entire family/community, but not dictating what that should be. Through effective listening, a prerequisite of effective leadership for the twenty-first-century leader, the community school's principal collaboratively accomplishes what is needed for the school and community— one who leads a community school as a comprehensive reform model. In other words, it is not the principal's vision for an effective school but rather what is the collective, all-inclusive vision for an effective school and how can schools work in tandem with the entire community to create such a place.

Network development and the mobilization of resources among organizational contributors are essential to collaborative effort. The building principal is often at the helm of the school's structural framework and appears hierarchical when charted. However, principals as cross-boundary leaders operate in a more complex environment of boundary spanning, collaboration, network development (and maintenance), and inter-organizational theaters. Williams (2002) argues that the collective benefits to public policy and practice are contingent upon understanding that "inter-organizational capacity is unlikely to flourish in organizational structures that are based on hierarchical control and power" (p. 150).

Relationships are key to building long-term commitments to the collective effort. The relationships necessary are often built informally and always with mutual respect for a particular purpose. Learning to span the various boundaries over time is critically important. Williams (2002) suggests that one element in establishing competency as a boundary-spanning network builder is the identification of particular factors, barriers, or conditions that are influential in determining the success or failure of collaborative encounters—critical performance factors such as a shared vision, communication, and teamwork. The entrepreneurial and innovative capacities of boundary spanners are emphasized by Challis, Fuller, Henwood, Klein, Plowden, Webb, Whittingham, and Wistow (1988) who highlight the defining characteristic of flexibility (Williams, 2002) as a central element to collaboration within the network. Leadbeater and Goss (1998) refer to these leaders as "creative, lateral thinking rule-breakers who frequently combine a capacity for visionary thinking with an appetite for opportunism" (Leadbeater & Goss, 1998).

Effective principals develop a shared vision with members of the entire community, convene the conversations, and insist on the inclusion of multiple voices to achieve the common goal of improving conditions so that student learning can remain the singular focus a school. The principal evokes and supports leadership in others, models and participates in collaborative practices by posing questions of the collaborators that facilitates the dialogue necessary to address the persistent issues preventing positive movement. Certainly, developing leadership capacity among multiple partners is central to understanding the evolving role of the principal in community schools. A principal going at it alone works against the undergirding philosophy of the Coalition for Community Schools, making it difficult to improve learning and enhance the well-being of children, families and communities.

Tulsa Area of Community Schools Initiative: A Model for School Reform

In the state of Oklahoma, one of the largest urban school districts and a neighboring suburban–urban district are engaged in a school reform initiative through collaborative partnerships to create educational systems that work for all students and families. In 2006, the mayor met with a diverse group of thirty individuals (representing Tulsa's private and public sector) to share and identify the educational issues impacting the city of Tulsa. Subsequently, the mayor invited the group to attend the National Coalition for Community Schools conference in Baltimore, Maryland. Upon their return, meetings with the entire group of 30 were held and they established a mission statement, developed a steering committee to present to the general session, and created the Tulsa Area of Community Schools Initiative (TACSI).

The formation of TACSI highlights the relationship between political activism and urban school reform. TACSI, similar to other education reform initiatives in cities like Chicago and Baltimore who are exemplars of urban regimes, "focuses on local urban actors who come together in coalitions around reform ideas and bring their independent, political, organizational, and economic resources to bear on these commitments" (Shipps, 2003, p. 842). TACSI's mission is to provide leadership and influence to engage local communities in creating and sustaining community schools that support academic success and strengthen children, families, and communities. As a collective of civic and business community, common and higher education, and local neighborhoods, TACSI organizes community-wide partnerships through the Community Service Council of Greater Tulsa and Office of Community Engagement at the University of Oklahoma. Through TACSI, both the public and private sectors focus on ways to work together to multiply their impact on school and community issues.

According to Stone (2001), the nature and context of urban school reform in cities will differ substantially in the ability to mobilize around education. In the city of Tulsa, a major impetus of civic capacity is the involvement of the philanthropic community. Tulsa has a long history of philanthropic and business activism that continues to play a major role in school reform efforts to improve communities and schools and increase student achievement. The philanthropic community takes a keen interest and is often at the forefront leading local educational and community development initiatives. In addition to the philanthropic community, city government, local businesses, religious

232

New Perspectives in Educational Leadership

and cultural organizations, higher education institutions, and civic and social service agencies are actively involved in taking public accountability for transforming schools and communities. This system-wide educational reform utilizes a political framework to build a high level of civic engagement in which actors both inside and outside of government come together to transform public schools (Blank, Berg, & Melaville, 2006; Shipps, 2003, 2008).

Presently, there are eighteen elementary schools participating in TACSI in the Tulsa and Union districts. Within Tulsa Public Schools, there are twelve schools, and in Union Public Schools, there are six participating schools. Union Public Schools is located in Tulsa and is considered a suburban–urban district because of population increase (i.e., urban sprawl) in recent years. As part of its strategic plan, TACSI's goal is to add more elementary schools to its network of community schools from Union and Tulsa. As with the national coalition, TACSI's strategies for scaling up and sustaining community schools entail (a) developing diverse financing, (b) changing policy and practice through technical assistance and professional development, (c) collecting evidence of student and family services, and (d) building broad-based public support (Blank, Berg, & Melaville, 2006, p. vii). These four strategies are critical for forging innovative working relationships toward the common goal of transforming traditional schools to community schools.

Modeled after the national Coalition for Community Schools, TACSI's leadership is premised on cross-boundary leadership. As previously discussed, growing community schools involves community leaders, leaders on the ground, and leaders in the middle (Blank, Berg, & Melaville, 2006). Under the auspices of the Metropolitan Human Services Commission, TACSI's governance structure includes *community leaders* who serve on the Community Schools Steering Committee (i.e., TACSI Community Partners, Office of Community Engagement—The University of Oklahoma, and the Community Service Council). In particular, the Community Service Council provides leadership to help the community work together to identify and address its health and human service needs. As such, they serve as an important network that links outside services that are important to schools as they seek to mobilize resources among organizational contributors. Another level of governance is *leaders in the middle* who make up the management team, which manages the community school implementation process. It consists of the community service council representation, as well as school district, city, and local government agencies; University of Oklahoma; and Conecciones (a Tulsa-based Hispanic education and workforce development organization) and meets monthly. In addition to community schools, the meetings focus on early childhood education and grant opportunities for local community groups and organization, in addition to funding sources for the operation, development, and evaluation of community schools. TACSI also meets monthly with community school principals in an implementation meeting attended by the principals and their community school coordinators (TACSI Governance Structure, 2009).

The third level of governance is *leaders on the ground*. Within TACSI, these leaders function at the local school sites, which include administrators, teachers, support staff, students, parents, representatives from the civic and business community, and neighborhood residents. They are appointed to the community site team to represent every sector of the school community and facilitate the development and maintenance of a shared educational vision for the school (Adams, 2008, p. 3). There is also a community school coordinator whose responsibilities are to facilitate the development, and implementation and management of community school efforts as they evolve from the school site team (p. 3). Presently, only 7 of the eighteen community schools have a coordinator.

The principal at each school site plays a critical role in building capacity and mobilizing resources to sustain a community school. In the eighteen schools in TACSI, these cross-boundary leaders provide leadership to manage school operations and community resources. They are at the forefront in confronting the day-to-day challenges and engaging their constituents to partner with them to accomplish their goal. The "go at it alone" philosophy dissipates because the responsibilities are too great for one person (i.e., the principal). Through the community site team and community school coordinator, these cross-boundary leaders are able to build multilevel leadership through democratic processes. Guided by a common agenda, leaders at the school site and in the community enable principals to more efficiently tackle the multitudes of issues pertaining to children and families. Over time, each community school builds an infrastructure to support change within and across systems to nurture and expand the community school philosophy. However, cross-boundary leadership ideally should be the normative practice of principals in community schools. Its enactment will vary based on the principal's philosophy, knowledge, and experience. Through professional development and opportunities to learn more about cross-boundary leadership, TACSI's principals will develop the leadership skills and practices needed for this new approach to leadership.

Now in its third year, the community schools in TACSI face increased pressure to produce results. In particular, funders from both the public and private sector want to see the impact of their support. In addition to the cross-boundary principals, the management team plays a critical role in communicating with partners and providing reports on incremental successes that are occurring at each school site. In particular, they are working with the evaluation team at the University of Oklahoma to study the stages of community school development. The core components of Community Schools are cross-boundary leadership, holistic programs, services and opportunities, family and community engagement, and community-based learning. The evaluation team, under the direction of Curt Adams, a faculty member of The University of Oklahoma department of educational leadership and policy studies, has developed a longitudinal research design for TACSI that uses integrated methods to measure the implementation and effectiveness of the community school model. There are two phases of the research: phase one measures the stages of development for each community school component within TACSI schools, and phase two measures changes in learning conditions and outcomes that can be attributed to the community school model. The research design will test the efficacy of the community school model for changing learning conditions and performance outcomes within TACSI schools.

Implications for Practice and Policy

In urban cities, the persistence of urban school failures has confounded the professionals as well as civic leaders and government officials. Reforming public schools, in particular urban schools, is attainable through the collective agency of schools and social service agencies, business, religious, and cultural organizations, and postsecondary or higher education institutions (Fusarelli, 2008; Mossberger & Stoker, 2001; Shipps, 2003, 2008). In the case of TACSI, it has developed a community and civic-based constituency working collaboratively to transform schools and communities.

The structure of community schools reflects an urban regime as applied in urban regime theory. Their capacity to structure community schools' agendas with civic resources and governmental capacity, and develop relationships between them further explicates the functionalities of urban regime theory (Shipps, 2008). The role of power extends beyond decisions made by principals, superintendents, or mayors but also includes businesses, civic organizations, or service agencies as members of the coalition. New relationships and institutions to reform school governing arrangements lie outside the system as much as within and constituents work together to create this "power to create" change collaboratively as opposed to power needed to resist change (Shipps, 2008).

As elaborated earlier in the chapter, urban regime theory (Mossberger & Stoker, 2001; Shipps, 2008, 2006; Stone, 1989, 1998a, 1998b, 1998c) offers a new way of thinking about community schools in relation to cross-boundary leadership. The literature on urban regime theory is used as a lens to examine the evolving role of the principal in fostering cross-boundary leadership (CBL) and spanning boundaries to transform the organizational culture, how CBL is developed and sustained over time to meet the holistic needs of students, and improve the quality of life for families and communities. In the field of educational leadership, further studies on urban regime theory as it pertains to school governance merit serious consideration. Likewise, the emerging model for school leadership—cross-boundary leadership, and the sustainability of community school governance, merit further study.

The United States continues to voice urgency for reshaping failing schools (Duncan, 2009; Dillon, 2009); yet effective models of sustained improvement in student achievement must be carefully studied. Community Schools as a comprehensive reform model and its unique twenty-first-century cross-boundary leadership framework must prove itself as a sustainable model equipped with the tools for developing and building coalitions for the improvement of entire school communities—all for the benefit of students, families, and communities.

Schools for the twenty-first century, community schools require collaborative involvement and engagement from multiple and diverse constituents—families; teachers; school leaders; district leadership (i.e., school boards); business; faith-based, nonprofit, charitable, and social services organizations; and political actors. Leadership that can bring these diverse groups together to develop a common purpose is required as the community school model becomes the transformational model of school reform for the twenty-first century. The development of the leader to lead across boundaries in a collaborative, all-inclusive style is paramount to transforming effective schools—community schools for the twenty-first century.

References

Adams, C. (2008). *Conceptual definitions of community schools DNA*. TACSI Evaluation Design. Unpublished report.

Blank, M. J., Berg, A. C., & Melaville, A. (2006). *Growing community schools: The role of cross-boundary leadership*. Washington, DC: Coalition for Community Schools.

Blank, M. J., Berg, A. C., & Melaville, A. (2003). *Making the difference: Research and practice in community schools*. Washington, DC: Coalition for Community Schools.

Blase, J., & Blase, J. (1999). Implementation of shared governance for instructional improvement: Principals' perspectives. *Journal of Educational Administration, 37*(5), 476–500.

Bulkley, K. (2007). Bringing the private into the public: Changing the rules of the game, and new regime politics in Philadelphia public education. In K. Bulkley & L. Fusarelli (Eds.), The politics of privatization in education: The 2007 yearbook of the Politics of Education Association [Special issue]. *Education Policy, 21*(1), 155–184.

Burns, P. (2003). Regime theory state government and a takeover of urban education. *Journal of Urban Affairs, 25*(3), 285–303.

Brunner, C., Kunessh, L. G., & Knuth, R. A. (1992). What does research say about interagency collaboration? Retrieved June 3, 2009 from http://www.ncrel.org/sdrs/aeras/stw_esys/8agcycol.htm.

Camburn, E., Rowan, B., & Taylor, J. E. (2003). Distributed leadership in schools: The case of elementary schools adopting comprehensive school reform models. *Educational Evaluation and Policy Analysis, 25*, 347–373.

Challis, L., Fuller, S., Henwood, M., Klein, R., Plowden, W, Webb, A., Whittingham, P., & Wistow, G. (1988). *Joint approaches to social policy*. Cambridge: Cambridge University Press.

Children's Aid Society (2001). *Building a community school* (3rd ed.). New York: The Children's Aid Society's National Technical Assistance Center for Community Schools.

Coalition for Community Schools, (2006). *A handbook for state policy leaders—Community schools: Improving student learning/strenthening schools, families, and communities*. Washington, DC: Coalition for Community Schools-Institute for Educational Leadership.

Coalition for Community Schools. (n.d.). Retrieved November 12, 2008, from www.thecommunityagenda.org.

Dillon, S. (2009, June 02). *Access World News*. Retrieved July 2, 2009, from NewsBank: http://infoweb.newsbank.com

Dryfoos, J. G. (1995). Full service schools: revolution or fad? *Journal of Research on Adolescence, 15*(2), 147–172.

Dryfoos, J. (2002). Full-service community schools. Creating new institutions. *Phi Delta Kappan, 83*(5), 393–400.

Duncan, A. (2009). Schools need to become centers of communities. A conversation with Charlie Rose. Retrieved May 5, 2009, from http://www.youtube.com/watch?v=TLQNFnUhWh w&feature=fvw.

Educational Resource Service. (1998). *Comprehensive models for school improvement: Finding the right match and making it work*. Arlington, VA: Education Research Service.

Firestone, W. A., & Shipps, D. (2005). How do leaders interpret conflicting accountabilities to improve student learning? In W. A. Firestone & C. Reihl (Eds.), *A new agenda for research in educational leadership* (pp. 81-100). New York: Teachers College.

Fusarelli, B. C. (2008). The politics of coordinated services for children: Interinstitutional relations and social justice. In B. S. Cooper, J. G. Cibulka, & L. D. Fusarelli (Eds.), *Handbook of education politics and policy* (pp. 350-373). New York: Routledge.

Goertz, M. E., Floden, R. E., & O'Day, J. (1995). *Studies of education reform: Systemic reform: Volume I: Findings and Conclusions.* Washington, DC: U. S. Department of Education.

Hannaway, J., & Kimball, K. (1998). *Reports on reform from the field: District and state survey reports.* Washington, DC: The Urban Institute.

Harkavy, I., & Blank, M. J. (2003). A vision for learning beyond testing and choice. *Reclaiming Children and Youth, 11*(4), 211-215.

Heller, M. J., & Firestone, W. A. (1995). Who's in charge here? Sources of leadership for change in eight schools. *Elementary School Journal, 95,* 65-86.

Hula, R. C., Jackson, C. Y., & Orr, M. (1997, March). Urban politics, governing nonprofits, and community revitalization. *Urban Affairs Review, 32,* 459-489.

Jean-Marie, G. (2008). Leadership for social justice: An agenda for 21st-century schools. *The Educational Forum, 72,* 340-354.

Leadbeater, C., & Goss, S. (1998). *Civic entrepreneurship.* London: Demos.

Mangin, Melinda M. (2007, August). Facilitating elementary principals' support for instructional teacher leadership. *Educational Administration Quarterly, 43*(3), 319-357.

Melaville, A. (1998). *Learning together: The developing field of school-community initiatives.* Flint MI: Institute for Educational Leadership and National Center for Community Education.

Marshall, C., & Oliva, M. (2009). *Leadership for social justice: Making revolutions in education.* 2nd ed., Upper Saddle River, NJ: Prentice Hall.

Mossberger, K., & Stoker, G. (2001). The evolution of urban regime theory: The challenge of conceptualization, *Urban Affairs Review, 36,* 810-835.

Muijs, D. (2007). Leadership in full-service extended schools: communicating across cultures. *School Leadership and Management, 27*(4), 347-362.

Murphy, J. (2005). *Connecting teacher leadership and school improvement.* Thousand Oaks, CA: Corwin.

Murphy, J., Beck, L. G., Crawford, M., Hodges, A., & McGauphy, C. L. (2001). *The productive high school: Creating personalized academic communities.* Thousand Oaks, CA: Corwin.

Orr, M. (1996). Urban politics and school reform: The case of Baltimore. *Urban Affairs Review, 31,* 314-345.

Panasonic Foundation. (2007, December). Breaking the links between race, poverty and achievement). Retrieved December 22, 2008 from http://ucea.org/html/strategies/13_01_2007.pdf.

Pechman, E. (1994). *Implementing schoolwide projects: An idea book for educators.* Washington, DC: U.S. Department of Education, Planning and Evaluation Service.

Peterson, K. D. (2002). The professional development of principals: Innovations and opportunities. *Educational Administration Quarterly, 38*(2), 213-232.

Prestine, N. A., & Nelson, B. S. (2005). How can educational leaders support and promote teaching and learning? New conceptions of learning and leading in schools. In In W. A.

Firestone & C. Reihl (Eds.), *A new agenda for research in educational leadership* (pp. 46-60). New York: Teachers College.

Rothstein, R. (2004). Class and schools: Using social, economic, and educational reform to close the Black-White achievement gap. New York: Teachers College.

Samberg, L., & Sheeran, M. (2000). *Community school models*. Washington, DC: Coalition for Community Schools.

Shipps, D. (2008). Urban regime theory and the reform of public schools: Governance, power, and leadership. In B. S. Cooper (Ed.), *Handbook of education politics and policy* (pp. 89-108). New York: Routledge.

Shipps, D. (2006). *School reform, corporate style: Chicago 1880-2000*. Lawrence: University Press of Kansas.

Shipps, D. (2003). Pulling together: Civic capacity and urban school reform. *American Educational Research Journal, 40*(4), 841-878.

Spillane, J. P., (2006). *Distributed leadership*. San Francisco: Jossey-Bass.

Spillane, J. P., Halverson, R., & Diamond, J. B. (2001). Investigating school leadership practice: a distributive perspective. *Educational Researcher, 30*(3), 23-28.

Stone, C. N. (2005). Looking backward to look forward: Reflections on urban regime analysis. *Urban Affairs Review, 40*(3), 309-341.

Stone, C. N. (2004). It's more than the economy after all: Continuing the debate about urban regimes. *Journal of Urban Affairs, 26* (1), 1-19.

Stone, C. N. (2001). Civic capacity and urban education. *Urban Affairs Review, 36*, 595-619.

Stone, C. N. (1998a). Political leadership in urban politics. In G. S. In D. Judge, *Theories of urban politics* (pp. 96-116). Thousand Oaks, CA: Sage.

Stone, C. N. (1998b). Regime analysis and the study of urban politics. *Journal of Urban Affairs, 20*(3), 249-260.

Stone, C. N. (1998c). *Changing urban education*. Lawrence, KS: University Press of Kansas.

Stone, C. N. (1989). *Regime politics: Governing Atlanta, 1946-1988*. Lawrence: University Press of Kansas.

Stone, C. N., Henig, J., Jones, B. F., & Pierannuzi, C. (2001). *Building civic capacity: The politics of reforming urban schools*. Lawrence: University Press of Kansas.

Trevillion, S. (1991). *Caring in the community*. London: Longman.

Tushman, M., & Scanlan, T. (1981). Boundary spanning individuals: Their role in information transfer and their antecedents. *Academy of Management Journal, 24*(2), 89-305.

Woods, P. A. (2005). *Democratic leadership in education*. Thousand Oaks, CA: Sage.

Woods, P. A. (2004, January-March). Democratic leadership: Drawing distinctions with distributed leadership. *International Leadership in Education, 7*, 3-26.

Woods, P. A. (2003). Building on Weber to understand governance: Exploring the links between identity, democracy and "inner distance." *Sociology, 37*, 143-163.

Williams, P. (2002). The competent boundary spanner. *Public Administration, 80*(1), 103-124.

✠ CHAPTER 12

Leaders of the New School: Exploring Teacher-Leadership and the Future of School Reform

Camika Royal and James Earl Davis

Understanding teaching as leadership and the need for *teacher-leaders* is increasingly important to the future of school reform. Since A *Nation at Risk* brought national attention to the pervasiveness of under-performing public school students and teachers in the early 1980s, teacher quality has been a nationwide concern for political pundits, policy makers, education stakeholders, and opinionated taxpayers alike. For more than twenty years, school districts have debated the best ways to improve what students learn and how they achieve (e.g., Schneider & Buckley, 2003; Saporito, 2003; Ball, 2002; Gamoran, 1996; Kantor, 1991; Rist, 1973). Huge sums of money have been diverted toward school districts for this effort, with little change and even less success having occurred in classrooms (Rorrer, Skrla, & Scheurich, 2008; Ball, 2002; Wellisch, MacQueen, Carriere, & Duck, 1978). Sadly, most school district reforms are symbolic political moves that have little impact on classrooms and even less input from teachers (Wilms, 2003).

Nieto's (2003) belief that teachers are becoming even more scrutinized is supported as school systems attempt to fool-proof education systems through stringent, standardized, mechanized, and heavily scripted curricula, though such top-down reforms do precious little to improve the structure and culture of schools and classrooms (Rorrer et al., 2008; Wilms, 2003). Nor do these efforts inspire or encourage teachers to perform better at their jobs (Wilms,

2003). Rather, they demoralize teachers and devalue their work. In order for schools to be truly transformed into places where learning happens at high levels for all students enrolled, regardless of race, ethnicity, gender, special needs, or socioeconomic status, teaching capacity must be enhanced.

Teachers as Leaders

Since teachers are critical to educational success in classrooms, schools, and communities and key to creating and sustaining meaningful school reform, this chapter describes a much-needed shift in U.S. education from thinking of *teachers as workers* to imagining *teachers as leaders* (Searby & Shaddix, 2008). Essential to this shift is the subtle yet important distinction of discussing "teaching" and not "teachers," and debating what teachers *do* and not who they *are*. While some may consider teachers as culpable for much of what ails schools (Warren, 2002; Tschannen-Moran & Woolfolk Hoy, 2001), blaming any single party within the contemporary context of public education in the United States ignores the variety of factors that create and sustain educational inequality and underachievement in schools and school systems.

As such, this chapter is not about blaming teachers. Rather, it aims to contextualize the complicated, multilayered, intricate work that excellent public school teaching requires and present "new" ways of constructing, understanding, and embodying teaching that advance the leadership of the teachers our students, schools, and communities desperately need and deserve. It respects the difficult, arduous work of public school teachers, knowing that teaching is a labor that one may sometimes love and, as with any profession, occasionally feel otherwise.

After describing the current educational climate in the United States, with particular attention to implications for urban schools and districts in an era of accountability, we discuss new entrepreneurial endeavors in education. These include: Teach For America, The New Teacher Project, the Teacher Advancement Program, New Leaders for New Schools, and the Knowledge Is Power Program, which are ever gaining favor and greater access to supply more teachers/teacher-leaders and/or create more schools in urban and rural areas. These relatively recent educational advances have at their foundations notions of teacher-leadership as essential to the success of schools and students' academic achievement. Next, we explain what we mean by "teaching as leadership" and use the high standards of two notable professional organizations as examples. We then explore professional learning communities and the roles of teacher-leaders within them as collective efforts to improve student achieve-ment and school performance. The inadvertent costs of these elements are also described. Lastly, we examine the multiple reasons why some of these teacher-leaders may not remain in their schools. To close, we consider the im-plications of the teacher-leadership issues explored here in relation to the new presidential administration and the future of school reform.

Assessing the Educational Climate in the United States

"The climate in most city schools is unrelievedly negative. Teachers are tired, and many feel defeated."

—Lois Weiner

The current educational climate in the United States is rife with efforts to make teachers more accountable for student achievement. Teachers are, there-fore, mandated by the federal government to be "highly-qualified," although each state determines how teachers achieve this status (Copenhaver-Johnson, 2007; Darling-Hammond & Berry, 2006). Not surprisingly, the number of highly qualified teachers in wealthier districts is often much higher than in poor urban districts (Honowar, 2008). Districts are scrambling to get highly qualified teachers not just to teach in their districts, but to teach in the schools in which they are assumed to have the most impact—where student achieve-ment is painfully low (Argue, Honeyman, & Shlay, 2006). In tandem, a cul-ture of crime and punishment exists for public schools. Stagnant or declining academic performance is treated as a crime; students, teachers, and faculty are criminalized, punished with the removal of funds and resources needed to improve students' academic performance.

Lipman (2004) has referred to this system of monitoring students' and schools' academic performances on these tests as "spectacle and surveillance." This culture can wreak havoc on the efficacy levels and subsequent perform-ances of school actors, causing or reinforcing various emotional responses in educators, impacting how they view the profession and themselves in the pro-fession (Taylor, 2006; Aronson, 2004; Rex & Nelson, 2004). Furthermore, most school districts know next to nothing about the effectiveness of the teachers they employ. A recent study entitled "The Widget Effect" (2009) demonstrated that common teacher evaluation systems are useless in distin-guishing strong, solid, and weak teaching practices, nor do they foster profes-sional development for teachers not meeting expectations. In fact, most teachers receive high ratings, even in schools that continue not to make adequate yearly progress (Weisberg, Sexton, Mulher, & Keeling, 2009). As such, though the scores students earn on standardized exams are well known and thoroughly documented, it remains difficult to truly attribute students' success or lack thereof to their teachers or to measure how well teachers perform the task of increasing what students know, are able to do, or how they think.

In addition to the constant conundrum of student achievement in under-resourced schools, other elements remain a challenge. Jones (2005) discussed that "urban school systems have suffered from high teacher and administrator turnover; high student mobility; dilapidated building infrastructures; and woefully inadequate human, fiscal, and material resources to meet all of the needs of the diverse student populations" (p. 7). Despite changes in student, educator, and school accountability, issues in teacher recruitment and retention remain for large urban school districts (Neild, Useem, Travers, & Lesnick, 2003; Neild, Useem, & Farley, 2005; Useem, Offenberg, & Farley, 2007; Argue et al., 2006; Mac Iver & Vaughn, 2007). Though district officials often know the types of efforts they believe would remedy these issues—such as new teacher induction, new teacher coaches, and incentives for teachers—often because of chronic underfunding and other budgetary issues, these programs are often cut (Useem et al., 2007). Moreover, the recent worldwide economic downturn has sent many states and school districts, especially those already financially strapped, into a tailspin, considering teacher layoffs and other ways to conserve funds (McNeil, 2009a, 2009b; Jacobson, 2009; Sawchuk, 2009a). All this in the broken, dysfunctional, inadequately staffed, and underfunded urban public schools where faculty and students attempt to achieve and meet the standards set for them in this era of accountability (Anyon, 2005; Kozol, 1991).

Teacher Performance, Incentives, and Accountability

Widely debated and hotly contested, educational accountability as advanced by the No Child Left Behind (NCLB) Act of 2001 is comprised of state standards, unified curricula, and the measurement of student learning by state-sanctioned multiple-choice exams. Proponents of NCLB purport their desire to ameliorate the underperformance of black, Latino, and low-income students, through this accountability system. If judged by its purest intentions, the goals of NCLB are lofty and ideal, goals for which the nation, states, and local districts should strive; that all students would have an opportunity at an excellent education, combined with the possibility that they might all strive for and attain excellence, with none as the standard bearer but excellence, regardless of their race, gender, native tongue, or socioeconomic status. NCLB is implemented by using students' state test scores and other indicators, such as school attendance rates, as the measuring tool by which positive or negative consequences are bestowed on schools and school actors. It aims to be "performance driven, test driven, measurable, and statistical" in order to evaluate how students, teachers, and schools perform and to make them do better (Lee, 2008, p. 610). However, even with these efforts at improving instruction for students, Ramanathan (2008) wrote, "there is little real indication that the law has made progress correcting the performance gap" (p. 306).

The Performance Gap

Academic achievement has been closely tied with wealth and underachievement tied to poverty (e.g., Bond, 1981; Lee & Wong, 2004). Indeed, Harris (2007) found that schools containing students with few economic challenges were 89 times more likely than schools with mostly high-poverty students to have test scores rendering them high performing. In addition to the legacy of economic, racial, social, and academic problems present in the large, underresourced, urban districts of major cities, low public faith in public schools has led to disinvestment in public schooling (Countryman, 2006; Mirel, 1998; Rury, 1999, Perlstein, 2004; Phillips, 2005; Birger, 1996; Alvarez, 2003; Schneider & Buckley, 2003).

Educational researchers have long foretold of the "brutal pessimism" and low expectations with which many students in underresourced schools are regarded (Hilliard, 2003, p. 141; Kurz, Woolfolk Hoy, & Hoy, 2007; Hoy, Tarter, and Woolfolk Hoy, 2006). In areas with relatively high concentrations of poverty, such as Philadelphia, Baltimore, Chicago, Gary, or New Orleans, where more than 80 percent of public school students receive free or reduced lunch, students' high academic achievement on state-mandated exams is less likely. Further confounding this situation, according to Harris and Herrington (2006), "the gap in achievement has shifted steadily from being an indicator of educational inequity to being a direct cause of socioeconomic inequality" (p. 210).

Teacher Incentives

Questions abound regarding whether teacher investment is the culprit in low student achievement, assuming that if these educators care more about the outcomes produced by students, they will work harder and will yield better instruction, more learning, and higher student test scores. This perspective assumes that educators view students' academic performances on standardized tests as a direct result of the instruction individual teachers provide for students in their classroom experiences. Following this supposition, a system of punishments have been employed for chronic underperformance, such as publishing school performance rates, restructuring school staffs, removing school leadership, and the reallocation and/or withholding of federal funds, among other components (Vergari, 2007). While these negative consequences may not inspire school actors, the performance incentives currently implemented in various locations throughout the nation may.

Incentive systems take many forms and may pay for the following: to attract teachers to hard-to-staff schools and subject areas; for teachers' involvement in professional development activities and acceptance of leadership roles in their schools and communities; to reward individual teachers or whole school staffs for the academic achievement of their students (Grier & Holcombe, 2008; Carr, 2008; Honawar & Olson, 2008; Flannery & Jehlen, 2008; Dillon, 2008; Keller, 2008). Financial incentives are implemented, organized, and distributed in various ways: some are used for recruiting teachers and some are used to retain them; some are paid to individual teachers and others are awarded to entire school staffs. Still, both systems of negative reinforcement and positive rewards suggest that educators subscribe to, and will therefore respond to, a market-economy view of education. However, some argue that paying teachers additional money for doing their jobs well insults them and cheapens the profession because of the assumption that teachers are willfully withholding their best instructional efforts and will perform better—or produce greater results in the form of higher test scores—when their pay increases. Performance pay may also decrease community and may encourage competition among educators (Rothstein, 2009).

To combat this sentiment, nonmonetary incentives are idealized as ways to reward what is perceived as greater teacher effort through giving continuing education reimbursements, advancing a teacher's step position on district pay scales, or providing grants for classroom- or school-based projects or programs designed, developed, or led by teachers. Whether through reward or punishment, in this era of accountability, teacher performance is judged by what students demonstrate they have learned on standardized exams. With teacher employment depending on student performance, many fear opaque, unfair evaluation processes that do not consider the distressing conditions in which some teach (Koops & Winsor, 2006; Anyon, 2005; Kozol, 1991). Even in the presence of financial incentives, high student test scores remain elusive for some.

Still, school districts around the nation have a host of possibilities to challenge previous, long-standing arrangements of American schooling systems. As some educators become frustrated by the lack of options and opportunities for students from disadvantaged backgrounds and concerned with what may appear as the inability or apathy of traditional school systems and ordinary educators, these educators form collaborations with other forward-thinking teacher-leaders to create new prospects for schooling and teacher-leadership.

Entrepreneurial Endeavors in Education

"The profession must . . . provide concrete ways for teachers to experience advancement if they are to commit to long-term careers."

—Becky Bobek

During the 1990s, several educational entrepreneurial endeavors were embarked upon that have served to change how education happens for some students, educators, and communities throughout the nation. Teach For America (TFA), The New Teacher Project (TNTP), New Leaders for New Schools (NLNS), the Teacher Advancement Program (TAP), and the Knowledge Is Power Program (KIPP) are some examples of organizations committed to dealing with altering underperformance in public schools to meeting the needs of all students, and these organizations are ever gaining favor and greater access to supply more teachers/teacher-leaders and/or create more schools in urban and rural areas. These relatively recent educational thrusts have at their foundations notions of teacher-leadership as essential to the success of schools and students' academic achievement. Instead of viewing teachers as deficient, complacent, or unable to render high results for students, these organizations focus on the locus of control within single individuals and position teacher-leaders as the single most important entities in changing school cultures, classroom behaviors, and student achievement.

Teach For America

Teach For America (TFA) was born as the senior thesis of a Princeton graduate after the emergence of *A Nation at Risk* and numerous popular films about urban blight and subsequent school failure of the 1980s and 1990s (Anyon,

2005; Kozol, 1991). Modeled after the Peace Corps, TFA markets itself as the opportunity for recent college graduates to teach for at least two years in underresourced communities, with the potential to learn and lead for a lifetime as a result of this experience (Kopp, 2003). Though it began with just 500 teachers in six locations around the country, TFA currently exists in 29 urban and rural regions with more than 6,000 new TFA teachers in classrooms in 2009 and over 20,000 alumni who have entered the education field through it. Their model is: new teachers—termed "corps members"—attend a five-week intensive summer training program in partner school districts where they participate in courses on instructional planning and delivery, classroom management and culture, literacy, and diversity. TFA corps members also teach summer school while getting coached and mentored by experienced former corps members and school district-employed teachers. TFA purports that "Education inequity is our nation's greatest injustice" and it encourages interested would-be teacher-leaders that they have the capacity to change this situation (Teach For America, n.d.).

Knowledge Is Power Program

Knowledge Is Power Program (KIPP) schools were started by two Teach For America alumni in 1995 to maintain high academic standards for students in underserved communities. Though it started as one middle school (grades five through eight) in Houston, Texas, and one in Bronx, New York, this network of charter schools has grown to almost seventy schools nationwide, now including elementary and high schools. Their mottos for faculty and students include: "All of us will learn," "Work hard," and "Be nice." Their methods include ten-hour school days, Saturday classes, and mandatory summer school for all. This intense environment lends itself to teachers who display leadership by taking on tasks that go beyond the scope of the traditional classroom teacher role. KIPP aims to get all their students to attend college, and they urge their students to attend private and college-preparatory high schools to accomplish this goal (Matthews, 2009; KIPP, 2008).

The New Teacher Project and New Leaders for New Schools

After earning a master's degree in public policy from the Kennedy School of Government at Harvard, another TFA alumna and some colleagues formed the nonprofit organization The New Teacher Project (TNTP) to aid school districts facing enormous challenges staffing their schools and classrooms with individuals who could and would teach all students effectively. They aim to collaborate with and support school districts in their quests to determine the most appropriate course of action based on district needs and context (The New Teacher Project, n.d.). Similarly, New Leaders for New Schools unites with school districts to improve the leadership capacity of urban schools. However, it does not limit itself to merely "principal training." Instead, like TFA, it couches itself as a movement, for teacher-leaders to expand their excellence beyond the confines of their classrooms to whole schools for the sake of increased student achievement (New Leaders for New Schools, n.d.).

Teacher Advancement Program

Another educational entrepreneurial reform effort is the Teacher Advancement Program (TAP). Its founder says he should have called it a system rather than a program (Sawchuk, 2009b). It creates pathways to leadership for classroom teachers while infusing schools and their educators with clear, high expectations for teaching practices and instructional behaviors (both from the classroom instructors and their appraisers) in order to transform student achievement in schools. In addition to constant mentoring, coaching, and instructional feedback, all educators in TAP schools are compensated when student achievement increases. Advocates for TAP, like those who support TFA, TNTP, and NLNS, view this system as a mechanism to transform traditional understandings of educators' work as isolated, individual, and independent.

All these entrepreneurial efforts provide opportunities for educators early in their careers to experience leadership opportunities to impact the type of growth they want to see in their classrooms and their schools. While "public schools are extraordinarily resistant to change . . . conflicts between teacher unions on the one hand and school boards and administrators on the other over issues of pay and working conditions have made it all but impossible to build consensus about how to redesign the schools' outdated systems of instruction" (Wilms, 2003, p. 607), these organizations understand that teachers are leaders who use their strengths, talents, and work to dramatically change the conditions of their classrooms, their schools, and students' lives.

Redefining Teaching as Leadership

Thus far in this discussion of teaching as leadership, we have described an attempt to lead schools into high student achievement for all via the No Child

Left Behind Act and its state testing programs. We have also presented education innovators who identified specific quandaries in schooling structures and practices that they set out to rectify. Teach For America, the Knowledge Is Power Program, The New Teacher Project, New Leaders for New Schools, and the Teacher Advancement Program all typify what we mean by teaching as leadership. High expectations for performance and use of data to measure whether or not those standards are being met are common denominators of teaching as leadership. Additionally, the missions and visions of TFA, KIPP, TNTP, NLNS, and TAP suggest the crucial role of individual educators' capacities to lead if schools are to be reformed. This type of leadership abandons traditional notions of educational hierarchies housed within the roles of the principal, school board, superintendent and other central office bureaucrats.

Teaching as leadership is not about management through mandates. Instead, it requires teachers to be self-governing individuals who lead their classrooms and inspire their colleagues through personal responsibility, vision, humility, professionalism, and a deep faith in the capacity of others to ensure high academic success for all students, regardless of community context (Barth, 2001). Teacher-leaders are knowledgeable and supportive, knowing that their colleagues' teaching performances and students' achievement are a direct reflection of the collaboration and coaching they receive (Martin, 2007; Anderson, 2004). Specifically, teacher-leaders are often educators in the "second stage" of their careers with four to ten years of teaching experience (Johnson & Donaldson, 2007). Though they may remain full-time classroom instructors, they may serve as master teacher, testing coordinator, grade-level chair, content specialist, department head, professional developer, or school growth facilitator, etc. (Firestone & Martinez, 2007). The work of teacher-leaders matters most because their colleagues often look to them as the models for instructional excellence against which they measure themselves.

Standards for Teaching as Leadership

"[T]he tragedy in life does not lie in not reaching a goal. The tragedy lies in having no goal to reach. It is not a disgrace not to reach the stars, but it is a disgrace to have no stars to reach for. Not failure but low aim is sin."

—Benjamin E. Mays

Presently, there is a culture of complacency around teaching quality that currently exists for and in public schools throughout the nation. The National Council on Teaching Quality (2008) and The New Teacher Project (2009) both argued that state and district standards are often a vague arrangement of the lowest common expectations for educators, making the bar for teaching quality extremely low (Cohen, Walsh, & Biddle, 2008; Weisberg et al., 2009). This does not provide much for traditional classroom educators to strive for. In Table 12.1, consider two ambitious examples of high standards held for teaching practices.

Table 12.1 Teaching Standards

National Board of Professional Teaching Standards Five Core Propositions	Teach For America's "Teaching As Leadership" Framework for Teacher Effectiveness
1. Teachers are committed to students and their learning. 2. Teachers know the subjects they teach and how to teach those subjects to their students. 3. Teachers are responsible for managing and monitoring student learning. 4. Teachers think systematically about their practice and learn from experience. 5. Teachers are members of learning communities.	1. Teachers set an ambitious vision of students' academic success. 2. Teachers invest students and their families in working hard toward the vision. 3. Teachers plan purposefully to meet ambitious academic goals. 4. Teachers execute those plans thoroughly and effectively. 5. Teachers work relentlessly to meet high academic goals for students. 6. Teachers continuously reflect and improve on leadership and effectiveness.
(National Board of Professional Teaching Standards, n.d.)	(Teach for America, n.d.)

National Board Certification is for teachers at the pinnacle of their careers, and those who earn this status are revered nationally as the best among America's public school teachers. Teach For America teachers are just beginning in the profession. Yet, the standards held for educators affiliated with both of these organizations demonstrate a shared understanding of teaching as complex, arduous, harrowing, and rewarding, as is leadership. In fact, both sets of standards have redefined teaching as leadership. Educators affiliated with either organization, who aspire to meet these standards, are ambitious, professional, student-centered leaders who recognize students as whole people with lives that extend beyond the academic content taught and the exams they take.

They are insatiable constant learners who know their area of focus and know how to get students to understand what they teach. They emphasize equity, appreciating and teaching to individual differences, not treating all students as if they are the same. Resourceful, relentless, and resilient, they employ multiple instructional methods and understand that their job is not done until every student has mastered the skills, understood the content, and demonstrated sophisticated ways of thinking. Ambitious yet realistic, analytical though quick-thinking, they know intelligence is malleable and that all students can achieve academically at high levels, regardless of context or condition. Conscientious and deliberate, they collaborate with other educators, parents, and community members and are reflective reformers of their practice, never becoming undone by the conditions in which they may teach. These teachers lead their students and encourage their colleagues to understand that context must not predict outcomes. Leadership is chiefly needed for educators to reach these high professional expectations. If meaningful school reform is to occur within American public schools, rigorous standards should be held of all educators, not just those who seek to be exceptions to the rule of mediocrity (Cohen et al., 2008; Weisberg et al., 2009). With universally high standards for teachers and the framework of teaching as leadership, teachers must look beyond the narrow confines of their own classrooms and their own students to take responsibility for elements elsewhere in their school buildings.

Teacher-Leaders and Professional Learning Communities

"Coming together is a beginning; keeping together is a process; working together is a success."

—Henry Ford

Teachers must be re-imagined as leaders and teaching understood as leadership if the student achievement crisis that faces our most underresourced and underserved communities is to be reversed. While some perceive accountability through state testing as the advancement of rote learning and an affront to critical thinking, teacher-leaders understand that poor performance on any assessment from any of their students is unacceptable. As research on educator resilience has demonstrated, "Teacher and teacher-leader success were defined in terms of student achievement being the same as or higher scores on reading or mathematics than the respective state average" (Patterson, Collins, & Abbott, 2004, p. 4). Therefore, they do not bemoan standardized tests; they recognize that these exams merely provide one set of data about students' performance levels (Henning, 2006; Lieberman, Saxl, & Miles, 2000).

As sites of reflection, collaboration, and collective improvement, Professional Learning Communities (PLCs) insist on and inspire the action-oriented collaboration and collective inquiry of educators in pursuit of the constant improvement of their school. PLCs are all about proactive, positive responses to the data that schools generate about the whole school and students' academic and behavioral performances, and educators in PLCs are focused on the school as the unit of positive change in the lives of students (DuFour, 2004; DuFour, Eaker, & DuFour, 2005). NCLB has made student performance data more available, which can be used to improve instruction and students' learning. In PLCs, educators see themselves as responsible for the learning of all students in the school. Educators work together to ensure all students learn, even when it does not happen the first time. "Professional dialogue" propagates throughout these PLCs; transparency, shared decision-making, collective responsibility of school staff, and de-personalized interpretation of teachers' instruction and student performance data is ever-present (Du Four, 2004). Nieto (2003) found that a committed professional community is one of the most important things that keeps highly devoted educators teachers going.

This type of cooperation has been empirically tested to yield moderate increases in student achievement. In the hierarchical linear modeling analysis of fourth-grade classes in 47 elementary schools in a large urban district, Goddard, Goddard, and Tschannen-Moran (2007) found that teacher collaboration resulted in higher math and reading test scores than in the schools where teacher collaboration was less existent. Educational accountability can be tied to greater cohesion among school staffs when they unite to ensure teachers teach and students learn. Still, maintaining a cohesive community of learning professionals in the midst of uncertain outcomes for students may have high costs for teacher-leaders.

Costs of Teacher-Leadership

"Among educators there has to be an acknowledgement that any effort to transform institutions . . . must take into consideration the fears teachers have when asked to shift their paradigms . . . [T]here can be, and usually is, some degree of pain involved in giving up old ways of thinking and knowing and learning new approaches."

—bell hooks

While Professional Learning Communities can be cadres of highly committed educators, they require teacher-leaders to ask and face self-critical questions about student achievement in one's classroom and the classrooms of colleagues, even when the answers yielded are unpleasant and difficult to own (Lieberman et al., 2000). There can be no shutting of doors, not just because of the spirit of PLCs, but also because of the consequences rendered from lack of achievement under NCLB, which may jeopardize the careers of all educators in a school (Bowman, 2004). To be a teacher-leader is to be in a constant state of discomfort.

When their instructional success is known, they risk being alienated by peers who covet their achievements. Because of their achievement, teacher-leaders often persist between the tension of remaining as high-performing classroom teachers and moving beyond those walls to coach their colleagues' instruction, ever uncertain that their efforts will produce better results for students. For those who are out of their classrooms performing specialized roles, the stakes are even higher because their success rests in the work of others. To make matters worse, opaque hiring and appointment processes may create jealousy among colleagues. Because many school systems have inaccurate methods of measuring teaching quality, traditionally, teaching effectiveness has been conflated with teaching experience (Cohen et al., 2008). Teacher-leadership positions have sometimes, thus, been yielded to teachers with the most classroom experience. Within these seniority-laden systems, resentment may arise that young teachers are viewed as school leaders (Johnson & Donaldson, 2007; York-Barr & Duke, 2004). Additionally, there may be unclear lines of authority for teacher-leaders as they instruct, coach, and assess their colleagues without having power to hold them accountable for noncompliance with recommendations for improvement (York-Barr & Duke, 2004).

Instructing through specialized roles requires teacher-leaders to challenge, encourage, urge, and celebrate their peers; to offer commendations and cautions; to exhibit constant sensitivity to the personal and professional needs of team members. In many teacher-education courses on classroom management, would-be educators are taught about the ethics of caring: the notion that students' misbehaviors are addressed in a way that does not attack the student but preserves her dignity. This is done so soon-to-be teachers learn the importance of being firm and holding high expectations for behavior while communicating to students that, though they are welcome in the classroom, their misbehavior is not. This is a civilizing, humanizing effort. Likewise, teacher-leaders must consider their colleagues' deficits but always capitalize on their assets and preserve civility, collegiality, and dignity of their colleagues, especially in the midst of conflicts, toward the goal of improved teaching quality and higher student achievement and school community outcomes (Warren, 2002; Dickar, 2008). In short, teaching as leadership requires humility and noticing colleagues' unexpressed needs (Noddings, 2006). Navigating school cultures entails patience and precise action. It may also necessitate the teacher-leader superseding his or her own comfort for that of others or potentially sacrifice his or her effectiveness.

Reframing teaching as leadership has costs for teacher-leaders, but there are also potential risks for school communities as paradigmatic and practice shifts occur. Though most schools have within them educators who remain classroom instructors for thirty-year careers, teacher-leaders who embody the qualities we have described may begin to imagine their potential impact as they move beyond the confines of the school in which they work. When teaching is viewed as leadership, the insatiable nature of these educators may manifest as a constant search to conquer the next barrier to students' achievement.

Teacher-leaders aspire to watch the excellence they help create at work, and they may feel buoyed by the improvements they see in the classrooms of others (Barth, 2001). They stay within their schools when they believe they are growing professionally, are being groomed by great mentors, have opportunities for advancement, and are trusted and supported in their work (Firestone & Martinez, 2007). When these elements are not in place, teacher-leaders may question the competence of their own administrators to lead and the capacity of their school to education all students well. These questions may cause them to seek to become administrators as another manifestation of teacher-leadership.

There are several issues that may lead to teacher-leaders' premature transitions from their schools. Among these issues is the mass exodus of colleagues, school leadership through dictates, administration resistant to questioning, political maneuvering, and high test scores at all costs—even to the detriment of the health and work–life balance of educators. Even if their schools highly value these teacher-leaders, the presence of these forces may drive them to leave their schools, in spite of their significance within their school communities and how they enhance student achievement and school culture. These disincentives reflect old perceptions of teachers as non-thinking, isolated implementers of classroom instruction. Operating according to these old constructs in this new era of school reform damages the potential of teaching as leadership and destroys possibilities of eradicating school performance inequities. Underserved for far too long, urban school students can ill afford to remain the victims of adults who refuse to shift their paradigms toward constant learning and shared leadership.

Future Possibilities of Teacher-Leadership

Student achievement for the masses will not improve without changes in teaching behaviors and the thinking that examines, critiques, and guides those behaviors. Schools will reform when the conceptualization and implementation of teachers' work redefines teachers as leaders and teaching as leadership (Phelps, 2008). This is especially important given the implications of the teaching as leadership issues explored here in relation to the new presidential administration. While it is uncertain how the No Child Left Behind accountability system will fare under President Obama's administration, the suggestion is that incentives and merit pay programs will expand for high-quality teacher-leaders who can demonstrate their effectiveness through their students' academic outcomes and the relationships they foster with their colleagues and school communities. Furthermore, educational entrepreneurs will continue to gain greater access to supplying teacher-leaders to schools and to creating or managing schools: the Obama administration favors charter schools, many of which are prideful that they employ teachers who view themselves as leaders, and there is increasing public distrust of bureaucratic school districts in the face of prolonged underperformance. Prior embodiments of teaching as solo endeavors will succumb as teachers understand their domain as enlarged for the sake of collective impact.

Conclusion

School district–wide opportunities and conditions for teacher-leaders to lead, learn, and grow are paramount if schools are to be reformed. Principal training to identify strong educators, to develop them into teacher-leaders, and to create teaching as leadership conditions, is of chief concern. These conditions include transparency, shared decision-making, collective responsibility, civility, capacity building, trust, and depersonalized analyses of instruction and student performance data (Christman, Brown, Burgess, Kay, Maluk, & Mitchell, 2009). These fundamentals do threaten previous schooling power arrangements, but this alteration also means that schools may actually be reformed toward equity instead of continuing to replicate inequities (Hambright & Franco, 2008; Rorrer et al., 2008).

Striving to surpass high standards for achievement and appraising strides toward the goal for teacher-leaders and students is the hallmark of a community where teaching is understood as leadership. In this new culture of improvement, no one is exempt from scrutiny. Teacher-leaders embrace it as an opportunity to demonstrate their accomplishments and to highlight the work that must keep happening if school reform is to be a fact of our society. When teaching as leadership and teachers as leaders are the solid facts of our schools instead of the imagined, educators, schools, and the communities they inhabit will be transformed, and the academic achievement and subsequent prospects for the students they serve will be transfigured.

References

Alvarez, R. L. (2003). "There's no such thing as an unqualified teacher": Unionization and integration in the Philadelphia public schools. *The Historian, 65*(4), 837–865.

Anyon, J. (2005). *Radical possibilities.* New York: Routledge.

Anderson, K. D. (2004). The nature of teacher leadership in schools as reciprocal influences between teacher leaders and principals. *School Effectiveness and School Improvement, 15*(1), 97–113.

Argue, K., Honeyman, S., & Shlay, A. B. (2006). *Separate and unequal: The distribution of instructional resources in the School District of Philadelphia, 2001–2005.* Philadelphia: Research for Democracy.

Aronson, J. (2004). The threat of stereotype. *Educational Leadership, 62*(3), 14–19.

Ball, A. F. (2002). Three decades of research on classroom life: Illuminating the classroom communicative lives of America's at-risk students. *Review of Research in Education, 26,* 71–111.

Barth, R. S. (2001, February). Teacher leader. *Phi Delta Kappan,* 443–449.

Birger, J. (1996). Race, reaction, and reform: The three Rs of Philadelphia school politics, 1965–1971. *Pennsylvania Magazine of History and Biography, 120,* 165–216.

Bobek, B. L. (2002). Teacher resiliency: A key to career longevity. *The Clearing House, 75*(4), 202–205.

Bond, G. C. (1981). Social economic status and educational achievement: A review article. *Anthropology & Education Quarterly, 12*(4), 227–257.

Bowman, R. (2004). Teachers as leaders. *The Clearing House, 77*(5), 187–189.

Carr, N. (2008). The pay-for-performance pitfall. *American School Board Journal, 195*(2), 38-39.

Christman, J. B., Brown, D., Burgess, S., Kay, J., Maluk, H. P., & Mitchell, C. (2009). *Effective organizational practices for middle and high school grades: A qualitative study of what's helping Philadelphia students succeed in grades 6–12.* Philadelphia: Research for Action.

Cohen, E., Walsh, K., &Biddle, R. (2008). *Invisible ink in collective bargaining: Why key issues are not addressed.* Washington, DC: National Council on Teaching Quality.

Copenhaver-Johnson, J. (2007). Rolling back advances in multicultural education: No child left behind and "highly qualified teachers." *Multicultural Perspectives, 9*(4), 40–47.

Countryman, M. J. (2006). *Up south: Civil rights and black power in Philadelphia*. Philadelphia: University of Pennsylvania.

Darling-Hammond, L., & Berry, B. (2006). Highly qualified teachers for all. *Educational Leadership, 64*(3), 14–20.

Dickar, M. (2008). Hearing the silenced dialogue: An examination of the impact of teacher race on their experiences. *Race Ethnicity and Education, 11*(2), 115–132.

Dillon, N. (2008). The merit scale. *American School Board Journal, 195*(4), 28–30.

Du Four, R. (2004). What is a professional learning community? *Educational Leadership, 61*(8), 6–11.

Du Four, R., Eaker, R., & Du Four, R. (2005). Recurring themes of professional learning communities and the assumptions they challenge. In R. Du Four, R. Eaker, & R. Du Four (Eds.) *On common ground: The power of professional learning communities* (pp. 7–29). Bloomington, IN: National Education Service.

Firestone, W. A., & Martinez, M. C. (2007). Districts, teacher leaders, and distributed leadership: Changing instructional practice. *Leadership and Policy in Schools, 6*, 3–35.

Flannery, M. E., & Jehlen, A. (2008, March). Salary trends: Where is your pay plan heading? *NEA Today*, 38–41.

Gamoran, A. (1996). Student achievement in public magnet, public comprehensive, and private city high schools. *Educational Evaluation and Analysis, 18*(1), 1–18.

Grier, T. B., & Holcombe, A. A. (2008, April). Mission possible: a North Carolina school district solves the problem of recruiting and retaining teachers in its most challenging schools. *Educational Leadership*, 25–30.

Goddard, Y. L., Goddard, R. D., & Tschannen-Moran, M. (2007). A theoretical and empirical investigation of teacher collaboration for school improvement and student achievement in public elementary schools. *Teachers College Record, 109*(4), 877–896.

Hambright, W. G., & Franco, M. S. (2008). Living the "tipping point": Concurrent teacher leader and principal preparation. *Education, 129*(2), 267–273.

Harris, D. N. (2007). High-flying schools, student disadvantage, and the logic of NCLB. *American Journal of Education, 113*, 367–394.

Harris, D. N., & Herrington, C. D. (2006). Accountability, standards, and the growing achievement gap: Lessons from the past half-century. *American Journal of Education, 112*, 209–238.

Henning, J. (2006). Teacher leaders at work: Analyzing standardized achievement data to improve instruction. *Education, 126*(4), 729–737.

Hilliard, A. (2003). No mystery: Closing the achievement gap between African Americans and excellence. In T. Perry, C. Steele, and A. Hilliard (Eds) *Young, gifted, and Black: Promoting high achievement among African-American students* (pp. 131–165). Boston: Beacon Press.

hooks, b. (1994). *Teaching to transgress: Education as the practice of freedom*. New York: Routledge.

Honawar, V. (2008). Performance-pay studies show few student achievement gains. *Education Week, 27*(27), 7.

Honawar, V., & Olson, L. (2008). Advancing pay for performance. *Education Week, 27*(18), 26–31.

Hoy, W. K., Tarter, C. J., & Woolfolk Hoy, A. (2006). Academic optimism of schools: A force for student achievement. *American Educational Research Journal, 43*(3), 425–466.

Jacobson, L. (2009). State budget chills send shivers through K-12 circles. *Education Week*, 28(12), 19.

Johnson, S. M., & Donaldson, M. L. (2007, September). Overcoming the obstacles to leadership. *Educational Leadership*, 8-13.

Jones, B. A. (2005). Forces for failure and genocide: The plantation model of urban educational policy making in St. Louis. *Educational Studies*, 37(1), 6-24.

Kantor, H. (1991). Education, social reform, and the state: ESEA and federal education policy in the 1960s. *American Journal of Education*, 47-83.

Keller, B. (2008). Houston, Denver move into next stage of pay plans. *Education Week*, 27(23), 12-13.

KIPP. (n.d.). About KIPP. Retrieved June 11, 2009, from http://www.kipp.org/01/.

Koops, J. B., & Winsor, K. A. (2006). Creating a professional learning culture through faculty evaluation. *The Journal of Evaluation*, 186 (3), 61-70.

Kopp, W. (2003). *One day, all children . . .The unlikely triumph of Teach For America and what I learned along the way*. New York: Public Affairs Books.

Kozol, J. (1991). *Savage inequalities*. New York: Harper Perennial.

Kurz, N., Woolfolk Hoy, A., & Hoy, W. K. (2007, April). *Predictors of academic optimism: Teachers' instructional beliefs and professional commitment*. Paper presented at the annual meeting of the American Educational Research Association, Chicago, IL.

Lee, J., & Wong, K. K. (2004). The impact of accountability on racial and socioeconomic equity: Considering both school resources and achievement outcomes. *American Educational Research Journal*, 41(4), 797-832.

Lee, J. (2008). Is test driven external accountability effective? Synthesizing the evidence from cross-state causal-comparative and correlational studies. *Review of Educational Research*, 78(3), 608-644.

Lieberman, A., Saxl, E. R., & Miles, M. B. (2000). Teacher leadership: Ideology and practice. In *The Jossey-Bass Reader on Educational Leadership* (1st ed.). San Francisco: Jossey-Bass.

Lipman, P. (2004). *High stakes education: Inequality, globalization and urban school reform*. New York: Taylor & Francis.

Mac Iver, M. A., & Vaughn, E. S. (2007). "But how long will they stay?" Alternative certification and new teacher retention in an urban district. *Educational Research Service Spectrum*, 25(2), 33-44.

Martin, B. (2007). Teacher leaders: Qualities and roles. *The Journal for Quality and Participation*, 30(4), 17-18.

Matthews, J. (2009). *Work hard. Be nice: How two teachers created the most promising schools in America*. Chapel Hill, NC: Algonquin Books.

McNeil, M. (2009a). Budget pain dampening K-12 efforts. *Education Week*, 28(16), 1-2.

_____. (2009b). Districts scrounge for low-pain budget cuts. *Education Week*, 28(18), 6-7.

Mirel, J. (1998). After the fall: Continuity and change in Detroit, 1981-1995. *History of Education Quarterly*, 38(3), 237-267.

National Board for Professional Teaching Standards. (n.d.). The five core propositions. Retrieved July 1, 2009, from http://www.nbpts.org/the_standards/the_five_core_propositio.

Neild, R., Useem, E., Travers, E., & Lesnick, J. (2003). *Once and for all: Placing a highly teacher in every Philadelphia classroom: What we know and need to do*. Philadelphia: Research for Action.

Neild, R., Useem, E., Farley, E. (2005). *The quest for quality: recruiting and retaining teachers in Philadelphia.* Philadelphia, PA: Research for Action.

New Leaders for New Schools. (n.d.). The program. Retrieved July 1, 2009, from http://www.nlns.org/Mission.jsp.

Nieto, S. (2003). *What keeps teachers going?* New York: Teachers College Press.

Noddings, N. (2006). Educational leaders as caring teachers. *School Leadership and Management,* 26(4), 339-345.

Patterson, J. H., Collins, L., Abbott, G. (2004). A study of teacher resilience in urban schools. *Journal of Instructional Psychology,* 31(1), 3-11

Perlstein, D. H. (2004). *Justice, justice: School politics and the eclipse of liberalism.* New York: Peter Lang.

Phelps, P. H. (2008). Helping teachers become leaders. *The Clearing House, 81*(3), 119-122.

Phillips, A. E. (2005). A history of the struggle for school desegregation in Philadelphia, 1955-1967. *Pennsylvania History: A Journal of Mid-Atlantic Studies, 72,* 49-76.

Ramanathan, A. (2008). Paved with good intentions: The federal role in the oversight and enforcement of the Individuals with Disabilities Education Act (IDEA) and the No Child Left Behind Act (NCLB). *Teachers College Record, 110*(2), 278-321.

Rex, L. A., & Nelson, M. C. (2004). How teachers' professional identities position high-stakes test preparation in their classrooms. *Teachers College Record, 106*(6), 1299-1331.

Rist, R. C. (1973). *The urban school: A factor for failure.* Cambridge: MIT Press.

Rorrer, A. K., Skrla, L., & Scheurich, J. J. (2008). Districts as institutional actors in educational reform. *Educational Administration Quarterly, 44*(3), 307-358.

Rothstein, R. (2009). The perils of quantitative performance accountability. In EPI Series on Alternative Teacher Compensation Systems, No. 1. *Teachers, Performance Pay, and Accountability: What Education Should Learn from Other Sectors* (pp. 67-99). Washington, DC: Economic Policy Institute.

Rury, J. L. (1999). Race, space and the politics of Chicago's public schools: Benjamin Willis and the tragedy of urban education. *History of Education Quarterly, 39*(2), 117-142.

Saporito, S. (2003). Private choices, public consequences: Magnet school choice and segregation by race and poverty. *Social Problems, 50*(2), 181-203.

Sawchuk, S. (2009a). Layoff policies could diminish teacher reform. *Education Week, 28*(22), 12-15.

Sawchuk, S. (2009b). TAP: More than performance pay. *Education Week, 28*(27), 25-27.

Schneider, M., & Buckley, J. (2003). Comparing DC charter schools to other DC public schools. *Educational Evaluation and Policy Analysis, 25*(3), 203-215.

Searby, L., & Shaddix, L. (2008). Growing teacher leaders in a culture of excellence. *Professional Educator, 32*(1), 1-9.

Taylor, E. (2006). A critical race analysis of the achievement gap in the United States: Politics, reality, and hope. *Leadership and Policy in Schools, 5,* 71-87.

Teach For America. (n.d.). Our history. Retrieved June 11, 2009, from http://www.teachforamerica.org/about/our_history.htm.

_____. (n.d.) Homepage. Retrieved June 11, 2009, from http://www.teachforamerica.org-index.htm).

_____. (n.d.). Teaching as leadership framework. Retrieved July 1, 2009, from http://www.teachforamerica.org/corps/teaching/teaching_leadership_framework.htm.

The New Teacher Project. (n.d.). About us: Our history. Retrieved June 11, 2009, from http://www-.tntp.org/aboutus/our_history.html.

Tschannen-Moran, M., & Woolfolk Hoy, A. (2001). Teacher efficacy: Capturing an elusive construct. *Teaching and Teacher Education, 17*(7), 783–805.

Useem, E., Offenberg, R., & Farley, E. (2007). *Closing the teacher quality gap in Philadelphia: New hope and old hurdles.* Philadelphia: Research for Action.

Vergari, S. (2007). Federalism and market-based education policy: The supplemental educational services mandate. *American Journal of Education, 113,* 311–339.

Warren, S. R. (2002). Stories from the classrooms: How expectations and efficacy of diverse teachers affect the academic performance of children in poor urban schools. *Educational Horizons, 80*(3), 109–116.

Weiner, L. (1999). To teach or not to teach in an urban school? *English Journal, 88*(5), 21–25.

Weisberg, D., Sexton, S., Mulhern, J., & Keeling, D. (2009). *The widget effect.* New York: The New Teacher Project.

Wellisch, J. B., MacQueen, A. H., Carriere, R. A., & Duck, G. A. (1978). School management and organization in successful schools (ESAA In-Depth Study School). *Sociology of Education, 51*(3), 211–226.

Wilms, W. W. (2003, April). Altering the structure and culture of American public schools. *Phi Delta Kappan,* 606–615.

York-Barr, J., & Duke, K. (2004). What do we know about teacher leadership? Findings from two decades of scholarship. *Review of Educational Research, 74*(3), 255–316.

✠ CHAPTER 13

Transforming Leadership Preparation for Social Justice: Dissatisfaction, Inspiration, and Rebirth— an Exemplar

C. Cryss Brunner, Karen Hammel, and Michael D. Miller

> The projects that we feature . . . reflect the sweeping visions of designers and archi-
> tects whose job, in a sense, is to be dissatisfied with what has come before: [the] old
> and inappropriate. . . . Each project . . . represents some sort of *radical transformation*
> [our emphasis]; but only once a year do we show you the . . . stages of this amazing
> process. We do it to remind you that no project is hopeless, no task too overwhelm-
> ing. [Anything] that seems beyond redemption is, in fact, capable of being dramati-
> cally reborn. Such transformations may begin with dissatisfaction, but they always end
> with well-deserved pride. Between the two comes inspiration—which is what we're of-
> fering here.
>
> —Paige (2003, p. 38)

In education, we are not lacking dissatisfaction—dissatisfaction with schools, teachers, administrators, *and* even with the reform efforts meant to correct our dissatisfactions. In fact, contemporary public school reform focused on high achievement for *every* child began as early as 1970 and continues today. And while "criticism of the ways in which men and women are prepared for school leadership positions enjoys a long history" (Murphy, 1992, p. 79), a critical eye was not turned on educational administrators in light of their connection to reform, or on their preparation programs as related to reform until the mid-1980s (Griffiths, 1988; Griffiths, Stout, & Forsyth, 1988; Murphy, 1992; Peterson & Finn, 1985). Once under scrutiny, preparation programs were found seriously wanting (See Campbell, et al., 1987; Cooper & Boyd, 1987; Culbertson, 1964; Farquar, 1977; Glass, 1986; Gregg, 1969; Hallinger, Leithwood, & Murphy, 1993; McCarthy, 1999b; Moore, 1964; Murphy, 1990, 1991, 1992; Silver, 1982).

The primary reason for the eventual attention on educational leadership preparation programs was the broad-based agreement that because school leadership roles affect participant learning, achievement for each child should be central to their purpose (Cambron-McCabe, 1993; Leithwood, 1994; Yukl, 1994). Thus, it is not surprising that standards-based reform initiatives have spread from standards for participants to standards for teachers and administrators (McCarthy, 1999a). As a result, educational leadership preparation programs are under pressure to produce administrators who can lead reform that equalizes and improves education for all participants (Kohn, 1998; Peebles, 2000). In no small measure, preparation programs need transformations that help rectify dissatisfactions with school leaders.

To that end, this chapter will focus on an innovative approach to leadership preparation that results in the dramatic shift in thinking necessary for administrators and others (Nadler & Tushman, 1995; Heifetz & Laurie, 1997) to co-create democratic, socially just learning organizations (Beck & Murphy, 1997; Peebles, 2000)—organizations in which shared, participatory decision-making occurs (Anderson, 1998; Leithwood & Duke, 1999). Thus, the threefold purpose of this chapter is to (a) identify a particular dissatisfaction with school leaders, (b) describe an innovative approach—inspired by social justice—to this dissatisfaction, and (c) highlight evidence that the approach provides an experience of "rebirth" or change for participants. For our discussion, we organize the chapter using the three stages of radical transformation identified in the chapter's beginning quote—dissatisfaction, inspiration, and rebirth.

The First Stage—Unyielding Dissatisfaction: The Challenges of Shared Decision-Making

In our quest for transformed leaders and preparation programs, we find ourselves in the first broad stage of radical transformation—dissatisfaction. In order to discuss of this first stage, we narrow our focus to a particular dissatisfaction—authentic participatory decision-making—that remains an important, yet unsuccessful part of reform efforts that advance social justice.

On one hand, some educational literature suggests that shared decision-making supports social justice. For example, Gary Anderson (1998) states that "many advocates of poor and disenfranchised groups claim that participation of any form holds out the possibility of greater accountability from educational institutions that have tended to at best ignore them and at worst pathologize them" (Anderson, 1998, p. 582). On the other hand, Anderson continues, some researchers at more micropolitical levels have provided documentation of the "ways participation is subverted even when diverse groups are brought to the table" (Henry, 1996; Malen, 1994; Malen & Ogawa, 1988: Mann, 1974).

In their study, Malen and Ogawa (1988) found that even under ideal conditions in which teachers and parents should have been able to have substantial influence on significant decisions, the following occurred:

> First, although the site councils are authorized policymakers, they function as ancillary advisors and pro forma endorsers. Second, teachers and parents are granted parity, but principals and professionals control the partnerships. Third, although teachers and parents had access to decision-making arenas, their inclusion has maintained, not altered, the decision-making relationships typically and traditionally found in schools. (p. 256, cited in Anderson, 1998, p. 582)

Thus, research documents the misuse and ineffectiveness of shared decision-making (see also, Delpit, 1994; Oakes, 1985; Popkewitz, 1979; Weiler, 1990) in its various forms, including the problems related to site-based management (SBM) (see Kahne, 1994; Malen & Ogawa, 1988; Newmann, King, & Rigdon, 1997). Several concerns with shared decision-making, identified by research, are related to power relationships and the redistribution of decision-making authority (Malen & Ogawa, 1988; Malen, Ogawa, & Kranz, 1990; Ogawa, 1994; Reitzug & Capper, 1996; Wohlsetter, Smyer, & Mohrman, 1994). In the face of this documentation Anderson (1998) suggests, "the discourse of participation has been absorbed into educational institutions in ways that are often manipulative and nondemocratic" (p. 586). And yet, he continues:

> I am not arguing that this cooptation of participatory discourse for nondemocratic ends is always done with Machiavellian intentionality. In many cases, attempts at increased participation are sincere but poorly conceived and implemented or caught up in a larger institutional and societal logic that is antithetical to norms of participation. Shifting our notions of participation may require not only understanding the contradictions, inauthenticities, and ideological agendas of the current discourse of participation but also creating new discourses that address broader democratic issues of social justice and are do-able, in the sense that they address current barriers to participation at both micro and macro levels. (p. 586)

In the remainder of Anderson's insightful article, he outlines a framework for moving toward what he refers to as "authentic participation" (p. 587). His framework consists of five central questions: "(a) Participation toward what end? (b) Who participates? (c) What are relevant spheres of participation? (d) What conditions and processes must be present locally to make participation authentic (i.e., the micropolitics of participation)? (e) What conditions and processes must be present at broader institutional and societal levels to make participation authentic (i.e., the macropolitics of participation)?"

In a discussion of the fourth question—"What conditions and processes must be present locally to make participation authentic?"—Anderson (1998) states, "Lipman (1997) found that participatory school restructuring cannot transform the educational experiences of marginalized participants unless changes occur at both personal and societal levels. She argues that educators' beliefs and assumptions, as well as relations of power in schools and communities, must be challenged" (p. 591). Anderson continues by quoting Lipman, who wrote,

> Without multiple voices, without authorization and support to reexamine critically the very core of beliefs and practices related to disempowered participants, without a public agenda which challenged the culture and power of dominant interests, teachers had few tools to begin to critically examine prevailing ideologies and political and structural arrangements. Thus, race and class divisions, exclusion, silencing, and lack of engagement across differences were seemingly unmitigated by new opportunities for collaboration. (p. 32)

In sum, opportunities for collaboration do not necessarily in themselves support social justice. Other things must occur. To begin, we agree with Lipman when she asserts that school leaders' personal beliefs and assumptions be critically challenged in light of ones that support authentic participatory reform and socially just decision-making processes. Going further, we advance that school leaders need targeted learning opportunities and experiences aimed at evoking deep essential insights for particular *ontological shifts*. In short, a capacity for social justice including authentic participatory decision-making relies on transformed foundational beliefs. The next section describes an innovative leadership preparation approach that provides experiences designed to encourage ontological shifts in its participants.

The Second Stage—Inspiration: A Promising Innovation [1]

> Increasingly, those involved in research and training in educational leadership have acknowledged the need for better information on how expert school leaders think

about what they do. This is essential to understanding the conditions under which they take action, a prerequisite to the design of effective training. (Hallinger, Leith-wood, & Murphy, 1993, p. 71)

Often literature that focuses on educational leadership preparation or development, as well as the fundamental cognitive changes required for people to become the type of leader needed in today's schools, ends with the question: What must preparation programs include that will change people from what they are to what they must become? Other literature works to answer this question by advancing that leadership preparation itself must move from the past decades' major paradigm that cast leaders as managers. Instead, it is suggested, principals and other administrators need preparation experiences that transform them from "individual people, role" and "a discrete set of individual behaviors" (Lambert, 1998, p. 6) into capacity builders who hold the aim of shared leadership (Peebles, 2000).

The message is clear, leadership preparation programs need to provide experiences that *transform* participants for the type of "leadership that represents the transcendence of self-interest by both leader and led" (Burns, 1978; cited in Leithwood & Jantzi, 1999, p. 453).[2] To be sure, "[t]ransformational approaches to leadership have long been advocated as productive under conditions fundamentally the same as those faced by schools targeted for reform (Leithwood, 1994; Yukl, 1994). Considerable evidence makes the point that transformational practices do contribute to the development of capacity and commitment (e.g., Yammarion, Dubinsky, & Spangler, 1998)" (Leithwood & Jantzi, 1999, p. 452). But, how are preparation programs going to provide the transformational experiences that this literature describes?

In response to this question, we are in the beginning stages of retooling leadership preparation programs to provide the transformational experiences aimed at building the authentically participative, decision-making capacity within school leaders, As stated in Brunner, Hitchon, and Brown (2002),

> The primary purposes of this project are: (a) to address the current concerns about the misuse and ineffectiveness of shared decision-making, specifically ones related to power relationships, [constructions of identity], and the redistribution of decision-making authority through the development of, what we refer to as, technologically delivered *Experiential Simulations* (ES); and (b) to change the face of higher education preparation programs to meet and adapt to the challenges of the future. For as Schank (2002) suggests, "The virtual schools that will arise to take the place of current institutions will attract participants less because of the credentials they bestow than because of the experiences they offer" (p. 211). In particular, we are convinced that in order to facilitate participatory school restructuring, educational leaders need targeted

and personal learning opportunities—delivered through ES in virtual school—to develop the insights and skills necessary to create and support collaborative practices
and decision-making spaces in which all community members are included—practices
and spaces in which leaders' understandings of power are conceptualized as shared
rather than as over others. (pp. 12–13)

In order to achieve the first aspect of our purposes, we have developed the
Experiential Simulations previously mentioned. In these pursuits, we have
joined others who are evaluating current technological developments that allow individuals to interact in virtual reality (Kopernik et al., 1997; Massaro et
al., 1998; Morishima et al., 1990; Scott & Leong, 2000; Tabor, 1997).

Our research-based work is grounded in theoretically driven classroom experiences and exercises developed between 1994 and 1999 (for full discussion,
see Brunner, 2002). In the past, in order to teach about conceptions of power
and their inter- and intra-relationship to constructions of difference and collaborative decision-making during courses, Brunner led participants through
classroom-based experiences in which participants uncovered their own conceptions of power. In addition, participants were asked to creatively alter their
own personal backgrounds (education, family, occupation) in order to escape
constructions of difference/identity related to these pieces of background information. These classroom activities, while successful at some levels, were
limited by the physical presence of the participants. Constructions of differ-
ence/identity (related to gender, race, class, and other categories of difference)
and assumptions about power—within decision-making settings—were more
difficult to unpack and make explicit in order to set them aside. Because of
the difficulties noted above, to develop the ES we have taken advantage of the
computer's visualization capabilities to (a) keep individuals' identities hidden
and (b) present individuals to others with a modified persona (MP). There is
little doubt that position/race/gender plays an enormous role in how we respond to each other (See Larson & Ovando, 2001). In fact, our evaluations
have shown that even when all parties are aware (as a part of informed con-
sent) that their identities are being altered, their interactions differ substantially when their positions, race, and/or gender are completely hidden or
appear to each other to be modified.

Using standard online course development tools—Web site, chat room,
threaded discussion, video and audio clips—an instructional plan was developed in which course participants, first with real identities masked and later
altered completely, met online for the first third of the course to collaborate
on an assigned decision-making task (the simulation). The ES involved the

immersion of participants in an environment in which they are perceived by the others (in the environment) to have an identity unlike their "true" identify [for example, women may be men; whites may be people of color]. The altered identity reflects a gender/racial/class/positional identity other than that to which they are accustomed. While interacting with others in this virtual environment, participants "walk in the shoes" of others whose social constructions are different from their own. The interactions occur in carefully designed leadership/policy-forming situations, intended to illustrate how perceptions and understandings of others' identity shape the way leaders enhance or restrict others' participation in decision-making. At the same time, through private communication with the instructor, course participants reflect on questions posed related to identity (gender, race, class, etc.) constructs, power conceptions, and the decision-making processes at play with the group.

In brief, the design of the ES described in this chapter, consists of several steps (full details are too extensive to include in this chapter): (a) Before classes begin, participants are interviewed individually by the instructor and asked to answer questions aimed at determining individuals' conceptions of power and its use. These questions are grounded in Brunner's (see 2002) research on power. During the interview, participants are informed that their identities will be masked in multiple ways during the chat sessions. (b) During the first third of the course, MP participants meet in carefully designed chat room experiences that immerse them in policy decision-making processes that are a part of addressing and accomplishing a specific problem-based task. (c) Between and during online chat sessions, participants answer reflective questions focused on power dynamics, identity constructions, the process of decision-making during task work, and their own role and actions during the sessions. In order to answer some of the questions, they are required to analyze the transcripts from each of the online sessions. They also are asked to read articles that are appropriate for the work online. (d) Online class sessions are followed by face-to-face sessions. (e) At the end of the course, individual exit interviews are conducted by the instructor. Questions are open-ended and focused on gaining insights into participants' understandings and critique of the course experiences.

In the last section of the chapter, a narrative from one participant who experienced the innovative preparation program offers evidence that the inspired, innovative approach has potential to "radically transform" leaders' thinking about power and decision-making and to "rebirth" them in ways that support socially just, authentically participative leadership.

Stage Three—Rebirth: An Exemplar of Radical Transformation

In this leadership (superintendency) preparation class, technology closed the gap between the dissatisfaction with current preparation programs and the necessary rebirth of educational leaders. The class combined technology with sound theoretical principles of transformation—anticipation, absence of control, and reflection (Wong et al., 2000)—to create the acquisition of new knowledge. As one participant, Kelly (pseudonym), recalled, "I logged on not knowing what to expect. I had read the 'task' and thought little of it." In this section, testimony based on the experience of Kelly provides an exemplar to illustrate how her deeply seated, ontological conceptions of power were challenged to the extent that she felt a strong need to change—she became dissatisfied with her own practices during decision-making sessions.

To begin the preparation process, one-on-one interview/informational meeting's between each participant and the professor and individual technology orientations prior to the first scheduled online meeting created the sense of anticipation for participants that is essential for transformation. The anticipation resulting from condensed course information along with technology-related anxiety introduced the tenet that control would not be "owned" by either participant or professor throughout much of the program. While in the chat space, Kelly strongly felt the lack of ownership, even her own. As she stated:

> Surely Cryss would be using [the task] in some interesting way to get us to think about leadership. But I was wrong. Cryss, it turns out, was absent altogether. I took this class to learn from her, to be challenged by her! But she was nowhere to be found except snippets of rules and prompts to take a break. Hell of a lot of good that was. Worse yet, everyone seemed to be taking this task very seriously, as if that is what they came for! What the hell were they thinking? Who gives a rip about some fictional district with some fictional crisis? Surely not me.

In addition to lack of ownership, the a priori and then later experiential understanding that the course environment relative to identity was in motion was the catalyst that moved participants to experience "the opposite of control" (Wong et al., 2001). It was upon experiencing "the opposite of control" that Kelly moved into the first stage of radical transformation—dissatisfaction. She pointedly describes her feelings,

> I remember crawling into bed that night feeling so tense and tired. The chat session, though unproductive, took a great deal out of me and I couldn't figure out why. I told my husband that it was awful, and that I was awful in return. I don't like what I

turned into there, I would tell him. I wanted to be funny and lighthearted, but people took it as sarcastic and caustic. I wanted to help, but no one listened, so I got loud and abrasive. I wanted to be done, but no one responded, so I offered to just do it myself. I thought I had made some good contributions, but they were tossed aside when "O" [the letter given one participant instead of a name; all participants we given a letter of the alphabet] the great goddess of goodness and light came on the scene to rescue everyone. I didn't like the shame that came over me as I thought about who I was, and how I had nothing truly valuable to contribute.

While terms such as learner preference and self-determination have long held places in the ranks of constructivist teaching principles, seemingly, less attention has been given to its invaluable counterpart, "'opposite of control.' We . . . make the point that transformative experience . . . can only occur when the distance and distinction between person and world decreases, rather than increases" (Wong et al., 2000). For as Dewey, (1934; cited in Wong et al., 2000) stated,

> The uniquely distinguishing feature of esthetic experience is exactly the fact that no such distinction of self and object exists in it, since it is esthetic in the degree to which organisms and environment cooperate to institute an experience in which the two are so fully integrated that each disappears. (p. 6)

Thus, "opposite of control" is defined as one's acceptance that external forces outside of one's own intention continuously change rather than the belief that one "has no control," (Wong et al., 2000). Described by the alpine skier who with gravity's momentum travels across the mountain's contour; it is the space occupied when external forces acting upon a person harmonize with their level of intentional exploration. Again, Dewey (1934) from Wong et al. (2000),

> The esthetic or undergoing phase of experience is receptive. It involves surrender. But adequate yielding of the self is possible only through a controlled activity that may well be intense. In much of our intercourse with our surroundings we withdraw; sometimes from fear, if only expending unduly our store of energy; sometimes from preoccupation with other matters, as in the case of recognition. Perception is an act of the going-out of energy in order to receive, not a withholding of energy. To steep ourselves in a subject-matter we have first to plunge into it. When we are only passive to a scene, it overwhelms us and, for lack of answering activity, we do not perceive that which bears us down. We must summon energy and pitch it at a responsive key in order to take in. (p. 53)

Kelly moved quickly into the "undergoing phase" of the experience. She talked about her "surrender" to the intense, controlled activity,

Despite my attempts to draw allies and support for my behavior in the chat room, no one was willing to team up. No one would tell me who they were. None were willing to plot a course of action to carry into the next week so we could complete the task and get on with it. Every one of them was irritated; every one of them spoke negatively about that first night. They all dealt with it differently than I wanted to, though. They maintained a commitment to Cryss's plan, where I was quite done with Dr. Brunner and her stupid class, thank you very much. Sadly, then, without the support of my cohort, I remained alone.

Because the online meetings of the superintendency preparation class were characterized by a chat space saturated with possibilities; amplified by virtue of being without voice, context, or identity, through the hours and sessions to come, participants surrendered to the anonymity posed by technology while at the same time, acting upon it. Kelly spoke clearly about her efforts to act upon the experience,

> I went into the second week ready to sit back. I was going to do nothing, say little. I would contribute my summary and stand back. That plan didn't work well. I couldn't do it. I could not shut up. I told myself that I could not sit by and waste this class while everyone else goofed around and had a big group hug. So week two went by much like the first. The task was coming together slowly, "O" saved the group from certain death, and I was put in my place on occasion for being mean. I had the same resentments, the same conversations with my husband and continued to pursue my cohort to support me—with the same result.

During the chat sessions, participants openly debated ideals of leadership and other issues related to the task at hand, while allowing their internal beliefs to unfold. As opportunities for reflection grew, participants faced various personal truths for the first time. In the end the true test of transformation rested upon each participant's ability to expose and her/his readiness to reflect on what each saw. At this stage, Kelly began to understand what the process invited. She explained, "There was no real excuse for my behavior. There was no reason for getting angry. There was only me. I was starting to get it, that I was creating my own experience, and I felt very alone." Kelly continued with further reflection:

> Most often when I am alone I know the person I'm with. I have clear views of [Kelly] the professional, [Kelly] the teacher (who is different, by the way), [Kelly] the friend, the wife, the mother, the student. I am many, many different things. I was comfortable being many different people. And they are very different. People who know me as a Mom, however, would be shocked at the way I run over people at work. And people at work assume I am a cold disciplinarian with total control over my husband and children. When I speak of it to myself, I am comforted by those distinctions.

> Sometimes I think it's plain old fun, like acting or playing a game. I know that either
> way, my heart is protected. I am nurtured and loved so beautifully at home, and I do
> not want that vulnerability at work. The dangers are too great. This plan was working
> for me.

Clearly, the ES offered densely packed experiences during long online sessions. The final component of transformation critical to the program was the opportunity to reflect. Participants were asked to analyze the transcripts of chat/decision-making sessions and document their reflections through question sets to the instructor. After her analysis of the transcripts, Kelly reflected:

> At any time, I could have chosen to be positive, to shut my mouth, to lift someone
> up, to ask good questions or just walk away. But I did not. I was a leader in that chat
> space. I exercised a great deal of influence. I truly feel that because of my own forceful
> personality, I was the most offensive and hurtful person there. I really am a leader.
> And I am ashamed of the way I lead. . . . I am an administrator. People look to me for
> guidance and example. And they see anger and force and power mongering. They see
> me.

At the conclusion of the online portion of the class, participants met in face-to-face classes promoting further release of significant inter- and intrapersonal findings about leadership and power through discussion and presentation. Kelly expressed her inner struggle as face-to-face classes took place:

> I cannot simply be me and take responsibility for that, because I hurt people. I cannot
> be someone else, because I don't know how. I have to be someone different, yet I am
> not yet ready to face that or come to terms with what that would mean.

Because she had been successful in her career, it was doubly difficult for Kelly to think about a change. This is not an unusual set of circumstances for educational leaders. Change can be dangerous, especially if one has been successful (by whatever measure) in the past. Kelly, who was a newly hired administrator at the time of the class, talked about this tension:

> I did a great job. I am a highly skilled teacher. I am able to handle and welcome every
> participant who walks into my classroom. I love teaching. I know Due Process and
> Special Education Law better than anyone I know. I have recruited and mentored
> new staff. I have contributed tirelessly to the development of a broad spectrum of in-
> clusive services for Special Education students. I was active on countless committees. I
> brought in grants to finance my vision of services. Whenever I asked something of the
> director of special education or the principal, I almost always got it. I became very
> powerful and, I believe, respected in my role. Things were looking really good!

Upon her experience in the class, Kelly moved beyond her defense of her past practice. As she put it,

I was ashamed of my behavior, my attitude, and my lack of respect for others. . . . I was ashamed that, not only could I not identify just one other person in that chat room, I did not care to know the others. I was ashamed that intelligence was not enough. Sarcasm and wit were not enough. The willingness to work harder and faster than anyone else was *still* [original emphasis] not enough. The only conclusion that I could possibly draw was that I was not enough. For a superhero, that was a defeating blow . . . . I cannot imagine another setting where I would have failed so bitterly. I have been, by most accounts, quite successful. For whatever reason, I had been rewarded richly in my professional life.

In fact, once willing to let go of her defense of past practices, Kelly moved further. She remembers,

I began to reach out a little. I engaged in side conversations with cohort members in the class. I tried to be so casual, like it was nothing really, but "I feel like this . . . ." To my surprise, I found someone who had felt the same way. It was not the class that brought her to this same place, but she knew what I meant. She wanted to get together and talk about it sometime, with others as well. She knew that it was a lonely and difficult journey. And the cloud began to lift. It was that ten-minute conversation at break that made all the difference. From that point on, the pieces began to come together.

With the cycle complete, participants recognized a larger picture of themselves as educational leaders and of their connection to the world through anticipation, "the opposite of control," and reflection. Without the use of technology, however, we assert this experience would not have happened. Kelly agrees.

Technology, it turns out, was a significant piece of this experience. It gave me something I would never have thought to ask for: solitude. The chat room gave me the loneliest and most profound professional experience of my life. It took away the task. It took away the politics and power structure. It took away work culture and environment. There was no history and no future. Expectations were gone for all who shared the space. I brought only one thing into the chat room: me. The only things I could take away were connections and relationships. But I walked out as alone as the day I walked in. I cannot imagine another way to bring an experience down to the most essential of human interactions.

Thus, while this exemplar provides the evidence from only one case, it can be said that the ES evoked for/in Kelly the three stages of radical transformation. She became deeply *dissatisfied* with her leadership practices, was intensely *inspired* to alter her practices, and reflected that her foundational, ontological beliefs were altered to the degree of *rebirth*. She beautifully expressed these stages:

One would be hard pressed to tell me that what I was doing was not working. A book could not have informed me, a class of relative strangers could not have confronted me, and rich philosophical discussion would not have enlightened me. Nor could I have produced it, orchestrated it, manipulated or demanded it on my own. I had to drown in it. . . . While the door to my office provided a clear escape route, the chat space did not. I could confess to my husband, seek out my cohort and rally my supporters at work; but I could not find a way out of the rising waters of the chat room.

In the end, it took this technology to stop time and space. I can imagine nothing else that could strip me of the power of intellect and ego. This technology called on my heart for answers. It was in coming up empty handed that I was faced with the challenge of a lifetime: developing relationships that require more humor than sarcasm, that can get things done better than I can do them on my own and generate power I have yet to imagine. *That* [original emphasis] journey has just begun.

Notes

1   Portions of this discussion are taken from Brunner, Hitchon, and Brown, (2002).
2   It is not the intent of this chapter to review the literature on "transformational leadership." For a brief, yet fairly comprehensive summary, see Leithwood and Jantzi (1999). On page 453, for example, they write:

> Current educational leadership literature offers no unitary concept of transformational leadership. Kowalski and Oates (1993), for instance, accept Burns' (1978) original claim that transformational leadership represents the transcendence of self-interest by both leader and led. Dillard (1995, p. 560) prefers Bennis' (1959) modified notion of "transformative leadership—the ability of a person to reach the souls of others in a fashion which raises human consciousness, builds meanings and inspires human intent that is the source of power." Leithwood (1994) used another modification of Burns, this one based on Bass's (1985) two-factor theory in which transactional and transformational leadership represent opposite ends of the leadership continuum. Bass maintained that the two actually can be complementary. Leithwood identified six factors that make up transformational leadership. Hipp and Bredeson (1995), however, reduced these factors to five in their analysis of the relationship between leadership behaviors and teacher efficacy. Gronn (1996) noted the close relationship, in much current writing, between views of transformational and charismatic leadership, as well as the explicit omission of charisma from some current conceptions of transformational leadership.

3.   Small portions of the discussion in this section are taken verbatim from Brunner, Hitchon, and Brown (2002).

References

Anderson, G. L. (1998). Toward authentic participation: Deconstructing the discourses of participatory reforms in education. *American Educational Research Journal, 35*(4), 571-603.

Bass, B. M. (1985). *Leadership and performance beyond expectations.* New York: The Free Press.

Beck, L., & Murphy, J. (1997). *Ethics in educational leadership programs: Emerging models.* Columbia, MO: University Council of Educational Administration, Inc.

Campbell, R. F., Fleming, T., Newell, L. J., & Bennion, J. W. (1987). *A history of thought and practice in educational administration.* New York: Teachers College Press.

Bennis, W. G. (1959). Leadership theory and administrative behavior: The problem of authority. *Administrative Science Quarterly, 4,* 259–260.

Brunner, C. C. (2002). Professing Educational Administration: Conceptions of Power (Three Parts). *Journal of School Leadership, 12,* 693–720.

Brunner, C. C., Hitchon, W. N. G., & Brown, R. (2002). Advancing social justice as a part of educational leadership development: The potential of imaging technologies. *On The Horizon, 10*(3), 12–15.

Burns, J. (1978). *Leadership.* New York: Harper & Row.

Cambron-McCabe, N. (1993) Leadership for democratic authority. In J. Murphy (Eds.), *Preparing tomorrow's school leaders: Alternative designs,* (pp. 157–176). University Park, PA: University Council for Educational Administration.

Cooper, B. S., & Boyd, W. L. (1987). The evolution of training for school administrators. In J. Murphy & P. Hallinger (Eds.), *Approaches to administrative training* (pp. 3–27). Albany: State University of New York Press.

Culbertson, J. A. (1964). The preparation of administrators. In D. E. Griffiths (Ed.), *Behavioral science in educational administration* (Sixty-third NSSE yearbook, Part II, pp. 303–330). Chicago, IL: University of Chicago Press.

Delpit, L. (1994). *Other people's children: Cultural conflict in the classroom.* New York: New Press.

Dewey, J. (1934). *Art as experience.* New York: Perigree.

Dillard, C. B. (1995). Leading with her life: An African-American feminist (re)interpretation of leadership for an urban high school principal. *Educational Administration Quarterly, 31,* 539–563.

Farquar, R. H. (1977). Preparatory programs in educational administration. In L. L. Cunningham, W. G. Hack, & R. O. Nystrand (Eds.), *Educational administration: The developing decades* (pp. 329–257). Berkeley, CA: McCutchan.

Glass, T. E. (Ed.) (1986). *An analysis of texts on school administration 1820–1985.* Danville, IL: Interstate.

Gregg, R. T. (1969). Preparation of administrators. In R. L. Ebel (Ed.), *Encyclopedia of educational research* (4th ed., pp. 993–1004). London: MacMillan.

Griffiths, D. E. (1988). *Educational administration: Reform PDQ or RIP.* (Occasional paper, no. 8312). Tempe, AZ: University Council for Educational Administration.

Griffiths, D. E., Stout, R. T., & Forsyth, P. B. (1988). The preparation of educational administrators. In D. E. Griffith, R. T. Stout, & P. B. Forsyth (Eds.), *Leaders for America's schools: The report and papers of the National Commission on Excellence in Educational Administration* (pp. 284–304). Berkeley, CA: McCutchan.

Gronn, P. (1996). From transactions to transformations: A new world order in the study of leadership. *Educational Management and Administration, 24*(1), 7–30.

Hallinger, P., Leithwood K., & Murphy, J. (1993). *Cognitive perspectives on education leadership.* New York: Teachers College Press.

Heifetz, R. A., & Laurie, D. L. (1997). The work of leadership. *Harvard Business Review, 75*(1), 124–134.

Henry, M. (1996). *Parent-school collaboration: Feminist organizational structures and school leadership.* Albany: State University of New York Press.

Hipp, K. A., & Bredeson, P. V. (1995). Exploring connections between teacher efficacy and principals' leadership behaviors. *Journal of School Leadership, 5*(2), 136–150.

Kahne, J. (1994). Democratic communities, equity, and excellence: A Deweyan reframing of educational policy analysis. *Educational Evaluation and Policy Analysis, 16*(3), 233–248.

Kohn, A. (1998). Only for my kid: How privileged parents undermine school reform. In *Phi Delta Kappan, 79*(8), 569–577.

Kopernik, A., Tuleweit, W., Wingbermuehle, J., & Weik, S. (1997). 3D-speaker-modeling for new videoconferencing services: Templates vs. adaptive triangulation. *ITG-Fachberichte, 143*, 671–673.

Kowalski, J., & Oates, A. (1993). The evolving role of superintendents in school-based management. *Journal of School Leadership, 3*(4), 380–390.

Lambert, L. (1998). *Building leadership capacity in schools.* Alexandria, VA: Association for Supervision and Curriculum Development.

Larson & Ovando, (2001). *The color of bureaucracy: The politics of equity in multi-cultural school communities.* Belmont CA: Wadsworth/Thompson Learning.

Leithwood, K. (1994). Leadership for school restructuring. *Educational Administration Quarterly, 30*(4), 498–518.

Leithwood, K., & Duke, D. L. (1999). A century's quest to understand school leadership. In J. Murphy & K. S. Louis (Eds.), *Handbook of research on educational administration: A project of the American Educational Research Association* (pp. 45–72). San Francisco: Jossey-Bass Publishers.

Leithwood, K., & Jantzi, D. (1999). Transformational school leadership effects: A replication. *School Effectiveness and School Improvement, 10*(4), 451–479.

Lipman, P. (1997). Restructuring in context: A case study of teacher participation and the dynamics of ideology, race, and power. *American Educational Research Journal, 34*, 3–37.

Malen, B. (1994). Enacting site-based management: A political utilities analysis. *Educational Evaluation and Policy Analysis, 16*(3), 249–267.

Malen, B., & Ogawa, R. (1988). Professional-patron influence on sit-based governance councils: A confounding case study. *Educational Evaluation and Policy Analysis, 10*(4), 251–270.

Malen, B., Ogawa, R. T., & Kranz, J. (1990). What do we know about school-based management? A case study of the literature—a call for research. In W. H. Clune & J. F. Witte (Eds.), *Choice and control in American education, Vol.2: The practice of choice, decentralization and school restructuring* (pp. 289–342). New York: Falmer Press.

Mann, D. (1974). *The politics of administrative representation: School administrators and local democracy.* Lexington, MA: Lexington Books.

Massaro, D. W., Cohen, M. M., Daniel, S., & Cole, R. A. (1998). Developing and evaluating conversational agents. *WECC 98. Workshop on embodied conversational characters* (pp. 137–147). Palo Alto, CA: FX Palo Alto Lab,

McCarthy, M. M. (1999a, Winter). How are school leaders prepared: Trends and future directions. *Educational Horizons,* 74–81.

McCarthy, M. M. (1999b). The evolution of educational leadership preparation programs. In J. Murphy & K. Seashore-Louis (Eds.), *Handbook of research on educational administration: A project of the American Educational Research Association*, (pp. 119–139). San Francisco, CA: Jossey-Bass.

Moore, H. A. (1964). The ferment in school administration. In D. E. Griffiths (Ed.), *Behavioral science and educational administration* (Sixty-third NSSE yearbook, Part II, pp. 11-32). Chicago, IL: University of Chicago Press.

Morishima, S., Aizawa, K., & Harashima, H. (1990). A real-time facial action image synthesis system driven by speech and text. *Proceedings of the SPIE–The International Society for Optical Engineering, 1360 Part 2*, 1151-1158.

Murphy, J. (1990). Preparing school administrators for the twenty-first century: The reform agenda. In B. Mitchell & L. L. Cunningham (Eds.), *Educational leadership and changing contexts of families, communities, and schools* (Eight-ninth NSSE yearbook, Part II, pp. 232-251). Chicago, IL: University of Chicago Press.

Murphy, J. (1991). The effects of the educational reform movement on departments of educational leadership. *Educational Evaluation and Policy Analysis, 13*(1), 49-65.

Murphy, J. (1992). *The landscape of leadership preparation: Reframing the education of school administrators.* Newbury Park, CA: Corwin Press, Inc.

Nadler, D. A., & Tushman, M. L. (1995). Types of organizational change: From incremental improvement to discontinuous transformation. In D. A. Nadler, R. B. Shaw, A. E. Walton, & Associates. *Discontinuous change: Leading organizational transformations* (pp. 15-34). San Francisco: Jossey-Bass Publishers.

Newmann, F., M., King, M. B., & Rigdon, M. (1997). Accountability and school performance: Implications from restructuring schools. *Harvard Educational Review, 67*, 41-74.

Oakes, J. (1985). *Keeping track: How schools structure inequality.* New Haven, CT: Yale University Press.

Ogawa, R. (1994). The institutional sources of educational reform: The case of school-based management. *American Educational Research Journal, 31*, 519-548.

Paige, R. (2003). Note from the Editor-in-Chief. *Architectural Digest: The International Magazine of Interior Design, 60*(2), 38.

Peebles, L. D. (2000). Millennial challenges for educational leadership: Revisiting issues of diversity. In P. M Jenlink & T. J. Kowalski, *Marching into a new millennium: Challenges to educational leadership* (pp. 190-211). Lanham, MD: Scarecrow Press, Inc.

Peterson, K. D., & Finn, C. E. (1985). Principals, superintendents and the administrator's art. *The Public Interest, 79*, 42-62.

Popkewitz, T. (1979). Schools and the symbolic uses of community participation. In C. Grant (Ed.), *Community participation in education* (pp.114-139). Boston, MA: Allyn & Bacon.

Reitzug, U. C., & Capper, C. (1996). Deconstructing site-based management: Possibilities for emancipation and alternative means of control. *International Journal of Educational Reform, 5* (1), 56-59.

Schank, R. C. (2002). Are we going to get smarter? In J. Brockman (Ed.), *The next fifty years: Science in the first half of the twenty-first century*, (pp. 206-215). New York: Vintage Books.

Scott, S. D., & Leong, S. T. (2000). Combining expressions and speech in talking head models, *Challenges of Information Technology Management in the 21ˢᵗ Century. Information Resources*

Management Association International Conference (pp. 707–708). Hershey, PA: Idea Group Publishing.

Silver, P. F. (1982). Administrator preparation. In H. E. Mitzel (Ed.), *Encyclopedia of educational research* (5th ed., Vol. 1, pp. 49–59). New York: Free Press.

Tabor, J. (1997). Talking heads. *IEEE-Multimedia, 4*(3), July–September, 81–83.

Weiler, H. (1990). Comparative perspectives on educational decentralization: An exercise in contradiction. *Educational Evaluation and Policy Analysis, 12*(4), 433-448.

Wohlsetter, P., Smyer, R., & Mohrman, S. A. (1994). New boundaries for school-based management: The high involvement model. *Education Evaluation and Policy Analysis, 16*(3), 268–286.

Wong, D., Packard, B., Girod, M., & Pugh, K. (2000). The opposite of control: A Deweyan perspective on intrinsic motivation in "After 3" technology programs. *Computers in Human Behavior, 16*, 313–338.

Wong, D., Pugh, K., & Dewey Ideas Group at Michigan State University, (2001). Learning science: A Deweyan perspective. *Journal of Research in Science Teaching, 38*(3), 317–336.

Yammarion, F. J., Dubinsky, A. J., & Spangler, W. D. (1998). Transformational and contingent reward leadership: Individual, dyad, and group level of analysis. *The Leadership Quarterly, 9* (1), 19–27.

Yukl, G. (1994). *Leadership in organizations: Third edition.* Englewood Cliffs, NJ: Prentice-Hall.

✠ CHAPTER 14

"Yes We Can": Social Justice Principals Navigating Resistance to Create Excellent Schools[1]

George Theoharis

Principals successful at creating more equitable and socially just schools encounter significant resistance and barriers to their work. Much of this resistance comes from larger societal norms of deficit thinking that play out in schools and school systems designed to maintain disparities for historically marginalized students. While all educators should play a role in changing the larger societal and systemic landscape that influences schools and schooling, the job of the school principal is largely one of a middle manager that impacts the education of students at her/his school site. This requires effective principals to have a sophisticated understanding of macrolevel resistance at the local and immediate level—the daily management and work of K-12 schools—and how this resistance informs the work of educators, and in turn, the educational experiences and outcomes of their students.

The purpose of this chapter is to examine how seven principals who led urban schools and came to the principalship to enact an agenda for equity and social justice navigated the resistance they faced as they created more equitable and excellent schools through social justice leadership. It begins with a definition of social justice leadership, followed by a description of the principals who were studied, the ways they advanced their agenda for equity and excellence, and the resistance they faced. This chapter then focuses upon a discussion of how these leaders navigated that resistance as a result of their beliefs, agency, vision of social justice, and an array of professional and personal strategies.

Defining Social Justice Leadership

In this chapter, I define *social justice leadership* in the context of K-12 education to mean that school leaders are focused on addressing and eliminating marginalization in schools. Practically, this means leaders advocate, lead, and keep at the center of their practice and vision issues of race, class, gender, disability, sexual orientation, and other historically and currently marginalizing conditions in the United States. In doing so, inclusive schooling practices for students with disabilities, English language learners, and other students traditionally segregated in schools are also necessitated by this definition (Theoharis, 2007, p. 222). This definition is not universal, but grounded in the daily realities of education leadership (Bogotch, 2002).

Social justice leadership is not bureaucratic management of school; it is not maintaining the norms of schools and districts where disparate social and academic student outcomes persist, and it moves beyond even effective instructional leadership. In theory, this means taking the needs (academic and emotional) of those who have historically struggled in school, those who have been valued less in the educational system, and those who have been in one way or another excluded and denied the full benefits of education, and both advocating for and with these students. In practice, this involves creating schools and systems that place the needs of marginalized students at the center of the design of inclusive structures, policies, and classroom practice. This chapter features seven principals who lived this definition of social justice leadership in their daily work in schools.

The Principals and the Study

I sought out principals not only committed to agendas for educational equity and social justice, but who were also successful in advancing them, using the following four criteria: (a) led a public school, (b) possessed a belief that promoting social justice is a driving force behind what brought them to their leadership position, (c) advocated, led, and kept at the center of their practice/vision issues of race, class, gender, language, disability, sexual orientation, and/or other historically marginalizing conditions, and (d) had evidence to show their work produced a more just school. Using purposeful and snowball sampling, I identified eighteen principals, spanning three states, to participate in this project. Seven of the original eighteen met the selection criteria although one ultimately chose not to participate, leaving six principals to take part in the project. In designing this study, I borrowed from the tradition of autoethnography (Cole & Knowles, 2001) and included myself, a principal committed to equity and social justice, as a seventh principal for this project. In doing so, this work combined a qualitative methodology with principles from autoethnography, which numerous scholars have used as a methodological tool (Cole & Knowles, 2000; Dews & Law, 1995; Ellis, 2004; Jackson, 1995; Meneley & Young, 2005), enabling me to make this work more personal and reflective.

This project lasted over several years and included at least three and as many as eight in-depth interviews with each of the principals, a review of documents from their schools (calendars, handbooks, meeting minutes, news articles, data charts, etc.), site visits, discussions/interviews with school staff and families, a detailed field log, convening the principals in small groups of 2–4, and a group meeting of all the principals. I had full access to the school and materials from my own experiences (including my personal calendar and journals), but additionally collected data on my experience by completing interviews and site visits with the assistance of another researcher. In writing about the principals in this chapter, I write in the third person using pseudonyms, even when speaking of my own experiences. I did this because I am only one in a group of equity-oriented principals. Changing to the first person would have exerted a particular power, shifting the focus to my experience over the experiences of the group of principals committed to social justice leaders.

Advancing Equity and Excellence

I continue this chapter with a brief description of the ways in which these leaders advanced their equity-oriented agenda. This meant these leaders worked to: (a) increase inclusion, access, and opportunity, (b) improve the core-learning context, and (c) create a climate of belonging. Those three aspects together became the combined ways they raised student achievement (Theoharis, 2009), resulting in more equitable and socially just schools. While this work was messy and ongoing, it is important to understand the progress these leaders made in creating more equitable and excellent schools. In increasing inclusion, access, and opportunity, these leaders eliminated pullout and self-contained programming for students with disabilities and students learning English to create inclusive services for all students who received support in heterogeneous groups. They also detracked their math programs. Additionally they increased rigor of the content being taught, access to the range of curricular and co-curricular opportunities, increased student learning time, and increased accountability systems for the achievement of all students.

Second, they worked to improve the core-learning context. The *core learning context* is used to describe the daily teaching and curriculum used in the general education classrooms but used by all staff including general education teachers, special education teachers, English Language Learner teachers, teaching assistants, special area teachers, etc. These leaders saw a strong connection between social justice for both students and teachers and improving the teaching and curriculum. They made progress in their equity-oriented agenda as they addressed issues of race, provided ongoing staff development focused on building equity, hired and supervised through an equity lens, adopted common research-based curricular approaches, and empowered staff. This combination pushed beyond the traditional, yet essential, aspects of instructional leadership.

Additionally, they created a climate of belonging in their work to make their schools more equitable and excellent. They made a purposeful connection between climate and school discipline. In this regard, they built warm and welcoming climates, fostered community-building in each classroom, reached out intentionally to the community and marginalized families, incorporated social responsibility into the school curriculum, and utilized a proactive and process approach to discipline. These leaders moved beyond lip service about climate and diversity to building a school culture that embraces diversity and connects in meaningful ways with the community. The seven principals purposefully developed a climate where all staff members were deemed important, where students learned to respect each other, and where the diversity of families was valued, not marginalized.

In combining their efforts to increase inclusion/access, improve the core-learning context, and create a climate of belonging, these seven principals saw marked improvement in student achievement. Student achievement as measured by local, state, and national assessments rose significantly under their leadership. For example, the achievement of students learning English (ELL) rose from no ELL students achieving at grade level to over 90 percent achieving at grade level. They saw an increase from 68 to 79 percent of students attending postsecondary education. They saw the achievement of all students and all demographic groups of students steadily rise on state tests from as little as 15 percentage points gained to as much at 45 percent more students performing at grade level (e.g., from 60 percent reading at grade level to 75 percent, or 33 percent of African American students reading at grade level to 78 percent). While imperfect, their work made important strides in creating more equitable and excellent schools. It is important to note that while great progress was made, none of these schools were "utopia," and none of these leaders viewed their equity-oriented leadership as heading toward a fixed destination. Their work and progress was ongoing and messy. While this project brought a wealth of data, the focus in this chapter is on the resistance the leaders faced in their equity-oriented work and the ways in which they navigated that resistance to create more equitable and excellent schools.

Facing Resistance

These principals' efforts to create more just and equitable schools were met with significant resistance. Substantial literature reports on the various resistances, barriers, and countervailing pressures to school change and more specifically to equity-oriented reform (Brown, 2004; Larson & Murtadha, 2002; Shields, 2004; Skrla, Scheurich, Garcia, & Nolly, 2004). These principals reported that this work felt like a constant uphill struggle. For the purpose of this chapter, I use the term resistance to refer to all of the barriers, countervailing pressures, tensions, and realities that detract from leading to create more equitable and just schools. These leaders described this resistance as "enormous," "never ceasing," and "often unbearable."

The data showed that resistance to their equity and social justice agenda came from two primary locations: within the school/community and from the district and beyond (Theoharis, 2007). The resistance from within the school/community in turn derived from the enormity of daily work of the principalship, the momentum of the status quo, obstructive staff attitudes and beliefs, and insular/privileged parental expectations. The resistance from the district and beyond took the forms of unsupportive central office administrators, fellow principals who lacked the will or skill to advance an equity-oriented agenda, a lack of financial, human and professional development resources provided to schools by federal, state and local funding streams, harmful state and federal regulations, and principal preparation programs that did not focus on equity or justice concerns. For example, obstructive staff attitudes in four of the schools took the form of teachers not wanting students with special education labels to be their responsibility. Additionally, an example of harmful regulations was the ways state English as a second language and federal Title I policies were written that promotes removing particular students from the general education core curriculum and instruction.

There were times when the principals took a particular action and it was met with a specific resistance, this can be understood as cause and effect resistance. However, many of their practice/successes in advancing social justice are not necessarily connected neatly with specific resistance(s) they faced—nonlinear resistance. And while these leaders did develop strategies to navigate this resistance they faced, again this was not linear. In other words, these leaders did not always do "A" and therefore faced resistance "B" and then could enact strategy "C." Advancing their social justice agenda was messy and not straightforward as was the resistance they faced in this work. Many of these forms or locations of resistance were not necessarily targeted at one particular event or strategy the principals used but were dynamic and overlapping. They were ongoing and appeared as one principal said, "at every turn." The principals reported a significant physical and emotional toll as well as a persistent sense of discouragement as a result of the ongoing resistance they faced. One shared that, "[Leading for social justice] tore at my soul. I knew this job would be hard, but I had no idea it would shake me to the core." The resistance these leaders faced requires much more elaborated consideration then space permits (see Theoharis, in press a; 2009). However, these leaders navigated this resistance and maintained their equity and justice agenda.

Navigating Resistance

While facing harsh and varied resistance, these seven leaders possessed and developed ways to navigate this resistance. This ability and desire to do this work resulted in the leaders using various strategies (bringing people together, providing support for their staff, and engaging in self-care) to move through the resistance. Yet perhaps the most important driver of the ways in which they navigated the resistance was their personal belief that as principal they were responsible for inequitable schools they inherited when they arrived and for changing them as well as their personal sense that they *could* actually do that.

Responsibility, Agency, and Imaginative Vision

In my work locally and nationally in public K-12 schools, I feel a growing sentiment held by many educators that "there is nothing we can do" about the problems, achievement gap, inequitable structures, low morale, disparate access and achievement for students with disabilities and students learning English, and disconnect with families/community. I hear this in many ways from school principals, teachers, district administrators, parents, community members, and superintendents. These diverse players in creating more equitable and excellent schools express feelings of being blocked by students' home lives, economic realities, district policy, state regulations, school administrators, teachers unions, and a list of other issues and people. This is formidable resistance that many schools face and leads many school leaders into submissive inaction or ineffective action. In stark contrast to this, the seven principals in this study completely rejected the "there is nothing we can do" sentiment. In part, their success at navigating this resistance was their belief that it was their responsibility to make their schools more equitable and excellent. They felt, and acted accordingly, that they needed to advocate for and improve the education that their marginalized students received.

These principals were working in the same era and facing the same policies, the same economic and home realities for their students, the same state mandates, the same teacher's unions, the same disgruntled staff, and the same district administrators as their educator colleagues around the country, yet they held firm to their belief that they were indeed responsible for making these inequities better. With this sense of responsibility came a personal sense of agency or efficacy. This agency meant not only did they believe they were responsible for challenging the inequities and injustices they encountered in their schools, but that they actually could *do* something about it. And in fact they did.

In many cases, this sense of responsibility and agency manifested itself in the vision these leaders brought to their schools—a vision not of superficial change or new programs or the latest educational buzzwords. They maintained a vision that there was something better, as in the words of one principal: "I knew there was a better way to organize, run, and teach at our school. It could be done *now*—not in two years when the budget conditions might change, not in ten years when policy and personnel had changed, but now." In working toward a better way, these leaders embodied a bold imaginative vision (Theoharis & Causton-Theoharis, 2008). This combination of responsibility, agency and belief in a better way led to a creativity to imagine, design, and create things for their school that they had not seen before and for which they did not have models to replicate. For example, two of the leaders created inclusive service delivery for ELL students, without ever seeing this in practice or reading about it elsewhere. Three principals de-tracked their previously tracked math program without immediate models to do that. They believed in a better way and could imagine it without ever seeing it before.

While impossible to quantify these beliefs (responsibility, agency, and imaginative vision) or the impact of each, these seven principals relied on them to navigate the resistance that many schools face concerning disparate realities and disparate education. This sense of responsibility brought a sense of burden that took a toll physically, emotionally, and professionally on these leaders (see Theoharis, 2009). From that increased burden developed a means to navigate resistance that impedes and even halts the kinds of reforms these leaders and their staffs created.

Bringing People Together

A key aspect of how the principals navigated resistance was their ability and efforts to bring people together. One way to look at this is that these principals in various ways organized groups around them to further their agenda and sustain themselves. First, they found other leaders to build a supportive administrative network. Thus, an important step in navigating resistance became building and maintaining connections with other school leaders who held similar beliefs about equity and justice. Finding, sharing, and supporting other leaders engaged in social justice action nourished these principals by providing support, reassurance, varied perspectives grounded in equity, an opportunity to help someone else, and an easing of the isolation of the position.

Also, they brought school staff together to make key decisions, and in doing so, developed a shared sense of commitment and responsibility. All seven leaders set the equity direction or vision for improvement at the school, yet led in a very collaborative and democratic manner. One principal summarized, "I set the course, but together my staff and I figured out how we were going to get there." This involved shared decision-making leadership teams, staff taking on new roles running meetings, setting staff meeting agendas, and making important decisions about their school curriculum program. Through these avenues, the staff and principals engaged in collaborative planning to solve problems, but also to plan new initiatives, adopt new curricula, and create new service delivery structures. Within this democratic and empowering style, these principals carried a spirit of trust in their leadership. While they were very present and visible in classrooms and around their school, they did not micromanage their staff and trusted them to make sensible and competent professional decisions. By having multiple staff deeply involved in the equity work of the school, this avenue of bringing people together spread out the burden of resistance to all those involved and reduced resistance as well.

They developed relationships with many school, family, and community stakeholders that helped further their work and sustain them. This avenue of bringing people together helped navigate resistance in that with these increased networks these principals were more connected to the school community, thus helping sustain them. This also meant that both marginalized families and families traditionally involved in school developed a greater sense of trust in and connection with these leaders. One principal likened these relationships to "money in the bank." He explained,

> When I develop meaningful relationships in the community, families are more apt to work with me and support a new direction for the school—even if they did not wholeheartedly agree, they resist less when they feel heard, when they feel connected, when they trust the person running the school.

These leaders relied on and purposefully maintained their own social and family networks outside of school that provided emotional support for them and gave them additional outlets to contribute and feel valued. Some principals volunteered in their own community in different ways, and all seven were purposeful about making time for and prioritizing their life outside of school. While they admitted it was often after a ten-hour or longer workday, they yet maintained a social or family support network that helped them navigate the resistance.

Creating supportive structures in school, building relationships with school staff and families, and maintaining social/family networks were integral aspects of organizing people around the school leaders to support this work and assist the administrator in navigating resistance. The ways in which the leaders brought people together did both in all of these schools and for all of these principals. While the context and the stakeholders would be different, bringing people together can clearly be a strategy that other current and future leaders utilize as they navigate resistance in their efforts to create more equitable and just schools.

Supporting Staff

In addition to their beliefs and their ability to bring people together, navigating resistance meant providing multiple kinds of support for staff. This was important, as it built trust with staff members, helped staff gain new knowledge and skills that changed their practice, positioned more staff to be agents of change in their teams and classrooms, and created a stronger staff community. This support took a variety of forms. First, like all good instructional leaders, these principals provided and facilitated professional development for their staffs. This professional learning was focused around equity goals or needs. It involved the effective ways in which professional development is carried out—ongoing coaching, time for planning and reflection, and the inclusion of all staff. A major part of the ways in which they provided professional development involved the use of time.

Across the board, these leaders created teams of professionals who were expected to collaborate to inclusively meet the needs of all learners. They were thus adamant that the school schedule was created to give these teams common planning time multiple times a week. They also provided ongoing support to these teams through subject area experts, collaboration facilitators, and differentiation coaches. Additionally, they provided as much additional time for professional development and team planning through the use of paying for after-school time, sub-release time, and summer learning. This was instrumental to navigating resistance as it conveyed the expectation for learning new roles and skills and provided the time and learning to make that happen.

Their support for staff not only aided in navigating resistance, but combined with the previously discussed commitment to bring people together, allowed them to lead in a democratic manner with empowered staff. Along with that empowerment, these leaders engaged in ongoing and purposeful appreciation of staff members. Just as empty praise is ineffective with young people, these leaders were committed to sincere and specific appreciation of their respective staff, which they conveyed in multiple ways: staff meetings, newsletters, classroom visits, personal notes, and staff events. Additionally, they worked to create a culture of appreciation among staff by making time for staff appreciation both publicly and privately.

While the ways in which these leaders supported their staffs are not different from what other good principals do, they are discussed here not only in terms of instructional leadership, but based on the importance of being able to navigate resistance. It was important for staff to learn new skills, not only for the skills themselves, but to also ease the resistance to their efforts in creating more equitable and just schools. An empowered and appreciated staff was a fundamental aspect of their approach to leadership and worked to defuse resistance by creating an improved school culture and staff of people who trusted each other and their principal.

Engaging Coping Strategies

The fourth avenue the seven leaders took to navigate resistance was coping strategies. All seven of the principals were already or learning to be purposeful about coping with the resistance they were facing. In this chapter, coping strategies means actions the principals took that allowed them to maintain their individual sanity in order to continue enacting their equity-oriented agenda. These strategies were distinct from the ones previously discussed in that they were not about how they approached their daily work, but rather, keeping themselves going and emotionally together. The principals explained that these coping strategies did not make the resistance go away, but they felt these strategies helped them continue with this work.

All seven leaders engaged in different forms of coping, although they all used some form of physical activity, like running, walking, biking, or playing basketball, as a way to let off steam about their work. All were purposeful about making sure they left work at their school (albeit they often drew this line about leaving their work after a ten-hour day). In doing this, the carved-out time for activities not relating to school gave them joy or refueled them (e.g., golf, pleasure reading, yoga, entertaining friends, playing musical instruments). Some of the principals engaged in community service or volunteer projects that gave them a tangible sense of accomplishment. Additionally, a few engaged in the potentially harmful behavior of increasing the amount of social drinking of alcohol.

The strategies the principals in this study shared are not a checklist for current and future social justice leaders to complete in order to counter the resistance they face. While certain ideas that these leaders utilized may resonate with particular administrators needs and lives, there is real danger in viewing these strategies as a finite list of tasks to complete. Although the principals in this study found their strategies helped navigate the resistance they faced, they did not suggest them as a cure; it was a messy and ongoing process. Still these strategies do provide other future and current leaders with entry points into how to maintain their sanity while furthering their justice work. Sharing and discussing these strategies not only allows for leaders to learn new ways to navigate resistance and fulfill their duties, it opens an important conversation that shows the vulnerable and still-learning side of leaders.

A Final Word—Yes We Can

These principals maintained their own level of responsibility for the oppression of marginalized students and found creative answers to address inequitable school realities. They created both necessity for change and the leadership to have teachers assume new roles and responsibilities. They brought people together to collaboratively plan to address disparate achievement, lack of access, and a poor climate between and among staff, families, fellow administrators, and community members. These leaders met harsh and varied resistance as they engaged in creating more equitable and just schools, but they developed their own strategies to maintain themselves, their commitment, and this work.

As a participant and researcher, it became apparent to me that these principals found relief from facing and navigating resistance by *working on* personal and professional self-care. It was not that they exercised and felt better about their work or found a network of supportive colleagues and were suddenly able to restructure their school, or provided professional development and could suddenly cope with the intense anger they faced. Rather, it was messy and ongoing. It was a process of approaching their jobs in sometimes slightly different ways and in sometimes radically different ways. It was a process of learning how to protect and maintain their lives outside of their schools as well as their spirits.

In the end, it came back time and time again to the beliefs these leaders held. They held themselves responsible for the conditions—both the good and unjust ones at their schools. They took ownership of the changing conditions that were inequitable. They felt a calling and that it was their job to create more equitable and excellent schools. And they embraced their agency in both imagining a better way and achieving it. Taken collectively, these social justice principals embodied the notion that when it comes to the question of whether or not educational leaders can successfully create more equitable and excellent schools, the response is "yes we can."

Note

1   Portions of this chapter adapted from Theoharis (2009; in press, a; in press, b).

References

Bogotch, I. (2002). Educational leadership and social justice: Practice into theory. *Journal of School Leadership, 1(2),* 138–156.

Brown, K. M. (2004). Leadership for social justice and equity: Weaving a transformative framework and pedagogy. *Educational Administrative Quarterly, 40*(1), 79–110.

Cole, A. L., & Knowles, J. G. (2000). *Researching teaching: Exploring teacher development through reflective inquiry*. New York: Allyn & Bacon.

Cole, A. L., & Knowles, J. G. (2001). *Lives in context: The art of life history research*. Walnut Creek, CA: Alta Mira Press.

Dews, C. L. B., & Law, C. L. (Eds.) (1995). *This fine place so far from home: Voices of academics from the working class*. Philadelphia: Temple University Press.

Ellis, C. (2004). *The ethnographic I: A methodological novel about autoethnography*. Lanham, MD: Alta Mira Press.

Jackson, M. (1995). *At home in the world*. Durham, NC: Duke University.

Larson, C., & Murtadha, K. (2002). Leadership for social justice, In J. Murphy (Ed.) *The educational leadership challenge: Redefining leadership for the 21st century* (pp. 134–161). Chicago, IL: University of Chicago Press.

Meneley, Y., & Young, D. (Eds.) (2005). *Autoethnographies: The anthropology of academic practices*. Toronto, ON: Broadview Press.

Shields, C. M. (2004). Dialogic leadership for social justice: Overcoming pathologies of silence. *Educational Administration Quarterly, 40*(1), 111–134.

Skrla, L., Scheurich, J. J., Garcia, J., & Nolly, G. (2004). Equity audits: A practical leadership tool for developing equitable and excellent schools. *Educational Administration Quarterly, 40*(1), 135–163.

Theoharis, G., & Causton-Theoharis, J. (2008). Oppressors or emancipators: Critical dispositions for preparing inclusive school leaders. *Equity and Excellence in Education, 41*(2), 230–246.

Theoharis, G. (2007). Social justice educational leaders and resistance: Toward a theory of social justice leadership. *Educational Administration Quarterly, 43*(2), 228–251.

Theoharis, G. (2009). *The school leaders our children deserve: 7 keys to equity, social justice, and school reform*. New York: Teachers College Press.

Theoharis, G. (in press a). "At every turn": The resistance principals face in their pursuit of equity and justice. *Journal of School Leadership*.

Theoharis, G. (in press, b). Sustaining social justice: Strategies urban principals develop to advance justice and equity while facing resistance. *International Journal of Urban Educational Leadership*.

✠ CONCLUSION

From New Perspectives to New Practices: Where Will Our Imagination Lead Us?

Linda C. Tillman

The introduction to this book is titled "Re-Imagining Educational Leadership: New Perspectives and Contextual Considerations in the Field." It is a title that is particularly appropriate for the book and for the field of educational leadership. More importantly, the ideas, concepts, and theoretical and empirical work presented in this book can help us to re-imagine both educational leadership and the U.S. educational system and society. They should also compel us to reflect on the promises and challenges facing school leaders in a complex racial, cultural, social, political and economic society.

The current U.S. educational and societal context necessitates that school leaders carefully consider a multitude of factors that threaten to leave unimaginable numbers of K-12 students underserved and undereducated in the richest and most powerful nation in the world. These factors include an unstable economic climate, increased numbers of children who live in poverty, are homelessness, and who suffer from emotional trauma; the shortage of teachers generally and a lack of content-certified teachers in key subject matter areas (e.g., science, math, special education); and a shortage of school leaders. All of these factors add to the complexity of school leadership. Authors in this book write about these and other issues that must be considered if we are to re-imagine and re-conceptualize educational leadership in ways that will lead to the *education* (rather than schooling) of *all* children regardless of race, class, gender, and other markers of difference. Theoretical constructs, changing demographics, social cultural contexts, equity, excellence, access to postsecondary education, and the moral imperative to lead in ways that are not only socially just, but which also identify and address social injustice are explored from a variety of perspectives.

Some of these topics have been written about in other books and articles as well as in conference presentations. Yet it is imperative that we continue to investigate and interrogate what roles school leaders need to play in changing education generally and the field of educational leadership specifically so that *all* children can be beneficiaries of what this country and its educational system has to offer. Clearly, the chapters in this book will advance our conversations and our knowledge and can help us to develop strategies to re-imagine the field.

But even as some scholars continue to address critical issues in education and educational leadership, one issue that remains a constant in U.S. education and society could negate our efforts to re-imagine educational leadership: the pervasiveness of racism and its consequences for an educated society. Discussions about the impact of racism are rarely politically correct. Individuals tend to avoid direct conversations about racism, scholars in the field of educational leadership rarely address racism directly in their writings, and teachers, leaders, parents, community members and students are often discouraged from identifying racism as a direct or indirect cause of inequitable schooling (e.g., funding disparities, inadequate facilities, lack of resources), the achievement gap, the overrepresentation of students of color in special education (especially African American males), and the underrepresentation of students of color in advanced placement and gifted classes. Other consequences including the lack of racial diversity in the field of educational leadership among professors, graduate students, and school leaders are also subjects that are overlooked or deemed as secondary in importance to topics such as leadership theory, even when leadership theory may have little influence on the educational outcomes of students.

While it may be more comfortable to avoid discussions about the impact of racism on the field of educational leadership, what are the consequences of our silence? If we truly advocate leadership practices that directly address and meet the needs of *all* children, can we really afford *not* to engage in discourse that is intended to name racism when we see it and experience it? How can we prepare school leaders to work in racially and culturally diverse school and community contexts if our leadership preparation programs include only cursory content that fails to go beyond a superficial treatment of race, racism, and social injustice? How will school leaders become culturally aware and culturally proficient if there are limited opportunities for honest conversations about race and racism in leadership preparation classes? How can we move the current rhetoric of social justice in educational leadership from theory to practice without addressing issues of race and racism? Additionally, in a field that is primarily Eurocentric in membership, theory and practice, when will we begin to address the issue of the privileging of voice? Can we re-imagine a field where all voices are heard and respected on the subject of racism, the one issue that continues to be perverse and pervasive in U.S. education and society?

As we re-imagine the field of educational leadership, can we also re-imagine an educational system in which educational leaders become advocates for *all* children regardless of their race, where racial and cultural differences are accepted (rather than tolerated), where educational leaders advance a vision of equity and excellence that is the rule rather than the exception, and where theory really does merge with practice? Scholars and practitioners will likely offer a variety of perspectives on the prevalence of racism in K-12 schooling and postsecondary education, as well as in society in general. Some will name racism, identify its victims and attempt to engage in discourse and practice that is intended to circumvent racism in schools. Others will claim that we live in a post-racial America, that racism is no longer a divisive issue, and that it certainly does not exit in K-12 schools and leadership preparation programs. But in a supposed postracial America, the incidence of hate groups has increased tremendously since January 2009. I cannot be convinced that the threats of violence and acts of violence will not spill over into schools—the very places where children should be in safe, nurturing, racism-free environments.

In our efforts to re-imagine educational leadership, it will take more than casual conversations, presentations at conferences, and scholarly writing to protect children from the devastating social, emotional, and academic effects of racism. But the process of re-imagining educational leadership can start with some simple and honest premises. None of these premises are new, but they are worth revisiting if we are to heed Sonya Horsford's call to re-imagine the field of educational leadership. First, we must take time to think about what educational leadership should be, rather than an over-reliance on what we want it to be or what it has always been. If our collective goal is to design and implement leadership preparation programs that will train competent, committed and caring leaders who will work on behalf of all children, then we must be about the business of continuously reviewing our programs rather than holding on to and reinforcing theories and course content that is designed exclusively for those students whom we feel comfortable teaching or whose perspectives we share, rather than all students. We must be committed to the education of all children and our commitment must be evidenced in our teaching, course content, and classroom discourse. If we believe that all children can perform at the highest academic levels, this belief should be reflected in how we train future school leaders—an asset- versus a deficit-oriented approach. We must approach our work as educational leadership professors with an ethic of care—care for our students and care for the children and communities that they are being trained to serve. We cannot disconnect the realities of a society that underserves and undereducates the majority of its students of color simply because we specialize in qualitative or quantitative research, feminist research, organizational theory, or leadership for social justice. Individually and collectively, our work should lead to recommendations for the social, emotional, racial, cultural, economic, and academic well-being of all children. Social justice does include issues of race and racism.

The body of scholarship in this book is a positive step in the process of re-imagining educational leadership and society. This work can also been seen as a challenge to us to begin the difficult, but necessary work of looking inward, looking at our own beliefs and values and looking at how we conduct ourselves in our interactions with our students and colleagues. Where will our imagination lead us? Will we allow ourselves to imagine a field that names racism and its consequences or will we continue to remain in our safe ivory tower spaces because the system works for us? Will we consider that the field of educational leadership will not change in a positive direction as long as students and faculty of color continue to be marginalized in leadership preparation programs? Will we consider that personal biases about race and culture do impact our teaching and often influence how future leaders form their opinions about students and faculty of color? If we are satisfied with the field as it is, there is no need to re-imagine it. If we are not, there is much work to be done.

Linda C. Tillman
Professor of Educational Leadership
University of North Carolina at Chapel Hill

✠ CONTRIBUTORS

Enrique Alemán, Jr. is Assistant Professor of Educational Leadership and Policy and a faculty fellow with the Center for Critical Race Studies at the University of Utah. Dr. Alemán has published articles in *Harvard Educational Review*, *Equity & Excellence in Education*, and *Educational Administration Quarterly*. His research and teaching interests include critical race and Latina/o critical theory, politics of education, community-engaged scholarship, and Chicana/o and Latina/o educational issues.

Bruce G. Barnett is a Professor in the Educational Leadership and Policy Studies Department at the University of Texas at San Antonio. His research interests include leadership preparation programs, mentoring and coaching, reflective practice, leadership for school improvement, school-university partnerships, and the realities of beginning principals. Bruce currently conducts international research and serves as the Associate Director of International Affairs for the University Council for Educational Administration.

Jeffrey S. Brooks is an Associate Professor of Educational Leadership and Policy Analysis at the University of Missouri. His research focuses on socio-cultural dynamics of educational leadership practice and preparation. Dr. Brooks is Editor of the *Journal of School Leadership* and Series Editor of the Information Age Publishing *Educational Leadership for Social Justice* Book Series.

C. Cryss Brunner is Associate Professor of Organizational Leadership, Policy, and Development at the University of Minnesota. Dr. Brunner conducts research on identity, power, superintendency, technology, and leadership preparation, which has appeared in more than 50 scholarly chapters and articles. In addition to sole-authoring one book, and editing two books (one with Lars Bjork), she is co-author of the book *Women Leading School Systems: Uncommon Roads to Fulfillment* (2007), with Margaret Grogan.

Kevin Burr is Area Superintendent for High Schools for Tulsa Public Schools and doctoral student in educational leadership at the University of Oklahoma. He has served twenty years as a high school principal and four years with Southern Regional Education Board and High Schools That Work. His research interests include urban high school reform, educational leadership, reflective practice, and professional learning communities.

Camille Wilson Cooper is an associate professor in the Department of Educational Leadership & Cultural Foundations at the University of North Carolina at Greensboro. Dr. Cooper's research on critical and culturally relevant perspectives of school-family relations and leadership has appeared in journals such as *Educational Administration Quarterly* and *Teachers College Record.*

T. Elon Dancy II is Assistant Professor of Adult and Higher Education at the University of Oklahoma in Norman. His research agenda investigates race, gender, and culture in colleges and universities, as well as other educational settings. Dr. Dancy is Editor of *Managing Diversity: (Re)Visioning Equity on College Campuses* and author of *The Brother Code: Manhood and Masculinity among African American Men in College.*

James Earl Davis is Professor in the Department of Educational Leadership and Policy Studies at Temple University with affiliate appointments in African American Studies and Women Studies. His research focusing on educational policy, urban school reform, higher education, and race and gender studies has appeared in *Gender & Society, Peabody Journal of Education,* and *Review of Research in Education.*

Fenwick W. English is the R. Wendell Eaves Distinguished Professor of Educational Leadership at the University of North Carolina at Chapel Hill. He is a former department chair, dean, and vice-chancellor of academic affairs and superintendent of schools in New York. Dr. English is the author or co-author of twenty-six books. He also served as a member of the University Council of Educational Administration for seven years, as President in 2006-07, and is a member of the NCPEA Executive Board.

Lance D. Fusarelli is Professor of Leadership, Policy and Adult & Higher Education at North Carolina State University. His recent works include: *Effec-*

tive Communication for School Administrators (Rowman & Littlefield, 2007) and the *Handbook of Education Politics and Policy* (Routledge, 2008). His research interests include the superintendency and the politics of education.

Karen Hammel is an adjunct professor in teacher preparation at Hamline University in St. Paul, Minnesota, and special education teacher in Minneapolis Public Schools. Her research interests are social justice, power, identity, personal transformation and educational leadership.

Sonya Douglass Horsford is Assistant Professor of Educational Leadership at the University of Nevada, Las Vegas. Her research interests include the social context of educational leadership, educational policy and politics, and school leadership in the post-civil rights era. Her work has been published in *The Urban Review, Journal of Negro Education,* and *International Journal of Qualitative Studies in Education.*

Gaetane Jean-Marie is Associate Professor in Educational Leadership at the University of Oklahoma. Her research interests include cross-boundary leadership, urban school reform, educational equity, and women and educational leadership. Her research has been published in peer-reviewed journals and presented at national conferences. She has a forthcoming co-edited book, *Educational Leadership Preparation: Innovation and Interdisciplinary Approaches to the Ed.D. and Graduate Education* (2010, Palgrave).

Wayne D. Lewis is an Assistant Professor in the Department of Educational Leadership Studies at the University of Kentucky. Wayne's research is in the areas of school choice, school-community collaboration, and education politics. He earned a PhD in Educational Research and Policy Analysis at North Carolina State University.

Leslie Ann Locke is a PhD student at Texas A&M University in the Department of Educational Administration and Human Resource Development. Her research interests include equity and access in public schools for historically marginalized populations, conceptualizations of academic success held by students and teachers, and systemic racism.

Patrice A. McClellan is Assistant Professor and Director of the Masters of Organizational Leadership program at Lourdes College. Dr. McClellan teaches Diversity, Social Justice and Leadership as well as Organization Development and Change. Her research focuses on leadership preparation, multicultural organization development, and socially just learning environments in higher education.

Kathryn Bell McKenzie is Associate Professor of Educational Administration and Human Resources at Texas A&M University in College Station. Her research foci include Equity and Social Justice in Schools, School Leadership, Qualitative Methodology, and Critical White Theory. During her more than twenty years in public education, Dr. McKenzie was a classroom teacher, curriculum specialist, assistant principal, principal, and Deputy Director of the University of Texas/Austin Independent School District Leadership Academy.

Mark T. Miles is Assistant Superintendent for School Improvement in the Park Hill School District in Kansas City, Missouri. He previously served as Assistant to the Superintendent and Principal of Plaza Middle School in Park Hill and a social studies teacher and assistant administrator in Missouri's Columbia Public Schools. He earned his doctorate degree in Educational Leadership and Policy Analysis at the University of Missouri.

Michael D. Miller is an Assistant Professor of Teacher Education at University of Wisconsin-River Fall, where he conducts research on the intersection of community engagement, diversity and equity in the context of pre-service teacher preparation. He is the recipient of the *Community-Based Practitioner Award* by Wisconsin's Campus Compact.

Elizabeth Murakami-Ramalho is an Assistant Professor in Educational Leadership and Policy Studies at the University of Texas-San Antonio. Her research focuses on urban and international educational leadership to include organizational learning and ecology, leadership dynamics, and hybrid identities/communities. She prepares professionals through graduate-level courses in school leadership, social justice and diverse settings, school change, and principal preparation in urban areas.

Gary O'Mahony is Director of O'Mahony & Associates Consulting, which provides state-based and regional programs in leadership for aspirant leaders, principals, and school teams. Formerly a primary school principal and Project Director at the Australian Principals Centre, Gary is involved in international research and program development, co-authoring books on school improvement, and presenting workshops in Australia, the United States, New Zealand, and Canada.

April L. Peters is an Assistant Professor in the Department of Lifelong Education, Administration and Policy at the University of Georgia. Her research interests include mentoring for early career administrators, African Americans in school leadership, and the principalship.

Camika Royal is a PhD candidate in Urban Education at Temple University. Her dissertation focuses on Black educators in Philadelphia, and her research interests include the sociopolitical context of schools and school districts for urban educators. She has taught middle and high school at Lincoln University of PA and worked for Teach For America.

Verna Ruffin is Assistant Superintendent for Curriculum and Instruction in Tulsa Public Schools and doctoral student in educational leadership at the University of Oklahoma. She has served as area superintendent, principal, and assistant principal in school districts in Texas and Louisiana. Her research interests include cross-boundary leadership, community schools, innovative schools, building trust within communities of learners, and restoring hope through community engagement.

George Theoharis is a faculty member in the Teaching and Leadership Department at Syracuse University. His research involves school leadership, the principalship, equity, school reform, and inclusive schooling. He is author of *The School Leaders Our Children Deserve: 7 Keys to Equity, Social Justice and School Reform* (Teachers College Press.)

Linda C. Tillman is Professor of Educational Leadership at the University of North Carolina at Chapel Hill. Her research interests include mentoring, leadership theory, the education of African Americans in K-12 and post-secondary education, and the use of racially and culturally sensitive qualitative research approaches. Dr. Tillman is Editor-in-Chief of the *SAGE Handbook of African American Education*; co-editor of *African American Perspectives on Schools: Building a Culture of Empowerment* (with Len Foster); and 2009 recipient of the Jay D. Scribner Mentoring Award from the University Council for Educational Administration.

✠ INDEX

M. Christopher Brown II, *General Editor*

The *Education Management: Contexts, Constituents, and Communities* (EM:c³) series includes the best scholarship on the varied dynamics of educational leadership, management, and administration across the educational continuum. In order to disseminate ideas and strategies useful for schools, colleges, and the education community, each book investigates critical topics missing from the extant literature and engages one or more theoretical perspectives. This series bridges the gaps between the traditional management research, practical approaches to academic administration, and the fluid nature of organizational realities.

Additionally, the EM:c³ series endeavors to provide meaningful guidance on continuing challenges to the effective and efficient management of educational contexts. Volumes in the series foreground important policy/praxis issues, developing professional trends, and the concerns of educational constituencies. The aim is to generate a corpus of scholarship that discusses the unique nature of education in the academic and social spaces of all school types (e.g., public, private, charter, parochial) and university types (e.g., public, private, historically black, tribal institutions, community colleges).

The EM:c³ series offers thoughtful research presentations from leading experts in the fields of educational administration, higher education, organizational behavior, public administration, and related academic concentrations. Contributions represent research on the United States as well as other countries by comparison, address issues related to leadership at all levels of the educational system, and are written in a style accessible to scholars, educational practitioners and policymakers throughout the world.

For further information about the series and submitting manuscripts, please contact:

Dr. M. Christopher Brown II | *em_bookseries@yahoo.com*

To order other books in this series, please contact our Customer Service Department at:

(800) 770-LANG (within the U.S.)
(212) 647-7706 (outside the U.S.)
(212) 647-7707 FAX

Or browse online by series at www.peterlang.com